The Transformation of the Classical Heritage

Peter Brown, General Editor

PACHOMIUS

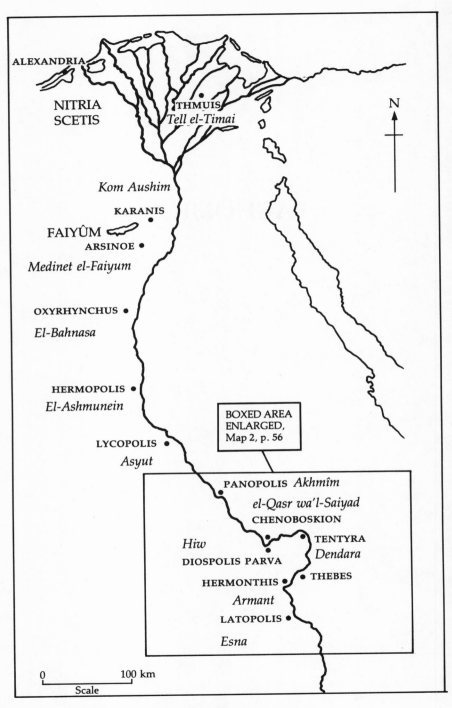

MAP 1. *EGYPT, showing Graeco-Roman and modern names.*

PHILIP ROUSSEAU

PACHOMIUS
The Making of a Community in Fourth-Century Egypt

UNIVERSITY OF CALIFORNIA PRESS
Berkeley · Los Angeles · London

University of California Press
Berkeley and Los Angeles, California

University of California Press, Ltd.
London, England

© 1985 by The Regents of the University of California

Preface to the Paperback Edition © 1999 by
The Regents of the University of California

First Paperback Printing 1999

Library of Congress Cataloging in Publication Data

Rousseau, Philip.
  Pachomius.

  (The Transformation of the classical heritage; 6)
  Bibliography: p.
  Includes index.
  1. Pachomius, Saint.   2. Monastic and religious orders—History—Early church, ca.
30–600.   3. Asceticism—History—Early church, ca. 30–600.   I. Title.   II. Series
BR1720.P23R68   1984   270.2′092′4   83-9285
ISBN 0-520-21959-7 (pbk. : alk. paper)

Printed in the United States of America

1 2 3 4 5 6 7 8 9

FOR THE FOUR
WHO TEACH ME MOST
ABOUT *KOINONIA*

Αὕτη δέ ἐστιν
ἡ ἀγάπη τοῦ θεοῦ
τὸ συμπάσχειν ἀλλήλοις

Vita Prima, 42

CONTENTS

LIST OF MAPS AND FIGURE

ABBREVIATIONS

All secondary works are referred to in the notes by short title. Fuller details will be found in the Bibliography.

A longer account of the primary source reference system is given in the notes to Chapter II.

Some texts use a dual numbering system. III (6), specifying Armand Veilleux's translation of a Sahidic *Life*, e.g. S[1], means "Fragment III, or Section 6"; 6 (12), specifying his translation of the *Paralipomena*, means "Chapter 6 or Section 12." The original editors (Lefort and Halkin) use only the Section numbers.

Cross references occur in two forms: "Chapter I, n. 43," which refers to the note; and "Chapter I, at n. 43," which refers to the text.

Am	Arabic *Life* of Pachomius, ed. É. Amélineau.
Bo	Bohairic (Coptic) *Life* of Pachomius, ed. L-Th. Lefort.
CJP	"Catechèse sur les six jours de Pâque" = Pachomius, *Instruction on the Six Days of the Passover*, ed. L-Th. Lefort, trans. A. Veilleux. *See* Chapter II, n. 1.
CMR	"Catechèse à propos d'un moine rancunier" = Pachomius, *Instruction Concerning a Spiteful Monk*, ed. L-Th. Lefort, trans. A. Veilleux. *See* Chapter II, n. 1.
CSCO	*Corpus scriptorum christianorum orientalium.*
CSEL	*Corpus scriptorum ecclesiasticorum latinorum.*
Dion.	Latin *Life* of Pachomius, translated from Greek by Dionysius Exiguus, ed. H. van Cranenburgh.
Ep.	*Letter.* The author (Pachomius, Jerome, etc.) is specified in each case.
G[1], G[2], etc.	The various Greek *Lives* of Pachomius, ed. F. Halkin. G[1] is the most frequently cited, and is referred to in the text as the *Vita Prima*.

GCS	*Die griechischen christlichen Schriftsteller der ersten Jahrhunderte.*
HE	*Historia ecclesiastica.* The author (Eusebius, Socrates, etc.) is specified in each case.
HL	Palladius, *Historia Lausiaca*, ed. C. Butler, referred to in the text as the *Lausiac History*.
HM	Rufinus, *Historia monachorum in Aegypto.* There are two versions: Latin, in *PL* 21.387–462, and Greek, ed. A-J. Festugière. I cite the Latin version unless I specify otherwise.
Nau	Anonymous apophthegmata (numbered), ed. F. Nau. *See* Bibliography, "Sources," *Apophthegmata*.
P, PInst, PIud, and PLeg	The various sections of the *Rules* of Pachomius: the *Praecepta, Praecepta et Instituta, Praecepta atque Iudicia,* and *Praecepta ac Leges. See* Chapter II and Bibliography, "Sources," Pachomius, *Rules*.
Paral.	The *Paralipomena*, ed. F. Halkin: additional biographical anecdotes about Pachomius.
PG	J. P. Migne, *Patrologia graeca.*
PL	J. P. Migne, *Patrologia latina.*
Ruppert	F. Ruppert, *Pachomianische Mönchtum.*
S¹, S², etc.	The various Sahidic (Coptic) *Lives* of Pachomius, ed. L-Th. Lefort.
script. copt.	Scriptores coptici (series in *CSCO*).
TU	*Texte und Untersuchungen zur Geschichte der altchristlichen Literatur.*
VBr, VTh	Hypothetical early *Lives* of Pachomius (*Vita Brevis*) and Theodore (*Vita Theodori*). *See* Chapter II.

PREFACE

Pachomius deserves our attention not simply because of the events he set in train, but also because of personal qualities. If we regard him as a founder of the community life within the tradition of Christian asceticism, we should not be surprised to find him resourceful and inventive. But he displayed talents that were neither exhausted nor entirely honored by the institutions and the reputation that survived him. He showed above all an understanding of the human heart and of what was required in those who wished to form and guide it. It was an understanding not always shared or even recognized by his successors. We would be mistaken, therefore, to treat him only as a pioneer, quickly superseded in the history of monasticism by men more articulate and more influential—Basil, Evagrius, Jerome, Augustine, or Cassian. By the time he died in 346, he had achieved in Upper Egypt something peculiar to himself, which rewards investigation regardless of what a later generation made of it. Indeed, it is wise to bypass those who came after, insofar as that is possible, and allow him to stand free, speaking for himself.

The present work comes closest to being a biography. It is not a general history of early monasticism, nor even a history of monasticism in Egypt alone. Reflecting on the first few chapters of my *Ascetics, Authority, and the Church*, I can see that attachment to a theme and haste toward later figures encouraged me to overlook basic elements of Pachomius's personality and achievement. Heinrich Bacht's *Das Vermächtnis des Ursprungs*, too, being focused on Horsiesios, Pachomius's eventual successor, inevitably raised the question of why a work like the *Liber Orsiesii* should be regarded as "original," why we should accept a late-fourth-century attitude as a just measure of the "Pachomian" ideal. The result was a second thorough reading of the Greek and Coptic *Lives*. I was anxious to discover just how much reliable information about Pachomius they were likely to contain. I wanted to know also whether Pachomius had been justly assessed by those who came after him, and in particular whether they had fully appreciated all that he had attempted or talked about in his lifetime. My task was made easier by the researches of Armand Veilleux and Fidelis Ruppert; and the appearance of Veilleux's English translation of all the Pachomian material was a fortunate antecedent to my own enterprise.

Direct access to Pachomius is difficult. An inquiry into the sources at our disposal is presented in Chapter II, but the crux of the matter is that most of those who wrote about him had little if any personal acquaintance with the man and interests or convictions that were often rather different. Yet it became increasingly clear to me that the roots of the biographical tradition can be reached, and that we discover there someone with much more to offer than rules, anecdotes, or a "cenobitic movement." We discover also a man unlike the pioneer of general histories— harsh, efficient, the drill-sergeant of the ascetic life, presiding without humor over a small empire of teeming, unreflective communities. Pachomius was, on the contrary, a man of caution and doubt, yet ready to experiment and to adapt to circumstance and personality. He was humble and generous. Above all he was a shrewd judge of character, and able to mold without tyranny those who trusted him.

For those reasons it seemed to me important to do him greater justice. He should interest us today not simply as the remote initiator of traditions now more familiar, but as a source of ideas and social forms as yet not wholly tested by Christian ascetics. Many persons distant from our own time and from our own habits of thought are yet entirely relevant to our needs. They deserve a new audience simply because their full worth has gone unrecognized both in their own day and in the centuries since. Pachomius is such a man.

Some background is required to explain Pachomius's social and intellectual attitudes and the audience he was addressing in his various endeavors. This I attempt to provide in Chapter I; but, as I explain more fully there, a temptation to be too ecclesiastical or too broad-ranging in my reference had to be avoided. I have assumed the reader's acquaintance with histories of the church and of the Roman Empire. In Chapter II, as mentioned already, I describe the sources upon which we have to rely in our study of Pachomius himself and assess their reliability, emphasizing in particular the different chronological layers of composition, which demand an interpretation most cautious.

The biography begins in Chapter III, where I describe what Pachomius was trying to achieve in founding his monasteries and the halting yet subtle steps by which he did so. The impression is of a man less idio-syncratic than one might have expected, less isolated from the religious and civil structures of his time and place. It is an impression sustained throughout his life. He never felt that he had succeeded, or that he had established a definitive model of the ascetic life, which he had merely to defend thereafter and to propagate.

In Chapters IV, V, and VI, I give some account of life in the Pacho-mian monastery: its daily order, the degree to which practice was subject to rule, and how authority was acquired and exercised. Although some conformity resulted from Pachomius's precepts, and although obedience was valued highly, chief emphasis was placed on the sense of personal responsibility each monk had to acquire for his spiritual progress—a re-sponsibility encouraged by the intimate and perceptive guidance of his religious leaders.

Those observations prepare us for Chapter VII, in some ways the center of the work. There I attempt to identify the goal of the ascetic life, as presented to the "Pachomian monk" who emerges from the previous chapters. That there was an inner dimension to the Pachomian ideal has itself been insufficiently admitted. What Pachomius hoped for most, in his subjects as in his own life, was a clear vision of the self as a creature of God, a vision involving both knowledge and control. Only the humil-ity and concern encouraged by the common life could lead to such a vision.

With the two remaining chapters, we enter again upon a broader stage. In Chapter VIII, I examine the ways in which the Pachomian mon-astery was related to the society around it: to the local village or town community and to the church and its leaders. There the connections be-tween ascetic and citizen suggested as possible in Chapter I are made more precise. The dialogue between those who "left the world" and those who remained in it is a bond overlooked by too many. Pachomius's convictions, spiritual and institutional, took shape as a response to the shortcomings, but also to the necessities, of his fellow Egyptians. Chap-ter IX treats of Pachomius's successors, or rather of the process of succes-sion itself. For in the very act of bequeathing his achievement to others, Pachomius exposed his own weakness and was forced to let some things fall into abeyance. Thus much that was "un-Pachomian" survived in Up-per Egypt, and much remains for us to resurrect or rescue.

Whatever portrait we achieve will appear to be from the side, from an angle. The nature of the sources makes this inevitable: we discover the man as he addresses others. Pachomius was above all a teacher, by example as much as by word. It is often his effect upon others that tells us most about his conviction and self-image. The characters in an anec-

dote, and the reporters themselves, are indispensable witnesses to his
personality. Yet it is still Pachomius we are talking about, rather than
"Pachomianism." I feel it is fair that the reader should put the book
down with some impression of an individual rather than of a corpus of
ideas or a pattern of shared behavior. That is certainly my intention.

The reading and reflection that first contributed to the structure of
the book and the formation of my arguments was essentially a solitary
task, though I owe a great deal to the support of my family, the stimulation of my students, and the kindness of my Auckland colleagues. But I
completed the work, with more intense revision and expansion, while
holding a Fellowship at Dumbarton Oaks. The diversity and extent of its
resources, the learning and kindness of its resident scholars, the help-
fulness of all its staff, and the peacefulness and beauty of its setting must
make this one of the most delightful institutes to work in. My debt ex-
tends far beyond the completion of this book.

But I must record in a special way what I owe to the elected Fellows
of that year, in particular to Marie Taylor Davis and Brian Daley. They
showed me at all times the generosity and affection of true friends and
the perception of the best of colleagues. Each read the book with great
attention, and offered extensive comment, which has made the text im-
measurably better than it might otherwise have been.

The final typescript was prepared for publication by Mrs. Freda
Christie. Her skill is matched only by her generosity and humor.

I offer my thanks finally to the University of California Press, particularly to my editors, Peter Brown, Doris Kretschmer, Mary Lamprech,
and Paul Psoinos. They have shown great patience with a sluggish writer,
never flagged in their encouragement, and corrected many a fault and
error.

My greatest and most intimate debts are recorded in my dedication.

Auckland
Christmas, 1983

PREFACE TO THE
PAPERBACK EDITION

To publish a paperback edition of a work written nearly fifteen years ago represents some confidence and courage. I hope the decision will not be mistaken for complacency. I find the main arguments of the book still tenable; but I must offer, of course, some account of subsequent research, which might modify the portrait I presented in 1985. I reiterate my belief that Pachomius is accessible to the historian, and I emphasize again his hesitant and fragile achievement, his shrewdness of judgment and depth of understanding, and the distinctness of principle and practice that he maintained in the fluid and mixed society of the fourth-century Thebaid. My confidence has to contend, nevertheless, with some criticisms. I anticipated them to some degree; but more recent debate and my own reflections prompt me now to alter the emphasis here and there, to make some points more forcefully and others with greater caution.

I want to concentrate on three issues. First comes the question of accessibility. What sources (if any) give us a reliable impression of Pachomius himself? The Coptic and Greek *Lives* were written well after his death. The problem is not simply one of memory (although that has to be taken into account) but also one of context. As with most ascetic writing, we have to recognize lateral relations: the post-Pachomian and even non-Pachomian audiences addressed, and the later preoccupations betrayed or disguised. Second, what of Pachomius's models, enemies, and allies—the broader ascetic culture within which he devised his experiments? Gnostics, Melitians, and Manichees all reflected an "ascetic imperative" and were widely dispersed in Egypt. We must remain sensitive to the influence they may have brought to bear upon Pachomius and his admirers. Finally, what degree of withdrawal, even of visible difference, marked out the monk among the Christians of Egypt? We read of an ordered regime, of walled-in communities, of economic self-sufficiency; yet, even in the Pachomian sources themselves, and certainly in other types of evidence, there are signs of engagement, exchange, familiarity, and location that call into question, at least in the earlier part of the fourth century, the image of segregated "monks" and "monasteries" that might have seemed prevalent or desirable to a later generation.

Those issues are addressed in the book. Chapter I provides some account of Manichees and Gnostics, and assesses their likely impact on the Pachomian world. Chapter II distinguishes between reliable and unreliable anecdotes and portrayals. Chapters III and VIII provide evidence of a certain social untidiness, a blurring of the frontier between ascetics and Christians generally. Other scholars, however, have continued to raise questions on all those fronts. Assumptions, therefore, have gained currency that still need resisting; fresh discoveries, on the other hand, invite fuller detail and adaptation. Each problem, moreover, affects the next. The reliability of later texts is governed by the battles they felt obliged to fight: against rival styles of ascetic practice, against deceitful or erroneous imitators, against those prepared to compromise the rigor of their dedication or withdrawal. That engagement with those ostensibly "outside" the received Pachomian tradition forces us in turn to map somewhat differently the territory thus shared or contested, and to wonder whether distinctions were as sharp on the ground as they appear in the written accounts.

On the reliability of the sources, James Goehring put the matter succinctly ("New Frontiers," pp. 239–40): "The fact that the *Vitae* preserve an accurate account of the movement's external historical events does not guarantee that they represent with equal accuracy the developments and changes in the more internal matters of practice and belief." He added, "The sources composed in the period under Theodore and Horsiesios tell us as much about the period of their composition as about the earlier period they purport to describe." It was not Goehring's direct intention, but this opinion, coming hot upon the publication of *Pachomius* (although formulated some two years before, and reflected in his "Vision of Heresy"), struck close to the roots of my own assurance. Goehring described, in his *Letter of Ammon*, what he clearly considered a more reliable source (as Derwas Chitty had done before him). Ammon, a bishop in the late fourth century, included an account of his three-year stay at Phbow during the time of Theodore some decades before. Those who follow L.-Th. Lefort in doubting the value of the work will continue to insist that Ammon's memory was at once unreliable and clouded by subsequent experience of the ascetic life elsewhere in Egypt. Unfavorable comparisons, on the other hand, with the terminology and narrative of the *Lives* depend danger-ously on prior confidence that the *Lives* are more worthy of trust. Unfor-tunately, neither the dates nor the circumstances of the surviving biogra-phies can be determined with precision. If Ammon's "letter" is genuine, therefore, it is entirely possible that it was written before them.

I do not think, in fact, that Goehring's book has greatly strengthened Ammon's claim. After a scrupulous rehearsal of all the arguments against the text, especially those of Lefort, it is plain that doubts survive. Goehring comes close to admitting in the end that cautious skepticism is still a good policy. His study is valuable, however, for the light it throws on the increasing (although probably later) engagement of Pachomian monks with the authority structures of the church, and in particular with Athanasius and other bishops of Alexandria. It also brings home the vari-ety of oral and written traditions that must have emerged between Pa-chomius's death and the formation of the surviving *Lives*. The report given by Ausonius and Elourion in the "letter" itself is a good example. Regard for Athanasius and his successors was certainly expressed more forcefully by Theodore than by Pachomius. Ammon's Theodore had been clearly, as Goehring put it, captured by the church once and for all. So had Ammon! We have to acknowledge, furthermore, that the biographical tra-dition as a whole was charged with the anxieties and prejudices of Theodore and Horsiesios, which were reflected in comparable ways among other Pachomians like Pgol and Shenoute. In regard to the accu-rate recollection of Pachomius among his successors, I think I adhered, nevertheless, to Goehring's own principle: each story must be "examined individually", to determine which offers "the truest reflection of the primitive tradition" (*Letter*, p. 23; see my p. 44).

We come, second, to the question of heterodoxy. Those who wish to establish a link between Pachomius (or rather his successors) and the Gnostic "library" from Nag Hammadi have to grapple with the question of why the famous codices were buried. Does the apparent collection of the documents in one place (among tombs, close to Chenoboskion) offer assurance about their coherence with one another, about the original place or places of their compilation (in Coptic), and about the fear or in-difference of those who hid them (supposing that "hide" is the apposite term)? I am still convinced that the answer is no. Once a connection with the Pachomians had been alleged on the basis of their location and the na-ture of the cartonnage (see my pp. 26–28), burial had to be explained either as a symptom of heterodox monastic fear in the face of ecclesias-tical disapproval or as a gesture of indifference, once the material had been deemed no longer useful. Neither possibility has been convincingly defended. The hare was started, of course, by Jean Doresse himself (*Livres secrets*, p. 155), although his argument was that Gnostics had done the burying, faced with the rising influence and the "strict orthodoxy" of the Pachomian communities. Ever since then a scholarly tradition has developed in which the bold speculations of one author become the secure suppositions of the next (a transition occasionally achieved within a single article.)

I was neither exhaustive nor detailed in my treatment of this tradition, but repeated reading, and attention to more recent reflections, have not encouraged me to reach different conclusions. Torgny Säve-Söderbergh's suggestion is certainly unlikely—that the codices were used by orthodox Christians, probably monks, to combat error rather than to embrace it, and then thrown away when the threat of error dissipated. Frederik Wisse was right enough in that respect ("Gnosticism and Early Monasticism"). Unfortunately, he then dug his own grave because he linked the Pachomians not with a central Gnostic culture, as some (although only some) of the codices illustrate, but with "writings on the periphery" and "the gnostic world view" (p. 431). One ends up in such a case with vague assertions that any number of Christians might have accepted. Even on a practical plane, ascetic rigor was a virtually universal phenomenon (Stroumsa, "Ascèse et gnose", p. 147). Wisse placed further hope in accounts of opposition to Pachomius. Whether Pachomius was thus criticized in matters of doctrine is very uncertain; but the problem is that he obviously disagreed with his critics! Charles Hedrick ("Gnostic Proclivities") used a similar appeal to surviving evidence of diversity and disorder. None of it, by his own admission, was connected with theology: it had much more to do with conflicting attitudes to the exercise and recognition of authority (Veilleux, "Monasticism and Gnosis", p. 274.)

Wisse's most stimulating speculation was that Pachomian communities might have welcomed gnosticizing Christians who had found a separate defense of their practices or beliefs either less than satisfying or increasingly dangerous. (The notion was anticipated by Hedrick, whose views, however, are briskly undermined by Alexandr Khosroyev, *Bibliothek*, pp. 88–89.) Wisse was led from there to search for a development (passing in his case through the world of Hieracas) that would illustrate, if not explain, a transition from traditional full-blown Gnosticism to the community asceticism of the fourth century and beyond (p. 440). In differing forms, that line of argument crops up repeatedly—not that I would readily accept it, especially when confirmed by the judgments of Khosroyev, *Bibliothek*, pp. 86-88. What it does do is provide a new agenda for argument.

Meanwhile Clemens Scholten and Khosroyev himself have offered additional reflections. Scholten attempts a precarious balance. He believes that the Nag Hammadi texts could have been used by monks, but he acknowledges a radical difference between Gnostic and Pachomian asceticism. He doubts that a Pachomian community would simply have manufactured blank codices for sale (and I now agree with that), but he does not reach his conclusion on the basis of supposed monastic references in the cartonnage fragments. Khosroyev is more consistent in his skepticism. In "Bemerkungen," he argues that the vocabulary of the codices (especially their occasional use of "father" and "son") is not monastic; that one should not confuse those who may have written the material with those who may have used it; and that editorial modifications (which are not difficult to identify) are not a reliable key to the intentions or circumstances of the original authors. His *Bibliothek* provides even greater detail. He sees little point in seeking out Gnostics among the Pachomian communities. Not only is the evidence lacking: there is little reason why Gnostics should have sought out such a refuge (pp. 84–85). Pachomians, for their part, were unlikely to have found a use for the codex material (pp. 89–90). There were plenty of other ascetic groups that could have indulged in rivalry or accommodation (pp. 71–78), and mutual relations among differing religious enthusiasts, Christian or otherwise, were in this period more complex than some scholars have been willing to take into account (pp. 97–102). The Pachomians themselves had sharply different views, even though their "orthodoxy" was, as many writers have been quick to suggest, a matter more of praxis than of theory (pp. 79, 90; a point made even more strongly by Stroumsa, "Ascèse et gnose"; see also Böhlig and Markschies, pp. 143–45). He is anxious to show that, above all, while Gnostics, socially as well as theoretically, fled an evil and chaotic material world, vitiated by its evil creator, Christian monks sought to change their situation by deliberate and prolonged effort, distancing themselves from others only to avoid distraction. Their search for perfection, encouraged by the providence of a single God, was conducted within the broader framework and general aspirations of the whole Christian community.

I mention on pp. 26–27 Athanasius's *Festal Letter* 39, issued in 367, and directed against erroneous books. That incident has proved particularly attractive to those supporting the "Gnostic connection". It was already brought into play by Doresse, and appealed to by Säve-Söderbergh and Wisse. Theodore, in the Coptic sources (see my n. 88, p. 27), had the letter translated into Coptic and lodged within the monasteries, and it has been suggested that such an intrusion on Athanasius's part led Gnostic sympathizers to bury their codices. However, Athanasius's letter was concerned with establishing a canon of scripture, for both the Old and New Testaments, and it is hard to imagine that in this instance the Nag Hammadi cache would have been automatically considered the direct object of his anxiety (Khosroyev, *Bibliothek*, pp. 90–91). Alberto Camplani (*Lettere Festali*) considers that the sheer breadth of Athanasius's reference, in this letter and in others, makes it impossible for us to focus on Gnostics. The metropolitan was more intent upon discrediting Melitians, who were attracting support in distant areas over which it was hard to maintain control. An alliance with the Pachomian communities, loyal and watchful, would have been a great asset. Although Athanasius's *Letter to the Monks*, like his correspondence with Horsiesios (see my pp. 189–190), was addressed to those practicing a "solitary'" life (*PG* 26. 1185), he was still able to exhort them to adopt almost a pastoral attitude to "those who believe in Christ", when they saw them consorting with heretics (1188A).

Melitians certainly complicated, and may even have confused, the ascetic scene. They were prone, according to Athanasius, to set themselves apart. He, on the other hand, as both Annik Martin and David Brakke have shown, wanted to create and sustain a single church community (*Festal Letter* 5). The Melitians, however, were also ascetic, and therefore admirable and attractive. Their communities, whatever their size or location, would have looked little different from ascetic groups of more orthodox persuasion, especially in the earlier part of the century (Camplani, pp. 264f; Goehring, "Melitian Monastic Organization", p. 389). Thus an episcopal urge to unite may have rendered less detectable the distinctiveness previously abhorred. (The plot thickens: R. M. Grant suggested mutually formative contacts between Melitians and Manichees when both groups were condemned by the persecutors to the mines, "Manichees and Christians," pp. 435–36.) It is probably unwise to suppose either that Melitians provided a model for Pachomius or, conversely, that they were directly weakened by his more successful enterprise. However, some of the Melitian texts presented by H. I. Bell (*Jews and Christians*, pp. 38–99) clearly refer to full-blown monasteries. (Goehring, "Organization," argues for the existence of a unified network of such communities, akin to the Pachomian *koinonia*.) Others of Bell's texts suggest a contrasting proximity to village and town. When, in the next generation, Shenoute took up his pen against error, the memory of Athanasius and the Melitian threat was still operative (Orlandi, "Catechesis"), although it is not always easy to identify precisely the opponents Shenoute had in mind (Origenists, yes, but others with too speculative a temper or too radical a self-denial). Some have thought he was aiming consciously at what Nag Hammadi had stood for (Dwight Young, "Milieu"), while others make the point that Melitians were probably as fond of apocryphal literature as any Gnostic—more confusion (Camplani, pp. 275f).

The most striking elision between orthodox ascetic groups and others has been suggested in relation to the Manichees. Ludwig Koenen's "Manichäische Mission" was particularly daring in its generality. Manichaean infiltration into Egypt in the later third century represented for him the very *Vorgeschichte* of Christian monasticism (p. 93). He also saw an affinity between Manichaean beliefs and the material discovered at Nag Hammadi (p. 95). (Giancarlo Mantovani makes the arrival of Manichees in Egypt a harbinger of the religious syncretism that, for him, the apparent muddle of the Nag Hammadi corpus represents, pp. 597f). The Aramaic and Syrian roots of the religion allowed Koenen to point to analogies of ascetic terminology and behavior linking Manichees and Christians (p. 99 and n. 36)—justly enough, although earlier connections with Qumran and the Essenes seem less secure (pp. 101–102). Unfortunately, he was too ready to translate Manichaean terms for "houses" or "dwellings," and for "house leader," into Christian terms like "monasteries" and "abbot," which were scarcely established terms in Pachomius's time anyway (pp. 97–99; he was particularly keen to see a link between Manichaean "houses" and the house-system of Pachomius, p. 101; see my pp. 28–31.) What is interesting, although Koenen did not make the connection, is the missionary character of these Manichaean groups: for in Egypt and elsewhere Christian ascetics adopted a pastoral role—not merely by accepting clerical and episcopal office, but also by catering more generally for the spiritual welfare of laypeople and playing a liturgical role in local churches. Having made his connections, however, Koenen concluded on a note of caution, admitting the differences he had been more inclined to dismiss on an earlier page (p. 104–5). He failed to ask what those differences implied about the Pachomians themselves. To say that development from one religious group to another is not ruled out is to underestimate the care with which Christian ascetics asserted their distinctiveness vis-à-vis "other beliefs" and monasteries not of the "same faith" (p. 105).

A comparable approach was adopted by Stroumsa ("Monachisme et "marranisme"). He also feels that in the confrontation between Christian and Manichee (as in *Life of Antony*, 68) we stumble upon a *Vorgeschichte* of later rivalries (p. 300 in *Savoir et salut*). Oddly enough, he uses an approach almost opposite to that adopted in "Ascèse et gnose": even though the theological differences between Christians and Manichees were, by his own admission, great, we should not imagine them to have been thereby separated one from the other on the ground (p. 302; see Ries for an account of what *encrateia* meant to Manichees, which was very different from Christian interpretations, and Heuser and Klimkeit for an accessible picture of Manichaean theology, as revealed in the Coptic sources). Stroumsa is also ready to trace a line from the Manichees to Pachomius through the Nag Hammadi *milieu* (pp. 302–3). Yet, he criticizes Koenen and others for being too hasty in their use of monastic terminology. He wants only to identify a necessary catalyst—necessary to explain the "sudden" and widespread development of fourth-century asceticism (pp. 303–5). The catalyst, Manichaeism, does not function for Stroumsa, however, as it did for Koenen: rather, Pachomius is seen as a reaction to what the Manichaean missionaries were attempting to achieve (p. 309). Then, like Wisse's Gnostics, the Manichees go underground, merging with their former rivals while keeping their "secret" teachings to themselves (p. 310–11). Stroumsa repeats his arguments in "Manichaean Challenge," without evident modification. The Manichees "must have looked for a hiding-place in the ascetical communities in the desert, i.e. [!], in the Pachomian monasteries" (p. 309). Many of Khosroyev's arguments render this argument equally insecure.

Obviously, Manichaeans were active in Egypt and emphasized ascetic rigor. I mentioned the literary attacks made upon them, quite apart from their proscription by law (see my pp. 32–35). I would add now Athanasius's warning letter to Amoun (*PG* 26. 1169–76), addressed broadly to "brothers" and "ascetics," and concerned with false notions about bodily purity and the dignity of marriage. One looks in vain, however, for secure evidence of social interaction with Christians (Stroumsa, "Monachisme et "marranisme," p. 300). We might have looked for contrary evidence in the more recent discoveries at Kellis, a substantial town in the Dakhleh Oasis, abandoned or destroyed around 400. It certainly sheltered a Manichaean community, although numbers are uncertain, and the abundant nonreligious texts link it with the society of the oasis more generally. The community itself, however, by the editors' admission, had nothing monastic about it (Iain Gardner and others, *Kellis Literary Texts*, 1). The material makes constant reference to family relationships and economic activity—not unlike some of the Melitian texts in Bell's *Jews and Christians*. What the excavations have suggested so far about relations among Manichees in Egypt more broadly, however, is meager and obscure (Gardner and Lieu, "Narmouthis . . . to Kellis"). With reference to Pachomian connections, the most obvious point is that the Kellis community was remote and, judging by the surviving correspondence, fearful—quite in contrast to the confident Christian monasteries abutting the villages and trade routes of the Nile valley.

In the end, all speculation about Pachomians and heterodoxy has to be tested by a reexamination of the surviving sources—particularly those relating to Theodore and Horsiesios. This I hope to undertake in the near future; the task is too big for a mere introduction. A few observations, however, might prove useful. Pachomius certainly faced opponents; but, even as opponents, they are never easy to identify as either Manichees or Gnostics. He was allegedly easygoing, when admitting to the *koinonia* already existing ascetic communities. However, as we have seen, his pre-occupations were more practical than theological, and about practical matters, such as the pursuit of material security, he could be very strict. The striking confrontation with "philosophers" from Panopolis (see my pp. 162–66) uses imagery too mixed to be usefully labelled Gnostic. Certainly, important distinctions were being made, even in the use of shared terminology (see Scholten, pp. 167–68; Bernward Büchler argues for a close link with Gnostics, *Armut*, pp. 140–45). There is a provoking passage in Bo 88; with references to impurity and wandering from monastery to monastery sowing discord, it is reminiscent of Athanasius and open to connection with either Melitians or Manichees. The story of Theodore and the *Festal Letter* of 367, in Bo 189, requires great care. A full analysis would certainly demand a close look at the terminology used, even though more general observations already made undermine a connection with Nag Hammadi. But these are piecemeal references: what is called for, as I say, is a fresh assessment of the broader spirituality revealed in all the material we can link with the successors of Pachomius.

The third issue, which in many ways is the broadest, can be handled more briefly. At least one reviewer took me to task for not paying more attention to the seclusion and self-protectiveness of the Pachomian communities. Secluded and protective they may seem at times, as presented in the later biographical sources, but there is also constant reference to the proximity of secular settlement, hospitality and travel, and involvement in the local economy, all of which contributed to the less ordered impressions I tried to preserve in Chapter VIII and elsewhere. Büchler's *Armut* may have overreached the mark: his Pachomius was radically different from other ascetics of his time in that he saw his chief task as a pastoral one, reaching out into the lay community on many fronts. Büchler's chief interests were, as his title suggested, economic, but he stressed also the extent to which exchange and generosity based on productivity and property were inspired by Pachomius's original desire to be the servant of all humanity, implying a concern that immediately and consistently extended beyond material ministrations.

Our growing knowledge of late Roman Egypt—based on an ever more penetrating study of non-literary papyri, on a more humble witness to civil relations and enterprise—offers a wider frame within which to place the whole range of ascetic devotion. (A general picture is provided by Roger Bagnall.) There is an image of the church at stake here. First, the theoretical basis of asceticism is brought closer to the baptismal obligations of every Christian—an emplacement of asceticism within the church that had its parallel in many other parts of the empire. Second, there is the sense that ascetics were visible and active within secular society: teaching, encouraging, and defending people, especially what used to be called the "common folk," although they were well able to censure the powerful or harness to their cause men and women of influence and standing. Whatever modification or restraint may have been given scope at a later date, the "monastic" world of Pachomius himself was, in its permeability, comparable to the more loosely structured and more urban-based enthusiasts we read of in non-Pachomian sources. And even a more direct successor like Shenoute teaches us how "engaged with the world" a coenobitic community could be—a pattern that continued to characterize eastern monasticism through at least the following two centuries. (Observe, as one less remote instance, the career of Apollo of Bawit, who shifted from solitude to association, continued for a long time to wander, engaged in a genuine apostolate, and ended up a master of monasteries: Orlandi, "Giustificazioni.")

Whatever acknowledgement of such a situation I might claim to have made (and I think I made a good deal), it still seems pale beside the assertions of Goehring, who has, in a substantial series of articles, placed Pachomius very firmly in the village world of the Nile valley ("Origins of Monasticism," "Withdrawing from the Desert," and "Monastic Diversity"). Both Pachomius and Antony received their first calling to a more rigorous life in that busy setting (Wipszycka, "Conversion"). I find Goehring's work very refreshing and frequently convincing, and I recognize that it must at least slow down in our minds the pace of the coenobitic tradition that claimed Pachomius as its founder and model. The arguments are grounded, of course, in Goehring's sense of which sources provide us with authentic information, a sense we have already explored, and about which some disagreement might persist. Nevertheless, it makes good sense of several texts and fits well with the papyrological work inspired by scholars like Françoise Morard, Ewa Wipszycka, and Edwin Judge. Martin Krause's "Möglichkeit" makes analogous points, showing how the very vocabulary of dedication and material renunciation can be found in both Pachomian sources and village and town papyri. "Coenobitism" (if one can argue for such a clear-cut category of organization) was not, therefore, a radical and promptly declared alternative to the "solitary life" (in itself a problematic term) but rather a more tentative and gradual alliance among men and women who nevertheless shared with devotees more independent than themselves, and indeed with many of the laity more generally, the fundamental and long established principles of ascetic commitment.

Because the biographies of Pachomius make such calculated reference to him, and because a book like Brakke's draws the ascetic communities into his unifying pastoral programme (exemplified in the *Festal Letters:* Camplani, pp. 200f), it is worth noting how much the material associated with Athanasius echoes this theme of softer boundaries. In his letter to Amoun, marriage and virginity are held side by side as "two ways," albeit the first is of lesser stature and the second elevated and angelic (*PG* 26. 1173BC). In his letter to Dracontius, in spite of his frequent use of the word *monachos* and its equivalents, the bishop warned against imagining that a distinction between the monastic world and the broader church community was in any way akin to the distinction between virtue and sin: monks failed in holiness as often as laypeople achieved it (*PG* 25: 524–533). The *Life of Antony* 68 highlights the danger of a world where so many different ascetic groups, some of them theologically wrong although worthy and indistinguishable in practice, could mingle in the countryside, challenging their peers and misleading the unsophisticated. A self-conscious and protective collusion with the like-minded was one response, but only one, to such threatening confusion (see my "Orthodoxy and the Coenobite").

Therefore, wherever readers find in this book signs of hesitation, experiment, shifting structure, cautious but ready hospitality, mobility, trade and exchange, pastoral concern, or involvement with civil and religious authority—all of which appear—they should view them in the fuller light provided by subsequent and more general studies of Egyptian church and society. They should also imagine that tighter regulation and more closely bonded communities reflected a success (if success it was) that only came with time, and often in response to newly perceived dangers of theological error, spiritual shallowness, and material temptation.

The overriding issue, therefore, is whether the book remains useful, or whether, in the light of more recent research, it is likely to mislead. There is no doubt that had I been writing after Goehring's work, following the next phase of Gnostic debate and paying more attention to Koenen or Büchler, I would have been more argumentative, and many of my opinions would have been more sharply expressed. I am confident, however, that my conclusions would not have been markedly different. There was something distinctive about Pachomius, and his convictions were built into the communities we read of in the *Lives*. Of all the issues on which more recent debate has focussed, the most fruitful, it seems to me, (and, I may add, the least securely resolved) is that concerning the relationship between heterodoxy and the coenobitic imperative. Theological controversy undoubtedly imposed new limitations on ascetic engagement with the church community, and the growth of monasteries in a stricter sense was undoubtedly part of a new response. That did not imply, however, a fearful withdrawal, for ascetics continued to claim, and to exercise, a moral and pedagogic authority in the Christian empire.

For those very reasons, there is no need to suppose that the monks themselves were, on a broad scale, heterodox—certainly not the Pachomians. I remain confident in that belief, in regard to Gnosticism for example, when I read again the assurances of fine scholars like Guillaumont and Veilleux. We are dealing, in Veilleux's words, with "two universes of thought that have evolved on parallel courses" ("Monasticism and Gnosis," p. 291). (Mantovani, "Tradizione dell'*enkrateia*", pursued the same line of thought. Encratism and Gnosticism have different histories, even though one is able to admit that the production of Gnostic documents in Coptic may have made the local situation in Egypt more confused, demanding clearer self-definition among those anxious to reject them.) However, in the face of encratite preoccupation with a flawed creator, who produced only bodies bonded to procreation, Pachomians and others espoused continence, for example, on more social and psychological grounds, dedicating themselves to singleness of purpose and the avoidance of distraction. (The task involved also a contrasting approach to the exegesis of Old Testament texts—a fruitful area for future research: Orlandi, "Giustificazioni," p. 359.) The dominant note was one of practicality, not speculation. Thus Guillaumont ("Célibat monastique") emphasized the moral concern of Christian monks, and Veilleux made a related point too often forgotten: "[Ascetical] practices can be understood only . . . if their motivations are perceived" ("Monasticism and Gnosis," p. 304).

I have kept until last one other recent work—Michael Williams's *Rethinking "Gnosticism"*—because in relation to Pachomius its implications may be far-reaching; certainly they are more substantial than I have yet been able to digest. He wishes generally to unscramble the rigid polarization that has encouraged scholars to limit to Gnostic circles the attribution of, among other things, certain rigorist tendencies, and to exclude from those same circles, on the other hand, all supposedly orthodox religious beliefs and inclinations. He restores, as a result, a less interrupted spectrum of opinion and practice across all those communities that regarded themselves, in one sense or another, as Christian, and in the process he allows any one group to appear more ambiguous or eclectic. Here, then, is a fresh opportunity to soften the boundary between the Pachomians and their ascetic rivals. But the argument goes further. Williams concludes to his own satisfaction that the Nag Hammadi codices should be associated with the Pachomian communities. Where he adds to the debate, as we have outlined it above, is in his contention that the codices display more coherence than has been hitherto supposed. Each volume appears to have been governed in its choice of included material by clearly identified principles of contiguous interest (pp. 247–60; the argument was developed in more detail in Williams's "Interpreting the Nag Hammadi Library"). Those principles, he suggests, reflect the characteristic interests of monks (pp. 260–61). Moreover, those monks (ostensibly Pachomians) were, by their novel associations (not always using, of course, material that need be described as "Gnostic"), reassembling what he calls the "shards" of a failed religious movement (p. 262). This would suggest to me that the ascetic ideology and the attitude adopted by Pachomians toward the wider community would have represented a much more contemporary seizure of opportunity than the sequence of influences conjured by Koenen, for example, would invite one to suppose. Far from being only the products of long tradition, orthodox or otherwise, the new coenobites of the Nile valley may carry us into a future that no one has yet charted. I suspect there are questions embedded here that will keep inquiry active for some time to come.

I should like to thank those colleagues whose warm comments made the issue of this paperback seem useful. I am grateful also to the Director and Fellows of Dumbarton Oaks, who have welcomed me back as a reader in their wonderful library. It seems fitting, and is certainly delightful, to be revisiting all these issues in the setting where the book first took shape.

Philip Rousseau
Catholic University of America
Washington, D.C.
December 1998

ADDITIONAL BIBLIOGRAPHY
(includes items overlooked in the original edition)

Armstrong, A. H. "Dualism: Platonic, Gnostic, and Christian." In *Neoplatonism and Gnosticism*, edited by Richard T. Wallis and Jay Bregman, pp. 33–54. Studies in Neoplatonism, Ancient and Modern, 6. New York: State University Press of New York, 1992.

Bagnall. Roger S. *Egypt in Late Antiquity*. Princeton: Princeton University Press, 1993.

Bianchi, Ugo (ed.). *La tradizione dell'enkrateia. Motivazioni ontologiche et protologiche*. Atti del Colloquio Internazionale, Milano, 20–23 April 1982. Rome: Edizioni dell'Ateneo, 1985.

Böhlig, Alexander, and Christoph Markschies. *Gnosis und Manichäismus. Forschungen und Studien zu Texten von Valentin und Mani sowie zu den Bibliotheken von Nag Hammadi und Medinet Madi*. Beihefte zur Zeitschrift für die neutestamentliche Wissenschaft und die Kunde der älteren Kirche, 72. Berlin and New York: Walter de Gruyter, 1994.

Brakke, David. *Athanasius and the Politics of Asceticism*. Oxford: Oxford University Press, 1995.

Camplani, Alberto. *Le Lettere Festali di Atanasio d'Alessandria*. Rome: CIM, 1989.

Emmel, Stephen. "Shenoute's Literary Corpus: a Codicological Reconstruction." In *Acts of the Fifth International Conference of Coptic Studies*, edited by David W. Johnson, 2: 153–62. Rome: CIM, 1993.

Gardner, I. M. F., and S. N. C. Lieu. "From Narmouthis (Medinet Madi) to Kellis (Ismant el-Kharab): Manichaean Documents from Roman Egypt." *Journal of Roman Studies* 86 (1996): 146–69.

Gardner, Iain, with S. Clackson, M. Franzmann and K. A. Worp (eds). *Kellis Literary Texts*, 1. Oxford: Oxbow Books, 1996.

Goehring, James E. "Melitian Monastic Organization: A Challenge to Pachomian Originality." In *Studia Patristia* 25, edited by Elizabeth A. Livingstone, pp. 388–95. Papers presented at the Eleventh International Conference on Patristic Studies held in Oxford, 1991. Louvain: Peeters, 1993.

―――. *The Letter of Ammon and Pachomian Monasticism*. Patristische Texte und Studien, 27. Berlin: Walter de Gruyter, 1986.

―――. "Monastic Diversity and Ideological Boundaries in Fourth-Century Christian Egypt." *Journal of Early Christian Studies* 5 (1997): 61–83.

―――. "New Frontiers in Pachomian Studies." In *The Roots of Egyptian Christianity*, edited by Birger A. Pearson and James E. Goehring , pp. 236–57. Philadelphia: Fortress Press, 1986.

―――. "The Origins of Monasticism." In *Eusebius, Christianity, and Judaism*, edited by Harold W. Attridge and Gohei Hata, pp. 235–55. Detroit: Wayne State University Press, 1992.

―――. "Pachomius' Vision of Heresy: The Development of a Pachomian Tradition." *Muséon* 95 (1982): 241–62.

―――. "Withdrawing from the Desert: Pachomius and the Development of Village Monasticism in Upper Egypt." *Harvard Theological Review* 89 (1996): 267–85.

Guillaumont, Antoine. "Gnose et monachisme: exposé introductif." In *Gnosti-*

cisme et Monde Hellénistique, edited by Julien Ries, with Yvonne Janssens and Jean-Marie Sevrin, pp. 301–310. Actes du Colloque de Louvain-la-Neuve (11–14 March 1980). Louvain-la-Nueve: Institut Orientaliste, 1982.

————. "Le célibat monastique et l'idéal chrétien de la virginité ont-ils des 'motivations ontologiques et protologiques'?" In *La tradizione dell'enkrateia,* edited by Ugo Bianchi (q.v.), pp. 83–107. Rome: Edizioni dell'Ateneo, 1985.

Hedrick, Charles W. "Gnostic Proclivities in the Greek *Life of Pachomius* and the *Sitz im Leben* of the Nag Hammadi Library." *Novum Testamentum* 22 (1980): 78–94.

Heuser, Manfred, and Hans-Joachim Klimkeit. *Studies in Manichaean Literature and Art.* Nag Hammadi and Manichaean Studies, 46. Leiden: Brill, 1998.

Khosroyev, Alexandr L. "Bemerkungen über die vermütlichen Besitzer der Nag-Hammadi-Texte." In *Divitiae Aegypti. Koptologische und verwandte Studien zu Ehren von Martin Krause,* edited by Cäcilia Fluck, Lucia Langener, Siegfried Richter, Sofia Schaten, and Gregor Wurst, pp. 200–205. Wiesbaden: Ludwig Reichert Verlag, 1995.

————. *Die Bibiothek von Nag Hammadi. Einige Probleme des Christentums in Ägypten während der ersten Jahrhunderte.* Arbeiten zum spätantiken und koptischen Ägypten, 7. Altenberge: Oros Verlag, 1995.

Koenen, Ludwig. "Manichäische Mission und Klöster in Ägypten." In *Das römisch-byzantinische Ägypten,* edited by Günter Grimm, Heinz Heinen, and Erich Winter, pp. 93–108. Akten des internationalischen Symposions, 26–30. September 1978, Trier. Aegyptiaca Treverensia, 2. Mainz am Rhein: Philipp von Zabern, 1983.

Krause, Martin. "Zur Möglichkeit von Besitz im apotaktischen Mönchtums Ägyptens." In *Acts of the Second International Conference of Coptic Study,* edited by Tito Orlandi and Frederik Wisse, pp. 121–33. Rome: CIM, 1985.

Lieu, Samuel N. C. *Manichaeism in the Later Roman Empire and Medieval China. A Historical Survey,* 2nd edition. Wissenschaftliche Untersuchungen zum neuen Testament 63. Tübingen: J. C. B. Mohr, 1992.

Mantovani, Giancarlo. "La tradizione dell'*enkrateia* nei testi di Nag Hammadi e nell'ambiente monastico egiziano del IV secolo." In *La tradizione dell'enkrateia,* edited by Ugo Bianchi (q.v.), pp. 561–602. Rome: Edizioni dell'Ateneo, 1985.

Martin, Annik. *Athanase d'Alexandrie et l'église d'Égypte au IVe siècle (328–373).* Rome: École française de Rome, 1996.

O'Neill, J. C. "The Origins of Monasticism." In *The Making of Orthodoxy. Essays in Honour of Henry Chadwick,* edited by Rowan Williams, pp. 270–87. Cambridge: Cambridge University Press, 1989.

Orlandi, Tito. "Gli apocrifi copti." *Augustinianum* 23 (1983): 57–71

————. "A Catechesis against Apocryphal Texts by Shenute and the Gnostic Texts of Nag Hammadi." *Harvard Theological Review* 75 (1982): 85–95.

————. "Giustificazioni dell'encratismo nei testi monastici copti del IV–V secolo." In *La tradizione dell'enkrateia,* edited by Ugo Bianchi (q.v.), pp. 341–68. Rome: Edizioni dell'Ateneo, 1985.

Ries, Julien. "L'*enkrateia* et les motivations dans les *Kephalaia* coptes de Medinet

Madi." In *La tradizione dell'enkrateia*, edited by Ugo Bianchi (q.v.), pp. 369–391. Rome: Edizioni dell'Ateneo, 1985.

Rousseau, Philip. "Orthodoxy and the Coenobite." In *Studia Patristica* 30, edited by Elizabeth A. Livingstone, pp. 241–58. Papers presented at the Twelfth International Conference on Patristic Studies held in Oxford, 1995. Louvain: Peeters, 1997.

Scholten, Clemens. "Die Nag-Hammadi-Texte als Buchbesitz der Pachomianer." *Jahrbuch für Antike und Christentum* 31 (1988): 144–72.

Stroumsa, Gedaliahu G. "Ascèse et gnose. Aux origines de la spiritualité monastique." *Revue Thomiste* 89 (1981): 557–73. Reprinted in his *Savoir et salut. Traditions juives et tentations dualistes dans le christianisme ancien*, pp. 145–62. Paris: Éditions du Cerf, 1992.

———. "Monachisme et 'marranisme' chez les Manichéens d'Egypte." *Numen* 29 (1983): 184–201. Reprinted in his *Savoir et salut. Traditions juives et tentations dualistes dans le christianisme ancien*, pp. 299–14. Paris: Éditions du Cerf, 1992.

———. "The Manichaean Challenge to Egyptian Christianity." In *The Roots of Egyptian Christianity*, edited by Birger A. Pearson and James E. Goehring, pp. 307–19. Philadelphia: Fortress Press, 1986.

———. "Titus of Bostra and Alexander of Lycopolis: A Christian and a Platonic Refutation of Manichaean Dualism." In *Neoplatonism and Gnosticism*, edited by Richard T. Wallis and Jay Bregman, pp. 337–49. Studies in Neoplatonism, Ancient and Modern, 6. New York: State University Press of New York, 1992.

Timbie, Janet. "The State of Research on the Career of Shenoute of Atripe." In *The Roots of Egyptian Christianity*, edited by Birger A. Pearson and James E. Goehring , pp. 258–70. Philadelphia: Fortress Press, 1986.

Turner, John D., and Anne McGuire (eds). *The Nag Hammadi Library after Fifty Years*. Proceedings of the 1995 Society of Biblical Literature Commemoration. Nag Hammadi and Manichaean Studies, 44. Leiden: Brill, 1997.

Veilleux, Armand. "Monasticism and Gnosis in Egypt." In *The Roots of Egyptian Christianity*, edited by Birger A. Pearson and James E. Goehring, pp. 271–306. Philadelphia: Fortress Press, 1986.

———. "The Origins of Egyptian Monasticism." In *The Continuing Quest for God: Monastic Spirituality in Tradition and Transition*, edited by William Skudlarek, pp. 44–50. Collegeville: Liturgical Press, 1982.

Williams, Michael Allen. "Interpreting the Nag Hammadi Library as 'Collection(s)' in the History of 'Gnosticism(s)'." In *Les textes de Nag Hammadi et le problème de leur classification*, edited by Louis Painchaud and Anne Pasquier, pp. 3–50. Actes du Colloque, Québec, 15–19 September 1993. Bibliothèque copte de Nag Hammadi, section "Études," 3. Québec: Presses de l'Université Laval; Louvain: Peeters, 1995.

———. *Rethinking "Gnosticism": An Argument for Dismantling a Dubious Category*. Princeton: Princeton University Press, 1996.

Wimbush, Vincent L., and Richard Valantasis (eds), with Gay L. Byron and William S. Love. *Asceticism*. Proceedings of an International Conference held at Union Theological Seminary, New York, 1993. New York: Oxford University Press, 1995.

Wipszycka, Ewa. "La conversion de saint Antoine. Remarques sur les chapitres 2 et 3 du Prologue de la Vita Antonii d'Athanase." In *Divitiae Aegypti. Koptologische und verwandte Studien zu Ehren von Martin Krause,* edited by Cäcilia Fluck, Lucia Langener, Siegfried Richter, Sofia Schaten, and Gregor Wurst, pp. 337–48. Wiesbaden: Ludwig Reichert Verlag, 1995.

Worp, K. A., with J. E. G. Whitehorn and R. W. Daniel (eds). *Greek Papyri from Kellis:* 1 (P. Kell. G) nos. 1–90. Oxford: Oxbow Books, 1995.

Young, Dwight W. "The Milieu of Nag Hammadi: Some Historical Considerations." *Vigiliae Christianae* 24 (1970): 127–37.

· I ·

EGYPT

Egypt has proved to be for historians one of the most exciting provinces of the later Roman Empire. Its physical characteristics were then, as now, striking enough. They combined the almost magical good fortune of the Nile, with its regular flooding and fertile banks, and the thrill of the imagination that follows naturally on a contemplation of the desert scene. The country had a long, well-documented history reaching back thousands of years before its inclusion in the Roman world. It had absorbed and enhanced a variety of races and cultures, notably the Hellenistic society encouraged by the conquests of Alexander the Great. It provided a rich soil for the development of religious ideas. Most prominent on the pagan side was the cult of Isis. In the Christian era, a bewildering variety of Egyptian speculations and so-called heresies perturbed the wider church for several centuries but offered it also immense intellectual stimulation. The province was a font of scholarship as well as of enthusiasm. The most enduring philosophy of the late antique world was that of an Egyptian, Plotinus. For Christians, the compilation and interpretation of sacred writings owed most to Egyptian Jews and to their own Clement and Origen of Alexandria.[1] And finally, Egyptians could claim in many ways to have invented the monastic life.

The task of introducing a reader to this productive and influential country is beset with inconvenience and danger.[2] Thanks to the nature

1. Plotinus was born at Lycopolis at the very beginning of the third century, Clement and Origen some fifty and twenty years before.
2. For a selection of general reading on the later Roman Empire, see the introduction to the Bibliography. I would only add here that, if I take frequent issue with H. I. Bell in these pages—both his *Egypt from Alexander the Great to the Arab Conquest* and his *Cults and Creeds in Graeco-Roman Egypt*—it is because his work has rightly won respect and exerted enormous influence. And if I appeal with equal constancy to the revisions of C. H. Roberts, *Manuscript, Society, and*

of the climate and soil—dry and preservative—historical evidence, when it does survive, often survives in abundance. But archaeology in Egypt has suffered much from the robber and the amateur, and in other ways from a heavy and understandable emphasis on its most distant past. The monastery of Apa Jeremias at Saqqara, the refuse dumps of Oxyrhynchus, the tombs of Nag Hammadi: these may seem to offer a very full picture of life and thought in later Roman Egypt. We shall mention them all again. But, quite apart from special difficulties in interpreting what they tell us, such sites are isolated and far-flung, like small if richly vegetated islands in a great ocean of ignorance.

We have constantly to face the fact that of some areas we know a great deal, while of many others we know nothing. One may take this to mean both areas in a geographical sense and areas of experience or activity. That uneven distribution of the evidence has often been obscured in more general studies of the province, particularly those by historians anxious to discover patterns of economy or administration. Confident assertions have survived for generations. Their logic has not necessarily been careless or deceitful, but little alternative material has been available with which to contradict them. What is called for is great caution before we assume that what was said or done in one village or ascetic community will have been said or done in any other.

But students of monasticism and of Pachomius in particular cannot content themselves with an equally isolated corpus of evidence, shutting themselves up, so to speak, in the ascetic household. As we shall see in Chapter II, the very nature of the ascetic literature will not allow so literal an escape from the province at large. Several features of Egyptian life are likely *a priori* to have had some bearing on the development of monasticism—the relationship between Egyptian towns and the imperial government on the one hand and the countryside around them on the other, the associated relationship between those educated in the Greek tradition and those of more local and perhaps more limited culture, the character and stability of the rural economy, and a variety of religious traditions that one might label (sometimes unwisely) pagan, Jewish, gnostic, heretical, or orthodox. These last contributed to the general "religious climate" of the Thebaid in the early fourth century and could have provided specific models for anyone like Pachomius engaged upon experiments in ascetic community and practice.

Summarized in that way, such features of Egyptian life look temptingly like the components of a general survey. Let it be stressed again,

---

Belief in Early Christian Egypt, it is because his deceptively slim volume marks a major step forward in our knowledge of Egyptian Christianity.

therefore: the evidence in each case is particular and disjointed. Rather than contribute toward a fully delineated context in which to place Pachomius, the evidence points to times and places where monastery and world may occasionally have met. It helps us to acquire not so much a framework as a further set of questions to ask of our ascetic evidence, questions which that evidence might not otherwise have prompted. How did Pachomius regard the structures and demands of civil and religous authority? How strict a distance did he keep between himself and the life of town and village? What was the nature and purpose of his own rural industry? How much did he derive from Jewish, or gnostic, or Manichaean traditions? How much, rather, did he fear or suspect them? To what extent did his Coptic heritage preclude his adopting Greek ideas?

So this chapter cannot be taken just as an introduction. In talking of town councils, of taxation and agriculture, of language and literature, of exegesis, liturgy, dualism, or mythology, we shall be focusing precisely on scattered elements of Egyptian life where, so to speak, the monastic modes—the concepts, the aspirations, the patterns of behavior—were already beginning to take on a distinctive contour within the social landscape before men suddenly took to the fringes of the settled world and started to look like monks as we now think of them.

Perhaps the most remarkable feature of the Egyptian province in Pachomius's lifetime was its growing unity, brought closer to fulfillment by the recent military and administrative policies of Diocletian, emperor from 284 to 305. We shall say a little more about them in a moment. The resulting stability and peace would have done much to ease the development of monastic institutions.[3]

The process of unification had already been noticeably furthered by Septimius Severus, emperor from 193 to 211. Prior to the third century, the towns of Egypt had enjoyed little of the political life characteristic of other centers in the Eastern Empire. The province seemed for that reason unusual in ancient eyes, provoking, for example, the famous taunt of Tacitus, "insciam legum, ignaram magistratuum."[4] In 199 or 200, Seve-

3. For Diocletian in Egypt, see Jacqueline Lallemand, *L'Administration civile de l'Égypte, passim*; but for the importance of this "new beginning", see esp. pp. 5f, p. 39 n. 4, and p. 97. Still useful on important antecedents is J. G. C. Anderson, "The Genesis of Diocletian's Provincial Re-organization," *Journal of Roman Studies* 22 (1932): 24–32.

4. Tacitus *Histories* 1.11. See Lallemand, *Administration*, p. 15.

rus decided to allow to Alexandria and to each *metropolis* (the urban center of a *nome*, or administrative district) a βουλή, or council, of its own. His purpose was undoubtedly to render more efficient the collection of taxes rather than to encourage the ambitions of local worthies, and the *territoria*, the districts around the towns, were retained under the central control of the provincial government.[5] But members of the new βουλαί quickly acquired responsibilities within the *territoria*, at least as agents of that government if not in their own right. The increased status of the towns encouraged in its turn the establishment in them of bishoprics. That ecclesiastical network and the new rapport between town and country paved the way for developments after Diocletian, when the *metropoleis* gained the added responsibility of administering the *territoria* themselves.[6]

The Severan reforms were modified in their effect by grave disruptions, in the form both of invasion and of usurpation, that almost destroyed the empire before the century had closed. Egypt suffered from about 250 onward at the hands of local "barbarian" intruders, Libyans and Blemmyes. This was a pressure less dramatic, perhaps, than that exerted by Germans and Goths on the northern frontiers of the empire.[7] A greater threat was posed by revolt and secession, most famously in the annexation of Egypt in 270 by Zenobia of Palmyra.

That originally small oasis chiefdom, situated on the border between Syria and Mesopotamia, had benefited from its strategic importance partly as a source of skilled manpower in the reformed army of Severus and partly as a frontier position against the new power of Sassanid Persia after the decline of Parthia. By the reign of Gallienus (260–68), its ruler, Odenathus, could claim leading military authority in the East. Sudden bereavement exposed in his widow, Zenobia, what proved to be an entirely rational ambition, which nevertheless far outstripped her husband's office. As well as Egypt and numerous territories in Syria and Mesopotamia, she successfully seized a large part of Asia Minor, and declared herself Augusta. Rome lost in the process almost a third of its domains. This blow followed closely upon the secession of Postumus in 259, which had carried away (and would continue to do so for some

5. Lallemand, *Administration*, pp. 24, 96; C. R. Whittacker, "Agri Deserti," in *Studies in Roman Property*, ed. M. I. Finley, p. 142.

6. Lallemand, *Administration*, p. 96; Bell, *Cults*, p. 86; E. R. Hardy, *Christian Egypt: Church and People*, p. 41. We may attach importance also to Caracalla's *Constitutio Antoniniana* (A.D. 212/13), which extended Roman citizenship to all free inhabitants of the empire.

7. Lallemand, *Administration*, p. 31. On the longer-term implications, see A. M. Demicheli, *Rapporti di pace e di guerra dell' Egitto romano con le popolazioni dei deserti africani*.

twenty years) whole sectors of the Western Empire. There was also the abiding humiliation of the emperor Valerian's capture alive during battle against the Persians in 260.

Zenobia was not allowed to maintain her position, thanks not to her own incompetence but to the arrival at last of an emperor, Aurelian, capable of reversing the disasters of almost half a century. His recapture of Egypt, however, beginning in 271, was gradual, complicated by the fact that some had welcomed Zenobia and others regretted her departure.[8]

The readiness of Egypt to revolt on its own account came to the fore again under Diocletian, during the prefecture of L. Domitius Domitianus.[9] We shall have occasion to note some detailed incidents in the revolt, which have been taken to reveal Manichaean activity in the province.[10] But the chief result of Domitianus's aspiration was the personal intervention of Diocletian himself. The rebels were crushed. More important, reforms were set in train that gave Egypt greater cohesion and bound it more closely to the empire as a whole. The policies of Severus were brought to a logical conclusion. Intervening disruptions, and the incidence of rebellion above all, affected considerably the final form of the new administration. Unity was achieved not only by reaching down from on high and thus radiating bureaucracy, for it had been precisely the servants of the government who had proved most unreliable in the preceding decades. A man's area of command was to be diminished, his access to military resources severely restricted. The new unity depended also, paradoxically, on division. Within the smaller arenas of authority, loyalty would call not only for obedience to those above but for a fuller sense of local responsibility. Those were the changes that brought *metropolis* and *territorium* into their new relationship whereby the βουλαί received (for their pains!) full control, especially fiscal control, over the surrounding rural communities.[11] The changes provided also a fresh opportunity for influence among the now widely established episcopate.

8. For the intrigues of the prefect Aemilianus and the rebel Firmus, see Lallemand, *Administration*, p. 32. The evidence of the *Historia Augusta* requires some care. Consult, as an *entrée*, J. Schwartz, "La Place de l'Égypte dans l'*Histoire Auguste*," in *Bonner Historia-Augusta-Colloquium (1975/1976)*, pp. 175–86; and, more generally, T. D. Barnes, *The Sources of the Historia Augusta*.

9. The date is disputed, between 295 and 298: see Lallemand, *Administration*, p. 35, and more recent literature cited below.

10. See below, at n. 96.

11. Lallemand, *Administration*, p. 96; Germaine Rouillard, *L'Administration civile de l'Égypte byzantine*, p. 3. A. K. Bowman emphasizes more carefully the oppressiveness of that development, not least in that rural officials might have been drawn from local towns but were not always answerable to local councils; see his *The Town Councils of Egypt*.

Pachomius grew up, then, in a country forced to acknowledge the identity it was acquiring within the wider Roman world. The administrative structures of the Tetrarchy, coupled subsequently with religious toleration under Constantine, gave Egypt's Christian leaders in particular the chance to play a part in affairs beyond their province. The career of the patriarch Athanasius (elected in 328, died in 373), so vital to the fortunes of monastic pioneers, is a vivid illustration of that development. At a lower level, so to speak, we may remind ourselves that one of the earliest definitely Christian letters found in Upper Egypt had been sent to Arsinoë via Alexandria from Rome itself.[12] But that exciting contact with greater affairs and centers of power gained considerable dignity from the growing cohesion and informed self-confidence within the province itself. The ecclesiastical and civil authority of Alexandria continued to impose upon towns farther south even after their hundred years of local responsibility and self-esteem. A weakening distinction between the urban and the rural, the inevitable result of Diocletian's understanding of municipal duties, carried the lines of communication far into the countryside. The voice of Alexandria, whether at church councils or at the imperial court, accordingly carried something of the vigor and loyalty of Egyptian peasants. Pachomius, far from rejecting such social and political developments, relished the opportunities of the age. His taste for federation, his enduring proximity to riverside communities, his heavy emphasis on productivity and self-reliance, and his devotion to the theology and to the patriarch of Alexandria all make sense to us only within the framework provided by Diocletian's empire.

It is important to keep the notion of unity firmly in mind when examining parcels of evidence more local or specific in character. Unity af-

12. J. van Haelst, "Les Sources papyrologiques concernant l'église en Égypte à l'époque de Constantin," in *Proceedings of the Twelfth International Congress of Papyrology*, ed. Deborah Samuel, p. 497 (see Bibliography under "International Congress of Papyrologists"). See also H. Musurillo, "Early Christian Economy: A Reconsideration of P. Amherst 3(a)," *Chronique d'Égypte* 31 (1956): 124–34, which includes the text. For further implications, see Roberts, *Manuscript*, p. 9; his doubts about van Haelst's conclusions are on p. 1 n. 2. For Athanasius, see W. H. C. Frend, "Athanasius as an Egyptian Christian Leader in the Fourth Century," *New College Bulletin* 8 (1974): 20–37; E. P. Meijering, *Orthodoxy and Platonism in Athanasius*; J. Roldanus, *Le Christ et l'homme dans la théologie d'Athanase d'Alexandrie*. For Arianism, see M. Simonetti, *La Crisi ariana nel IV*

fected, for example, much more than administration. It is no longer possible to suppose that the Hellenistic culture of Alexandria inspired only
a few Greek-speaking notables in the southern *metropoleis* and confirmed
a sharp distinction between people of their standing and the Egyptian
peasantry.[13] Nor should we continue to suggest for associated reasons
that Christianity also ventured only slowly beyond the Delta, encroach-
ing cautiously upon the countryside, "the concern of a small minority
. . . quite separate . . . from the Egyptian χώρα."[14] As is often the case,
such views were already undermined by careful reflection while still
being aired in more general studies.[15] Recent research provokes an important quickening of suspicion.[16] The evidence of letters and literary or
biblical texts preserved among the papyri of the third and earlier centuries now suggests very strongly that there had been for some time extensive contact at a cultural level between Alexandria and the towns of
Upper Egypt, a contact not restricted to the wealthy, the traveled, or the
erudite. The Christian material in particular points often to a surprising
level of education.[17] The style of presentation in some of the Christian
documents is closely related to more mundane and secular examples,

---

secolo. Two more recent works have provided some controversy: T. A. Kopecek,
A History of Neo-Arianism, and R. Lorenz, *Arius Judaizans?*

13.   Representative of that view is Bell, *Cults*, p. 63.

14.   Still the opinion of van Haelst, "Sources papyrologiques," p. 500.

15.   In this, as in other matters, *caveats* were anticipated by A. D. Nock. See
his 1944 essay, "Later Egyptian Piety," reprinted in his *Essays on Religion and the
Ancient World*, ed. Z. Stewart, 2:566–74, esp. pp. 567f, where he discusses the
wide radiation of Greek culture and its association with Coptic (on which more
below). J. W. B. Barns, in a 1966 lecture, "Egyptians and Greeks," continued to
emphasize the fiscal disadvantages of the non-Greek population, but doubted
that there was any deep division between Alexandria and Upper Egypt in the
Christian sphere.

16.   That is the predominant emphasis in Roberts, *Manuscript*. Note the important and favorable review of his book by T. C. Skeat, *Journal of Theological
Studies*, n.s., 31 (1980): 183–86; and, for some interesting contrasts, that by
W. H. C. Frend, *Journal of Ecclesiastical History* 31 (1980): 207–8. H. C. Youtie has
provided some examples from family law, which suggest that whatever desire
there may have been on the part of the Roman government to separate the races
(if such a phrase has meaning) was constantly frustrated by independent, contrary, and successful ambitions among the local population: "'Απάτορες: Law vs.
Custom in Roman Egypt," in *Le Monde grec. Hommages à Claire Préaux*, ed. J. Bingen et al., pp. 723–40 (see Bibliography under "Bingen").

17.   The process was not linked exclusively with the expansion of Christianity. For what may be implied by the quality of the *Acts of the Pagan Martyrs*, see
the comments and bibliography of Roberts, *Manuscript*, p. 3. For more general
discussion, including reference to the Christian material, see pp. 8f, 63.

suggesting as an audience what we might risk describing as a middle or bureaucratic class. These documents were directed toward liturgical and catechetical uses in the community rather than towards the drawing rooms of the polite and intellectually curious.[18] We even find a knowledge of Latin, which long persisted as the language of administration.[19] Beyond the readers and writers for whom we have clear evidence, we must allow also the existence of a passive culture, in the sense that many would have been able to speak Greek and appreciate its value in more than practical terms without being part of the technically literate community. The famous Aurelius Isidorus of Karanis, for example, could read but could not write.[20]

Such evidence for a growing access to culture among the up-country population must be related closely to the political and administrative changes we have already described. The very opportunities provided by increased municipal responsibility in rural areas set in motion two other processes that forged more firmly the cultural links between Greeks and Egyptians. First, there was intermarriage.[21] Second, closely connected, there was a desire among many "countrymen" to be enrolled as *metropolitai* within the citizen body of the local town. They did not do so merely in order to enter the magic circle of the urban Greek and escape the fiscal burdens supposedly endured by an oppressed peasantry. Tax advantage in such enrollment was doubtful. The arrival of these new citizens set in motion other efforts, made largely by those already townsmen, to enter the exclusive and hereditary "gymnasium" class. Success in such an application meant that the state and the municipality confirmed a claim to long-standing family involvement in urban culture and affairs, opened the door to the best education and a chance of influence

18.   For the "middle class," see Roberts, *Manuscript*, p. 3. Some scriptural texts were obviously for the few, pp. 11f, but see by contrast pp. 15, 20. On the practical nature of the material, see p. 10 n. 3, p. 22.

19.   Roberts, *Manuscript*, p. 10, uses the phrase, "something of a rarity," referring to the care with which a Greek scribe, copying the New Testament Book of Hebrews, preserved the Livy already written on the other side of his Oxyrhynchus roll. But see the Latin letter translated into Greek, no. 160 in *Kölner Papyri*, ed. B. Kramer et al., 3:168–71 (see Bibliography under "Sources: Kramer"); and Lallemand, *Administration*, p. 40.

20.   A. E. R. Boak, "An Egyptian Farmer of the Age of Diocletian and Constantine," *Byzantina Metabyzantina* 1 (1946): 42. Boak's analysis was extended in "Village Liturgies in Fourth Century Karanis," in *Akten des VIII. internationalen Kongresses für Papyrologie*, pp. 37–40 (see Bibliography under "International Congress of Papyrologists") and completed, with H. C. Youtie, in *The Archive of Aurelius Isidorus*.

21.   The examples presented by Youtie suggest a wide field: see n. 16 above.

for the whole family, and granted them certain fiscal advantages. That anxious pretension makes it even more clear that the real social division in Upper Egypt was not between town and country but within the towns themselves, between those in the gymnasium class and those not. Persons eligible for gymnasium status were striving, in other words, to escape precisely the growing encroachment of the wealthier farmer upon the public life of their towns.[22]

Rather than imagine, therefore, some lofty and cautious importation of culture from "outside," we should note a readiness in the rural areas to share in the prosperity, status, and intellectual vitality of town life. And this was a local movement, not some gesture towards distant Alexandria or the world beyond. Perhaps for that very reason it did not automatically involve the rejection of what was "Egyptian" in people's lives. A local and traditional quality persisted, particularly of religion, even in such a heartland of Greek culture as the Faiyûm.[23]

The bond between town and country, fostered by increasing administrative responsibilities and illustrated by social and educational aspirations, helps us to understand in a new light another corpus of local evidence from the Egyptian countryside. Too many writers continued for too long to take for granted a readiness among Egyptians of this period to abandon society, and in particular the orbit of local rural economy, mainly under the burden of taxation. Such writers would see monasticism as associated with that abandonment, as a symptom of psychological depression and the rejection of human intercourse.[24] "Flight" of that sort did take place. Although it would be unwise to extrapolate from scattered examples, some distinct dossiers do exist.[25] But as one reads

22. For one series of carefully chosen examples, see P. Mertens, *Les Services de l'état civil et le contrôle de la population à Oxyrhynchus*, esp. pp. 121, 124, 127, 133. The whole trend is studied more generally in C. A. Nelson, *Status Declarations in Roman Egypt*. See also Bell, *Cults*, p. 60; *Egypt*, pp. 70f.

23. E. Bernand, "Epigraphie grecque et histoire des cultes au Fayoum," in *Hommages à la mémoire de Serge Sauneron, 1927–1976*, ed. J. Vercoutter, vol. 2, *Égypte post-pharaonique*, pp. 57–76 (see Bibliography under "Vercoutter").

24. Bell paints a traditional and gloomy picture, *Cults*, pp. 69f, and *Egypt*, pp. 76f. He took to task in a review A. C. Johnson and L. C. West, *Byzantine Egypt: Economic Studies*; see *Journal of Roman Studies* 40 (1950): 123–28, where he makes useful reference also to his own article, "The Economic Crisis in Egypt under Nero," ibid. 28 (1938): 1–8. But a modified view was vindicated, as already in Johnson's 1947–48 lectures, *Egypt and the Roman Empire*.

25. A famous, compact, and accessible example is Boak and Youtie's study of Karanis (Kom Aushim) already mentioned, *The Archive of Aurelius Isidorus*. As well as other material mentioned in n. 20, see Boak, "'Tesserarii' and 'Quadrarii' as Village Officials in Egypt of the Fourth Century," in *Studies in Roman Economic*

through the collected references to little men in little communities with close horizons, it becomes clear that one is dealing with an enclosed system. Everyone knew everyone else; everyone was expected to bear their fiscal and corporate responsibilities. If people abandoned their locality, it was widely known where they had gone. "Flight" or "withdrawal" in those cases was rarely to the stark alternative of the desert and most often to another community identical in social and economic structure, usually close by. Its inhabitants and officials, harboring or welcoming the fugitive, were immediately besieged by a chorus of precise complaints from the home village and by demands for extradition.

The historian is now encouraged to paint a less dark and dramatic picture of the Egyptian countryside. Instead of oppressed or impoverished peasants seeking solitude or the protection of rich patrons on large estates, we have to acknowledge the persistence of small land-holdings at a time when farming was still seen as a profitable pursuit. The holdings themselves were not only small but scattered; this stemmed from the earlier third-century practice whereby independent peasant farmers had taken out small leaseholds on what was then crown land. One of Diocletian's major economic reforms was to transfer those parcels entirely to private possession. That did not prompt the immediate development of great estates such as were characteristic of later Byzantine Egypt or akin in economic terms to the *latifundia* of the Western Empire. Before the large privately owned estate came what was in effect a peasant cooperative. Farmers were forced to collaborate both in production and in the payment of taxes before they could create among themselves any more rigid social hierarchy. That was one impetus behind the new village economy encouraged by Diocletian. And when the emperor fused all other rural areas into a second new category, of "public land," small-scale farmers were eager to cultivate that as well. The returns from their other, personal, lots, therefore, cannot have been negligible, since they were accepting, in this second case, a tax on public land ten times higher than that on their private holdings. We should view in this context the new anxiety, which we can detect in some papyri, about the fulfillment of expectations in crop-yields and taxes. What Diocletian did was to make each village responsible for the fiscal productivity of *all* the land around it, whether public or private, farmed or fallow.

This economic and political climate provided a rich opportunity for

and Social History in Honor of Allan Chester Johnson, pp. 322–35 (see Bibliography under "Coleman-Norton"); and Boak and Youtie, "Flight and Oppression in Fourth-Century Egypt," in *Studi in onore di Aristide Calderini e Roberto Paribeni*, 2:325–37 (see Bibliography under "Arslan").

anyone ready to emphasize productive corporate enterprise.[26] Pachomian monastic organization, in other words, could well have been another step in the process: one type of opportunism among several others,
certainly, but not necessarily a despairing escape from economic circumstance. Once we entertain that possibility (which of course we shall have
to assess more carefully), we are forced to reexamine also what we may
have imagined to be the deeper psychology of the monastic vocation. It
is too easy to speak of "some permanent tendency in the Egyptian temperament and the geography of a country in which the desert is everywhere at hand,"[27] or to conjure with the image of "endless leagues of
desert" that prompted "ancient memories and secret fears and supersti-
tions forgotten elsewhere."[28] If such fears were entertained, they could
only be characteristic of minds emotionally wedded to the safety of the
valley village; it was habits of collaboration, proper to the same environ-
ment, that some ascetics wished to transfer to their new monastic settings. Athanasius, who in his *Life of Antony* would coin the phrase "the
desert a city," set the tone in a much earlier *Festal Epistle* issued in 338, in
which he made pointed reference to Israel, the "people of God," who

> walked in the wilderness as in an inhabited place. For although, accord-
> ing to the mode of living customary among men, the place was desert;
> yet, through the gracious gift of the law, and also through their inter-

26. These judgments were already adumbrated by Boak, "An Egyptian
Farmer," esp. p. 45, and by Johnson, *Egypt and the Roman Empire*, esp. pp. 73f.
See now Whittacker, "Agri Deserti," and A. K. Bowman, "The Economy of Egypt
in the Earlier Fourth Century," in *Imperial Revenue, Expenditure, and Monetary Policy in the Fourth Century A.D.*, ed. C. E. King, pp. 21–40. In spite, perhaps, of his
intentions, I. F. Fikhman confirms that in the late third century even large land-
holders owned scattered properties and that those of more moderate wealth
were imitating their wide investment, rather than seeking refuge under the
patronage of men with compact estates: "Quelques données sur la genèse de la
grande propriété foncière à Oxyrhynchus," in *Hommages à Claire Préaux*, pp. 784–
90. On the development of fiscal responsibilities and the anxieties generated, see
Naphtali Lewis, *Leitourgia Papyri*, Transactions of the American Philosophical
Society, n.s., 53, no. 9 (1963); and "Exemption from Liturgy in Roman Egypt," in
Atti dell' XI congresso internazionale di papyrologia (1965), pp. 508–41 (see Bibliography under "International Congress of Papyrologists"). Useful information is also
contained in studies of later periods: J. Karayannopulos, "Entstehung und Bedeutung des Nomos Georgikos," *Byzantinische Zeitschrift* 51 (1958): 357–73 (and
see the résumé, "Collective Fiscal Responsibility in Egypt, Particularly in the Byzantine Period," *Bulletin of the American Society of Papyrologists* 3 [1965]: 16);
M. Loos, "Quelques remarques sur les communautés rurales et la grande pro-
priété terrienne à Byzance (VIIe–XIe siècles)," *Byzantinoslavica* 39 (1978): 3–18.

27. Bell, *Cults*, p. 99.
28. Bell, *Egypt*, p. 109.

course with angels, it was no longer desolate, but inhabited, yea, and more than inhabited.[29]

Pachomius would seize in particular on the note sounded by "the law" that gave cohesion and a sense of identity to the Jewish people. The monastic movement, as he perceived it, was to retain that supposedly classical quality, an emphasis on community. Whatever personal relationship with God he might wish to encourage was to be discovered, explored, and expressed in a public and corporate context. In making the point, Pachomius was moving in a tradition much older than that of withdrawal in the face of economic difficulty. If we are seeking earlier Egyptian analogues to the monastic life, perhaps it *is* to the devotees of Serapis or the *therapeutai* of Alexandria that we should look, religious groups who never did entirely lose, as we shall see in a moment, their association with city life.[30] Or we may take note of chance evidence from cities farther south: the case, for example, of a Ptolemagrius at Panopolis, where Pachomius would later found more than one monastery. Here was a prominent citizen who engaged, with his family, in a life of philosophy and horticulture outside the town. That still allowed him the public practice of religious devotion within his old community and encouraged him on the basis of moral principle to entertain friends hospitably in his suburban retreat.[31] Just how different were Christian ascetic settlements? Archaeology, even at sites more eremitical than those of Pachomius, reveals habitation entirely comparable to the better class of secular rural dwelling, geared to a complex economy and a degree of social intercourse.[32] In only a short time, such communities, benefiting from well-organized labor and the generosity of admirers, could themselves become *patroni*, attracting the peasant in flight as easily as any rich landowner or successful χωρίον.[33] To enroll oneself in the resur-

29.   Athanasius *Festal Epistles* 10, translated by H. Burgess, *The Festal Epistles of S. Athanasius, Bishop of Alexandria*, p. 74. For the text, see *The Festal Letters of Athanasius*, edited and with extensive preface by W. Cureton.

30.   F. Ruppert, *Das pachomianische Mönchtum und die Anfänge klösterlichen Gehorsams*, p. 65f. (Hereafter cited as "Ruppert.")

31.   C. Bradford Welles, "The Garden of Ptolemagrius at Panopolis," *Transactions of the American Philological Association* 77 (1946): 192–206. Pachomius's association with Panopolis will be discussed fully in Chapter VIII.

32.   Geneviève Husson, "L'Habitat monastique en Égypte à la lumière des papyrus grecs, des textes chrétiens et de l'archéologie," in *Hommages à la mémoire de Serge Sauneron*, 2:191–207. Further archaeological evidence will be discussed in Chapters II and IV.

33.   Lallemand, *Administration*, pp. 228, 231, referring to the *Theodosian Code* 12.1.63 (A.D. 370/73). The text does not immediately support all her suggestions, but proves that some monasteries exerted that attraction.

rected economy of Tabennesis (which was a deserted village, not a stretch of desert) was not to abandon society, but to transfer one's allegiance, as had many another "anchorite," from one rural community to another.[34]

The changing structure of provincial administration and the consequent relationship between town, village, and countryside have already suggested where there may have been points of contact between monastic experiment and society at large. The wider picture helps us to understand also several other developments within the Egyptian church. We have a rather different and very famous source of information, which we should now relate to the impressions already acquired: the historical writings of Eusebius of Caesarea. A dearth of evidence and a desire to make a point rendered him often helpless. We cannot take refuge as he did in mythology or misconception. But we have to accept that his account may have done much to shape the mind of the church, in Egypt as elsewhere, during the century in which monasticism developed. He also prompts us to look more closely, in the light of our other evidence, at leading figures and events in the Christian history of the province.

Take, for example, his portrayal of the early Christian community at Alexandria. He felt himself informed above all on that subject by the writings of Philo, who died about 50 A.D. That author's famous *therapeutai* Eusebius resolutely believed to be Christian. He was wrong, but—so importantly for his own generation—he was able by virtue of his error to present the young church as having been rigorously ascetic, open to philosophy, espousing poverty and a partial withdrawal from city life, and inspired by the first Christians of Jerusalem, as described in the *Acts of the Apostles*.[35] And we are therefore impelled to look at Philo's *De vita contemplativa* directly and to note those elements in his account that could, and in some cases could not, be taken as antecedents of monasticism as Pachomius embraced it.

34. H. Henne examines the differences between ἀναχώρησις in the administrative sense and in the monastic, but does not pursue his laudable conclusion that the latter "withdrawal" was by no means total: "Documents et travaux sur l'anachôrèsis," in *Akten des VIII. internationalen Kongresses für Papyrologie*, pp. 59–66.
35. Eusebius *HE* 2.16f. His works are critically edited by I. A. Heickel, E. Schwartz, Th. Mommsen and others in the *GCS* series. The *HE* is translated in the Loeb Classical Library by Kirsopp Lake and J. E. L. Oulton, and more recently by R. J. Deferrari. The *Praeparatio evangelica* is usefully edited and trans-

The *therapeutai* withdrew from the city in a measured and responsible way, carefully redistributing their property and avoiding the distracting conflict that characterized even the best-governed city.[36] They also rejected marriage and the family, often having tasted it—Eusebius would pick upon this chastity as a hallmark of their Christianity! They lived in "houses" (οἰκίαι) close enough for mutual security, but far enough apart to protect their contemplation.[37] Once a week they attended a general meeting, sitting in due order and addressed by the "eldest" (πρεσβύτατος).[38] In this way they lived a life that befitted free men, rejecting slavery as the source of evil and cherishing equality among themselves.[39] There is much that anticipates Pachomius in these descriptions, though notably absent is any mention of work (which Eusebius felt obliged to include, to be echoed by Cassian).

An even more arresting series of parallels emerges in Philo's treatment of the Essenes in the tract *Quod omnis probus liber sit*. The Essenes, of course, were not Egyptian, but Philo regarded this second work as a balance to the *De vita contemplativa*: one treated the contemplative life as practiced by the *therapeutai*, the other the active life of the Essenes. These last, according to Philo, "lived in villages" (κωμηδὸν οἰκοῦσι). In that consisted their rejection of city life. Some cultivated the land, others pursued crafts, partly for their own peace of mind, partly to be of help to others.[40] They shared with the *therapeutai* a hatred of slavery and a love of freedom; they, too, met once a week for allegorical and philosophical discussion.[41] Eusebius provides us with detailed extracts from Philo's *Hypothetica* also, which discuss the practicalities of Essene economy, the

---

lated by E. des Places. See also D. S. Wallace-Hadrill, *Eusebius of Caesarea*, and R. M. Grant, *Eusebius as Church Historian*; and consult the Bibliography for full details. The reference in the passage of the *HE* noted here is to Philo's *De vita contemplativa*, most conveniently available in the Loeb Classical Library, *Works*, trans. F. H. Colson, 9:113–69. The "myth" had a firm and monastic future: see Jerome *De viris illustribus* 8 (explaining Philo's "mistake" in failing to recognize the Christianity!), 11; id., *Ep.* 22.35; Cassian *Institutes* 2.5. Discussion in Roberts, *Manuscript*, p. 56 n. 3; A. Guillaumont, "Philon et les origines du monachisme," in his *Aux origines du monachisme*, p. 25. This latter essay contains in essence much that is said in the rest of Guillaumont's book.

36.   Philo *De vita contemplativa* 2.14, 2.18, 5.47.

37.   Ibid. 3.24.

38.   Ibid. 3.30f. Note the cheerfulness of the occasion in 8.66, and the attention with which the address was received in 10.78.

39.   Ibid. 8.69f.

40.   Philo *Quod omnis probus liber sit* 12.76. Again, see Colson (tr.), *Works*, 9:11–101.

41.   Ibid. 12.79, 12.82.

relationship between the Essenes' disciplined life and their freedom, and their escape from the distractions of marriage.[42]

Now it is necessary to keep firmly in mind the differences between those societies and the monastic communities of Upper Egypt. There lay two centuries and more between Philo's death and the emergence of Christian ascetics. Yet it is clearly important that a style of life so similar should have been available within the Egyptian tradition. The references to village settlement, manual labor, a structured community with a hierarchy of authority, and regular discussions of sacred teachings under the guidance of a superior cannot be dismissed as unconnected with later monastic patterns. One can understand why Eusebius was delighted to present Philo's narrative, and the ascetic practices it described, as a central element in the Egyptian church's history.[43] But our own more accurate perception raises a matter of even greater interest; for we can see that the tradition was in reality Jewish, and so we must ask to what extent Judaism had influenced Egyptian Christianity and for how long it continued to do so.[44] Recent study allows us to suggest, with care, a strong connection between the first Christians of Alexandria and the Jewish and Christian communities of Jerusalem—forged at the expense, that is to say, of the theology of Paul and John.[45] Perhaps not until the Jewish War under Trajan were Christians in Egypt able to dissociate themselves from their Jewish colleagues.[46]

The issue is too large to discuss here at length, but it tells us some-

42. Eusebius *Praeparatio evangelica* 8.11.1f. In addition to Guillaumont, "Philon," see the discussion by Nock in a 1943 review of F. H. Colson, *Philo*, vol. 9, "Philo and Hellenistic Philosophy," reprinted in *Essays*, ed. Stewart, 2:559–65. The relation between the *therapeutai* and the Essenes is carefully discussed by G. Vermes, "Essenes—Therapeutai—Qumran," *Durham University Journal*, n.s., 21 (1960): 97–115; "Essenes and Therapeutai," *Revue de Qumran* 3 (1962): 495–504.

43. Bell made justifiable comments in "Evidences of Christianity in Egypt during the Roman Period," *Harvard Theological Review* 37 (1944): 185–208; but a reading of Roberts, *Manuscript*, will now prompt more careful references to the sources.

44. This is not to suggest a direct link between Alexandria and the Essenes of Qumran: see Roberts, *Manuscript*, p. 44 n. 4; also F. de Cenival, "Les Associations dans les temples égyptiens d'après les données fournies par les papyrus démotiques," in *Religions en Égypte hellénistique et romain: Colloque de Strasbourg, 16–18 Mai 1967* (q.v.), pp. 5–19.

45. The burden of much in Roberts, *Manuscript*: see esp. pp. 43, 47, 49. Excellent also is N. de Lange, *Origen and the Jews*.

46. Roberts, *Manuscript*, p. 58. Frend laments his caution, Skeat his temerity: see n. 16.

thing important about the tradition we are attempting to unravel. Eusebius defended doggedly the notion that a single unbroken thread of orthodoxy ran through the history of the church. Once you admit that the ascetic movement so central to that history might possess Jewish (and still other) roots, a whole range of bewildering possibilities suddenly present themselves. Contemporary historians have delighted in the confusion. They mention, besides the Jews, the gnostics above all as important contributors to Christian development who accordingly blur the clear distinctions of "orthodox" history. One scholar at least is still determined to free the Jews of Alexandria from any taint of gnosticism, although he will admit that Judaism, especially under the influence of Hellenistic ideas, could take a variety of forms not always likely to encourage orthodoxy among Christian associates.[47] Other scholars more happily conflate a variety of traditions: Jewish and Christian asceticism in the *Gospel of Thomas*,[48] asceticism and gnosticism,[49] gnosticism and Pythagoreanism.[50]

After we have tasted those forbidden fruits, can Eusebius's desperate rigidity offer us anything of further value? The next link in *his* chain is the Catechetical School in Alexandria, the διδασκαλεῖον τῶν ἱερῶν λόγων, founded, he suggests, in the late second century by Pantaenus. Given the predilections of the School's more famous masters, Clement and Origen, the record of the *Historia Ecclesiastica* will do little to deter those enthusiasts who wish to find gnosticism in every quarter. It is true that Origen's theology in particular depended on considerable cosmological speculation and placed great value on spiritual knowledge. It would have made it easier for any man who thought himself a Christian to ignore the boundaries between himself and many a gnostic. But Eusebius may not have been entirely astray in suggesting that Pantaenus was intent upon *countering* gnostic influence, particularly that of his fellow countrymen Basilides and Valentinus. In doing so, he allied himself much more closely with Stoic thought,[51] and so reinforced the moral rigorism of early Alexandrian Christianity. He wished to cater for "citizens of the world with a creed of duty to the state and society," and to

47.   Roberts, *Manuscript*, pp. 43, 49. Gnosticism is discussed more fully below.

48.   Frend, "Athanasius," p. 26, although he may contradict himself on p. 29. He is referring to a fragment from Oxyrhynchus, not to any text discovered at Nag Hammadi. For a context, see Roberts, *Manuscript*, pp. 23f.

49.   Bell, *Cults*, p. 94. Eusebius would not have thanked him for involvement in the connection!

50.   R. M. Grant, "Early Alexandrian Christianity," *Church History* 40 (1971): 133–44.

51.   Eusebius *HE* 5.10.

encourage "self-sufficiency and public spirit." That kind of emphasis within the traditions of the Egyptian church would have been no less important, as an influence upon later ascetics, than the teachings of Philo or of Judaism more generally.[52]

If we regard at least some types of gnosticism as heresies within the Christian tradition, then it would be fair to see the Alexandrian School as a representative, indeed a champion, of the contrasting "orthodoxy" that would make such a judgment possible.[53] It stood above all for what has been called "common core Christianity," which had rejected docetism as a solution to the Christological conundrum, accepted the Old Testament as necessary and intelligible to Christians, and above all considered revelation as given to all, and not accessible merely to an elite.[54] To do so was to reject at least some Jewish and gnostic convictions. However Jewish early Alexandrian Christianity may have been, the traditions were now being made available to religious people who had become in their own minds quite distinct. And all the evidence already rehearsed in our earlier sections—for cultural and religious links between Alexandria and the rest of Egypt—will encourage us also to suppose that those insights, disciplines, and traditions were making their presence felt, in the late second and early third centuries, well beyond the Delta.[55]

For as far as Eusebius was concerned, we are still at this point in Alexandria. He could not believe that Christianity had ventured far beyond the city until he found evidence for a wider establishment of the episcopate. That fresh stage in his history began hesitantly with the patriarch Demetrius (188/89–231) and achieved clarity and unity only with Dionysius (249–65). Too many historians have contented themselves with this second start.[56] There has been a failure to link ecclesiastical

52. Roberts, *Manuscript*, p. 54; and see Nock's 1936 review, "The Milieu of Gnosticism," commenting on the first volume of H. Jonas, *Gnosis und spätantiken Geist*, and reprinted in *Essays*, ed. Stewart, 2:451.

53. Bell, *Cults*, p. 80.

54. The phrase is that of R. M. Grant, applied by Roberts where Grant would not! See *Manuscript*, p. 72. On the importance of this change of status, so to speak, in the Jewish scriptures, Nock remarked, "Had [the Septuagint] not been made, the Christian Church would have found it hard to retain its Jewish heritage after its separation from contemporary Judaism, and would have run a very grave risk of losing its identity, cohesion, and power to survive." "Later Egyptian Piety," *Essays*, 2:573. See also Bell, *Cults*, p. 46.

55. Add to the material discussed above the forceful example of Oxyrhynchus, Roberts, *Manuscript*, pp. 23f.

56. E.g., W. Telfer, "Episcopal Succession in Egypt," *Journal of Ecclesiastical History* 3 (1951): 1–13, criticized by Roberts, *Manuscript*, p. 4. Hardy is similar, *Christian Egypt*, p. 18: note that for him the Egypt administered by Dionysius is

events with the social and cultural unification of the province already well in train by the middle of the third century.

Two other misconceptions affect this stage of the account. One is connected with language, the other with the very notion of orthodoxy. If you have already decided that Alexandria was for a long time an isolated Hellenistic city, the breakdown of that isolation will take the form of, among other things, an exploration of a non-Greek world, a world as yet unready for inquiry and formulation. "It is impossible to say," runs a tell-tale phrase, "when Christianity first began to make an impression on the *Egyptian-speaking* populace." [57] This refers to the move beyond Alexandria: Upper Egypt is seen as predominantly Coptic, and Coptic, as a cultural vehicle, is seen as a late development, reflecting nationalist resentment in the face of Graeco-Roman oppression. The same will be thought of Christianity to the south.[58] Not until Athanasius are we expected to find, according to this type of analysis, a blend between "the Biblicism of the Copt and the philosophic theology of Alexandria." [59] And finally, with fatal care, the monastic movement is placed at the heart of this distinct, Coptic, nationalist Christianity.[60]

The first Coptic biblical scholar we know of was Hieracas. He was born as late as 270, at Leontopolis in the Delta, and was probably still alive in the middle of the fourth century. And he was not, as we shall see, noted for his orthodoxy.[61] But the way Coptic writers toward the end of the third century seized so quickly upon ideas from beyond Egypt, expressing them in a variety of dialects, indicates a longer-standing degree of skill and an informed contact with the Greek world.[62] Most important of all, it is now clear that monks were not the initiators of such a development, and that early Coptic was not intimately associated with

---

nationalist also. Dionysius was a disciple of Origen. For the dates of Demetrius, see B. M. Metzger, *The Early Versions of the New Testament*, p. 100.

57.   Bell, *Cults*, p. 88 (italics mine); but we may respect the greater caution of his "Evidences," p. 204.

58.   Clearly expressed by Bell, *Cults*, p. 66.

59.   See Frend, "Athanasius," p. 22. "Welded into harmony" is the phrase he uses. But in whose mind?

60.   Bell, *Cults*, p. 88; Hardy, *Christian Egypt*, p. 34.

61.   Metzger, *Early Versions*, in the important chapter, "The Introduction of Christianity into Egypt and the Translation of the New Testament," pp. 99–108.

62.   R. Kasser, "Y a-t-il une généalogie des dialectes coptes?" in *Mélanges d'histoire des religions offerts à Henri-Charles Puech* (q.v.), pp. 431–36. See also his "Les Dialectes coptes et les versions coptes bibliques," *Biblica* 46 (1965): 278–310, summarized in English by Metzger, *Early Versions* pp. 127–32. His comments will now qualify the observations of J. Doresse, *Les Livres secrets des gnostiques d'Égypte*, 1:160.

gnostic or heretical writing. Quite apart from the detectable appeal of orthodoxy in Upper Egypt, the immediate binding of Coptic texts into codex form, scotching the sleights of the interpolator, may indicate a taste for authoritative tradition.[63]

Pachomius and his associates were markedly attached to orthodoxy. There is no reason to think that attachment is merely a gloss imposed on the texts by later compilers. The association between Athanasius and ascetics of many types is well and independently documented; he noted at a very early stage in his episcopal career a clear link between the pursuit of perfection and the support of the doctrine of his church: "And as when brother is helped by brother, they become as a wall to each other; so faith and godliness, being of kindred growth, hang together; and he who is occupied in the one, of necessity is strengthened by the other."[64]

Because of the variety we can now discern in early Alexandrian Christianity, the concept of orthodoxy may hinder us most in understanding the spread of that religion to other parts of the country. "Orthodoxy" is a judgment, not a description. For the historian preoccupied with sound, triumphant doctrine and canonical leadership, Alexandria is made to peer anxiously south, finding not only a cultural desert, linguistic barriers, and a lack of hierarchical structure, but also an abundance of gnostics.[65] The evidence for such a conclusion is thin and late; furthermore, a logical flaw is at work here. If Egyptians reveled in dissent and mystification, then either they were reacting to a clear corpus of orthodox ideas, in which case not all Egyptians were so impetuous, or else we are dealing, as in Alexandria itself, with nothing more than a variety that predated definitions, in which case the impetuosity was not so heretical! It is dangerous amid such variety to talk of heresies as "blind alleys or forms of incipient lunacy," which the church had the "uncommon degree of horse sense" to condemn. That is like watching the rerun of a race while fixing your eyes confidently on the outsider you now know to have won as he inches unexpectedly forward along the fence. The only question we have the right to ask is simply, why did late Roman religious sentiment eventually take, on the larger scale, the form it did, a form still so characteristic of the ancient world?[66]

63.   Roberts, *Manuscript*, pp. 64–69. See his "The Codex," *Proceedings of the British Academy* 40 (1954): 169–204.

64.   Athanasius *Festal Epistles* 11 (A.D. 339), trans. Burgess, *Festal Epistles*, p. 92.

65.   W. H. C. Frend, "The Gnostic Sects and the Roman Empire," *Journal of Ecclesiastical History* 5 (1954): 35. The text is cautious; the footnote is not!

66.   See Bell, *Cults*, pp. 90, 95; *Egypt*, p. 106. At issue here are the assumptions of W. Bauer, *Orthodoxy and Heresy in Earliest Christianity* (originally pub-

The problem presents itself particularly with reference to gnosticism. To summarize gnosticism here would be difficult.[67] It was not specifically Egyptian, and not exclusively Christian. To put the matter at its simplest, the gnostic will stress knowledge as the supreme religious experience and will suggest that such knowledge is open only to a few. In order to preserve or explain that exclusive note, he may resort to highly symbolic and mythological language. In the process, what is "known" religiously has less and less to do with the world of sense experience.

To regard gnosticism as some religious norm against which Christian orthodoxy fought a beleaguered and intolerant battle, only lately successful, is to exaggerate matters on both sides. It is better to suggest that much first-century religious thought and behavior could be labeled gnostic and that upon that world, as upon Judaism itself, the appearance of Jesus and his followers forced a variety of adaptations. "The emergence of belief in a specific Redeemer [and particularly in "a supernatural being who had appeared on earth"] could give a wholly new importance to speculations about cosmogony and the Primal Man," and hence "precipitated elements previously suspended in solution."[68] The

---

lished in German, 1934), translated under the editorship of R. Kraft and G. Krodel. The work is usefully taken to task by J. F. McCue, "Walter Bauer and the Valentinians," *Vigiliae Christianae* 33 (1979): 118–30.

67.   Nor can we mount a detailed criticism of the extensive literature. The following provide a good introduction, but adopt a variety of approaches, which cannot be equally reliable. An excellent place to start would be Nock, "Gnosticism," in *Essays*, ed. Stewart, 2:940–59. An idea of the debates involved can be gained from the anthology *Gnosis*, ed. R. Haardt, trans. J. F. Hendry. A recent and outstanding major study is K. Rudolph, *Die Gnosis*. Two sets of collected papers are invaluable: G. Quispel, *Gnostic Studies*, 2 vols., and H-C. Puech, *En quête de la gnose*, 2 vols. Different views can be gained from R. McL. Wilson, *The Gnostic Problem*; K. Koschorke, *Die Polemik der Gnostiker gegen das kirchliche Christentum*; and Elaine Pagels, *The Gnostic Paul* and *The Gnostic Gospels*.
Central to our Egyptian interest is the discovery of gnostic texts at Nag Hammadi. The best guide to the early years of interpretation is J. Doresse, *Les Livres secrets des gnostiques d'Égypte*, vol. 1. To this I shall refer, but an English translation is available, *The Secret Books of the Egyptian Gnostics*. The codices themselves are available in *The Facsimile Edition of the Nag Hammadi Codices*, 12 vols.; English translation in *The Nag Hammadi Library in English*, edited under the directorship of J. M. Robinson. A very searching review of the whole enterprise was presented by R. A. Kraft and Janet Timbie, *Religious Studies Review* 8 (1982): 32–51. See also the many papers in the series "Nag Hammadi Studies."
68.   A. D. Nock, "A Coptic Library of Gnostic Writings," *Journal of Theological Studies*, n.s., 11 (1958): 321, and "Gnosticism," in *Essays*, ed. Stewart, 2:958. On the link with Judaism, Quispel is particularly useful, *Gnostic Studies*. Gnosticism was not the result of a confrontation between paganism and Christianity, but much more a part of the general religious atmosphere that made such a vari-

consequent adaptations were often accepted in the early period as both Christian and orthodox and were rendered suspect only to later generations. We are dealing, in the initial stages of development, with "the aggregate of a series of individualistic responses to the religious situation."[69] Only later theologians in the tradition of Irenaeus and Hippolytus systematized opponents and forced them to define themselves vis-à-vis the tradition of the theologians' choice. In the process, they set up on the surface of "ecclesiastical history" a series of misleading milestones marking the supposed advance of the pristine faith. Those whom they attacked, like Basilides, were in no way so systematic and were most reluctant to be forced into some heretical corner. They preferred to develop their ideas orally and to interpret for disciples as best they could the intricacies of scripture.[70] Valentinus, who was the best-known gnostic within the Christian tradition, was only very slowly driven into opposition, as even the *Gospel of Truth* makes clear. By the time we come to the much later documents peculiar to the so-called Nag Hammadi library, the clarity of those earlier "heretics," with their greater moral seriousness and their avoidance of bizarre mythology, offers a refreshing and rational contrast. Later Egyptian gnosticism had left such great traditions far behind, and that would have been reason enough for its finding itself at odds with Christianity.[71]

The Christians themselves in fourth-century Egypt had had enough time to establish themselves with some confidence as distinct from gnostic groups. The debates initiated by Irenaeus had been known of in the

---

ety of theological positions possible. And precisely because they subscribed to that tolerance, martyrdom was a puzzle to gnostics. That apparent distaste for needless heroism did not spring from some "heretical" desire on their part to oppose the institutional church. Compare Frend, "Gnostic Sects," p. 35 (referring to Origen *Contra Celsum* 3.12), with his more acceptable emphasis on gnostic syncretism, which made it more a rival to Christianity than a heresy within it, pp. 31f.

69. Nock, "Gnosticism," p. 954.

70. A point much emphasized by Rudolph, *Gnosis*, esp. pp. 330ff. The practice is reminiscent of monastic catechesis, as discussed in Chapter IV. More clearly than anyone, Rudolph has made self-knowledge the central element in gnosticism, pp. 130ff.

71. See K. Grobel, *The Gospel of Truth: A Valentinian Meditation on the Gospel*, and H-C. Puech, "Plotin et les gnostiques," in *Les Sources de Plotin* (q.v.), pp. 178–79. For the dating, see Doresse, *Livres secrets*, pp. 163ff. The whole point is taken up from a specifically Egyptian viewpoint, and against Bauer, by Roberts, *Manuscript*, pp. 49f, strongly supported by Skeat in his review (see n. 16). J. Doresse, *Des hiéroglyphes à la croix*, tries to find specifically Egyptian elements in Egyptian gnosticism. It is clear that his examples are much too late to have definitely affected Pachomius's age.

province, perhaps well before his death shortly after 200,[72] but very few at the time would have been so clear-headed as he. The lines of battle laid down in books did not always correspond to those on the ground. "We may surmise that for much of the second century [the Church in Egypt had] no strong central authority and little organization; one of the directions in which it developed was certainly Gnosticism, but a Gnosticism not initially separated from the rest of the Church."[73] The way religious curiosity and the documents that fed it were reaching beyond the enclaves of original speculation did most to promote a more confident and informed body within the Egyptian church. Once again we establish the link with the unity of the province and the growing influence of town life. "Behind this group of papyri [namely, the earliest Christian manuscripts of Egypt] it is not difficult to envisage the men familiar to us from the documentary papyri in the Arsinoite or Oxyrhynchus: tradesmen, farmers, minor government officials to whom knowledge of and writing in Greek was an essential skill, but who had few or no literary interests."[74] By the time we reach the "orthodox" of Pachomius's day, we find that, whatever their suspicions of contemporary gnostics, they retained a link with that broader past, which had often been gnostic in its less-defined way. We should not imagine that mainstream Christianity had by then purged itself completely, forcing all gnostics into peripheral conventicles. The "precipitated elements" mentioned above continued to appear throughout the religious world. Heretics were not alone in their enduring need to structure in more detail their attachment to wisdom! But at the same time, some exaggerated inclination to personal vision, some elitist complacency, would isolate this or that group of people who might in the earlier period have continued to survive more peaceably within the central body of the church.[75]

It was not only Christians who at once shared and rejected the gnostic world. There were pagan gnostics also, and pagans who viewed these with suspicion. It is clear from an examination of, say, the Hermetic tradition that there were plenty who thought of themselves as neither Christian nor gnostic, and yet repudiated material rewards, longed to be released from the power of fate, to gain spiritual knowledge, to achieve purity of heart and union with God. They had enough in common with

72. Roberts, *Manuscript*, pp. 23, 53.
73. Ibid., p. 71.
74. Ibid., p. 21; see above at nn. 17f.
75. This renders less adequate the categories of R. McL. Wilson, "From Gnosis to Gnosticism," in *Mélanges Puech*, pp. 423–29. We shall discuss a specific confrontation between Pachomius and the non-Christian world in Chapter VIII at nn. 64f.

gnostics and with Christians to know where they wished to draw the lines between them.[76]

One of the most famous opponents of gnostic thought was a third-century Egyptian pagan, the philosopher Plotinus. His teaching did not have more influence in Egypt than elsewhere (he spent his most productive years in Italy), but his ideas had certainly affected some of the early biographers of Pachomius and may have penetrated the province more generally during his lifetime.

What type of gnosticism Plotinus had in mind when making his criticism is not clear.[77] Porphyry hints in his *Life* of the philosopher that it was that of the so-called Sethians, although he is not so specific as to mention the name. The implication would allow us to associate Plotinus's comments with some of the documents in the Nag Hammadi corpus. The *Enneads* themselves—that is to say, Porphyry's edition of Plotinus's works—seem to refer to an earlier, Valentinian mode of thought.[78] A sentence in Porphyry's biography, still in the context of Plotinus's attack on gnosticism, increases the confusion: Γεγόνασι δὲ κατ' αὐτὸν τῶν Χριστιανῶν πολλοὶ μὲν καὶ ἄλλοι, αἱρετικοὶ δὲ ἐκ τῆς παλαιᾶς φιλοσοφίας ἀνηγμένοι. With the comma where it is, Plotinus's best-known translator has taken this to mean, "There were in his time many Christians and others, and sectarians who had abandoned the old philosophy." But some commentators have wished to suggest that Christian gnostics alone were in view. Their translation would be rather, "There were in his time a wide variety of Christians, and in particular sectarians who had abandoned the old philosophy." It would certainly be difficult to make "others" go with "sectarians," moving the comma; and even the first translation avoids such a choice. What matters most is that, however the translation runs, the word "sectarians" (αἱρετικοί, literally, "heretics") refers to these people's abandonment of the "old philosophy"—i.e., paganism—and not necessarily to any distinction between themselves and the orthodox church.[79]

76. The material outlined in n. 67, and on paganism more generally in the introduction to the Bibliography, will offer sufficient background. See also Bell, *Cults*, pp. 75f, and Doresse, *Livres secrets*, p. 7.

77. His anti-gnostic essay was in four parts, scattered by Porphyry in the *Enneads* but reassembled by R. Harder, "Eine neue Schrift Plotins," *Hermes* 71 (1936): 1–10. Combine, therefore, *Enneads* 3.8, 5.8, 5.5, 2.9 (in that order), and see Porphyry's *Life of Plotinus* 16.

78. Puech, "Plotin et les gnostiques," pp. 161f, 173f.

79. So Puech, "Plotin et les gnostiques," p. 163, supported by E. R. Dodds in the discussion following the paper, p. 175. See also A. H. Armstrong, "Man in the Cosmos: A Study of Some Differences between Pagan Neoplatonism and Christianity," paper 22 in his *Plotinian and Christian Studies*, pp. 6–8.

For the student of Christian asceticism, the attack Plotinus mounts is well worth examining. His first emphasis is on power, in the sense of personal energy, talent, and initiative. It represents a value and goal in life worthy of greater attention than knowledge. What people have within themselves will count for more in the end than what they see or know. Advancing this position, the first section of his anti-gnostic treatise reveals Plotinus as a moralist, intent always upon the practical demands implied by his philosophy.[80]

He pursues the same theme in the next section, since the power we harness in our own lives has to be directed, he says, most of all toward subduing ourselves in preparation for what he calls "inner comeliness, the truly personal" (τὸ εἴσω κάλλος αὐτοῦ). Understanding and perception, therefore, when they come, are not to be thought of merely as the acts of some spectator. They are linked much more with self-possession and with a person's ability to see divinity within.[81]

For that reason Plotinus insists on a unity between the knower and the known, which means in this case between the moral and religious individual and the divine order or person. He had no time for the dramatic and anxious religiosity so characteristic of the gnostics—the sense of estrangement in the face of the material world and the consequently urgent attempt to reach out from a situation of human doubt, inadequacy, and imperfection. To make such a transition from one world to another would inevitably contaminate (if that were possible) the divine itself. We cannot approach the divine, Plotinus says, as if it lay completely beyond ourselves. We must grow to appreciate its persistent presence in our lives and persons.[82] Plotinus, for a Platonist, was surprisingly optimistic about the world and about human nature. Gnostics, on the other hand, regarded them as inescapably chaotic and evil.[83] It is the unity of the person that he emphasizes once again, and the worthy destiny of the body. Darker expectations are firmly rejected.[84]

The most remarkable conclusion in Plotinus's final essay is that we must make an effort in our moral lives, unlike the complacent and disdainful gnostics, and that we must do so in the light of a treasured past. Gnostics laugh at those who venerate "beings whose worship they in-

80.   Plotinus *Enneads* 3.8, esp. sections 3–4, 9–10. The place of δύναμις in ancient religion is perceptively handled by A. D. Nock, "Studies in the Graeco-Roman Beliefs of the Empire," in *Essays*, ed. Stewart, 1:33–48. See also H-C. Puech, "La gnose et le temps," *Eranos Jahrbuch* 20 (1951): 68f.

81.   Plotinus *Enneads* 5.8.2 and 10.

82.   Ibid. 5.5.1–2 and 8.

83.   These passages mark, for Puech, a movement in Plotinus away from dualism and pessimism: "Plotin et les gnostiques," p. 184.

84.   Plotinus *Enneads* 2.9.1–2, 4, 13, 15.

herit from antiquity." Like Epicurus's, their doctrine "scorns every law known to us; immemorial virtue and all restraint it makes into a laughing stock." Plotinus criticizes them for "reviling and seeking in their own persons to replace men honoured by the fine intelligences of ages past." "Instead of insulting those venerable teachers," he says, "they should receive their doctrine with the respect due to the older thought and honour all that noble system." [85] Those were precisely the criticisms leveled against the gnostics by orthodox Christians.

A defense of tradition represented the clearest distinction between the gnostics and all their opponents. Gnosticism was essentially an antihistorical religion. The very notion of time was associated with enslavement in the system of the visible, material world from which every gnostic looked to escape. Christians also hoped for a saving revelation, but they stressed, for the most part, that the revelation was public, universally available, and dependent above all on the fact that in the person of Jesus God had immersed himself in human history. They rejected also the gnostic suspicion that the creator and the redeemer were at odds with one another in the cosmos.[86] Revelation and salvation for Christians were part of a plan, long foreseen and fully understood by both Jesus and his Father and unfolded in the record of human progress. Hence arose the importance, which we have already noted, of a textual tradition, above all of the Bible, which was thought to illustrate and authenticate the progress of revelation, or salvation history. That was what made a gnostic writer's links with his past models so different from that, say, between Coptic monks and the biblical scholarship of Christian and Jewish Alexandria: the gnostic was simply toying with literary types and themes. The interplay between a speculative mind and what came to be thought of as the canon of scripture would have been a discipline foreign to him. As Athanasius pointed out, gnostics "indeed refer to the Scriptures, but do not hold such opinions as the saints have handed down." [87]

There is an uncanny similarity between the teachings of Pachomius and the points raised by Plotinus. The moral emphasis on action, the search for self-possession and inner vision, the respect for the body, a sense that the past was important as a buttress to the community in which one grew: all these convictions will recur in the chapters that fol-

85.   Ibid. 2.9.6, 9, 15. The translations throughout have been those of S. MacKenna, *The Enneads*.

86.   These are points developed fully by Puech, "La gnose et le temps," esp. pp. 81f. Bell is also perceptive, *Cults*, pp. 91, 102.

87.   Athanasius *Festal Epistles* 2 (A.D. 330), trans. Burgess, *Festal Epistles*, p. 19.

low. The final point in particular deserves some emphasis. As we shall see in the early sections of Chapter III, and again in Chapter IX, Pachomius and his biographers were very conscious of their place within a doctrinal and institutional, but also specifically ascetic, religious tradition. They wished to make it clear in addition that there was now a "Pachomian" history with its own orthodoxy and its own authentic succession of leaders. At a more personal level, Pachomius defended passionately the conviction that men and women by their own efforts, their spiritual discipline, could change, could make progress, could create and live out a personal history of their own. That will form a central theme of Chapter VII. Such teachings were not peculiar to Pachomius, but they were drastically opposed to gnostic beliefs. To whatever extent he was conscious of such opponents, that attachment, so to speak, to the cause of time itself would have represented his most telling attack on gnosticism and perhaps his most valuable contribution to the history of Christian asceticism.

And very conscious of opposition he must have been. He would not have read the *Enneads*! Not even his biographers need have done that. What they tell us, even so, discloses in itself how quickly a philosophic thesis might penetrate a provincial hinterland. There are other reasons Pachomius must have had explicit knowledge of gnostic ideas. The famous codices from Nag Hammadi—our own source of so much gnostic information—were found very close to Chenoboskion; this was Pachomius's native village and the site of one of his later monasteries. The connection has caused some excitement and as well some speculations that may be premature. At the time the discoveries were first being assessed, in the late 1940s, it seemed reasonable to stress that the find had been made away from the area settled by Christians in a burial ground they had abandoned. It was thought that the Christians might even have been ignorant of so "secret" a sect in the vicinity. Scholars were well aware, on the other hand, that Pachomian monks had been informed of dangerous texts circulating in Upper Egypt. Athanasius, in a *Festal Epistle* of 367, had been anxious to have such texts purged from monastic libraries if that should prove necessary. Theodore, Pachomius's successor, and general superior at the time, saw the implied conflict as one between a reliable tradition of exegesis and texts that had deviously attributed novel speculations to the "saints." This latter description could apply to some of the Nag Hammadi codices. Their burial at Chenoboskion, therefore, was thought to represent the last act of some group in rivalry or conflict with nearby monastic leaders, perhaps with Theodore and his subjects. Finally and fearfully, it was supposed, they were succumbing to the local triumph of orthodoxy in the late fourth or early fifth century.[88]

The situation was then complicated by the gradual extraction, unfolding, and eventual publication of the cartonnage of the Nag Hammadi codices—that is, of the paper used to pack their covers and bindings.[89] Some of the volumes were found to contain letters and other documents from a monastic setting. There were thought to be references to known Pachomian personalities, which might link the codices more directly with the community at Chenoboskion.[90] Hence the suggestion was made that the "library" had been collected or even compiled by the Pachomian monks themselves as a weapon against gnostic opponents and buried as either redundant or, after Athanasius's declared anxiety, too embarrassing to hold on to.[91] Even more daring was the suggestion that the texts pointed to the presence within the very monastery itself of gnostics who had ultimately been reconciled with the church by their incorporation in a community not inimical to their ideas and not dissimilar to their own former associations.[92] Evidence for so close a connection between gnostics and the community at Chenoboskion still seems very thin. There may have been a naive tolerance at work in that one monastery. The arguments put forward to date, however, are not sufficiently attentive to the cautions already expressed in this chapter and are based in part on assumptions about Egyptian gnosticism open

88.   So Doresse, *Livres secrets*, pp. 154f, 164f, 290f. The relevant Pachomian texts are the Bohairic *Life* 189, and the Sahidic *Life* 3ᵇ.4, trans. L-Th. Lefort, *Les Vies coptes de saint Pachôme*, pp. 205f, 370f. Fuller bibliographical references to these texts will be found in Chapter II. For Athanasius, see *Festal Epistles* 39, trans. L-Th. Lefort, *S. Athanase, lettres festales et pastorales en copte*, CSCO 151:31–40. The text bears out the reported interpretation by Theodore, although it is mainly preoccupied with the Melitians.

89.   The material was first displayed in *Facsimile Edition*, vol. 11: see n. 67.

90.   J. W. B. Barns, "Greek and Coptic Papyri from the Covers of the Nag Hammadi Codices," in *Essays on the Nag Hammadi Texts in Honour of Pahor Labib*, ed. M. Krause, pp. 9–17 (see Bibliography under "Krause"). Note also the cautious comment appended by E. G. Turner, ibid., pp. 17–18.

91.   So Barns and, to some extent independently, T. Säve-Söderbergh, "Holy Scriptures or Apologetic Documentations?" in *Les Textes de Nag Hammadi*, ed. J-E. Ménard, pp. 3–14. This is where, for example, the debate between Theodore and the "philosophers" of Panopolis (Akhmîm) acquires importance, as already noted by Doresse, *Livres secrets*, pp. 155f. The relevant text is the Bohairic *Life* 55, trans. Lefort, *Vies*, pp. 117f. See further in Chapter VIII.

92.   F. Wisse, "Gnosticism and Early Monasticism in Egypt," in *Gnosis: Festschrift für Hans Jonas*, ed. Barbara Aland, pp. 431–40 (see Bibliography under "Aland").

to suspicion on other grounds. Nor do they seem informed enough
about contrasting emphases in the Pachomian corpus and about ascetic
development in the fourth century more generally. In any case, further
reflection and a more careful examination of the texts has now vindicated those who expressed doubt about these early speculations. The
possibilities that remain are more mundane and revolve around the *economic* relations between the Chenoboskion community and its environs.
The monks could have bound someone else's material or could simply
have produced blank codices for the use of anyone who wished to buy
them. Otherwise we know too little about the circulation of wastepaper
or the production of codices to draw conclusions from such meager
evidence.[93]

To suppose that the Egyptian church, or indeed any other Christian
community in the empire, was divided simply between orthodox rig-
orists and gnostic speculators would be a grave error. The chief implication of our account so far must be that boundaries between religious
groups were slow to form, rarely clear-cut, and constantly adjusted. The
variety of religious behavior and belief should strike us most; Pachomius
would have found the spiritual resources available to him amid this variety both abundant and confusing.

The case of the Manichees also illustrates the fluid state of religious
traditions in the lifetime of Pachomius.[94] We have evidence of Mani-

93.   For second thoughts, see esp. J. C. Shelton's introduction to *Nag Hammadi Codices: Greek and Coptic Papyri from the Cartonnage of the Covers*, ed. J. W. B.
Barns et al. Turner appears to have been correct in his judgment that what was
previously taken (on the basis of photographs and a cautious peep) to have been
the exciting word μονή should in fact read κώμης, pp. 2f (see n. 90 above). Shelton is skeptical about any connection with Pachomius, pp. 5f. The best judgment
on how matters rest at the moment is that of Roberts in his review of the cartonnage facsimile, *Journal of Theological Studies*, n.s., 32 (1981): 265–66. It was particularly unwise of Wisse to be confident that monasticism "lacked at this time the
organization and the political muscle to be a serious threat to the gnostic sects,"
"Gnosticism and Early Monasticism," p. 433.

94.   This is not the place to present a summary of so major a religion. An
excellent introduction is provided by H-C. Puech in a revised version of a 1936
essay, "La Conception manichéenne du salut," reprinted in his *Sur le manichéisme,
et autres essais*, pp. 5–101. See also P. Brown, "The Diffusion of Manichaeism in
the Roman Empire," *Journal of Roman Studies* 59 (1969): 92–103. Major works of
varying quality are as follows: H-C. Puech, *Le Manichéisme: son fondateur, sa doctrine*; G. Widengren, *Mani and Manichaeism*, trans. C. Kessler; J. P. Asmussen,

chaean activity in Egypt, as we shall see. We also have textual accounts of Manichaean belief, which we can place tidily on the table, like the Jewish and gnostic material, and compare coolly with Pachomian and other monastic literature. But excitement at the evidence of Manichaean activity might be premature, and a comparison of texts might mislead us in suggesting clear distinctions and ideas. We need to observe more carefully how scattered are the references and how obscurely shaded were the differences between Manichees and those around them.

It is natural to make some connection between the Manichees and the gnostics, since both movements were preoccupied with a need to escape from the power of evil. A comparable connection also exists between Manichees and Christians. Mani was not, any more than the gnostics, simply a Christian heretic, but his theology did develop in the company of what would later be regarded as eccentric Jewish and Christian devotees.[95] Religious eccentricity, of course, was not peculiar to Egypt. What is more immediately interesting is the suggested link between Manichees and the revolt of Domitianus, already discussed in an earlier section. We have letters of one Paniscus, apparently an ally of Domitianus stationed in the southern center of his revolt. Paniscus asked his wife, who was still in the Faiyûm, to send him weapons and eventually to join him $\mu\varepsilon\tau\grave{\alpha}$ $\grave{\alpha}\nu\vartheta\rho\acute{\omega}\pi\omega\nu$ $\kappa\alpha\lambda\tilde{\omega}\nu$. It has been suggested that

---

X^{U}ĀSTVĀNĪFT: *Studies in Manichaeism*; L. J. R. Ort, *Mani*. An even wider background, which he has subsequently modified, is provided in two works by K. Rudolph, *Die Mandäer*, 2 vols., and *Theogonie, Kosmogonie und Anthropogonie in der mandäischen Schriften*. See also his *Gnosis*, pp. 349ff.

The main corpus of Egyptian material may be consulted as follows. Discoveries were introduced in C. Schmidt and H. J. Polotsky, *Ein Mani-Fund in Ägypten*. The texts are edited as follows: H. J. Polotsky, ed., *Manichäische Handschriften der Sammlung A. Chester Beatty*, vol. 1, *Manichäische Homilien*; C. R. C. Allberry, ed., *Manichaean Manuscripts in the Chester Beatty Collection*, vol. 2, *A Manichaean Psalm-Book*, part 2; H. J. Polotsky and A. Böhlig, eds., *Manichäische Handschriften der staatlichen Museen Berlin*, vol. 1, *Kephalaia*, gen. ed. C. Schmidt, with additional comment by H. Ibscher. See also A. Henrichs and L. Koenen, "Ein griechischer Mani-Codex," *Zeitschrift für Papyrologie und Epigraphik* 5 (1970): 97–216. My understanding of Manichaeism in Egypt has been greatly aided by the comments of Dr. David W. Johnson of the Institute of Christian Oriental Research, Catholic University of America.

95. This is an important implication of Henrichs and Koenen, "Griechischer Mani-Codex," accepted by K. Rudolph, "Die Bedeutung des kölner Mani-Codex für die Manichäismusforschung: vorläufige Anmerkungen," in *Mélanges Puech*, pp. 471–86. See further R. N. Frye, "The Cologne Greek Codex about Mani," in *Ex orbe religionum: Studia Geo Widengren* (q.v.), 1:424–29. We do not have to think of Manichees, however, as *successors* to the gnostics, whether in Egypt or elsewhere: see Frend, "Athanasius," p. 28.

those "good" men (to take the word καλῶν at its weakest) were a group
of the Manichaean "elect." The allusion is not obvious and certainly does
not offer clear proof that Manichees took part in political subversion.[96] It
does, however, alert us to other hints. At least one Manichaean text describes the visit to Egypt and the activities there of one Addai, Addas, or
Pappos, a personal emissary of Mani, who founded, especially in the
Thebaid, a number of mānistān (a word normally translated as "monasteries"). Naturally it would be exciting and important if we were able to
suggest, quite apart from any connection of Manichees with Domitianus, the presence of such communities, founded and enlivened by a
self-confident and proselytizing group apparently at just the time when
organized Christian asceticism was first making its appearance in the
province.[97]

Certain other considerations at present disallow such enthusiastic
suppositions. There is an all-important gap in time between those Manichaean activities and the foundation of anything approaching what we
could call a Christian monastery. Nor could we safely regard the Manichaean communities as antecedents to Christian ascetic groups. It is not
clear what mānistān in late third-century Egypt might have been; the

96.   For the original suggestion, without additional documentation, see
W. Seston, "L'Égypte manichéenne," Chronique d'Égypte 14 (1939): 368. He refers
to his own "Achilleus et la révolte de l'Égypte sous Dioclétien," Mélanges d'archéologie et d'histoire de l'École française de Rome 55 (1938): 184–200; but it does not add
much that is helpful. For the text, see J. G. Winter, Papyri in the University of
Michigan Collection: Miscellaneous Papyri, p. 278, no. 214, lines 25f.

Skepticism is precise in Jacqueline Lallemand, "Lucius Domitius Domitianus," Aegyptus 33 (1953): 97–104, and may have compelled J. Schwartz to content
himself with the phrase "une tendance possible," L. Domitius Domitianus, p. 128.
Doubts were also expressed by J. A. L. Vergote, "Der Manichäismus in Ägypten,"
in Der Manichaismus, ed. G. Widengren, p. 392 n. 17. There is useful reflection
on these events in H. Chadwick, "The Relativity of Moral Codes," in Early Christian Literature, ed. W. R. Schoedel and R. L. Wilken, pp. 135–53.

97.   The implications of the text concerned were most enthusiastically explored by Seston, "L'Égypte manichéenne," pp. 365f. See also Vergote, "Manichäismus." The text itself, known as M 2, was published in F. C. Andreas and W.
Henning, Mitteliranische Manichaica aus Chinesisch-Turkestan, 2:[302]. For English
translation with commentary, see Ort, Mani, pp. 62–67. See also the comments
in H. H. Schraeder, Iranica, pp. 68–83. P. Peeters, in a useful review of Schmidt
and Polotsky, Mani-Fund, suggested that there was no significant contact between Pachomius and such circles, Analecta Bollandiana 51 (1933): 396–99. For a
useful bibliography and comment, see Asmussen, X^UĀSTVĀNĪFT, p. 21 n. 29,
and his Chapter 5 n. 14, pp. 260f. That Augustine may have known of Addai is
suggested by W. H. C. Frend, "The Gnostic-Manichaean Tradition in Roman
North Africa," Journal of Ecclesiastical History 4 (1953): 20.

word means simply "dwellings."[98] Wherever they may have "dwelled" for a time, the Manichaean elect would have been very different from Pachomian monks, at least, since these elect were highly mobile, and dependent entirely (by definition, for theological reasons) on the support and therefore on the labor of others.[99]

An attempt to associate Manichaeans with the Melitians and thus to corroborate further their impact upon the Egyptian church is equally insecure.[100] The Melitian schism arose, in ways akin to Donatism in North Africa, because a party in the Egyptian church refused to compromise with those who had shown weakness during the years of persecution under Diocletian. Certainly there was a connection between these schismatics and some of the ascetic communities in Egypt. That connection, however, does not make them either clearly Manichaean or indeed exclusively Coptic or nationalistic.[101] Athanasius displayed a natural anxiety about the followers of Melitius, who had been bishop of Lycopolis, but it revolved for the most part around matters of discipline and in no way diminished his sympathy for and encouragement of ascetic developments.

So the Manichees present us with no clear-cut alternative to or direct antecedent of Christian asceticism in Egypt at that time. The snippets of information, always partial and obscure, simply prove again that in the decades prior to Pachomius's emergence upon the scene a wide variety of sometimes eccentric and sometimes ascetic experiments in religious life were under way. Only later, among those vaguely and often errone-

98. A more specific translation depended, for Andreas and Henning, on the interpretation of another text, M 36, p. [326], where the context, entirely different, is yet richer and more obviously religious: "*mānistān* bedeutet 'Wohnung,' speziell 'Wohnung der Erwälten' = 'Kloster.'" Their inspiration is betrayed by their appeal to W. Bang, "Manichäische Hymnen," *Le Muséon* 38 (1925): 30f, where much wider meaning was nevertheless admitted (although some earlier commentators, according to Bang, had suggested monastic parallels). The problem is complicated by the lateness of M 2, whose central Asian translators would have interpreted late third-century Egyptian events in the light of the more recent and, to them, more familiar confrontation between Manichaean missionaries and Buddhist ascetics; this is a point that emerges from S. N. C. Lieu, "Precept and Practice in Manichaean Monasticism," *Journal of Theological Studies*, n.s., 32 (1981): 153–73.

99. A point made very forcibly by Brown, "Diffusion," esp. pp. 101–2.

100. As by R. M. Grant, "Manichees and Christians in the Third and Early Fourth Centuries," in *Studia Widengren*, 1:435–36.

101. Handle with care, therefore, Hardy, *Christian Egypt*, p. 53. See Ruppert, p. 59f, and, more generally, H. I. Bell, *Jews and Christians in Egypt*, part 2, pp. 38ff.

ously informed, would it seem either possible or necessary to label any of them "Manichaean."

Eusebius, for example, has a fascinating story about Nepos, an early third-century bishop from the Arsinoite *nome*.[102] Nepos had encouraged the development of a closely knit community with ascetic values, a love of psalmody, and a devotion to hard work. He had also written a millenarian treatise, Ἔλεγχος ἀλληγοριστῶν, based on a literal interpretation of the *Apocalypse* and offering the hope of a material paradise devoted, as Eusebius put it, to "bodily indulgence." His later opponent Dionysius of Alexandria, in his Περὶ ἐπαγγελιῶν, thought that Nepos had been subject to Jewish influence. Dionysius deplored above all the man's repudiation of tradition, his claim that his work contained "some great hidden mystery," and his division of Christians into spiritual classes, only some of which were capable of understanding the resurrection or what it meant to be "like Christ." Dionysius was compelled to counter the lasting influence of Nepos in the surrounding villages, among people who were, as he admitted himself, of sound judgment and keen intelligence.

Clearly the Christian community created by Nepos fits exactly into the picture of the developing church in third-century Egypt that we have already outlined. We have the Jewish background, the informed up-country Christian, the expanding *metropolis*, the agricultural industry, the doctrinal idiosyncrasy. We also discover categories that might easily be labeled, especially by later commentators, monastic, or gnostic, or Manichaean. What Eusebius's account makes most clear, however, is that Nepos pursued what was for him an integrated set of ideas and pastoral programs. He was *sui generis*.

Another example of religious diversity, already touched upon during our discussion of the Coptic background, is provided by Hieracas. Epiphanius of Salamis, in his *Panarion*, a refutation of all heresies written in the 370s, linked Hieracas with both the Manichees and Origen— neither reference being intended as a compliment![103] According to this heresiologist, Hieracas encouraged a strict mode of life, insisted that paradise was open only to those who made a considerable moral effort, and was opposed to marriage and to the notion of a bodily resurrection. Epiphanius wrote that in his own day many of the "ascetics of Egypt" had come to follow Hieracas's lead.

But was it fair to suggest that Hieracas was a Manichee? Athanasius,

102.   Eusebius *HE* 7.24. This was precisely the area where Domitianus's supposed and possibly Manichaean supporters came from, and a center of Melitian loyalty at the time of Nicaea.

103.   Epiphanius *Panarion* 67.

in a letter on virginity, had warned that he ought to be numbered among heretics, particularly because of his teaching on marriage,[104] and we have a letter from another bishop in Egypt attacking Manichees for precisely those notions.[105] Without the benefit of such advice, how many would have thought of Hieracas as even heretical, let alone a Manichee? In any case, it is not sufficiently clear that Epiphanius, Athanasius, and the anonymous bishop were all focusing on the same aspects of religious behavior.

There are other examples of the variety of religious practices. Philostorgius reproduces the story of one Aetius, who had been an opponent of Athanasius, dodged in and out of a number of factions during the early years of the Arian controversy, and came to Alexandria itself to dispute with a Manichaean leader, Aphthonius.[106] The Manichee seems clearly defined in the account; equally characteristic of the period is the ambiguity and restlessness of his opponent. Then, too, Epiphanius, after discussing the Manichees and Hieracas, described a Syrian, Audius, who had been stirred by the abuse of wealth and by easy living in the church—just like Antony and like Pachomius's disciple Theodore. He was eventually driven to rebellion by the Council of Nicaea; his rebellion took the form of strong anti-clericalism coupled with a very rigorous ascetic program, which included the belief that one should labor to support oneself.[107] Even within the pages of the *Panarion* itself—a work not noted for its tolerance—a series of narrow but clear distinctions separated Audius, Hieracas, and the Manichees more generally; these distinctions were graciously admitted even a generation later by a man who had, of course, lived in Egypt himself. Only at the end of the century[108] were fewer people able to appreciate the varieties of behavior and allegiance possible in an earlier period, particularly in matters of elitism, dualism, virginity, hard work, and attitudes to the orthodox hierarchy.[109]

104.   Athanasius *Lettre aux vièrges*, trans. Lefort, *Lettres festales et pastorales*, pp. 65f.

105.   A. Adam, *Texte zum Manichäismus*, no. 35, pp. 52–54.

106.   Philostorgius *HE* 3.15.

107.   Epiphanius *Panarion* 70. Origenism figures here also, and the Jews!

108.   Though even then eccentric ascetics in Egypt could at least try to argue with Manichees: see the tale of Copres in Rufinus *HM* 9 (*PL* 21.426). He felt he might lose the verbal battle, so reverted to an ordeal by fire. The Manichee withdrew on singed soles.

109.   Peeters, in the review cited above, n. 97. Brown, "Diffusion," p. 100, repeats the account of Eutychius about an episcopal test for the discovery of Manichees, achieved by forcing monks to eat meat once a year. (There Manichees would draw the line, even if monks would not!) Brown has the wrong patriarch, Vergote, "Manichäismus," the wrong dates. Clearly the Egyptian bish-

Even in the early part of the century, however, some very precise criticisms were being leveled against Manichees. Those anxieties, more so than the vague allusions of later commentators, do tell us something about Pachomius's world. On the one hand, we have the pagan philosopher Alexander of Lycopolis, writing before Diocletian.[110] He deplored sectarianism, which he interpreted as a tendency to ignore doctrinal antecedents and to begin afresh with one's own insights amid a small band of devotees. The results of this tendency would be, and indeed were, irresponsible speculation, destructive rivalry, and a weakening of practical ethics.[111] Against Manichees in particular, Alexander's most telling thrust was the assertion that if one man could become perfect, then so could all—an attack, in other words, upon their elitism.[112] There is much in Alexander's work that recalls Plotinus's critique of the gnostics. And what in Alexander's eyes was the moral and social antidote to sectarian aberration?

> This was, I believe, correctly understood by Jesus, and this is why, in order that farmers and carpenters and masons and other skilled workers should not be excluded from the good, he instituted a common circle [κοινὸν συνέδριον] of all these people together, and why, by means of simple and easy conversation [διὰ ἁπλῶν καὶ εὐκόλων διαλέξεων], he led them towards an understanding of God and helped them to achieve a desire for the good.[113]

If there were Manichaean *mānistān* anywhere within Alexander's reach, the alternative he proposed to them was an evangelical society of skilled workers. The later achievements of Pachomius were much closer to the ideals of this Platonist than to anything Addai and his associates might have had in mind!

Somewhat later, Serapion, bishop of Thmuis in the Delta and a friend of Antony and Athanasius, also wrote a treatise against the Manichees. In his case the objects of attack seem to have been chosen simply so that

---

ops concerned had otherwise only the haziest notion of what a Manichee might think or do. See Eutychius *Annales* (*PG* 111.1023f). The original Greek is missing. The allusion, in Migne's text, to the Patriarch Timothy (A.D. 381–85) seems to reproduce faithfully both the Arabic and the Latin in Pococke's earlier edition (Oxford, 1658), 1: 514/515, but the broader context in which this small piece of information occurs is full of errors and fancies, and makes every detail open to doubt.

110.   See Alexander of Lycopolis *Contra Manichaei opiniones disputatio*, ed. A. Brinkmann, trans. P. W. van der Horst and J. Mansfeld. It was once possible to think Alexander a Christian bishop! That is not now accepted.

111.   Alexander *Disputatio* 1.

112.   Ibid. 16.

113.   Ibid.

he might construct an argument against the view that dualism could explain evil. Already the label "Manichee" was being more widely and more inaccurately applied. Serapion admitted that the error he abhorred was a κακία πολυειδὴς καὶ πολυσχεδής. He was obviously puzzled by what he still had to accept: the ideological and social ramifications of the dualist sects![114] What seems to have worried him most was the Christian guise adopted by so many of them. They were not a set of visibly differentiated rivals, but hidden within the church; that made them worse than even the gnostics.[115] Nevertheless, the main thrust of his work was theoretical, concentrating on the real possibility of conversion, on the relation between mind, soul, and body, and on the status of demons.[116] Much that he said recalls the teaching of Pachomius and the monastic developments with which his own generation was now entirely familiar. Serapion's writings serve to emphasize further the differences between Manichaean thought and that of Christian ascetic pioneers.

It is interesting to observe also how Serapion's own reputation was preserved by an even later generation. Socrates, writing toward the middle of the fifth century, recorded a statement made by Evagrius of Pontus, which would date, therefore, from the end of the fourth century:

> Sarapion, the angel of the church of the Thmuitae, declared that the mind [νοῦς] is completely purified by drinking in spiritual knowledge [πνευματικὴν γνῶσιν]; that charity [ἀγάπη] cures the inflammatory tendencies of the soul; and that the depraved lusts which spring up in it are restrained by abstinence [ἐγκράτεια].[117]

That combination—γνῶσις, ἀγάπη, ἐγκράτεια—is suspiciously more characteristic of Evagrius himself, but the traditions conflate even more,

114. Serapion of Thmuis *Against the Manichees* 2, ed. R. P. Casey. The text in *PG* 40.900–24 is truncated; Serapion's work has been confused with that attributed to Titus of Bostra (*PG* 18.1065ff). See also Casey, "The Text of the Anti-Manichaean Writings of Titus of Bosra and Serapion of Thmuis," *Harvard Theological Review* 21 (1928): 97–111. For some account of Serapion, see Athanasius, *Athanase d'Alexandrie: lettres à Sérapion*, ed. J. Lebon. For English translation of the latter text, see C. R. B. Shapland, *The Letters of Saint Athanasius Concerning the Holy Spirit*. (Serapion and Sarapion are names that will recur, owned by a number of churchmen, who are not to be confused!)

115. Serapion *Against the Manichees* 3.

116. Serapion's *Epistola ad monachos* (*PG* 40.925–42) suggests that he was less subtle when it came to the social practicalities of monasticism. The work is often vague, almost always predictable, and entirely self-congratulatory. That may remind us, however, that the majority of unsophisticated monks depended on straightforward images of renunciation as a basis for their confidence and sense of identity.

117. Socrates *HE* 4.23, translated in Bohn's Ecclesiastical Library. Cf. Serapion *Against the Manichees* 45.27.

for there would have been few gnostics who could not have had the same beliefs!

So it is worthwhile distinguishing between the general and often ill-informed or conflated categories of later commentators and the more various and quite particular anxieties and experiences of Pachomius's own contemporaries. It might have been possible for us to suggest that Pachomius sprang from a gnostic or a Manichaean or a pagan or a philosophical tradition, had something so clear-cut been available to him. But in fact, he was as idiosyncratic and as curious and selective as any of the figures we have plucked from the pages of Eusebius or Epiphanius. He never had the luxury of a single progenitor; nor could he enjoy, on the other hand, a doctrinal or social *carte blanche*. In that regard he experienced the advantages and frustrations of all great initiators. He had to exercise choice and occasionally had to react sharply in the face of a very complicated religious situation. Indeed, his very "orthodoxy" (as it would appear to successors) may have been no more than the ability to rise above the narrow heritage of one locality, to remain free and objective in the midst of the many religious experiments the province in his time afforded.[118]

But the province itself provides a framework nevertheless. In studying the Pachomian communities and the ideas and practices of their members we shall not be dealing with some stark alternative to Roman Egypt, or some exercise in rejection. The new and growing unity of the empire, the strengthening of a diocesan and institutional church, and the changes in rural economy and in the relative status of town and village enabled Pachomius to embark upon his own career of exploration, to build something coherent from the exciting range of religious experiments that were afoot in Upper Egypt. He belonged to the place: it was that rootedness that made him intelligible both to those whom he attracted and to those who felt compelled to argue against him.

118. The *Letter of Ammon* 12f, in *Sancti Pachomii vitae graecae*, ed. F. Halkin, refers to Pachomius's doubts in the face of divergent doctrine. Oddly enough, it is there his attachment to the hermit Palamon that proves his orthodoxy. More extensive references and discussion are given in Chapters II and III.

· II ·

THE SOURCES

It is always tempting to relegate to an appendix any detailed discussion of texts. In the case of Pachomius, that is particularly so, since the difficulties are numerous, convoluted, and the topic of lengthy dispute. It is wise to recall, therefore, the chief hope that lies behind this study: to produce not simply the account of a doctrine or movement but the portrait of a man. Knowing whether such a portrait is possible and how to proceed toward it will depend on our understanding how the available historical material came into being and how the various literary traditions developed. Those responsible for the production and growth of the texts in the first place were equally intent upon creating portraits. Until their skills and deceptions have been appreciated, a fresh presentation of our own will be impossible. Simply rifling the texts for information is not enough. Within those sources themselves, a debate was taking place as to how Pachomius should be portrayed. The results were not always reliable; indeed, they were often contradictory.

Biographies often depend in part on evidence provided by the subject—letters, at least, if not some original composition. With Pachomius we are poorly served. There are in addition to the *Rules*, which we shall discuss later, two Coptic "catecheses," or instructions to monks, which survive under his name.[1] The first, the *Instruction Concerning a Spiteful*

---

1. These were edited by L-Th. Lefort, in *Oeuvres de s. Pachôme et de ses disciples*, CSCO 159, 160, script. copt., 23, 24: "Catéchèse à propos d'un moine rancunier," text, 23:1–24, French translation, 24:1–26; "Catéchèse sur les six jours de Pâque," text, 23:24–26, French translation, 24:26–27. (Hereafter cited as CMR and CJP.) They are translated into English by Armand Veilleux in *Pachomian Koinonia*, 3:13–46 (CMR), and 47–49 (CJP). I make no pretense to competence in Coptic and have depended heavily on the comments and translations of other scholars. I shall almost always use Veilleux's translations throughout

Monk, may well provide clues to Pachomius's teaching, but the existing text is closely related to a sermon by Athanasius and is likely to have been subject to some reworking.[2] The second, an *Instruction on the Six Days of the Passover*, is probably original except for the closing lines, but. much briefer.[3]

So neither of these provides much information; the few additional Coptic fragments of this genre are too short and run-of-the-mill to add greatly to the picture. Similarly disappointing are the supposed *Letters* of Pachomius, which were translated into Latin by Jerome very early in the fifth century. He followed a Greek text, and Greek versions of some of the *Letters* still survive, together with Coptic fragments.[4] If such a collection, datable to the early 400s, could be confidently ascribed to Pachomius, it would naturally arouse our excitement. Unfortunately, it is not entirely clear that Jerome's supplier was directly in touch with an authentic Pachomian tradition in Upper Egypt. There are also signs that the existing text has been influenced by material produced between Pachomius's death in 346 and Jerome's compilation in 404. Finally, several of the *Letters* are written partly in a code that no one as yet has satisfactorily explained.[5]

It is not surprising, therefore, that our main approach to Pachomius will have to be by way of other material—in the first place, through the

this book. M. M. van Molle was particularly skeptical about the *CMR*, "Confrontation entre les règles et la littérature pachômienne postérieure," *Supplément de La Vie spirituelle* 86 (September, 1968): 395f. But this critique should be balanced by the observations of Ruppert, pp. 378f, 388f.

2.   A. Veilleux, *La Liturgie dans le cénobitisme pachômien*, p. 134. The Athanasian text was first edited, with French translation, by A. van Lantschoot, "Lettre de saint Athanase au sujet de l'amour et de la tempérance," *Le Muséon* 40 (1927): 265–92. For the link with Pachomius, see L-Th. Lefort, "S. Athanase écrivain copte," *Le Muséon* 46 (1933): 1–33, with extensive use of parallel French translation. See also his *S. Athanase, lettres festales et pastorales*, 19:110–20 (the "Pachomian" section beginning on 113); French translation, 20:88–98 ("Pachomian" from 91).

3.   Veilleux, *Liturgie*, pp. 134f.

4.   Latin edition of Jerome's text by A. Boon, *Pachomiana Latina*, pp. 77–101. Armand Veilleux has produced an English translation, reaching back to Coptic or Greek wherever possible, *Pachomian Koinonia*, 3: 51–83. For the implications of the Coptic fragments and the Greek translations, which help our understanding of some of the Latin, see H. Quecke, *Die Briefe Pachoms*. What follows is based on his analysis.

5.   Quecke discusses different theories extensively. A brief example from *Ep.* 2 will illustrate the difficulty: "Open your mouth and wash your face, so that your eyes see and you read the characters well. Watch yourself so as not to write δ over φ, lest your days grow old and your waters diminish. Remember and write ϑ and ρ, so that the ρ be well written."

various biographies that survive from his era. Here abundance itself creates a problem. A variety of languages is involved: mainly Coptic (both Sahidic and Bohairic), Greek, and Arabic. A number of *Lives* survive in each. The earliest modern commentators were quickly compelled, as they saw it, to decide whether Greek or Coptic had been the language of the first biography. Émile Amélineau decided in favor of Coptic and was quickly supported by Georg Grützmacher. A specific suggestion was that Sahidic texts predated Bohairic, the latter providing a basis for some Greek text earlier than any now known.[6] The contrary position, that the existing Greek predated Coptic versions, was adopted by Paulin Ladeuze; he was eventually followed by Karl Heussi and, much more recently, by Derwas Chitty.[7]

The early stages of the debate were bedeviled by an often prejudiced confusion over the relationship between the Hellenistic and indigenous cultures. We touched upon this in Chapter I. Ladeuze had found it hard to believe that Copts could initiate a literary tradition without Greek models. That argument was rendered obsolete in its details by the subsequent production of much better texts. L-Th. Lefort spent a lifetime editing and translating the Coptic material, arguing always for its priority. He suggested the existence of a now-lost Coptic source lying behind each of three biographical traditions: the Sahidic and Bohairic texts; the *Vita Prima*, or earliest existing Greek *Life*; and the sixth-century Latin translation by Dionysius Exiguus, which was closely associated with the supposedly second Greek *Life*, the *Vita Altera*.[8] His comparisons were aided by the labors of François Halkin, who edited the Greek *Lives* and made it clear in the process that the *Vita Prima* was almost certainly the first, and the only one usefully close to Pachomius's own time.[9]

6.   Émile Amélineau, *Monuments pour servir à l'histoire de l'Égypte chrétienne au IVe siècle*. Georg Grützmacher, *Pachomius und das älteste Klosterleben*.

7.   Paulin Ladeuze, *Étude sur le cénobitisme pakhômien*. Karl Heussi, *Der Ursprung des Mönchtums*. Derwas Chitty, *The Desert a City*. See further in n. 10.

8.   *S. Pachomii vita bohairice scripta* and *S. Pachomii vitae sahidice scriptae*. See the Bibliography, Sources, under "Lefort." He later published a complete French translation of all the texts, with extensive introduction, *Les Vies coptes de s. Pachôme et de ses premiers successeurs*. Armand Veilleux translated some of the Sahidic *Lives* into English in *Pachomian Koinonia*, 1:425–57. For his version of the Bohairic *Life*, see n. 9 following. Latin *Life* edited by H. van Cranenburgh, *La Vie latine de saint Pachôme, traduite du grec par Denys le Petit*, with Halkin's edition of the *Vita Altera* printed in parallel passage (see next note).

9.   *S. Pachomii vitae graecae*. The *Vita Prima* and the Bohairic *Life* are presented in English by A. Veilleux in *Pachomian Koinonia*, 1:23–295 (Bohairic), and 297–423 (Greek). (Chapters 115f of the Bohairic *Life* were in fact translated by Mark Sheridan; Veilleux was able to consult versions by Chitty of the *Vita Prima*, the *Paralipomena*, and the *Letter of Ammon*. The last two texts are discussed be-

With better texts and a clearer view of manuscript traditions, the debate about priority could enter a new stage; this was conducted for the most part by Chitty and Lefort. Chitty never relinquished his attachment to the Greek cause and viewed existing Coptic sources with suspicion. He and Lefort were often reduced to subjective judgments, but it says much for the scholarship of both men that, given the terms of their dispute, they had by the end of their lives probably identified and exploited every possible avenue of documented argument.[10] For progress, some new element had to be introduced.

This was done by Armand Veilleux, who used Arabic sources as clues to the earlier condition of Coptic texts.[11] He regarded as inescapable the conclusion that the original biography of Pachomius had been in Coptic. It was necessary to ask, therefore, whether any of our existing Coptic texts represented that primitive composition. Simply by comparing the sources as we now have them, it seemed clear that the so-called second and third Sahidic *Lives* could not have been part of any source or sources for the great Bohairic *Life* and its more closely associated Sahidic fragments.[12] The first Sahidic *Life*, however, did seem more primitive, and its present, truncated form could be safely augmented by reference to other texts.[13] It could be argued also that the tenth Sahidic *Life* and *its*

---

low.) There is a large gap in our existing Bohairic text, chapters 115–65. In his translation, Veilleux draws here on other texts and fragments, with additional modifications, as defended in his notes and in *Koinonia*, 1:4. This represents some advance on Lefort, *Vies*, p. 191 n. 4. It will also explain why, in my own notes, references to those "missing" sections of the Bohairic *Life* will often include allusions to Sahidic substitutes.

10.   See especially Chitty, "Pachomian Sources Reconsidered," *Journal of Ecclesiastical History* 5 (1954): 38–77; Lefort, "Les Sources coptes pachômiennes," *Le Muséon* 67 (1954): 217–29; and Chitty, "Pachomian Sources Once More," *Studia patristica*, 10:54–64. Another important contribution was made by A-J. Festugière, in his translation, with introduction, *La Première Vie grecque de saint Pachôme = Les Moines d'Orient*, 4:2. I summarized important aspects of the debate in my *Ascetics, Authority, and the Church*, pp. 243–47.

11.   Veilleux, *Liturgie*, to which refer for all that follows. Apart from early misgivings expressed by Chitty, the only detailed criticism of Veilleux's thesis is A. de Vogüé, "La Vie arabe de saint Pachôme et ses deux sources présumées," *Analecta Bollandiana*, 91 (1973): 379–90. Veilleux is unmoved in *Koinonia*, vol. 1.

12.   The Bohairic *Life* is very likely a translation of a Sahidic text akin to our fourth, fifth, and fourteenth Sahidic *Lives*. The Vatican Arabic *Life*, mentioned again below, appears to have translated that same text and shows further links with the sixth and seventh Sahidic *Lives*, together with that known as 3ᵇ. Because of these Sahidic connections, the whole tradition represented by the Bohairic *Life* is often referred to as SBo. Note that the numbers now attached to the Sahidic *Lives* imply nothing reliable about the order of their composition.

13.   As explained, with a chart, by Veilleux, *Liturgie*, pp. 41f.

associated fragments, part of a biography of Pachomius's disciple Theodore, were equally ancient.

So the published texts provided access to three sectors of what may be called the primitive tradition: the Bohairic *Life*, early Sahidic texts relating to Pachomius, and equally ancient texts, again Sahidic, relating to Theodore. Yet some more precise measures of antiquity were required. In pursuit of these, Veilleux turned to Arabic material—to "medieval" translations, that is, of earlier Greek and Coptic *Lives*, only some of which have otherwise survived in their original form. Those based on Greek proved scarcely useful, but two translations from Coptic, one in the Vatican and one in Gottingen (widely referred to as Av and Ag, respectively), were regarded by Veilleux as particularly important. Av has been published only in part, not all of that Pachomian, Ag not at all. Fortunately, an Arabic *Life* (referred to as Am) published by Amélineau is very closely related to Ag and can safely be used for purposes of reference.[14]

The usefulness of Veilleux's appeal rests on his suggestion that, from page 386 of Amélineau's edition, we can detect how the Coptic writer whom the Arab translates (γ in the table) turned suddenly to a new source.[15] Up to that point, his narrative had been focused in a straightforward manner on Pachomius and was clearly related to what we now possess in the Bohairic *Life*. He then proceeded to give a more tendentious account, concerned rather with Theodore and based on a different tradition, namely that reflected in (although not identical with) our present-day tenth Sahidic *Life*. This account continued until page 533 of the Arabic translation, at which point the Coptic writer appears to have returned to his first source. In other words, in the Arabic *Life* (Ag/Am) we have an independent witness, both to the Bohairic *Life* (and some of *its* sources) and to an early and separate biography of Theodore. We can also make new sense of the relation between them.

Veilleux had then to discuss the joins in the immediate Coptic source (γ) of Ag/Am; these joins were inevitably implied by his analysis. There were also significant repetitions. His conclusion was that the Arabic text revealed two distinct sources at an even earlier stage of the Coptic tradition: a life of Pachomius, which he named the *Vita Brevis* (*VBr*), and a life of Theodore (*VTh*). The *Vita Brevis*, he said, would have been a very plain account. The life of Theodore would have pleaded much more for unquestioning commitment to its hero's cause, on the basis especially of his almost miraculous perception.

14.   This is the first section of the text presented by Amélineau, *Monuments*, pp. 337–599.

15.   Reference to the genealogical table on p. 42 will clarify what follows.

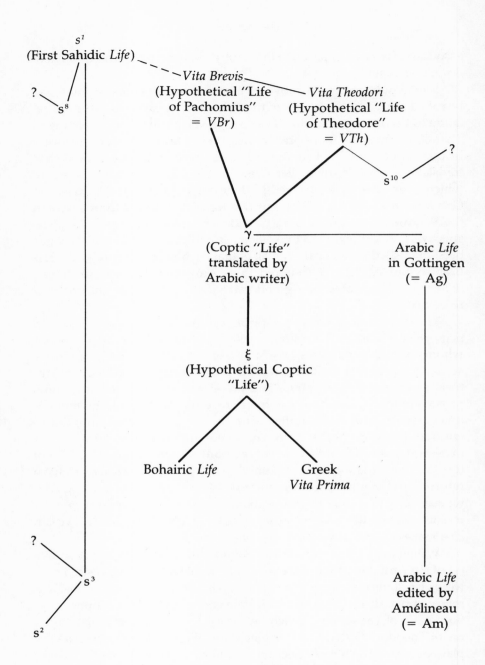

FIGURE 1. *Genealogical Table of Some of the* Lives *of Pachomius (based on that of Veilleux,* Koinonia, *vol. 1: 17)*

Several intricate questions remained. Could we be sure, for example, that any of the Coptic sources behind Ag/Am—remotely, *VBr* and *VTh*, and, more immediately, their Coptic amalgamation (γ)—were prior to our existing Bohairic *Life* and Greek *Vita Prima*? With a series of examples, Veilleux argued that these last sometimes fused together anecdotes that had apparently been separated in those primitive Coptic texts. That suggested to him that the Bohairic and Greek *Lives* were later—later even than the Coptic amalgamation (γ) immediately translated by Ag/Am. They may even have been dependent on a Coptic fusion later still (ξ in the table)—that is to say, a Coptic text that was itself dependent on the source translated in Ag/Am. This further point was reinforced by the fact that when we read in Ag/Am and in the tenth Sahidic *Life* incidents that are also recounted in both the Bohairic *Life* and the *Vita Prima*, these last two texts appear to have a common source, but a source distinct from whatever may lie immediately behind Ag/Am itself and the tenth *Life*. It would seem, therefore, that Ag/Am, on the one hand, and the Bohairic and Greek traditions, on the other, follow independently upon the primitive texts suggested by Veilleux. Hence the probability of a Coptic text (ξ) that was, first, prior to many of those we have now; second, a frequent source for both Bohairic and Greek *Lives*; third, intermediate between them and the text translated in Ag/Am (namely γ); and fourth, itself dependent on that text. There are some cases, not surprisingly, where the Bohairic *Life* is the only one to recount some incident. In those cases, Veilleux thought, it could have been drawing more directly upon the traditions embodied in Ag/Am and the tenth Sahidic *Life*.[16] But if the fusion argument was generally valid, then one of the few assurances that we were close to older Coptic sources would be agreement between the Bohairic *Life* and the *Vita Prima*. Veilleux remained very cautious about suggesting any direct access, on the part of the Bohairic *Life*, either to *VTh* or to the text translated in Ag/Am.

And what is the relation between the Bohairic *Life* and the *Vita Prima* themselves? For according to Veilleux's approach, gone were the days when one could be taken to depend on the other. There is cause for suspicion that the Greek text has summarized where the Bohairic has retained a fuller account (which could suggest a conscious modification, by the Greek writer, of our present Bohairic text, already available to him). On the other hand, there are passages which support the contention that the Bohairic tradition has added to what has been preserved in the Greek. (Of course, it could have done so quite legitimately, on the basis of evidence earlier than the *Vita Prima*.)

16.   For details, see Veilleux, *Liturgie*, pp. 76f.

Now Veilleux wished to avoid the danger here of slipping back into the debate about priority conducted by Chitty and Lefort. He insisted that such issues had to be gathered under the heading of relation to the common source determined by his analysis of Ag/Am. He was already inclined to trust more the Bohairic text in the light of two other factors: signs that Coptic was the older tradition and signs that the Bohairic *Life* might have bypassed in a few instances, as we have said, the source it shared with the *Vita Prima* and the source translated by Ag/Am—might have reached back, in other words, to *VTh*, if not to *VBr*. He was moved also by examples from the *Vita Prima* supporting a conviction that, at least where it stood alone, it was often a dangerous guide.

How does all that affect our use of the published texts? First, with the exception of the first Sahidic *Life*, it is not possible to arrange all our Coptic and Greek texts in one chronological order. Even if we could, an earlier version would not necessarily be a more reliable one. Where we have different versions of an incident, we have to respect them all. Reference to Ag/Am may help us to detect when the Bohairic *Life* and the *Vita Prima* are recounting the oldest and simplest traditions about Pachomius, when they depend on material more affected by controversies following his death, and when they or their source have confused incidents that should be distinct. Second, we shall feel confident when an incident occurs in both the Bohairic *Life* and the *Vita Prima*, especially when supported by reference to Ag/Am; moderately cautious when it is in the Bohairic *Life* alone; and distinctly nervous if it is found only in the *Vita Prima*.[17]

However, that scarcely resolves the historian's difficulty. Interrelating existing texts in such a complex way does not immediately reveal how or why the *Vita Brevis*, or for that matter any other early text, was first compiled. The *Vita Prima* is the only biography that stands back from events to give some account of its own genesis.

> We write these things although we have not seen him in the flesh, as we have said before. But we have seen those who were with him and of the same age. They knew these things accurately and they have recounted them to us in detail. Should anybody say, "Why did they not write his life?" our answer is that we did not hear them speak often about writing, although they had been with him and were of the same age and he was their father. But perhaps it was not yet the time. And when we saw that it was necessary to do so, that we might not forget altogether what we had heard about this perfect monk who is our father after all the saints, we wrote down a few out of many things.[18]

17.   This differs from the balance suggested in my *Ascetics*, where I was readier to accept the *Vita Prima* as an independent witness.

18.   *Vita Prima* (hereafter cited as G¹) 98. The passage is absent from the

Several points in this original statement deserve notice. The writer has depended on oral accounts, or at least his source has—a source he may have shared with the writer of the Bohairic *Life*. No written material was available: he was taking an initiative and being deliberately selective. About why the task had not been attempted before, he makes the reflection, "Perhaps it was not yet the time." Now, therefore, a time was felt to have come. So it is less likely that any early biography was based on an existing collection of brief anecdotes such as we find in the *Apophthegmata Patrum*.[19] (The sources of the so-called *Paralipomena* may have been of that kind; we shall discuss them briefly in a moment.) The impulse to fairly lengthy biography was earlier and marked the first literary step prior to more piecemeal written recollections (with the exception, perhaps, of some of the *Rules*). One steps straight from shared memories to a literary form. Perhaps only cenobites, with their sense of a corporate past and frequent opportunity for debate, could support so deliberate and self-conscious a venture. Moreover, the impetus came from within the group as much as from the literate observer. The writer of the *Vita Prima* itself appears to have known of Athanasius's *Life of Antony* and may even have been worried by it; but if we compare the *Vita Prima*'s opening section with that of the Bohairic *Life*, it is possible to suggest that the same may not have been true of their common source.[20]

So, in spite of its isolation on this point, the *Vita Prima* may reliably suggest two things: biography came to birth, as it were, immediately, and in response to a particular need. Those circumstances we shall discuss again in the final chapter; it deserves notice now that the need was felt very soon after Pachomius's death and may have been vital to the survival of his monastic legacy. Here it is precisely and reassuringly the Bohairic *Life* that helps us, describing how Theodore lamented the way the communities had abandoned the founder's teaching.

Bohairic *Life* (hereafter cited as Bo). See also G[1] 46, which also lacks an equivalent in Bo.

19.   There is little about Pachomius in the *Apophthegmata*, for details of which see the early chapters of my *Ascetics*.

20.   G[1] 2: "The life of our most ascetic and truly virtuous father Antony . . . as the most holy archbishop Athanasius attests in writing. For he wrote about him after his death, revealing at the same time . . ." Bo 2 reads simply, "Such was the virtuous life of our holy father Apa Antony. . . . We heard that of this kind was also . . ." A desire to portray Pachomius as a worthy rival of Antony is clear from G[1] 120. Bo is incomplete at that point, but may have been close to existing Sahidic sources, as used by Veilleux, *Koinonia*, 1:127f. The same effect is achieved in G[1] 136 and in S[5] 128 (used by Veilleux for Bo 134). (S[5] refers to the fifth Sahidic *Life*: further references will be on this model.) The *Life of Antony* is mentioned also in G[1] 99, but there is no equivalent in Bo.

Then he began to tell them of the life of our father Pachomius from his childhood on and of all the labors he underwent from the beginning when he established the holy *Koinonia*. [He told them of] the temptations of demons and how he snatched away from them the souls which the Lord gave him and of the revelations which the Lord disclosed to him. [And he told them] everything he had heard from that saint's mouth as well as those things he had seen with his own eyes.

He spoke to them as follows: "Listen to me, my brothers, and understand well the things I am telling you. For the man whom we are exalting is truly the father of us all after God. God established a covenant with him to save a great many souls by means of him. And us also the Lord has saved through his holy prayers. For he—I am speaking of our righteous father Pachomius—is also one of the holy men of God and one who did his will always and everywhere. I am fearful that we may forget his labors and actually be unmindful of who it was who made this multitude one spirit and one body."

Theodore continued,

"Perhaps some of you may think that they are giving glory to flesh. Not at all! Or on the other hand that our hope is placed in a man. By no means! Rather we glorify and we bless the Spirit of God which is in him. And indeed, if we also bless the flesh it is truly worthy of it, for it became a temple of the Lord. Not only is it fitting to act this way, but, we know besides, and we believe that his name is written in the book of life with all the saints. Now then, my brothers, I tell you that it is necessary and right for us to write of his labors from the beginning, of the perfection he achieved, of his way of life, and of all the ascetic practices he performed, so that his memory may remain on earth as also it remains forever in heaven. As the blessed Job also said, 'If only my words were written down and left in a book for ever!'"

The biographer later recounts,

The brothers who acted as his interpreters into Greek for those who did not understand Egyptian—because they were foreigners or Alexandrians—heard him speak many times about the way of life of our father Pachomius. Since they had paid full and precise attention to what he said concerning him, they wrote these things down for [the brothers]. For after our father Theodore finished speaking to them about him and praising him and all his labors, he used to sigh, saying to the brothers, "Pay attention to the words I am speaking to you, because a time is coming when you will not be able to find anyone able to recount them for you." [21]

Those were statements made at a moment of crisis, when Horsiesios had had to admit his failure as successor to Pachomius and Theodore had

21.   Bo 194, 196. The reference to the Greek interpreters is, of course, a tempting credential for the priority of the *Vita Prima*, but "many times" is an important qualification, as are also the implications of n. 18, not to mention the wider critical judgments provided by Lefort and Veilleux.

gained at last the leadership for which he had long seemed destined. Such disturbance and tension would clearly amount to special circumstance, in which the production of a biography could take on a public, almost political significance. We cannot regard the *Lives* simply as examples of a literary tradition, inspired by the biography of Antony or governed by pagan antecedents.[22] In its conception—and that is what we are discussing at the moment—the biographical tradition of Pachomius was peculiar to the *Koinonia*. It was marked by an anxious desire to preserve and defend, amid controversy and division, an endangered memory.

So we are not dealing just with interwoven layers of anecdote challenging the skills of the modern critic. We are faced with texts that were in themselves exercises in historical analysis. This also will affect the use we make of them. By the end of the fourth century it was possible for someone like the author of the *Vita Prima* to look back over the career not only of Pachomius but also of each of his immediate successors and to see a certain development in them. The concept of "Pachomian monasticism" began to take shape. But the development portrayed may not have been foreseen by Pachomius himself. It may have been less than characteristic of his own ambitions and policies. Indeed, the patterns detected by this writer or that may not have been the only ones within the Pachomian communities. We have already noted, and will observe further, that even Pachomius himself addressed a variety of audiences and had to cater for both the criticism and the admiration of very different contemporaries. So also with the *Lives*: once biography had been launched, it could be imitated in a variety of circumstances, built upon for a variety of reasons, and distributed to a variety of readers. And each *Life* could portray, and thereby defend, growth of one kind rather than another. Biography, therefore, could endow the "Pachomian experiment" with a degree of optimism and inevitability that might well have surprised both the founder and his close associates.

The implication is briefly stated but constantly embarrassing: we cannot read back from existing sources. Awareness of Antony in the *Vita Prima* is a case in point. Quite apart from its competitive tone, the biography makes much of the difference between Antony and Pachomius. But was this difference so original as the text implies? The compilers of our existing *Lives*, even the Coptic ones, may have had access to Athanasius's biography, recognizing it as a now famous, influential, and even rival text. But when Theodore expressed his anxieties and prompted the initial biographies, it had quite possibly not yet been written. Theodore

22. A literary background can be admitted, of course, but it must, by its nature, have affected more the later stages of the tradition.

died in 368, while the *Life of Antony* had appeared some ten years earlier; but his address in the Bohairic *Life*, quoted above, is likely to have been delivered only shortly after his appointment as superior in about 350. Antony at that time was not even dead, and one may question how clearly Pachomian monks would have distinguished themselves from his community at Pispir.[23]

We cannot, then, visit the *Lives* upon the contemporaries of Pachomius. It is not even enough to single out an anecdote—say, in the Bohairic *Life*—and assert in the light of the Arabic tradition that it reflects the earliest account likely to have found a place in the *Vita Brevis*. The context in which we now have to assess such anecdotes, which inevitably colors their content, is that of a biographical tradition. We are dealing not so much with biographies of individuals as with the account of what the authors regarded as an orthodox tradition within the Pachomian movement. Very often the first question to be answered is, by what stages did the followers of Pachomius reach the level of practice or spirituality revealed by the literary evidence? That they had always behaved or thought that way is a dangerous assumption.

Although that may seem a discouraging litany of *caveat*s, the *Lives* are nevertheless more reliable as a source of information than the *Rules*, translated by Jerome into Latin (with some other documents) in 404. A comparison of Jerome's text with some surviving Coptic fragments and with corresponding Greek compilations encourages the belief that Jerome was faithful to the scripts at his disposal; but those scripts represented a stage of development in "Pachomian legislation" reached more than a generation later than Pachomius's death.[24] There is evidence that

23. See *Life of Antony* 13, 48, 54. We shall say more about the similarity of Antony and Pachomius; see also my "The Desert Fathers," in *The Study of Spirituality*, ed. C. P. M. Jones, G. Wainwright, and E. J. Yarnold. A fuller bibliography on Antony appears in my *Ascetics*. Veilleux, *Liturgie*, p. 175 wants G¹ 120 to imply that Pachomius had been different from the beginning. His references to the work of H. Bacht are important, because they do not wholly support his own contention. See especially Bacht's "Antonius and Pachomius," in *Antonius Magnus Eremita*, ed. B. Steidle, pp. 66–107.

24. Latin edition in Boon, *Pachomiana*, pp. 13–74, to which should be added a preface to one section of the *Rules*, the *Praecepta et Instituta*, attributed to Horsiesios by Lefort, *Oeuvres*, 23:80, lines 23–32, and correctly identified by H. Bacht, "Ein verkanntes Fragment der koptischen Pachomius-Regel," *Le Muséon* 75 (1962): 5–18. All are translated by Veilleux, *Koinonia*, 2:141–95. Coptic frag-

parts of the collection were closely associated with or influenced by the work of Horsiesios, and others may indeed have sprung from *milieux* not immediately linked with Pachomius at all.[25]

Jerome's translation, in other words, may reveal practices and principles of organization not envisaged by Pachomius. That does not mean we dismiss the *Rules* out of hand. But we do need to ask whether it is possible to identify original layers, or at least individual prescriptions, that date back to the 340s and earlier. The most recent comprehensive attempt in that regard was undertaken in a series of articles by M. M. van Molle.[26] She was not altogether successful, but, although she met with considerable criticism,[27] her work deserves attention still. Jerome's version of the *Rules* contained four sections: *Praecepta*, *Praecepta et Instituta*, *Praecepta atque Iudicia*, and *Praecepta ac Leges*. That, it has been widely held, was more or less the order of their composition, the *Praecepta*, certainly, being considered the most primitive. The *Praecepta et Instituta*, which appear to contain instructions peculiar to certain officials, have been taken as at least partly dependent on the *Praecepta* and the *Praecepta atque Iudicia*. Mlle. van Molle proposed an almost complete reversal of that conclusion, seeing the *Praecepta atque Iudicia* as the most primitive regulations, and the *Praecepta* as very late and foreign to the spirit of Pachomius.

The whole argument rested on a comparison between the Latin translation and the surviving Coptic fragments of the *Praecepta et Instituta*. Certain words and phrases clustering around the term *monasterium* were allegedly absent from the Coptic, and therefore, it was supposed, intruded by Jerome. Further, it was therefore assumed that, even when Coptic comparisons were not available, such terms could be taken as intruded elsewhere in the collection, for example in the *Praecepta atque Iudicia*. Once "purified" of those intrusions, the two sections, especially

ments were presented by Lefort, first with a Latin translation in Boon, *Pachomiana*, pp. 155–68, and later in his own *Oeuvres*, text, 23:30–36; French translation, 24:30–37. There are fragments of Greek translations also, not exactly equivalent, known as the *Excerpta*, and printed in Boon, pp. 169–82.

25. Veilleux, *Liturgie*, pp. 117f; Ruppert, pp. 238f.

26. Especially "Essai de classement chronologique des premières règles de vie commune connue en chrétienté," *Supplément de La Vie spirituelle* 84 (February, 1968): 108–27; "Confrontation entre les règles et la littérature pachômienne postérieure," ibid. 86 (September, 1968): 394–424; and "Vie commune et obéissance d'après les institutions premières de Pachôme et Basile," ibid. 93 (May, 1970): 196–225.

27. A. de Vogüé, "Les Pièces latines du dossier pachômien: remarques sur quelques publications récentes," *Revue d'histoire ecclésiastique* 67 (1972): 26–27; Ruppert, esp. pp. 240f, but also 53f.

the latter, when compared with the *Praecepta*, appeared less "institutional," and therefore, according to the argument, more primitive. In particular, the supposedly early prescriptions envisaged a single community, not divided into the famous "houses" (which we shall discuss later), and certainly not a complex federation of communities.

Certain terminological inadequacies in Mlle. van Molle's comparisons were noted by her critics. Some will be mentioned in later chapters.[28] There are, however, more general objections to be raised. It is

28. See particularly the second part of Chapter VI. Controversy centers on the Coptic terms used for superiors: in the *Praecepta*, ⲣⲱⲙⲉ ⲛ̄ⲧⲥⲟⲟⲩϩⲥ̄, for what Jerome most often translated *pater*, and ⲡⲣ̄ⲛ̄ⲏⲓ̈, for *praepositus domus*; and in the *Praecepta et Instituta*, ⲟⲓⲕⲟⲛⲟⲙⲟⲥ. Mlle. van Molle wished the latter (translated "économe") to mean the superior of the (original) single house. In the former (and, according to her, later) regulations, that position was represented by the ⲣⲱⲙⲉ ⲛ̄ⲧⲥⲟⲟⲩϩⲥ̄ (which she translated "celui du rassemblement"), while each house (now one of several) had its ⲡⲣ̄ⲛ̄ⲏⲓ̈ ("chef de maison"). But she had to admit that the *Praecepta et Instituta*, in addition to the ⲟⲓⲕⲟⲛⲟⲙⲟⲥ, mentioned a specific "house" superior, which she referred to as "celui de la maison."

De Vogüé demonstrated how unnecessary and inaccurate it was to suppose two superiors, as in the *Praecepta et Instituta*, for only one house, "Pièces latines," pp. 39f. The whole question, as we shall see, was discussed fully by Ruppert, pp. 282f. Here it should be noted simply that Mlle. van Molle's judgments and translations, in "Classement chronologique," obscure many variations.

She does not discuss adequately the relation between the very precise ⲡⲣ̄ⲛ̄ⲏⲓ̈ of the *Praecepta* and the loose equivalents of *Praecepta et Instituta* 11, 13, 16, and 17. Having described the relation between "celui de la maison" and the "économe" in 11 and 13, she does not explain why the major superior in *Praecepta et Instituta* 12 (translated by Jerome as *pater*) is *not*, in the Coptic, ⲟⲓⲕⲟⲛⲟⲙⲟⲥ. Nor does she speculate sufficiently on the variety of terms apparently used by Jerome to translate this one word: *pater* in 5, 11, and 17; *pater monasterii* in 10 and 13; *maior* in 4; and *princeps* in 5. (It is not possible to correlate the *praepositus* of 18 with the disfigured Coptic now surviving.)

In spite of her declarations on p. 113, ⲟⲓⲕⲟⲛⲟⲙⲟⲥ *does* occur in the Coptic *Praecepta*, in 105, where Jerome has "eos quibus fratrum vesticulae commissae sunt" (she comments on that on p. 116!). The phraseology of 105 is very similar to that of 111, and there Jerome used *praepositi*.

(Jerome was not always consistent in his apparent rendering of ⲡⲣ̄ⲛ̄ⲏⲓ̈: he has *praepositus domus*, at least by clear implication, in *Praecepta* 96, 98, 104, 105, 115, and 122; *praepositus* in 98, 106, and 123; and *maior* in 97.)

Finally, on p. 116, Mlle. van Molle produces a list of functions for her "celui du rassemblement"; but in no case do we have a Coptic equivalent that enables us to be certain ⲣⲱⲙⲉ ⲛ̄ⲧⲥⲟⲟⲩϩⲥ̄ stood in any supposed original. What we do have, again, is a variety of terms employed by Jerome: *princeps monasterii* for 8, 23, 24, and 133; *pater monasterii* for 53 and 54; and *praepositus* again in 133. Only 54 has any equivalent in the *Excerpta* (LIII), which has simply κεφαλή.

These complexities should dissuade us from belief in a smooth transition from the ⲟⲓⲕⲟⲛⲟⲙⲟⲥ of the *Praecepta et Instituta* to the ⲣⲱⲙⲉ ⲛ̄ⲧⲥⲟⲟⲩϩⲥ̄ of the *Praecepta*.

clearly very risky to make assumptions about a now-lost Coptic original behind Jerome's *Praecepta atque Iudicia*. Jerome was not translating Coptic anyway. Nor can we be certain that our existing Coptic fragments pre-date his work. Arguing even more broadly, should we not ask whether development had taken place within each section of the *Rules* prior to Jerome's enterprise? That is, were his *Praecepta*, late or not, necessarily the original *Praecepta*?[29] Should we not ask, also, why Jerome retained in his collection those partly distinct but partly interrelated sections? What might the possibility of different audiences for the different sections imply—some of them, perhaps, non-Pachomian? Finally, is it certain that a supposed "spirit of the Gospel" will always predate "minor details of organization"? Is that "the normal order of progression in the history of institutions"?[30] It is surely just as possible that the *Praecepta atque Iudicia* represented a period of theological reflection, coming after the particularities of the *Praecepta*. None of these questions was approached by Mlle. van Molle with any seriousness: the very possibility of their being raised must threaten her logic.

That was not the end of the matter. Armed with her conviction that the *Praecepta* were late and the *Praecepta atque Iudicia* early, Mlle. van Molle pointed to links between the *Praecepta* and the *Lives*, and found the latter therefore open to suspicion. They were late also, and devoted mainly to a glorification of Theodore, who was accordingly to be associated with the "un-Pachomian" character of "later" levels of legislation.[31]

Unfortunately, these judgments about chronology continued to depend on Mlle. van Molle's understanding of the *Praecepta atque Iudicia*. Of course, what was required (and what Veilleux and others have since attempted) was an independent assessment of textual chronology within the tradition of the *Lives* themselves. Conclusions about that tradition might in their turn have corroborated the sequence reconstructed for the *Rules*. Instead, the *Rules* were used to suggest a date for the *Lives*, and errors in the former argument were visited upon the latter.

Although Mlle. van Molle's conclusions are unacceptable, there are interwoven in her arguments some laudable and useful convictions. First, she points to questions about the *Rules* that had not been raised with any forcefulness previously. Second, she makes it clear that the *Lives* (properly sorted out on their own) have to be used to assess the

29. We have to treat with some respect, therefore, the attempted subdivisions of Veilleux, *Liturgie*, pp. 126f.

30. Van Molle, "Classement chronologique," p. 120. Even more odd is her refusal to admit any trace in Pachomian literature of polemic, reform, "une volonté de retour en arrière": the careers of Horsiesios and Theodore argue quite the contrary.

31. Those were the main themes of her "Confrontation."

accuracy and development of the *Rules*, not vice versa. Third, in spite of her failures, she steadfastly presented readers with what we shall come to regard as the "true" Pachomius: not a ruthless or petty-minded governor of men and systems, but a spiritual guide intent upon a repentance and improvement that sprang from an accurate perception of self, a man ready to encourage the sharing of responsibility.[32]

The question remains, therefore, how much in the *Rules* dates from the years after Pachomius's death and with how much justice may we use them to deduce developments in Pachomius's own career?[33] Is it possible to lay bare one or more primitive layers in that collection, as we seem able to do in the *Lives*? We can accept that the legislation we possess represents "a gradual accretion of *ad hoc* rules to be fitted into a framework of daily life which is taken for granted, so that we have to infer it."[34] Such an inference would be inescapable if we were faced with the *Rules* alone. But the "framework of daily life" is presented by the *Lives* also, which thus provide clues about the legislation likely to have been formulated in the early stages of that "gradual accretion."

The references are scattered and inconclusive. The earliest description of the regulated life does not imply anything written: Pachomius simply issued very general instructions.[35] When he founded a monastery for women, he did write them rules, but there is no indication of what sort.[36] With the establishment of his second monastery at Phbow something more definite seems to be implied: "he enjoined them in writing, as a form of memorial, that no one should hurt his neighbor, but each should keep to his rule of conduct."[37] Yet there is no indication that the "rule of conduct" was also written, and the "memorial" could have been just a letter for the occasion. That may explain why the Arabic *Life* makes no mention of writing, though it does record the appointment of superiors at Phbow "accustomed to behave in accordance with his rules."[38] A clue to those situations may be provided by a Bohairic reference to "laws and traditions," some of them written, others learned by heart.[39] There is an interesting reference also to the annual meeting of all the monasteries, at which, "if one or the other needed to receive an ordinance, our father Pachomius would give it to them."[40] Again, the creation of written material is not to be taken for granted.

32. The burden of her "Vie commune."
33. Ruppert, pp. 234f.   34. Chitty, *Desert*, p. 21.   35. G[1] 24.
36. Bo 27.
37. G[1] 54. Bo 49 is equally vague, but with the additional complication of a vision. Only Thmoušons received anything approaching a written code.
38. Am, p. 378.
39. Bo 104.
40. Bo 71. G[1] 59 is clearly dependent on the *Praecepta*. G[1] 99 must be refer-

Some clear impressions emerge. There were general principles of behavior widely known and accepted among the Pachomian communities, but not necessarily written. Pachomius did write instructions, but normally on special occasions or in response to particular requests; on all such occasions nothing suggests a type of document different from our surviving *Letters* and *Instructions*. Government depended, in any case, on a constant series of visitations and gatherings both within each monastery and in the federation more widely.

What may we conclude, therefore? There is certainly no need to suppose that anything like the various *Praecepta*, as presented by Jerome, existed sixty years or more previously. Indeed, that is very unlikely. It would be almost impossible to judge what connection existed between Jerome's translation and any Coptic text we now possess. Deciding on an order of composition for the sections of his collection has proved very difficult. It certainly need not be the order in the common edition. Finally, we cannot assume that each section as it stood in 404 was in its original form.

In the light of what we find in the *Lives*, where layers of composition are clearer, we have first to decide what type of community Pachomius wished to establish and what type of authority he wished to exercise, both in person and through subordinates. Then we can place more trust in sections of the various *Praecepta* that reflect those wishes. In particular, we can attend more readily to prescriptions that seem *ad hoc*, not obviously part of some formally codified system but more closely associated with personal government or formation by letter and catechesis. Little else more definite can be expected.

There are very few other ancient sources that touch upon Pachomius personally. The *Paralipomena* must be regarded as parallel to the *Lives*. They show signs of having been influenced by a biographical tradition that was already established. Yet the disjointed anecdotes upon which they were based did not constitute necessarily a source always common to them and to the *Lives*; they may even have been compiled in circles unfamiliar with the communities of Upper Egypt.[41] They offer secure

---

ring mainly to material like the *Letters*. Even G¹ 122, referring to the time of Horsiesios, may not be talking about a written corpus.

41. Veilleux, *Liturgie*, pp. 21f, with further misgivings in *Koinonia*, 2:2, appealing to P. Peeters, "Le Dossier copte de S. Pachôme," *Analecta Bollandiana* 64 (1946): 263–67; text edited by Halkin, *Vitae*, pp. 122–65; English translation in

evidence only of fifth-century attitudes and recollections. The *Letter of Ammon* is also of doubtful value. Chitty resolutely defended the contrary opinion.[42] But even if the attribution of authorship is secure, and even if this Ammon was at Phbow, as he claimed, his concern was much more with Theodore than with Pachomius, and his account much affected by longer subsequent experience among ascetic groups of a very different sort.[43]

In fact it is quite surprising that any accurate recollection of Pachomius remained at all. This added problem of a non-Pachomian authorship may affect even the *Vita Prima*—like the *Rules* (and indeed the Bohairic *Life*), a product of the Delta. The *Vita's* detail and its general conformity to the Coptic traditions are all the more remarkable when we look at the other monastic sources of the period. Among the major Christian writers of that age, there was an extraordinary degree of ignorance not only about Pachomius but also about his legacy. Jerome was aware of a cenobitic tradition in Egypt but wrote of it in only the most general terms.[44] The *Historia Monachorum*, written probably by Rufinus at the turn of the century, is either silent about Pachomius's followers or obscures the distinction between their communities and those of a quasi-cenobitic nature on the Lower Nile.[45] The same is true of Cassian, whose experience of Egyptian monasticism was limited to northern areas, although he pretended to a knowledge of the "Tabennesiotes."[46]

Veilleux, *Koinonia*, 2:19–70. Of comparable nature are the two fragments edited by R. Draguet, "Un Morceau grec inédit des vies de Pachôme apparié à un texte d'Évagre en partie inconnue," *Le Muséon* 52 (1957): 267–306, and "Un Paralipomenon pachômien inconnu dans le Karakallou 251," *Mélanges Eugène Tisserant* (q.v.), 2, 1:55–61. Veilleux called these "Draguet, Fragments 1 and 2," *Liturgie*, p. 112, and translated them in *Koinonia*, 2:111–19. De Vogüé cast doubt on the value of the first, "L'Anecdote pachômienne du 'Vaticanus graecus' 2091: son origine et ses sources," *Revue d'histoire de la spiritualité* 49 (1973): 401–19, pointing to links with the *Apophthegmata* and the *Lausiac History*; and Veilleux allowed some modification, *Koinonia*, 2:4. But the arguments do not exclude an authentic tradition at the heart of the story, which is accepted by Ruppert as a convincing example of Pachomius's humility, pp. 166f. See Chapter V at n. 56.

42. "One of our most reliable accounts of Pachomius as he was remembered by his successors and described to the writer," *Desert*, p. 8, but "as he was remembered" is precisely the problem! See also his "Pachomian Sources Reconsidered," the opening sections. Text edited by Halkin, *Vitae*, pp. 97–121; English translation in Veilleux, *Koinonia*, 2:71–109.

43. Veilleux, *Liturgie*, pp. 108f.

44. Most famously to Eustochium in *Ep.* 22.34–36.

45. The closest he comes to a Pachomian reference is in *HM* 3 (*PL* 21.407f); see my *Ascetics*, p. 45. Other Thebaid references indicate only how varied the ascetic life was even there.

46. Passages are discussed fully by Veilleux, *Liturgie*, pp. 146f. See also the final chapters of my *Ascetics*, which treat of Cassian in detail.

Finally Palladius, in the *Lausiac History*, is even more unreliable, although his account of Pachomius remained for a long time the most famous, and possibly the most influential, in Christian literature.[47]

In the search for Pachomius himself, therefore, two principles must guide us. We shall accept a distinction between tradition and event. Even the earliest sources, while retaining accurate recollections, present them in anachronistic if not tendentious contexts. And we shall remain alert to development, not only from the time of Pachomius's death until the formation of our existing texts, but also within his own career. Both principles are forced upon us by the nature of the texts themselves. Their lateness entails their not reflecting in detail the practice of the 320s and 330s, and the probable circumstances of their first emergence has made them inevitably as much argumentative as descriptive.

So in spite of the calculated sharpness of focus in both the *Lives* and the *Rules*, we shall accept the notion that their later image of Pachomius—the "received history" of the Pachomian experiment—is an impression we might almost wish to avoid and certainly aim to unmask. We shall be prepared to discover, rather, a man feeling his way with caution and often without instant success, a man who nevertheless inspired admiration and loyalty among an increasing circle of followers, a man who used that admiration and loyalty to encourage among those followers a certain view of humanity, and perhaps of society—a view neither ready made nor to be imposed without question, but one that developed in pace with his own social experiments and his status as a leader in the eyes of others—a man above all uncertain of the future, for whom the history of Egyptian monasticism was not only not inevitable, but had not yet even begun.

47. See Veilleux, *Liturgie*, pp. 138f. Attention is focused on *Lausiac History* (hereafter cited as *HL*) 32f, and the sections concerned (in chapters 7, 18, and 32–34) are translated in Veilleux, *Koinonia*, 2:123–35. See also the important studies by R. Draguet, "Le Chapitre de l'*Histoire Lausiaque* sur les Tabennésiotes dérive-t-il d'une source copte?" *Le Muséon* 57 (1944): 53–145; 58 (1945): 15–95; and "L' 'Histoire Lausiaque,' une oeuvre écrite dans l'esprit d'Évagre," *Revue d'histoire ecclésiastique* 41 (1946): 321–64; 42 (1947): 5–49.

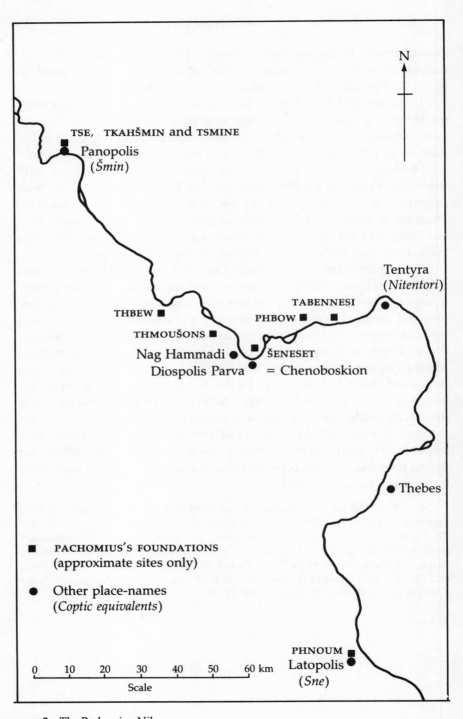

N

TSE, TKAHŠMIN and TSMINE
● Panopolis
(*Šmin*)

Tentyra
(*Nitentori*)

TABENNESI
THBEW ■   PHBOW ■   ■   ●
THMOUŠONS ■
Nag Hammadi ● ■ ŠENESET
Diospolis Parva ●   = Chenoboskion

● Thebes

■ PACHOMIUS'S FOUNDATIONS
(approximate sites only)

● Other place-names
(*Coptic equivalents*)

0   10   20   30   40   50   60 km
Scale

PHNOUM
■ ●
Latopolis
(*Sne*)

MAP 2. *The Pachomian Nile*

· III ·

FORMING THE COMMUNITY

As soon as we ask how Pachomius formed his first community, it becomes clear in what ways the sources might mislead us. As the previous chapter should suggest, it is no use searching in the *Rules* for evolution or change. Quite apart from the fact that they present the structure of monastic society in terms that Pachomius might not have known at first hand, they certainly do not allow us to estimate patterns of recruitment or expansion. Nor are the *Lives*, with their special pleading and taste for rewritten history, immediately reliable keys to development. They present the endeavors of Pachomius as part of God's general plan for the salvation of humanity. The *Vita Prima* refers to the promises made to Abraham, to the coming of Christ, to the church's mission of preaching to and baptizing the nations, and to the faith and vigor of the martyrs. Pachomius follows in that tradition: "salvation history" explains his arrival on the scene and provides him with a program.[1] The biographers suggest that he himself would at times speak of his work in those terms. He is made to describe an even flow of religious development from primitive animism, through the literal sacrifices of paganism and the Jewish temple, to the establishment of Christianity, whereby the incarnate Word of God became the consuming fire of true sacrifice. His listeners were undoubtedly intended to see themselves as latter-day participators in that purer dedication.[2] It is no surprise, therefore, that later

1. G[1] 1. Bo is missing at this point, but similar statements are made in Am, pp. 337–39. See Veilleux, *Koinonia*, 1: 266. Similar points are made in Antony's *Letters*, and in the *Life of Antony* (89): see my *Ascetics*, pp. 22f.
2. G[1] 34, Bo 29—during an analysis of Hebrews 9 (in itself a salvation history). It was that exegesis that first aroused the admiration of Pachomius's famous disciple Theodore. Compare the opening sections of *CMR*, and 18, and the introduction to *PInst* as presented by Bacht, "Verkanntes Fragment." (See table of abbreviations for methods of reference to sections of the *Rules*.)

traditions continued to present Pachomius as a successor of the prophets and apostles. The *Koinonia* itself—evoking that essentially communal
quality that Pachomius strove for—is interpreted as an instrument of salvation in the fullest sense, an image of the saving community God intended his church to be.[3]

Such declarations are no guarantee that Pachomius first saw himself
in such a broad historical setting, although he may have come to do so at
a later stage. So tendentious a view is of little help when we are trying to
decide precisely by what changes Pachomius transformed himself from
a pagan military recruit into the founder of a monastery at Tabennesi.
For those were the crucial years. We have to piece together a more prosaic chronology based on details in a variety of sources.

Pachomius was conscripted into the army during the war of 312/13
between Licinius and Maximin Daia. While billeted in Thebes, he was
impressed by the charity of local Christians, described to him as doing
"all manner of good to everyone."[4] "They treat us with love for the sake
of the God of heaven."[5] Pachomius then prayed to that Christian God,
promising that he would serve his fellows in the same way.[6] After his
release from the army, he was instructed in the Christian faith and baptized in the village of Chenoboskion, known in Coptic as Šeneset.[7] On

3. G[1] 98; compare G[1] 17. Festugière had misplaced anxieties about the
phrase that immediately follows in G[1] 98, ὡς καὶ οἱ λοιποὶ τοιοῦτοι κατὰ τόπον
εἰσίν. Veilleux has made sense with "those who are like him in various places,"
followed by allusion to God purifying the whole earth: it means that Pachomius
was not the only one in this tradition. Festugière modified the text to κατὰ τρό-
πον, and added "pères" to his translation, *Première Vie grecque*, p. 211. See also
G[1] 120. Neither passage is echoed in Bo.
4. G[1] 4. This is a better account than Bo 7; Festugière outlines the inconsis-
tencies, *Première Vie grecque*, pp. 15f. Useful, though, is the information in Bo
that Pachomius was about twenty years old. The passage also relates that the
event took place at Latopolis (where Theodore was later a monk, G[1] 33); but that
is a mistake: Veilleux, *Koinonia*, 1:267. For parallels, see H. I. Bell, *Jews and Christians in Egypt*, text no. 1919, lines 16f, 32f.
5. Bo 7.
6. G[1] 5: "Loving all men, I will be their servant." Bo 7 is also general, with
"humankind." But different texts give different impressions of this early prayer.
Implications are explored below; and see Veilleux, *Liturgie*, pp. 168f, and my *Ascetics*, pp. 57f (which overlooks the implications of Bo).
7. For details of all Pachomius's settlements and foundations, see L-Th.
Lefort, "Les Premiers Monastères pachômiens: exploration topographique," *Le
Muséon* 52 (1939): 379–407, and Derwas J. Chitty, "A Note on the Chronology of
the Pachomian Foundations," *Studia patristica*, 2:379–85. Reference to the map
facing p. 57 will be useful. Reference should now be made also to Bernward
Büchler, *Die Armut der Armen*. I regret, with some shame, that I did not discover
this book until my own work was completed. In spite of the specific title, it raises

the eve of his baptism he had a vision, in which he saw dew falling upon him from heaven, spilling into his hand in the form of honey, and flowing from there over the surface of the earth. A voice informed him that this was an augury for his future.[8]

He stayed at or near Šeneset for perhaps three years attempting to fulfill the promise of his first prayer by serving within the community. He attracted others to share his simple life of horticulture, public charity, and discussion.[9] But then he adopted a more ascetic life, associating himself with an older hermit, Palamon.[10] At some time in the course of their association,[11] while praying near the deserted village of Tabennesi, he heard a voice telling him to build a monastery there, with the prospect of attracting many followers.[12]

The experience demanded a change in Pachomius's relationship with Palamon. They made a formal agreement to remain in touch with one another. Palamon clearly acknowledged in Pachomius a new equality with himself, and therefore a certain independence.[13]

After Palamon's death, Pachomius was joined by his brother John. Their reunion was the first sign that his family understood what he was

many questions about Pachomius's motives. While not contradicting, I think, any of my major conclusions, it promises to carry the "Pachomian debate" another step forward.

8.   The interpretations of Veilleux (see n. 6) undermine the importance of augury. Note the variations on the significance of the earth. G[1] presents the ascetic life as the immediate aftermath of this experience.

9.   Only in Bo 8–10; but see below, at n. 19, and Veilleux, *Liturgie*, p. 169. The chronology of Bo may be confirmed by *Letter of Ammon* 12, with its reference to Alexander, patriarch of Alexandria from 312 to 328, which allows us to place the conversion of Pachomius in 313: see Veilleux, *Koinonia*, 2:107. An ascetic community at Šeneset later asked, as we shall see, to join the Pachomian federation. At the earlier date, according to Bo 8, the place was deserted, but that could mean simply that there were few inhabitants, rather than none at all. The text is referring to a place actually outside Šeneset, identified as Pmampesterposen, also the site, according to some versions, of a later Pachomian monastery. See Bo 51, as augmented by S[5], and Veilleux, *Koinonia*, 1:267. Chitty had grave doubts about the existence of this foundation; and his arguments are convincing, "Chronology," pp. 383–84.

10.   G[1] 6–11. Bo suggests that the earlier sojourn in the village area could not properly be regarded as an ascetic experience and follows with the observation, "Then he sought to become a monk and to give himself up to the anchoritic life" (10).

11.   It lasted, according to Bo 17 and S[3], for seven years. Arabic texts provide a variation. Perhaps it is here that one might shorten events to fit better Chitty's chronology.

12.   G[1] 12, Bo 17.

13.   G[1] 12f, Bo 17.

trying to do. The two carried out together vigorous religious exercises and kept the law of God, worked for the benefit of others, and provided an example to neighboring ascetics.[14] Then, in the light perhaps of another vision, Pachomius decided to erect more buildings in order to allow other anchorites to live with his brother and himself.[15] The two brothers quarreled over the proposal, John suggesting that it smacked of pride. Pachomius prayed for patience, but the problem was resolved only by his brother's death.[16]

After a further period of asceticism, resulting in purity of heart and the conquest of demons,[17] Pachomius began to attract ascetic followers in a more organized manner. The *Vita Prima* refers to one Hieracapollon, who stressed the importance of Pachomius's example as an encouragement and model for other ascetics and remained close to him (as Palamon had done), dying in one of his later monasteries. "They prayed not to be separated from each other for ever."[18]

The early Sahidic *Lives* provide a story, apparently distinct from that series of events, of how local villagers came to live with Pachomius, forming a little colony of anchorites; how they pooled their resources and ate food together, being in other respects independent; how they regarded Pachomius as their father, although they treated him with some disdain; and how he acted for the most part as their servant, remembering again his early promise at Thebes. All this seems to have covered a period of four to five years. It is hard to know where to place the anecdote in the sequence we have provided so far (if, indeed, it is

14.   All implied by G[1] 14. Bo 19 says slightly less of the neighbors, but the hint is there.

15.   The vision is suggested by S[1]; see further below. S[3] gives a fuller account, and implies that others had already begun to arrive. G[1] describes the expansion plans and the subsequent quarrel, as also Bo 19.

16.   John's death is mentioned in S[1], in the section numbered by Veilleux Fragment III (9), as also by Bo and S[3]. G[1] 15 passes over the death, but is otherwise closer to S[1] than is S[3]: it puts John clearly in the wrong. Pachomius's prayer obviously implies doubts in his own mind about his ability to achieve what John objected to. S[3], trans. Lefort, *Vies*, p. 62, is the only Coptic source to reproduce this prayer; but others have *lacunae* at this point, which may make S[3] less exceptional: see Veilleux, *Liturgie*, pp. 45f.

17.   G[1] 17–19 seems a reflective interpolation, reminiscent of the *Life of Antony* (Antony is mentioned in G[1] 22 as having had similar experiences), but there are parallels in Bo that are probably less dependent on the example of Athanasius's text.

18.   G[1] 20 (not in Bo). The quotation echoes his earlier agreement with Palamon. The phrase ἐν τῇ κοινωνίᾳ implies a monastic setting in some stricter sense. See also G[1] 123.

possible at all), but it may be referring, with some variations, to his earliest experiments at Šeneset before he met Palamon.[19]

In what must be the final stage of the story, the *Vita Prima* speaks of another vision, also probably at Tabennesi, which confirmed God's purpose "to minister to the race of men in order to reconcile them to himself."[20] Pachomius now decided to accept as his subjects any who wished to join him. He clothed them in the monastic habit and emphasized the radical way in which they thereby left the world. In Coptic versions he continued to act as their servant, seeing they were not yet ready to serve one another, but in the Greek text they come to appreciate his virtue, accept their community responsibility, and receive from Pachomius formal regulations about food, clothing, and sleep, all on the basis of scripture.[21]

At this point we have a monastery in some formal sense, but the chronology is based on a far from simple conflation of texts in different languages, which contradict each other in more than their account of events.

Take, for example, visions or similar supernatural experiences. Leaving aside for the moment Pachomius's first prayer and his baptismal vision of dew and honey, we note three such moments associated with the formation of the ascetic community. There is the voice at Tabennesi, which encourages (in both the Greek and the Bohairic accounts) the establishment of a monastery on that spot. This occurs during Pachomius's association with Palamon.[22] Then there is the vision (in the Sahidic *Life*), almost certainly of an angel, alluding to Pachomius's vocation as a servant of humanity in reconciling mortals to God.[23] Finally (John now being dead) we have what seems to be a further vision (this time in the Greek and Bohairic biographies), again of an angel, which refers in slightly different terms to service and reconciliation and which prompts Pachomius actually to build the monastery at Tabennesi.[24] One voice, therefore, followed by two angels.

Now it is possible that some, if not all, of those accounts refer to one

19. S¹ III (10f), which then peters out. See Veilleux, *Liturgie*, p. 170.
20. G¹ 23, Bo 22. Note that this is expressed as *God's* purpose, not, as in Dion., Pachomius's.
21. G¹ 24. On separation from relatives, see Bo 23, and further discussion below. The habit, σχῆμα, has already been mentioned in the company of Palamon, G¹ 6.
22. G¹ 12, Bo 17; see above at n. 12.
23. S¹ III (6); see above at n. 15.
24. G¹ 23, Bo 22; see above at n. 20.

experience. Where the *Vita Prima* speaks of the early voice at Tabennesi, other Greek traditions (as represented, for example, in the Latin translation by Dionysius Exiguus) speak of a vision and insert the full account (as given by Palladius in his *Lausiac History*) of tablets containing the *Rules* handed to Pachomius by an angel.[25] So the *other* experience in the *Vita Prima*, the vision mentioned above, could simply be a repetition of the "voice incident," the result of untidy compilation on the part of the author.[26] On the other hand, it does seem odd that anyone would have placed at such an early stage of Pachomius's life an experience (namely, the voice) more naturally connected with the establishment of Tabennesi than with asceticism in the company of Palamon. It could be, therefore, that this earlier incident, this voice, was, so to speak, the repetition, moved back in the text in order to explain, even to justify, the decision to withdraw from association with so holy an old man.[27]

However, it is possible also that the writer of the *Vita Prima* thought the account of two experiences, the voice and the vision, made perfect sense! The first Sahidic *Life* restricts itself to one vision and places it in the context of Pachomius's association with John.[28] It is precisely at that stage of the narrative that the author of the *Vita Prima* omits all reference to visions. With a certain logic, he places *his* angel close to the later formal founding of Tabennesi. In the earlier context, referring to association with Palamon, he restricts himself to a mere voice. It is a voice, nevertheless, that sets in motion a very real change in Pachomius's view of the ascetic life, a change without which the later foundation of Tabennesi would probably have been impossible. The author describes the urge to expand—the urge, as other texts tell us, that soured relations between Pachomius and John—as a wish to build further upon the instructions of the voice, rather than upon any experience more recent and spectacular (during, that is, Pachomius's collaboration with his brother).[29] Indeed, the author plays down the intervening period spent with John, precisely because it frustrated for a while the hopes that the voice had raised. With his eventual vision of an angel, he allows his pattern to reemerge: Pachomius was seeking by then to know not just the

25.   Dion. 12, although the chapter goes on to talk of a voice! See *HL* 32. Dion. still repeats this material, complete with angel, in 21, the chapter corresponding to G¹ 23. There is a hint at vision in the company of John in Dion. 15.

26.   So, characteristically, Festugière, *Première Vie grecque*, p. 109.

27.   Veilleux, *Liturgie*, p. 169 n. 9, says G¹ 23 is based on S¹, and then, for the reasons suggested, transferred back to G¹ 12.

28.   S³ has G¹ 12 material, but Veilleux, *Liturgie*, p. 41, would not include that passage as a primitive adjunct to the S¹ text.

29.   G¹ 15.

will of God (already revealed to him by the voice) but the "whole" (or perhaps "complete and final") will of God.[30]

So there is a sequence of emphases in the *Vita Prima* that may not entirely clash with the stark narrative of the Sahidic *Lives*. Pachomius desires to serve others, his future as a man of significance and influence is vaguely portended at his baptism, he is urged to pioneer experiments in the monastic life, and some final accession of clarity and confidence results in the formal incorporation of the Tabennesi community.

There are other complications. First is the tendentious character of the very visions and prayers themselves. In the *Vita Prima*, for example, Pachomius the soldier promises to serve all humanity. The vision on the eve of his baptism suggests, in all the texts, that his own spiritual gifts were to be placed at the disposal of a wide audience. The voice at Tabennesi speaks only, it is true, of a monastery and of monks, but the final vision of the angel recalls the early emphasis on service and association with the saving work of Christ. Reference to the beatitudes may also suggest that Pachomius saw himself engaged in little more than basic Christianity.

A glance at other passages will show that such a program was open to dispute. Not all admirers of Pachomius wished his followers or imitators to dedicate themselves to so extensive an apostolate.[31] Even the *Vita Prima* is cautious, omitting, for example, any suggestion that Pachomius after his baptism may have lingered at Šeneset for as much as three years before embracing a truly ascetic life.[32] It may have avoided, in other words, the embarrassment more freely admitted by the Bohairic author, according to whom Pachomius finally declared, "This service of the sick in the villages is no work for a monk."[33] The first Sahidic *Life* strikes, in the end, a similar note. Its single vision is concerned with service in a narrow setting, and the account of Pachomius's new community refers only to the neighborhood of a single village.[34]

A second complication, not unconnected with the first, arises from the relation between that Sahidic narrative and the account given in the

30.   Note the phrases of G[1] 21: "even before he had received perfect knowledge from the Lord," and "teach me your whole will." There are no equivalents in Bo.

31.   See n. 6, and the comments made by Ruppert, pp. 13–18.

32.   Information already discussed, and preserved in Bo 8–10.

33.   Bo 9. It is important to note, however, that this was a very specific reservation, that it did not result in any immediate change (see the opening of Bo 10), and that it was compromised by the scriptural quotations that follow.

34.   S[1] III (11) emphasizes the village connection. Compare the early experience of Antony, in the *Life of Antony* 2f.

Greek and Bohairic *Lives*.[35] All purport to describe Pachomius's first disciples. In all he is presented as a father.[36] He issues regulations for his followers. He acts above all as a servant—preparing meals, caring for the sick, attending generally to the material side of life. He admits that those first enthusiasts are not yet ready for full community life modeled on the Christian community portrayed in the *Acts of the Apostles*.[37] The main difference is that in the Sahidic *Life* his authority is rejected by his followers, his generosity is ridiculed, and he experiences some years of frustrating disdain. In both Greek and Bohairic texts his authority is recognized, his example admired, and his regulations accepted. Perhaps the latter accounts describe the resolution of a conflict left in the air by our fragmented Sahidic text.[38]

A third complication springs from the fact that the foundation of Tabennesi, as described in any text, cannot be seen as a radical change from earlier patterns of behavior. Pachomius had been involved in Christian groups of one kind or another throughout the previous ten to fifteen years. There was his residence close to Šeneset.[39] There is the fact that his years with Palamon were not years of isolation: other ascetics could join them, at least for a while,[40] they indulged in manual labor for the benefit of others in need,[41] and Pachomius continued to keep a wider world in his prayers.[42] That social context would have made the "voice" at Tabennesi not unnatural in its tone. Then in the company of his brother Pachomius continued to work for others.[43] At least one text suggests that

35. G¹ 24–26, Bo 23f.

36. More so in G¹. Veilleux, *Liturgie*, p. 170 seems wrong.

37. S¹ III (11) makes the allusion, with emphasis on "one heart and one soul." G¹ inclines more to mutual dependence, a point that Pachomius recalled, G¹ 112, discussed fully below.

38. Contested by van Molle, "Confrontation," pp. 404f. The Greek and Bohairic accounts, she says, offer later support for later rules, which reject the notion of a superior who serves; the whole issue is therefore glossed over. Quite apart from general misgivings discussed in Chapter II, it is wrong to impose institutional tidiness on this early period (which is what this article in particular tends to do), and short-sighted to ignore the later passages, in both Greek and Bohairic, that continue to describe Pachomius as a servant of his community.

39. He was close enough to care for travelers, Bo 8.

40. G¹ 8. Bo 14 says he "lived in a cell near them"; and later, referring to "all the neighboring brothers" and to "those on all that mountain," the text asserts that Palamon was "their father and comforter." In G¹ 13 these brothers and a local doctor advise Palamon in his sickness; see also Bo 16.

41. G¹ 6, Bo 10.

42. G¹ 11, not explicit in Bo 15. Their settlement was also near the village: see Lefort, "Premiers Monastères," p. 387. For the enduring breadth of Pachomius's intercession, see Bo 100f (not in G¹).

43. G¹ 14, Bo 19.

the two of them may have attracted further company. Certainly, in such an atmosphere, it would not have been illogical to prepare for the arrival of companions.[44] After his brother's death (according to the Greek tradition), he was joined in a close relationship by Hieracapollon, who remained with him throughout the period leading up to the formal founding of Tabennesi and beyond. The account of this association clearly implies that others lived close by, aware of Pachomius and inspired by his example. "Be valiant," urges Hieracapollon. "The devil knows that if carelessness overtakes you, he will also dominate us, for you are our model. Therefore endure, lest you have to answer for our blood if you are defeated."[45] The Sahidic texts confirm that almost certainly before the formal founding of Tabennesi (as envisaged in the *Vita Prima*) people could live in the company of Pachomius or under his influence, while still regarding themselves as anchorites.[46]

In other words, the formal establishment of a communal way of life did not represent a sudden lurch in a new direction. From the very beginning, even when we make allowances for the prejudices of the *Vita Prima*, Pachomius seems to have had in mind an asceticism closely bound up with a sense of obligation toward other people. We are not dealing with the mere rejection of village life followed by sudden disenchantment with the solitary vocation. Rather, we are faced with a ten-to-fifteen-year period of more complex experiment, failure, and growth; we need to ask by what shifts of emphasis or conviction that gradual development took place.

The clue lies in the relationships with Palamon, with John, and with Hieracapollon—or rather in the changes within those relationships. Pachomius and Palamon entered into a covenant together, a διαθήκη, agreeing for the time being "that we shall visit each other in turn, you and I, so as not to be separated from each other from now on."[47] The same point is made with regard to Hieracapollon: "they prayed not to be

44. S[3] mentions that others were arriving already.

45. G[1] 20, not in Bo.

46. S[1] III (10f). G[1] 23 has Pachomius μετὰ ἀδελφῶν, a reading that Halkin was content to accept. Veilleux, *Koinonia*, 1:311 suggests "his brother," and thinks, p. 409, that the plural was "probably a mistake," since the formal community is set up only in G[1] 24. Lefort, *Vies*, p. 60, had already had doubts. S[1] III (6) has "and his brother," drawn from S[3]. Bo 22 specifically says that Pachomius was "alone," as does Am. G[2] 21 omits reference to the place, and has reconstructed the passage extensively.

47. G[1] 12. Here it is Palamon who takes the initiative and abides by the decision for the rest of his life. Bo 17 is similar and stresses mutual respect without explicitly using a term equivalent to διαθήκη.

separated from each other for ever," and, as we have just seen, a firm declaration of mutual responsibility was involved in that agreement.[48]

The relationship with John seems somewhat different, involving antagonism resolved only by death. But there are clues in the Greek tradition to what lay behind that antagonism: John was "older according to the flesh."[49] The Latin translation by Dionysius (not following any known Greek text) says that John became "a true brother of Pachomius, imitating him."[50] John presumed, perhaps, upon some natural authority over his younger brother and Pachomius may have attempted, with some success, to assert a spiritual equality. In the light of those allusions, we might be drawn to place more faith in the Bohairic *Life* at this point. John is made to declare, "The Lord knows, my brother, that every day I used to say that I am your elder by the flesh, that was why every day I would call you my brother. From this day forward I will call you my father because of your firm faith in the Lord."[51]

What Pachomius seems to have striven for, in other words, was not mere association with others, nor even the service of others in some vague sense. He sought for a community built upon mutual respect and mutual support. That was to be the basic component of his *Koinonia* and will become, therefore, a central theme in our description of Pachomius; its implications and practical effects will be unfolded in the chapters that follow. Let us say, for the moment, that we shall discover in the members of the Pachomian community a readiness to work together in their daily tasks—to be described in Chapter IV—and, even more important, a readiness to encourage one another in the attainment of spiritual goals, and ultimately to accept responsibility for the interior development of their fellow monks. We can see those principles in the Sahidic descrip-

48.   G[1] 20. The notion of διαθήκη persisted in the Pachomian tradition: see Theodore's use of the Coptic equivalent in S[6] (text ed. Lefort, p. 275; trans. *Vies*, p. 328) used by Veilleux, *Koinonia*, vol. 1, to fill up his Bo 142 (the same word recurs several times in the passages following, and clearly sums up Theodore's understanding of the *Koinonia*). Bell, *Jews and Christians*, prints a text, no. 1917, pp. 81f, which sets up a διαθήκη between two monks, though the notion of equality is absent.

49.   G[1] 15, at precisely the moment of conflict, but Bo 19 does not mention the age factor.

50.   Dion. 14.

51.   Bo 20. This attempt to change a relationship "according to the flesh" may explain more fully the Sahidic and Greek expressions of dismay in Pachomius's prayers after his quarrel with John (dismay at his own anger, as much as at John's intransigence): "remove this fleshly thought," S[1] III (8); "O God, the mind of the flesh is still in me. I still live according to the flesh; alas for me!" G[1] 15. Bo 20 offers a more rational account than G[1] 21 of Pachomius's mastery over crocodiles (a feat that supposedly impressed his brother).

tion of the very first community: "He established for them the following rule: each should be self-supporting and manage his own affairs"; but that rather tense segregation was a temporary compromise, since he hoped that they would eventually "bind themselves together in a perfect *Koinonia* like that of the believers which *Acts* describes: 'They were one heart and one soul.'"[52] The apparently corresponding passage in the *Vita Prima* is more formal with reference to the monastic habit and to rules, but the same cautious elasticity is defended: "for the neophytes had not yet attained to such a disposition as to serve each other." Pachomius was confident that attitudes would change: "The merciful Lord himself, looking upon my poverty, will strengthen you or will bring others able to assist me in caring for the monastery."[53]

That is not to suppose, of course, that Pachomius did not acquire in the process some overriding authority, which was in itself influential in forming the communities of which he was a part. The new relationship, the mutual support, had to be accepted by others, and accepted on the basis of personal qualities recognized in Pachomius. His leadership we shall observe more closely in a later chapter, but the significance of his power over others is clear even in early anecdotes. "I believe," said Palamon, referring to the voice at Tabennesi, "that this has come to you from God." He had already expressed his amazement at the spiritual gifts Pachomius displayed—not only a complete dedication to practical asceticism, but also a heart purged of all but a love for the law of God.[54] John, in the Bohairic *Life*, was willing to call Pachomius "father."[55] Hieracapollon stressed the importance of his example for the ascetics around him.[56] Even in the first Sahidic *Life*, when Pachomius was reticent and his followers abusive, alternative hints are present: "they considered him trustworthy," "he was their father after God."[57]

What we should avoid supposing is that, after the founding of Tabennesi and its sister houses, the charismatic quality in Pachomius gave way to mere authoritarianism. Theodore is described, for example, as a γνήσιον τέκνον of Pachomius, a worthy and legitimate son, precisely be-

---

52. S¹ III (11).

53. G¹ 23–25. Without placing too much weight on a word, note that Veilleux's "disposition" translates διάθεσις, close to διαθήκη above; Bo 23 has the Coptic equivalent. On the general theme of mutual responsibility, see the closely related emphases of Ruppert, culminating on pp. 101 and 347f.

54. G¹ 9, 12, the latter implied in Bo 17.

55. Bo 20.

56. G¹ 20. The same is true of G¹ 14, Bo 21.

57. S¹ III (11). G¹ 17f describes the qualities involved: power over demons, and insight.

cause he became like him.[58] Theodore, of course, was a model disciple. It was to him among others that Antony addressed the words, "All of you have become as Abba Pachomius."[59] But the theme of sonship was emphasized more broadly in later sources.[60] Greek tradition would assert, with analogous effect, that once you had seen Pachomius you would never wish to leave him.[61] Nor was he ashamed to think of himself as a disciple in the older style. Palamon's teaching and practice on prayer, for example, he would still impart years later to his own followers.[62] He was happy to submit others to the same one-to-one relationship. So Theodore of Alexandria was placed at first under the instruction of an aged monk who could speak Greek.[63] The young Silvanos was to be instructed by old Psenamon, Pachomius himself being too busy to attend to the boy, and the terms of the arrangement recalled precisely the authority he had developed years before: "See, this is your father after God: do everything he does."[64] It is striking that the Arabic account should end with people approaching Silvanos as a charismatic master: "Abba Silvanos, our father: speak to me a word for my profit!"[65]

And what of later years? The establishment of the community at Tabennesi does seem to have represented more than a forceful emphasis

58.   G[1] 26; also in G[3] 45, and in the text supplied by Veilleux, *Koinonia*, vol. 1, for G[1] 33.

59.   G[1] 120. Bo is missing: see the scattered comments of Festugière, *Première Vie grecque*, beginning with p. 57.

60.   Pachomius was also a γνήσιον τέκνον, G[1] 98 (not in Bo; and see n. 3). For the attitudes of Theodore and Horsiesios, see G[1] 145, Bo 210, *Liber Orsiesii*, 46. The *Liber*, as translated into Latin by Jerome, is now edited, with German translation and extensive commentary, by H. Bacht, *Das Vermächtnis des Ursprungs*. A Latin text is also included in Boon, *Pachomiana*. Veilleux refers to the *Liber* as the *Testament of Horsiesios* and presents the revision of an English translation by Philip Timko in *Koinonia*, 3:171–224.

61.   G[3] 57. G[1] 31 is incomplete. Note that this final phrase is not in G[2] 27, and is not included by Veilleux in his translation, *Koinonia*, 1:318. He says, p. 411, that he is using MS Athos 1015. So does Festugière, *Première Vie grecque*, p. 22, and yet he does have the phrase in his translation, p. 175.

62.   G[1] 60, Bo 59.

63.   G[1] 94, Bo 89 (which makes it clear that the arrangement was not made just on the basis of language).

64.   Am, p. 522, reflected also in S[5] 93. The incident is not in Bo. Festugière prefers the account in G[1] 104f, against Sahidic versions and the *Paralipomena*; see *Première Vie grecque*, pp. 118–20. Am, pp. 518f is longer but similar; it mentions that Silvanos was sent specially to a separate monastery and is more specific about his spiritual weaknesses.

65.   Am, p. 533. Ruppert comments usefully, p. 125: Silvanos illustrates the growth of self-reliance that eventually needs no tutelage. That spiritual progression will be explored at length, in Chapter VII especially.

on mutual support or an increase in Pachomius's public reputation. Before he sees the angel, he is described in a variety of texts as having been associated with professional ascetics, yet after the vision, as the *Vita Prima* puts it, "he began to *receive* those who came to him."[66] What precisely was the difference in behavior implied by this ὑποδέχεσθαι? As well as bestowing upon them a monastic habit, Pachomius now questioned them closely whether they were able to "renounce all the world"; to renounce especially their families, "for this is to carry the Cross."[67] One might imagine these words to imply that going to Tabennesi meant not only associating with a striking personality and adopting a life governed by rule, but also crossing a clear line between one society and another. But we must avoid exaggeration. Relatives were closely involved in the process of adhesion to the monastic life. Members of one family might enter together, or successively within a short period.[68] Those "outside" were allowed to visit.[69] Men were allowed to call on their sisters in the women's monastery.[70] The very experience of first vocation appears to have depended on family support: the *Vita Prima* includes the interesting phrase, "after appropriately testing them *and their parents*."[71] It would be unwise to place too much weight on Theodore's severity, examined at revealing length, against his mother and his brother Paphnouti. His mother arrived at the monastery armed with at least one letter from a bishop, but because of the variety of accounts it is not clear whether she wanted simply to see her son, to share in his dedication, or to carry Theodore away. We shall return to the incident. Theodore was adamant: the gospel called for a strict and literal repudiation of one's family. Pachomius found it hard to deny that exegesis and was clearly embarrassed by the situation, but, in every version of the story, he counseled moderation.[72] What is more to the point is that Theodore is dis-

66. G¹ 24. The three stages of renunciation here will be discussed further. Note that "he introduced them to the life gradually"; and see Veilleux, *Liturgie*, pp. 223f.

67. A point echoed in Bo 23.

68. This had been the experience of both Pachomius and Theodore: see, e.g., G¹ 65, which will be discussed further, and Bo 27, as also the famous example of Petronios and his family, G¹ 80.

69. *P* 53–55.

70. Bo 27.

71. G¹ 24. See the useful discussion by A-J. Festugière, *Antioche païenne et chrétienne*, pp. 190f.

72. Bo 37–38 (where the mother receives no satisfaction). G¹ separates the two incidents, 37 (where the mother is more appeased) and 65. One should note that here, as in G² 33 and Dion. 31, his mother wanted to take Theodore away, which rather alters the situation, but in the later texts she stays on in the women's

played elsewhere as having developed humane attitudes on the issue.[73]

When we turn to the later evidence preserved in the *Rules*, the division between monastery and world appears somewhat sharper, for a wider variety of reasons. They were not new. All who wished to enter the monastery had to wait a few days at the gate: that is exactly what Theodore did.[74] They had to learn the Lord's Prayer and what psalms they could: just so much Pachomius had demanded of his disciples during the early days at Tabennesi, and so much he had done himself.[75] The postulants had then to be asked whether they were in a position to leave their families (a legal question, perhaps, as much as a psychological one), not to mention their property. Only then were they instructed in the rules of the monastery.[76] In a later *praeceptum* not necessarily dating from Pachomius's own lifetime, the *rudis*, as Jerome calls him, was first to be taught his responsibilities in the monastery and then, after his assent, some twenty psalms and a couple of epistles or some other useful scriptural texts. Non-readers were to be taught to read.[77] Later biographical texts reinforce that impression of a neat and tidy system. Pachomius is portrayed as asking the porter every morning whether anyone wished to leave the world,[78] and that world had become by that time an

---

monastery. *Verba seniorum* 34 has Theodore's sister arriving also; this is perhaps a confusion with Pachomius, *PL* 73.760f. The S[10] fragment adds nothing, in spite of van Molle's over-forceful assertions, "Confrontation," p. 421; and Am, p. 406 has Pachomius say that Theodore should unbend to the sorrow of his parents.

73.   *Letter of Ammon* 30, but note Draguet's "Fragment 2," "Un paralipomenon pachômien," pp. 55–61. The text is translated in Veilleux, *Koinonia*, 2:115–19. See also *Liturgie*, p. 112. Many later texts continued to discuss the issue. Dion. 46 may deserve trust, following, perhaps, the vision reported in G[1] 102/Bo 103: monks have an obligation to perform well, so to speak, in their relatives' eyes, not least because relatives have the right expectations, and will feel that the sorrow of parting is wasted in the case of failure. See also G[2] 71, and *Paral.* 9 (19). For a further discussion of attitudes to relatives, see Ruppert, pp. 142f.

74.   G[1] 35. *HL* 32.5 is hopelessly misinformed.

75.   Psalms at Tabennesi, G[1] 24 (Bo 23 is less specific); Pachomius's study of scripture with Palamon, G[1] 9, Bo 15 (which is better).

76.   *P* 49.

77.   *P* 139. For a critical discussion of the links between this prescription and *P* 49, see de Vogüé, "Pièces latines," pp. 58–61, referred to again below, n. 81. Veilleux thinks that *rudis* meant "pagan" to Jerome, *Liturgie*, p. 199, but it seems important that the context dwells upon illiteracy.

78.   G[2] 58 (not in Dion.); note what became a rather technical word for withdrawal, ἀποτάξασθαι, which may evoke the term ἀποτακτικός, used for some early ascetics. Both G[1] 28 and Bo 26 have the story in a shortened form. They state that novices stayed some time with the porter. Veilleux gives references to the *Rules*, *Koinonia*, 1:271.

increasingly defined and slightly fearsome antithesis of the monastery, representing a way of life that was burdensome as well as wicked.[79]

The question is, how quickly did this despairing view of the world develop? The allusions surviving in the *Rules* to the events of Pachomius's life are allusions to more intimate and haphazard prescriptions. Yet a sense of some break in one's life was, from the very beginning, part and parcel of involvement with the Pachomian community. The one note sounded in the biographies that helps us to be more precise is that of conversion. The first disciples were surprised and grateful to discover that holiness was not something determined at birth, but something you achieved through repentance, a change of heart. Pachomius himself, born a pagan, was proof of that, and the change was an experience his disciples wished to share.[80]

It is tempting to suggest, in the light of such early hints, that attachment to the community was synonymous with the embracing of Christianity itself. Of course there were pagan postulants, but we have noted in Chapter I how rash it would be to underestimate the number of Christians in Upper Egypt at that period. Many already baptized (including even clergy) applied to join the community, confident that they were taking a further and radical step in their religious development. The most famous example was Theodore himself. A probably reliable tradition states that he was born a Christian of Christian parents, and that what impelled him to embrace the monastic life was distress at the sight of his family's luxury.[81]

79. Dion. 23, with parallels in G^2 22. It would depend on how literally you took πονηρά: Dion. obviously did very much so, although note a possible confusion of *opera* and *onera*, and the way in which Dion. then goes on to talk about the alternative burdens of monasticism (as does G^2). Dion. 46 has *dura servitutis obsequia*, G^2 71 includes the notion *dura* only remotely, *Paral.*9 (19) even less, and Bo 23 not at all. G^1 25 is also faint in its impressions, but the idea of liberation from the world is there, with the allusion to Matthew 11.28, "Come to me all you who labour and are overburdened."

80. G^1 25. A wide degree of textual variation may prove the popularity of this anecdote: see G^2 22, with Dion. 23, and *Apophthegmata patrum*, Psenthaisius 1, *PG* 65.436–37. Comparable is *Letter of Ammon* 20, where the idea is blessed by the support of Antony. The same theme is treated at length in Bo 107, not in G^1, but parallel to Am, pp. 510f.

81. Bo 31. See also G^3 45, and the text used by Veilleux, *Koinonia*, vol. 1, for G^1 33. Here we touch upon the link between monastic "profession" and baptism, discussed at length by Veilleux, *Liturgie*, pp. 198f. His references provide a very weak base for the general picture of Pachomian spirituality he wishes to develop. De Vogüé, "Pièces latines," p. 61, was willing to accept P 49 as referring to the induction of non-Christians, but that was in conjunction with S^{10} which

A clear sense that monasticism was a unique form of devotion was also delayed and perhaps for a long time obscured by the existence of other ascetic groups around Tabennesi, Panopolis, and Latopolis. In addition to the references from the early years at Šeneset, there are several anecdotes that describe how Pachomius entertained or visited members of such groups, clearly enjoying a status among them unconnected with the leadership of his own communities and falling easily into the older role of quasi-eremitic colleague. (We should not imagine, of course, that Upper Egypt, when compared, for example, with Scetis, was monopolized by cenobites: the *Apophthegmata Patrum* record a number of *Thebaidi*.)[82] As we shall discuss further, the local bishop Sarapion suggested to Athanasius that Pachomius be placed "over all the monks in my diocese as father and priest."[83] He avoided that promotion, but to a guest at Tabennesi from the young Theodore's first community at Latopolis he was "the holy man, our father Pachomius."[84] So it was also in the case of "the father of a nearby monastery," who attempted to control his own subjects with the warnings of "our father Pachomius."[85]

Pachomius may have felt threatened at times by other ascetics. At an early stage of his life at Tabennesi, Theodore had complained that standards were higher in his old community and wondered whether he ought not to return to it. Pachomius was anxious to prevent him from doing so, foreseeing a likely cause of slander against his own monks.[86] As late as the writing of the *Vita Prima* such tensions still persisted. Pachomius was made to stand at the forefront of monastic history. The great Antony praised the degree to which he had improved upon the eremitic life. That was propaganda intended to allay misgivings. Antony

cannot carry the weight placed upon it by Veilleux. The several other passages quoted are vague or ambiguous. See Chapter I at n. 107 for an attitude close to that of Theodore.

82.   For Pachomius, G^1 40, Bo 40; G^1 76, to be discussed further; G^1 85. G^1 72 is another example, but confused: see Lefort, *Vies*, p. 31, and Festugière, *Première Vie grecque*, p. 38. Bo 67 suggests that this particular meeting (G^1 72) may not have taken place in the monastery. Am, p. 416 says it did, as also S^{10} (although this section is not included by Veilleux in *Koinonia*, vol. 1). The *Apophthegmata patrum* show relationships between hermits and cenobites from the hermits' point of view: Nisteroos the Coenobite, 2; Poemen, 6 and 70. On *Thebaidi*, John the Dwarf, 1; John of the Thebaid; Joseph of Panephysis, 3; Sisoes, 10.

83.   G^1 30, Bo 28.

84.   G^1 34, considerably clarified by Bo 29. To suggest with Festugière, *Première Vie grecque*, p. 116 n. 1, that there is no question here of jurisdiction (over Latopolis) is to miss the point.

85.   G^1 42, Bo 42 (which makes the contact of much longer standing).

86.   G^1 68. But was Theodore serious? There may be confusion with a story in G^1 66, but that is not straightforward either: see Bo 62f.

had still to be described as "light of all this world." He was allowed to hint that others before Pachomius had tried to initiate more cenobitic asceticism. Not that Pachomius would have denied it! And in a more vigorous Coptic version of the story, Antony had to defend himself against the inquiry why, if he admired Pachomius so much, he had not joined one of his monasteries himself.[87]

To the very end of his life, however, Pachomius defended his earliest emphases. During his trial at the Synod of Latopolis in the autumn of 345,[88] he said that it was rare in his young days to find ascetics in groups of two or three: a "community" of ten would have been the maximum. That was because they found it very hard, as he put it, "to govern each other in the fear of God."[89] The phrase explained why his own endeavor was more successful. He valued still the old notion of mutual support evoked by the words "govern each other." Important also was the fear of God, which we shall discuss much more in a later chapter. Instructive, again, is the tradition concerning Pachomius's sister. He invited her to join him in his experiment so that she might find mercy, self-knowledge, the reflection born of quietness, and (though last of all) an opportunity to live with others called to join her by the Lord.[90] Like mutual support and the fear of God, those would be recurrent emphases in Pachomian doctrine. They reinforce the impression that Pachomius's early disciples attached themselves much more to an attitude of mind, a spirituality, than to a mere system or regime.

So, even when we see Pachomius founding other monasteries, we should not imagine the mere transference or duplication of a ready-made institution. It is likely, of course, as the *Vita Prima* suggests, that by 330, when he had founded Phbow (which later became his headquarters), Pachomius had devised his system of superiors for both monasteries and "houses." That does not imply that their duties were as clearly defined as they are in the *Rules* translated by Jerome. Colonization was more in evidence than was legislation; what mattered was the appointment of the right kind of leader, rather than the publication of the right kind of rule.[91] In any case, the succession of subsequent foundations ca-

87.   G¹ 120, but the text suppresses the attack on Antony by Zacchaeus: see Bo 126f. We raised this topic in Chapter II at n. 22f. S⁵ 120f probably represents a clearer but later reflection on an enduring controversy, *pace* Festugière, *Première Vie grecque*, pp. 78f.

88.   Chitty, "Chronology," p. 379.

89.   G¹ 112. The institutional character of κυβερνῶσιν is much modified by ἀλλήλους. The Synod will be discussed fully in Chapter VIII.

90.   Bo 27. There is a gap at G¹ 32, which Veilleux, *Koinonia*, vol. 1, has supplied from MS Athos 1015.

91.   G¹ 54. Bo 49 gives a slightly fuller account, but is suspiciously more

tered for a surprising variety of circumstances. Particularly striking is the degree of cautious deliberation provoked by the opening of the communities to Greek-speaking ascetics from Lower Egypt.[92] System was also undermined by the fact that whole monasteries could apply for membership in the Pachomian network. This was the case with Šeneset/Chenoboskion under its superior Ebonh. Pachomius sent him "other brothers . . . having them remain there with the original brothers," but he retained Ebonh in command.[93] Perhaps he had known him from earlier years. The same pattern may have applied at Thmoušons, founded shortly afterwards.[94] Šeneset was the monastery from which Horsiesios came to rule the communities after Pachomius's death. Thmoušons was the center of an important revolt that prompted modifications during the years of government by Horsiesios and Theodore.[95] One cannot be sure, therefore, what strings were attached to those incorporations, quite apart from the misunderstandings that may have grown from them. The same doubt will surround the later foundation at Thbew, near Panopolis, which seems to have been a gift—in what form is not clear—from the father of Petronios, Pachomius's immediate successor.[96]

All that should make us wary when we try to assess the degree of assurance and consistency represented by the step-by-step formation of the various Pachomian communities. Of course there was an overall structure, and it was probably established quite quickly. Sheer numbers would have ensured this. If we can believe Palladius (and there is very little other evidence), Pachomius himself governed three thousand devotees. The two early foundations of Tabennesi and Phbow may have contained a thousand or more each. Other monasteries numbered perhaps two or three hundred inhabitants. By the end of the fourth century, the Pachomian communities totaled perhaps seven thousand members

---

formal, including another vision. G[1] is closer to Am, p. 378. For the slowness with which systems were duplicated, see Am, p. 523, and Veilleux, *Liturgie*, p. 130. For the location of Phbow, "another deserted village," and barely two miles from Tabennesi, see Lefort, "Premiers Monastères," p. 392.

92. Bo 89–91 is very full; see also G[1] 95, 111.

93. Bo 50 is more reliable than G[1] 54. On retaining the same superior, see Veilleux, *Koinonia*, 1:413.

94. So, clearly Bo 51; G[1] 54 less so. It is at this point that Bo 51 adds the account about Pmampesterposen: see n. 9. On the site, consult Lefort, "Premiers Monastères," pp. 399f.

95. On Horsiesios at Šeneset, see G[1] 114, 118–19, 129, Bo 146. On the revolt at Thmoušons, see G[1] 127. There will be further discussion in Chapters VIII and IX.

96. G[1] 80, Bo 56 (which makes it clear that, in the Greek, Pšenthbo is the subject of the verb ἔδωκεν). See Lefort, "Premiers Monastères," pp. 402f.

overall.[97] Pachomius established Phbow as a general headquarters, close to Tabennesi.[98] From there he would travel to visit all the other monasteries: in the early days, at least, he accepted overall responsibility for their material welfare.[99] Twice a year, at Easter and on the great Feast of Reconciliation on 13 August, a large number of monks (if not all of them) came to Phbow from the other monasteries.[100]

The figures are impressive, and so is the organization. But the very scale of Pachomian asceticism made for what one might call a federal attitude. As always in the history of a monastic movement, one must not forget to look at things from the viewpoint of the individual monk. Even within one monastery, the *Rules* arranged *praepositi* in a strict order of precedence.[101] Members of one house in the community were not allowed without special permission to communicate with those of another, let alone with monks from another monastery.[102] In the end, perhaps, it was those with whom one shared a house that filled one's institutional horizon.

Certain misconceptions can therefore be avoided. We do not witness in Pachomius's lifetime the prompt conversion of hermits to the cenobitic life, nor the ruthless supplanting of the solitary tradition by a cenobitic system. Nor are the Pachomian communities entirely uniform either in their economy (in the broadest sense) or in their location. The regularity of life displayed in the *Rules* is not to be taken as a clue to how the communities were originally formed.

What we do see is a man who tried gradually to define the best setting in which ascetics might support each other both spiritually and ma-

97.   *HL* 7.6 (3,000); 18.13 (1,400 at Tabennesi); 32.8 (1,300 at Phbow, 7,000 in all); 32.9 (two or three hundred in others).

98.   See n. 91 and G[1] 78. Chitty suggests, "Chronology," p. 381, that by moving to Phbow Pachomius avoided ordination (see n. 83). On the closeness of the two houses, see the short journeys by Pachomius and Theodore, G[1] 88, 96f.

99.   G[1] 83, Bo 58.

100.   G[1] 83, 122, which deal with the rendering of accounts. See also Bo 71. Festugière, *Première Vie grecque*, pp. 100 f, examines corresponding passages and concludes that we must accept the statements of the *Rules* and of Pachomius, *Ep.* 7, that this was also an occasion of forgiveness and reconciliation. Veilleux takes this as a later development, *Koinonia*, 1:229, as also Ruppert, pp. 323f. Van Molle, "Confrontations," pp. 400f, is obscure in her contradictions. She feels that the "grande célébration de pardon mutuel," described in *Ep.* 7, is "un usage inconnu de la tradition pachômienne"; and yet she describes it herself as a "pratique bien conforme à l'esprit des *Praecepta atque Iudicia*," which, according to her, as we saw in Chapter II, were early.

101.   *P* 59.

102.   *P* 85. See G[1] 59, which is not in Bo, nor precisely in S[3a], used by Veilleux, *Koinonia*, vol. 1, to supply for Bo 104.

terially. He saw the enterprise as the necessary fulfillment of New Testament demands of brotherly love. One result of the experiment was a growing distinction between the Pachomian community and the rest of society, ascetic as well as urban and lay. To involve oneself in this system of mutual concern, this *Koinonia,* was to effect in the end a radical change in one's life.

· IV ·

THE DAY'S ROUTINE

Having seen the communities formed, we need now to understand how, and according to what principles, the daily life of a monk was organized and controlled. This chapter and the two following should be taken together as an attempt to meet that need. Here we shall limit ourselves to a description of the basic timetable. Then we shall assess in Chapter V just how rigidly imposed the monastic order was, and how conformity was conceived and enforced. Finally, in Chapter VI we shall ask who was responsible for that achievement, and how they acquired and retained their positions of authority. In a sense we shall be reaching inward, from the visible practices of asceticism to the more structural and theoretical elements that inspired and maintained those practices. This may make for some repetition as we review different levels of the same accounts, but by the end of the analysis an integrated impression should be formed.

So how, within those new communities, did Pachomian monks conduct themselves? Were not their days, according to the commonest tradition, dominated by rule and firm government? The impression of order, complexity, and strict designation of role is derived most from later elements in the *Rules* and (most misleadingly) in the *Lausiac History* of Palladius. Our caution should by now be well rehearsed. Such texts offer no immediate guide to the practice of Pachomius's day, and may obscure from us the true feel of daily life in one of his monasteries.[1] We

1. A. H. M. Jones is not exceptional; he refers to "a communal life under strict discipline," involving "gangs," "foremen," and "highly organized industrial and agricultural concerns," *Later Roman Empire*, 2:929. His references, Chapter 22 n. 156, p. 1388, are mainly to Palladius. Ludicrously unjust to Pachomius is E. Amand de Mendieta, "Le Système cénobitique basilien comparé au système cénobitique pachômien," *Revue de l'histoire des religions* 152 (1957): 31–80. He deals, in the case of Pachomius, with a "système encore primitif, presque em-

need to recall not only the primitive customs but also what contemporaries regarded as essential to their community experience. When Theodore looked back on his younger days, he remembered chiefly the joy and peace that the monks preserved for one another. They had nothing but the word of God in their hearts and on their lips: "We were not conscious of living on earth but of feasting in heaven."[2] Reading the *Rules*, one might hardly have guessed it!

Yet the essentials can be discovered as Pachomius first defined them. They are easy enough to extract from early levels in the sources at our disposal. "They lived," as the *Vita Prima* puts it, "a coenobitic life. So he established for them in a rule an irreproachable lifestyle and traditions profitable for their souls. These he took from the holy Scriptures: proper measure in clothing, equality in food, and decent sleeping arrangements."[3] That early formulary brings us much closer to the central and enduring spirit of Pachomius's community.

Day began with the monks in their cells. There they had slept or kept a vigil propped up on special seats[4] since the end of the previous

---

bryonnaire et, à certains égards, monstrueux," p. 34. No serious comparison is attempted. On the central issues of love, the Bible, the supremacy of the cenobitic life, pp. 43f, Pachomius is not even mentioned; much the same is true when he writes of the relations between monasticism and the church, pp. 65f. Fuller reference to such notions, and necessary criticism, is provided by Ruppert, pp. 265f. Ruppert's work is indispensable to an understanding of order and authority in the lifetime of Pachomius. The required balance is also provided by, for example, W. Bousset, *Apophthegmata*, in the fourth and fifth chapters of his section on Pachomius (somewhat neglected by scholars), pp. 236–47; by Chitty, *Desert*, Chapter 2, "The Institution," pp. 20–28 (which would be a useful companion to this chapter); by P. Deseille, *L'Esprit du monachisme pachômien*, especially pp. xxxixf; and by A. de Vogüé, in his foreword to Veilleux, *Koinonia*, 1: vii–xxiii. One might note also at this point the material data provided by C. C. Walters, *Monastic Archaeology in Egypt*, esp. pp. 205f, on food, clothing, and artifacts. Little work has been done on Pachomian sites. *Miscellanea Coptica*, presented by Hjalmar Torp and others, is mainly iconographical and focused on the monastery of Apa Jeremias at Saqqara, but it contains useful comparative material and a good bibliography to augment references to Lower Egypt in my *Ascetics*. On clothing, see also G. Castel, "Étude d'une momie copte," *Hommages à la mémoire de Serge Sauneron*, 2:121–43 and plates.

2. G[1] 131. Bo is missing. There is no exact equivalent in S[6], but see the S[3] text used by Veilleux, *Koinonia*, vol. 1, for Bo 104. Athanasius, *Festal Letter* 14, voices the same sentiment: "for thus also the saints all their lives long, were like men rejoicing at a feast" (Eng. trans., p. 111).

3. G[1] 25, but for "irreproachable" ($\dot{\alpha}\pi\rho\dot{o}\sigma\kappa\sigma\pi\sigma\nu$) I would prefer "not calculated to cause offense." The allusion to scripture at such an "original" moment will prove important.

4. G[1] 79, P 87–88, based on Pachomius's own early practice (G[1] 14): "for a

evening's prayer.[5] In the early days they would have had a cell each;[6] no one was allowed to visit the cell of another without permission.[7] This degree of privacy was an important feature of Pachomian monasticism. Although the door could not be locked, there was always this one place where a monk could reflect without distraction. The cells were arranged in "houses," with twenty monks or more to a house.[8] What distinguished one house from another is not entirely clear. In some communities, or at certain periods, all who possessed one skill or exercised one responsibility may have lived together; but this could have been the case only when a wide variety of activities took place within each monastery, which was a later development, as we shall see.[9] Much of a monk's religious life revolved around his house, and its superior, the οἰκιακός or *praepositus*, was probably the most important man in his life.[10]

long time whenever he wanted to refresh his body with sleep after growing weary in keeping awake for prayer, he would simply sit on something in the middle of the place without leaning his back against the wall." These καϑισμά-τια, attested also by Cassian and Palladius, had a reclining back designed to make lengthy sleep unlikely; the sick and the elderly were probably dispensed from their use.

5. *P* 126, *PLeg* 2. For evening prayer, see below.

6. Ladeuze, *Cénobitisme pachômien*, pp. 263, 275f, questioning the accuracy of Palladius, *HL* 32.2, which has three in a cell. Chitty, *Desert*, Chapter 2 n. 26, p. 39, gives several references, not all of which are precise about numbers or quite to the point.

7. G¹ 59, not in Bo. The same applied to visiting other houses, *P* 112, *PLeg* 7 (although *P* 89 is more lenient). The cells were strong enough for a monk to sleep on the roof, *P* 87. The phrase in G¹ 76, ἐκοιμᾶτο ἔσω εἰς τὰς καλύβας, refers to huts built at harvest time (see also G¹ 51); this is probably what G¹ 77 refers to, with the phrase εἰς τὰς σκηνὰς αὐτῶν ("probably a blunder," Veilleux, *Koinonia*, 1:416), as also τὰ σκηνώματα in G¹ 126.

8. Jerome suggested forty, disputed effectively by Ladeuze, *Cénobitisme pachômien*, pp. 274f. Three or four houses constituted a "tribe" according to Jerome's gloss at *P* 15 (see Veilleux, *Koinonia*, 2:184 n. 9), but Ruppert doubts the accuracy of the reference, pp. 300f.

9. G¹ 28 might mean that each house performed a different task. The references, ostensibly to specialized houses, supplied by Chitty, *Desert*, Chapter 2 n. 31, p. 40, refer only to the sick and the preparation of food; but note the more favorable opinion of Ruppert, pp. 297f. Palladius thought different houses catered for different standards of monk, *HL* 32.4. This may have been a confusion on his part; the notion persisted in Dion. 25. On the slowness of development in this regard, see Veilleux, *Liturgie*, p. 130.

10. There is confusion in the terminology of G¹ 28. We begin tidily with an οἰκονόμος and a δεύτερος for the monastery, and an οἰκιακός and a δεύτερος for each house; the οἰκονόμος delivers the weekend catechesis proper to the superior of the monastery (see below). But then we have οἰκονόμοι in the houses, and the writer attempts clarity at the end with phrases like μεγάλος οἰκονόμος,

Around dawn[11] the monks would hear a horn or gong[12] calling them to morning prayer. This was the *synaxis* or *collecta*, which brought together in one place all members of the community. They would file in to occupy thir strictly allotted places.[13] The regular morning prayer consisted of extensive readings from scripture, followed at intervals by common recitation of the Our Father, and periods of silent reflection. Only on Sundays and other days when the Eucharist was celebrated was there any particular emphasis on psalms or singing. During the *synaxis* (presumably during the periods of scripture reading) the monks were expected to work quietly,[14] and it was during the *synaxis* that penance was performed for various faults against the rule.[15]

This type of monastic liturgy was different from that practiced elsewhere in Egypt, and not perhaps what we in the Latin West would expect, given the development of the monastic office as we know it since Benedict, with its heavy emphasis on the singing of the psalter. The opportunity to reflect and pray in silence, though still in a communal setting, seems a particularly well conceived stipulation, and the stimulus to that prayer and reflection was always a varied reading of the Bible. It made Pachomian practice less a contrast, perhaps, to the normal liturgical experience of the Christian layman.[16] It also made the act of commu-

and πατὴρ τῆς μονῆς. Veilleux is less worried, *Koinonia*, 1:410. Ruppert, pp. 282f, 290f, shows how difficult it is to plot a progression in the vocabulary of leadership—which would tell us little about role in any case. He emphasizes, p. 291, how remote the superior might seem, at "house level"; and see p. 321. Just how much authority *praepositi* enjoyed will be discussed in the two following chapters. Other *praepositi* could stand in for one absent, *P* 115.

11.   I follow Veilleux, *Liturgie*, pp. 299f. For Cornelios's practice at Thmoušons, see G¹ 60f; Bo 59 is slightly less explicit.

12.   The horn may be Jerome's error in *P* 3; but it recurs in *P* 9, which is echoed (independently?) by σάλπιγξ in the *Excerpta*, Boon, p. 171. The gong is mentioned in G¹ 61 (as also for meals, G¹ 52). *P* 23 suggests that such signals were made by the superior of the monastery.

13.   *P* 1, 4.

14.   *P* 4, 5. The opening of 5 could mean that this practice was restricted to the evening prayer in the house; this seems unlikely.

15.   G¹ 70, Bo 65; *P* 131 (although *P* 8, 135, *PInst* 6, 8 imply penance during meals). Jerome links the practice with the catechesis, *Ep.* 22.35, but this section of the letter is confused in several ways. Bo 87, however, makes the same connection, only under Theodore, and with no counterpart in G¹. On both morning and evening prayer, a useful English summary based largely on the views of Veilleux, together with other interesting information, is provided by R. Taft, "Praise in the Desert," *Worship* 56 (1982): 513–36. My thanks to Eugene O'Sullivan for this reference.

16.   See G¹ 29, Bo 25. Pachomius's links with church and society will be explored in Chapter VIII.

nal prayer more closely associated with the rest of the monastic day, during which the recitation of scripture and reflection upon it played a continuous part. Formal evening prayer and instruction by superiors we shall refer to in a moment, but monks would also recite texts while they worked (an activity described as *meditatio*).[17] They were constantly encouraged to discuss among themselves the reflections on scripture offered by their superiors,[18] and as they moved from one duty to another in the monastery, they turned over texts of scripture in their heads.[19]

This heavy emphasis on the recitation of texts points also to the use of books. All monks were expected to be lettered, and to learn at least some of the psalter and the New Testament.[20] Pachomius warned them against "the splendor and the beauty" of books, which could be "outwardly pleasing to the eye," but this was not so much an attack on ideas as an emphasis on a book's true worth—the contents rather than the appearance.[21] Books, like much other monastic property, were guarded very carefully by the *praepositus* of each house,[22] but they could be borrowed with permission for a week at a time.[23]

After morning prayer, monks returned to their cells to await instructions about the day's work.[24] One of the house *praepositi* would go to the superior of the monastery (this might not have been necessary every day) to inquire what work was to be done; he would then go around the various houses to see what fresh equipment or material they might need.[25] This was one of the responsibilities of the *hebdomadarius*. The houses took it in turns to organize the work in this way, as also to con-

17. *P* 36–37. The "simul meditabuntur" of *P* 116 might suggest recitation aloud, but the context demands silence; see also G[1] 89. In *P* 60, however, "aut . . . aut . . ." makes the activity seem an alternative to silence.

18. *P* 138; see 122, and G[1] 125. The point will recur when we discuss the evening timetable.

19. *P* 28, 59; G[1] 61, 88; Bo 34, 66, 99. On the central role of scripture, see Ruppert, pp. 128f.

20. *P* 139–40.

21. G[1] 63, not in Bo. The caution is directed also against food and clothing. It is tempting to raise the specter of possible anti-intellectualism in Pachomius and his associates; but there is little early evidence for later preoccupations, for example with the works of Origen, as reflected in Dion. 44, with parallels in G[2] 68 and *Paral.* 4 (7). G[1] 31 also attacks Origen, but again has no parallel in Bo.

22. G[1] 59. Other instances concern especially clothing: see *P* 66, *PLeg* 15.

23. *P* 25. Jerome in *P* 101 says books were counted every night, but this is not supported by the Coptic text. See also *P* 100. However, books were clearly popular: see *PInst* 2, 7, and note *P* 82.

24. *P* 19, 24.

25. *P* 24. See *P* 12, 111, 124, and Veilleux, *Liturgie*, p. 127. *P* 26 suggests that some such inquiry might have been conducted the previous evening.

duct certain parts of the liturgy (especially on Sundays), and to prepare meals and serve at table. They did this a week at a time, and were excused meanwhile from certain other duties.[26] It is worth noting that, in the early days, Pachomius made this arrangement precisely so that no one should become wedded to a particular routine, or over-identified with a particular skill, but should be ready to turn his hand to anything as the well-being of the community might require.[27]

Once the day's work had been planned and tools and material had been distributed, the monks in each house lined up to be led away to their place of work by their *praepositi*.[28] At such a moment we might most clearly picture them, wearing simple belted tunics, their arms bare, a goatskin and hood thrown over their shoulders (each hood bearing the sign of both monastery and house), rough boots for the working day, and perhaps a staff.[29] Only those engaged in the weaving of baskets, mats, or ropes would remain in the living quarters. The lining up and leading off seems regimental; it also hints at a diversity of labor. It brings to mind the most famous description of the Pachomian workforce (and also the most enduring in the Christian memory), recorded by Palladius in his *Lausiac History*. He suggests that the monks engaged in every sort of handicraft. Referring to Panopolis (without specifying which community), he mentions tailors, metalworkers, carpenters, cameldrivers, and fullers.[30] In another passage he writes more generally of husbandmen, gardeners, smiths, bakers, fullers, basketmakers, shoemakers, and copyists.[31] Here no numbers are mentioned; but in the earlier passage he makes it clear that, of a community of about three hundred, he is discussing only fifty-three men, more than half of whom are concerned with clothing.

More primitive texts do suggest, however, a certain amount of specialization, particularly in agriculture. The *villa* of the monastery, mean-

26. *P* 15; see G¹ 77, 125.
27. G¹ 28, although contradictions will be examined.
28. *P* 58, and perhaps 130, although Ruppert, p. 285, must qualify Veilleux, *Koinonia*, 2:191f: the words here, *ducem*/ἡγούμενον, refer probably to no one more exalted than the monk who was deputed to head the line. There will be further discussion of how and where the monks did their work in Chapter VIII, esp. at nn. 24f.
29. See Jerome's preface to the *Rules*, 4, and *P* 2, 81, 99. They also wore a mantle at night and during the *synaxis*, *P* 61. For laundry (weekly), see *P* 67f. It was as the monks went off to work that Theodore's mother watched them, Bo 37. Compare the information provided by Castel (n. 1 above).
30. *HL* 32.9.
31. Ibid. 12. The last-mentioned reminds us of the Nag Hammadi codices. See also the list of tasks in Am, pp. 377f.

ing in this case the stable area, was open only to people with relevant skills, herdsmen and plowmen especially.[32] Another closed shop, so to speak, was the bakery.[33] We have mentioned already an early passage in the *Vita Prima* that could suggest houses were at first distinguished by the tasks they performed: serving at table, cooking meals, caring for the sick, receiving guests, collecting material for work, and selling the produce of the monastery. But these denote services rather than skills; and the reference has to be coupled with the system of weekly rotation, and with the statement in that same chapter that monks were not to set their hearts upon any one type of activity, but hold themselves ready to obey whatever orders might be given them.[34]

Most primitive references to work in the Pachomian sources are concerned with basket making and the weaving of ropes and mats, together with the collection of materials necessary for the work and the marketing of the produce in nearby towns.[35] It is even suggested in one instance that the *praepositus* of each house should provide his monks with model baskets to copy![36] The mention of expeditions for the collection of rushes is particularly frequent. These may have been quite prolonged forays, with camping out in temporary shelters; that they stood out in people's memories may be proven by the anecdotes that cluster around them in the texts. It was while cutting rushes, for example, that Pachomius received the vision of the angel at Tabennesi.[37]

The enthusiastic and surely rather distracting diversity described by Palladius seems to have been a later development. There are signs that shortly after Pachomius's death controversy arose as to whether the simple economy of basket making and marketing should not give way to

32. *P* 108. The Coptic is more specific about *villa*, referring to "animal stalls"; and there are other variations. The item is omitted in the Greek *Excerpta*.

33. *P* 117. This was a rowdy venue, if one may trust G[1] 89, 121. The S[5] account, supplied by Veilleux, *Koinonia*, vol. 1, for Bo 138, is even funnier. See the comments of Festugière on this "bavardage à la boulangerie," *Première Vie grecque*, p. 47.

34. G[1] 28. G[1] 84 has a house at Phbow, with its own οἰκιακός, entirely responsible for the care of the sick. G[1] 26 may imply that services came before crafts.

35. *P* 5, 12, 26, 124. *P* 27 mentions the records kept of manufacture, to be presented at the great federation meeting in August (see Chapter III at n. 100). There is very little reference to marketing in those sections of the *Lives* that refer to Pachomius's lifetime. For information about the federation's boats and their use, see G[1] 113, and Veilleux, *Koinonia*, 1:419. One late text implies that over a two-month period a monk could weave five hundred mats: G[2] 67, Dion. 43.

36. *PLeg* 1. He was also supposed to show them how to eat, *P* 31. Theodore demonstrated techniques, G[1] 86.

37. G[1] 23. See n. 7, adding G[1] 71, *P* 80.

something a little more adventurous and profitable. It was on this issue that the monastery at Thmoušons under Apollonius virtually seceded from Pachomius's federation, raising a principle and presenting a difficulty that would preoccupy the government of his immediate successors.[38] The implication has to be that, in spite of the details provided by Palladius (presuming they are accurate), Pachomius himself was not the architect of a complex economic system, as is often suggested, and might have frowned upon the industry for which his followers in later generations apparently became famous.

The work that Pachomius demanded of his monks was "moderatus,"[39] and this consideration is reflected also in regulations about meals. There seem to have been usually two each day: the main meal during the working period and a lighter one in the evening.[40] Again a gong was sounded, and all met to eat together (with their boots off—a pleasing touch).[41] Eating was conducted in complete silence.[42] The meal appears to have consisted of bread and cooked vegetables; but other food may sometimes have been available or tolerated, and the sick were treated, in a place apart, with special consideration.[43] There was also an obscure morsel known as *tragematia* or κορσενήλιον, perhaps a dessert of dried

38.   G[1] 127. The dispute concerned much more than economy, and called into question the whole structure of the federation, the style of Pachomius's leadership, and his assumptions about the succession. The events will be discussed more fully in Chapters VIII and IX. The other monasteries were subject at first to supply and control from Phbow, G[1] 83.

39.   *PLeg* 3. *PLeg* 11, and perhaps *P* 10, imply consideration for a monk weary with work: see n. 46 below.

40.   Veilleux, *Liturgie*, p. 306. For the midday meal, see *P* 103.

41.   G[1] 52. Boots would be handed in after work, along with other tools, but they were removed even for lunch in the fields, *P* 65, 102. The influence of the house persisted at mealtime: no one should start eating before his *praepositus*, *P* 30.

42.   *P* 30, corroborated by Jerome, *Ep* 22. 35; *HM* (Latin) 3; Cassian, *Institutes* 4.17; and Palladius, *HL* 32.6. It is interesting that the supposed canons of Athanasius should include (67), "None among them shall talk while they eat, nor shall they, while they eat, raise their faces one toward another"—referring here to the expected conduct of priests in their bishop's household! See W. Riedel and W. E. Crum, *The Canons of Athanasius of Alexandria*, and note, for Pachomius, pp. xviii–xxii.

43.   G[1] 53, 69. Palladius, *HL* 32.11, mentions also cheese and olives. G[1] 55 and Am, pp. 376f may prove that such delicacies were available, although it is not clear that such was true of Thmoušons itself, to which the anecdote refers, but rather of what might come one's way while traveling, which is what Pachomius and his companions were doing here. Dried fruit is mentioned in G[1] 97 and *P* 75–77. See more generally *P* 71, 73, 80. *Paral.* 8 (15f) may provide reliable and similar information about fourth-century practice. Does G[1] 79 suggest that absti-

fruit, which was distributed to the monks after the evening meal. Palladius mentions meals in the houses, which was not the Pachomian practice, but he may have been thinking of the *tragematia*, which were intended for eating in the house and were supposed to last three days.[44]

The evening timetable is difficult to reconstruct. In addition to the meal, there was a period of instruction and brief community prayer; prayers were also conducted in each house before the monks retired for the night. A chapter in the *Vita Prima* provides us with a probably reliable outline: after the meal, Pachomius delivered his catechesis; there was a short prayer; the monks withdrew to their houses, repeating by heart passages from scripture; they then recited together, in the house, what were known as the "six prayers"; and these were followed by a discussion of the catechesis.[45] We know from other passages, both in the *Lives* and in the *Rules*, that the superior of each monastery delivered his catechesis normally only on Saturdays and Sundays (on Sundays twice). On Wednesdays and Fridays, which were fast days, a catechesis was delivered in the house by the *praepositus*. On these occasions, presumably there was no community meal in the evening and the monks went straight from work to their houses.[46] Discussion of the catechesis seems always to have taken place in the house, and particular emphasis was placed on the need to discuss the catechesis of the *praepositus*—partly no doubt because this was inevitably a more intimate occasion, and partly perhaps because his lesser authority invited a greater degree of inquiry and debate.[47] As for the "six prayers," a certain confusion and obscurity

---

nence from wine was exceptional? On the treatment of the sick (granted soup, fish, and perhaps even meat), see G¹ 53, 64. Palladius also says that the monks kept pigs to eat their scraps, *HL* 32.10.

44.   *HL* 32.2. Some may have been allowed to stay away from the common meal and eat more sparingly in the house under the supervision of the *praepositus*, *P* 79, but this would have been a temporary arrangement. For moderation in fasting, which will emerge in several anecdotes, see Ruppert, pp. 91f. Note also *P* 37f, G¹ 111 (not in Bo). *P* 28 is odd: it suggests a meal after the *collecta*. Could the tradition behind *P* 32 explain this? The corresponding item in the Greek *Excerpta*, XXXII, Boon, p. 173, has the phrase ὑστερίζων τῆς εὐχῆς τοῦ φαγεῖν, which must mean being late for the *grace*, before the meal.

45.   G¹ 58. G¹ 77 is similar, referring to Theodore's catechetical *début*—probably an evening occasion, since the outraged returned to their cells. For similar practices in other settings, see my *Ascetics*, p. 41.

46.   G¹ 28, Bo 26; *PInst* 15. "Disputatio" in *P* 20 refers to the same activity. On coming straight from work, see *PLeg* 11. The evening catechesis was regarded as very important: one might be absent only "gravissima necessitate," *PLeg* 12, and see *P* 22.

47.   *P* 122. The Coptic version does not reproduce the phrase "vicissim inter se," but then *P* 138 is emphatic on the point; and see *P* 19. Compare the

persists.[48] It seems reasonably certain that they were a minor version of the morning *synaxis*,[49] but given the fact that they were going to be followed by a discussion among the twenty or so monks present, there was probably less emphasis on periods of personal reflection.

This sequence of instruction, recitation, and above all discussion among those most closely known to one another may contrast with what can spring to mind when one thinks of monastic liturgy, even in its early days. Here was a real opportunity for growth in understanding, and one that would help a monk to relate what he heard to his immediate needs and circumstance. The individual's knowledge of himself in the light of scripture, fostered within a small and stable group: that was the hoped-for effect of the Pachomian day. Inner levels of the experience we shall examine in later chapters. At the practical level, it was a pattern of activity that flowed naturally into the more solitary reflections of a watchful night.[50]

---

custom at Latopolis, G¹ 34. Jerome also mentions these discussions, *Ep.* 22.35. It is in this light that one should judge the hesitation of Ruppert, pp. 351f.

48.   Veilleux has discussed the problems exhaustively, *Liturgie*, pp. 295f.

49.   *PInst* 14, *PLeg* 10; see Veilleux, *loc. cit.* (n. 48) and pp. 121f.

50.   There was no formal night prayer. Reference to such an occasion is restricted to the *Paralipomena*, which do not reflect Pachomian practice: see Veilleux, *Liturgie*, p. 24 n. 29, and pp. 302–5. Pachomius himself at times kept vigil, G¹ 22; G¹ 60f, Bo 59; G¹ 88, Bo 73. But these seem always to have been exceptional events.

· V ·

LIVING UNDER RULE

Having disclosed the surprisingly loose and simple structure of the monastic day in Pachomius's time, and, more important, the scope it allowed to intimacy and reflection, we are in a better position to understand what a life governed by rule might have felt like in those early days. Governed by rule it undoubtedly was, but we must remain cautious in judging what the phrase might mean. We have given in the previous chapter sympathetic attention to the role played by scripture in the structuring of the daily program and the guidance of spiritual development more generally, not to mention the constant meditation and discussion centered on the sacred text. Yet that may not be enough to dispel entirely the suspicion that there was in those communities a degree of regimentation scarcely palatable to a modern mind. A picture of Pachomian discipline can still be assembled that emphasizes ruthless conformity. Take the spectacular impression made upon Palladius by a Pachomian meal, during which, amid the crowd, each monk was isolated by silent attentiveness to his own plate.[1] The *Praecepta* corroborate the anecdote, insisting that at work or prayer each monk should keep his eyes lowered, and attend only to his own pursuit.[2] The loneliness that comes from being indistinguishable from one's fellows could hardly be more vividly described or imposed. Other dictates appear to reinforce that mood. Each monk's cell was to be so constructed that it could not be closed to others. He was alone, yet never alone.[3] We have noted already the walking in order of rank in silence,[4] the silence while working,[5] and

1. *HL* 32.6. See Chapter IV n. 42.   2.   *P* 7.
3.   *P* 107. Jerome's translation suggests that exceptions might be made for the aged and the ill.
4.   *P* 13, 20, 131; *PLeg* 3. Veilleux, *Koinonia*, 2:189, thinks *P* 65 is modified by the Greek *Excerpta*, where "order" is not emphasized. On silence, see *P* 34.
5.   *P* 60.

the allotment of a special seat at prayer, and possibly at meals, retained for life.[6] The greatest leveler of all was that the monks were dressed identically, and recommended to carry themselves with a "modesty and meekness" that was itself dictated by rule.[7]

But we must continue to attempt a more sensitive search for the deeper convictions reflected in the sources, convictions that mitigate the apparent ferocity of uniform legislation and suggest that conformity itself was not a dominant preoccupation. Even the passage about walking in rank occurs in a wider context. "Let there be peace and concord among them"—that first; "and let them willingly submit to the superiors." (We shall build on that "willingly" [libenter] as these chapters proceed.) Then comes the sentence about walking "according to their rank"; followed by the phrase "and competing with one another in humility." So brotherhood, mutual deference, and interior assent were all to be preserved amid the visible order.[8]

The "peace and concord" were the greatest values. Quite apart from a deep suspicion of office and dignity, which we shall examine later, Pachomius was intent, in his regularity, upon breaking down disruptive distinctions between man and man, such as may have existed before they entered his community, or may have arisen from varieties of age and talent. There is a revealing story in the Vita Prima (although it refers to Theodore, not Pachomius), in which a thief remains undiscovered and another is wrongly accused of his crime. The culprit, who eventually comes forward, was ὡς παρὰ ἀνθρώποις πιστός: the sort that people might normally trust. The monk first suspected of the crime was, on the other hand, χυδαῖος: "a little vulgar," which was why he had been suspected in the first place. The violent prejudice of his fellow monks was bad enough—they were all ready to expel him without further discussion—but in every version of the story, not even Theodore was willing to expose the true sinner, who confessed to him only secretly.[9] Attitudes that could prompt such hasty suspicion may have been hard to exclude completely, but it was worthwhile attempting to counter them. We know from other references that there would have been plenty of opportunity for both failure and cure. A monastery was likely to contain rather a

6. P 1, 49. The porter showed each postulant where to sit.
7. P 2, 81.
8. PLeg 3.
9. G¹ 92. Bo 75 and Am, pp. 455f are a little less "class conscious." Veilleux, Liturgie, pp. 72f, shows how these texts are interrelated and suggests that Am brings us closest to the original. It is interesting that there the guilty party, without admitting (at that stage) his guilt, attempts to divert community anger away from the one wrongly accused.

mixed bag of members with "diverse dispositions," including "neophytes who do not yet know what a monk is, and boys who cannot tell
their right hand from their left." [10] Such youngsters at least, "given to
games and idleness," the *praepositus* had thirty days to lick into shape
before presenting them for the approval of his superior. [11]

Even among the virtuous, variety in ascetic practice could be considered a danger. A passage in the Arabic *Life* reveals the reasoning behind
such a notion. A young monk had been praying and fasting beyond the
norm. The point made at once is that he did so to gain attention and
renown, not to please God. Pachomius is ready from the first to call his
practice good. What he deplores is the vanity that has seized him. "Obey
me," he says—the reason being that the sickened soul of the monk
needed special treatment. His command is, abide by the rule in prayer
(though you may continue to pray in your cell) and attend the common
meals (though you may eat less than you might). So the rule is at once
oriented toward the individual's need, and the command to obey is an
act of personal spiritual healing. There is even the suggestion that, were
it not for the vanity, asceticism beyond that envisaged by rule would
be entirely acceptable. However, the monk disobeys. That too must be
clearly interpreted. Pachomius is not angry, shocked, or affronted; he is
sad, because he knows what evil will follow. He repeats his warnings
"many times." At that stage deadlock ensues, because the monk simply
does not *believe* him. Only trust of that kind would have made submission intelligent and fruitful. Here we have an early tradition only partly
reflected in our Greek and Bohairic texts. The Greek obscures the careful
pedagogy and exalts obedience in a quite different way. "Brother," says
Pachomius, and these are his opening words, "the Lord says, I have
come down from heaven, not to do my own will, but to do the will of the
one who sent me. Therefore listen also to him who says this through
me." The Bohairic *Life* omits those sentences, but it is equally brief in its
treatment of the incident. Only at the end does it recall the emphasis of
the Arabic version (in words the Arabic does not reproduce): "The Lord
healed him; he opened the eyes of his heart so that he could understand
how he must behave, not as a fool but as one wise." [12]

10.   G^1 28; the diversity is implied in Bo 26, G^1 40, and to some extent Bo 40.
11.   *PLud* 13. Ruppert, pp. 339f, discusses this desire to break down in-
equalities.
12.   Compare with this the phrase in G^1 42, "Have you not come to seek
from me the will of God?"; this is also omitted by Bo (42). For the story discussed
here, see Am, pp. 420f, G^1 69, and Bo 64. Ruppert, pp. 392f, supports the supe-
riority of Am. Bo 102 has an interesting story, which makes similar points and
casts light also on the matter of expulsion discussed below. This is a longer ver-

So it was attention to the spiritual growth of the individual that inspired the *Rules* in the first place, and it was their fruitful application at an individual level that gave them meaning and value. A balance between conformity and excess was always sought for, but the fervor of those advanced in the spiritual life, when freed from vanity, was never discouraged. The *Rules*, therefore, provided a framework within which each monk could thrive. They were rooted in something more general than the piecemeal demands of the various *Praecepta*. Pachomius's desire to gain humanity, soul by soul, for God, his reference to scripture, the impact of his personal example: those are the forces, already noted in Chapter III, that explain the shape and language of the regular life.[13] And persistent in the ordered community was that "charismatic" presence of the founder, who interacted as much as possible with each of his followers. "If you cannot get along alone, join another who is living according to the Gospel of Christ, and you will make progress with him. Either listen, or submit to one who listens."[14] The choice was there. Pachomius meanwhile catered for both weak and strong, "approaching each on his own, and putting his soul to work according to his capacity."[15] Theodore would do the same: "speak with each of them privately, discussing their thoughts and their actions by means of the spirit of God that was in him."[16]

None of that should surprise us. Profound pedagogical skill had been manifest from the earliest stages of Pachomius's cenobitic endeavor. His first disciples had refused to obey him. "They treated him with contempt . . . they would contradict him openly and insult him." What did this mean? "The lack of integrity of their hearts toward God . . . the unworthiness of their soul"; they were endowed only with "a carnal mind, for not everyone chooses the fear of God." The emphasis, in other words, is on their inner state. And how does Pachomius react? "He admonished them often," as in the Arabic anecdote above. "He did not punish them, however, but on the contrary, he bore with them with great patience saying, 'They will see my humility and affliction and they will return to God reforming themselves and fearing him.'" Yes, he also drew up rules for

---

sion of G[1] 100/Bo 92; a parallel occurs in Am, pp. 495f. Neither Veilleux nor Ruppert discusses the interrelation, but Ruppert does speculate elsewhere, pp. 366f, that "obedience texts" could become more explicit with time, comparing, e.g., Bo 104 with S[3a] 260, Bo 206 with S[3b] 298, and G[1] 126 with S[3b] 306.

13.   See Ruppert, pp. 122, 271.

14.   *CMR* 17: see Chapter II n. 1. Ruppert, p. 378, defends this sentiment as characteristic of Pachomius himself.

15.   S[3], trans. Lefort, *Vies*, pp. 69f. See Ruppert, pp. 167f.

16.   Bo 195; G[1] 132 makes the same point. See Deseille, *Esprit*, pp. xliiif.

them, concerning common prayer and other matters less clearly speci-fied; but he did so κατὰ ἀνάγκην, according to their need or the de-mands of the moment. The account suggests not belligerence or re-venge, but a moderate, *ad hoc* attempt to lead them forward gently on the basis of what were, for the time being, only modest abilities and in-sights. His followers then realized that they were not going to get their way, and "they withdrew in fear"—not the fear of a tyrannical ruler, but the very different fear that sprang from guilt and humiliation.[17]

That distinction between two kinds of fear was obviously considered important. A fear that bears fruit, such as Pachomius hoped for in his first disciples, ὁ φόβος τοῦ θεοῦ, is commended in several passages. Titoue at Phbow prays, "Make me perfect in your fear."[18] Pachomius preaches more generally at Tabennesi, "Just as fire cleanses all rust and burnishes the objects, so the fear of God consumes every evil in man and burnishes him into a vessel for special occasions, sanctified, well pleasing to God and ready for any good work."[19] With perhaps a slight change of note, Horsiesios reiterated the theme. "And if that man is well disposed toward God and has simply been overcome through negli-gence, the merciful God puts into him His fear and the memory of pun-ishments; then the man will be vigilant in the future, guarding himself with great caution until the day of his visitation."[20]

Later texts, based on the early *Lives*, not only repeat such anecdotes but even clarify the distinctions involved. In Dionysius, echoed by the *Vita Altera*, Pachomius prays that his monks will develop a healthy fear of God (φόβος in the Greek), "so that recognizing your divine power, they may serve you in truth."[21] Here too he gives them rules, "privately, each for himself," and the text explains why: "so that they might at least like slaves fulfill commands and gradually by force of habit come like sons to labor for love." The *Vita Altera* presents the contrast in slightly different terms, trusting that the monks will come to enjoy παρρησία, a

17. S¹ III (11f) brings us closest to the event; G¹ 38 is pale but useful. S³ shows Pachomius chasing the rebellious monks from his community; Veilleux, in *Koinonia*, vol. 1, includes that passage in his version of S¹ as Fragment IV. Bo 24 tells us where they originally came from; there and in S³ reference is made to a local bishop. These are matters to be discussed in Chapter VIII. In G¹ 24 Pacho-mius is ready to serve his new disciples, preparing meals, greeting guests, and caring for the garden so that they can concentrate on reflection upon scripture.

18. G¹ 84. The phrase is not reproduced in Bo.

19. G¹ 96. Again, there is no exact equivalent in Bo.

20. G¹ 118; not quite the same in Bo 209. It is interesting to compare this teaching on "fear" with that of other desert fathers, which is not dissimilar: see *Apophthegmata patrum*, James 3; John the Dwarf 10.

21. Dion. 32.

word also denoting intimacy but suggesting freedom more than affection.[22] In the second stage of the story, the recalcitrant monks were possessed by a different spirit of fear, the πνεῦμα δειλίας, much more abject than the φόβος earlier commended (as in the *Vita Prima*). Dionysius explains even more explicitly: "they were led astray by a spirit of timidity that was not pure." Their departure left the community, on the other hand, "in the state of integrity proper to it."[23]

We can detect already the complex theories, allusions, and desires that lay behind apparently simple and uncompromising regulations. Some of the issues raised we shall have to pursue in later chapters: the problems that arose, for example, from the wide qualitative range of recruits to the monastic life; the theology of obedience that lay behind apparently impersonal legislation; above all, the tact of Pachomius the legislator, his recognition that a monk had to grow in freedom, that keeping rules was not an end in itself but an aid to that growth.

It is interesting to observe, for the moment, with what surprising accuracy even Palladius could identify and interpret those underlying considerations. On the one hand he allows his famous angel, handing the *Rules* to Pachomius, to insist that the prescriptions should conform to the strength of those called upon to obey them (a point repeated by Dionysius): "I arranged it this way so that even the little ones [τοὺς μικρούς] might achieve the fulfillment of the rule without grief."[24] In this he agrees with the texts already quoted. On the other hand he asserts, presuming it to be a Pachomian principle, "as for the perfect [τέλειοι], they have no need of legislation; for they have dedicated all their life to the contemplation of God by themselves in their cells."[25]

That judgment finds an echo in the *Vita Prima*. Having described the setting down of rules for the new monastery at Phbow, the text con-

22. G² 34. See the use of the word in *HL* 32.7: "a life of complete liberty." (Veilleux uses the word "confidence.")

23. Dion. 32. G² 34, with reference to this "integrity," ends with the biblical allusion to the remnant of Israel, καθαρὰ λοιπόν. Dion., along with G¹ 38, recalls a different text: "the rest grew as wheat does when the darnel is rooted up." Veilleux, *Koinonia*, 1:267, in his note on Bo 6, shows that Bo is fond of this text also, but it does not occur in Bo 24. Πνεῦμα δειλίας recalls 2 Tim. 1.7, although the contrast there is not with some other kind of fear, but with "power and love and self-control." The use of παρρησία alludes more to passages like 2 Cor. 3.12f, Eph. 3.12, Heb. 4.16 and 10.19, 1 Jn. 2.28, 3.21, and 4.17. The first distinction made, that between slaves and sons, is based on Rom. 8.12; but παρρησία is not mentioned there, and indeed the (slightly different) πνεῦμα δουλείας is rejected by Paul precisely because it leads to φόβος! How subtle these biographers were in their concatenation of biblical references.

24. *HL* 32.7; Dion. 22.

25. *HL* 32.7. For the relation between this and the text that follows, see my *Ascetics*, p. 71.

tinues, "Order is a good thing, although the perfect man [τέλειος] is irreproachable even amidst disorder."[26] The sentence is obscure, even in its context. It could mean that most monks will content themselves with obedience to rules, while a few more advanced will find no need for them. That is the impression created by Palladius. But the intention in the *Life* appears to be that the value placed upon "order" (τάξις) should be subject to some limiting qualification: good though it may be, those who are perfect will rise above it. What exactly is it that the perfect will rise above? Can we take "order" simply to mean the minute controls envisaged in the *Praecepta*? Not at all: what Pachomius puts "in writing" for Phbow is simply a "memorial"—"no one should hurt his neighbor, but each should keep to his rule of conduct." It is that reminder that the perfect learn to do without. There is no suggestion, therefore, that only a few will do so while the bulk of the community falls back upon detailed rules: none such yet existed. Only in the later sources do we gain that impression, since it was for those not yet perfect that the rules, in their eventual detail, were intended.

What we find implied, therefore, is not two levels of achievement within the community—almost, one might say, two permanent classes of ascetic—but a sense of growth, of relatively easy movement from one level of achievement to another, experienced by the majority. And the gentleness we have spoken about, the personal consideration in the application of rules, was among the stimuli that prompted that growth. Apart from concern for the sick, which we shall touch upon later,[27] much is revealed by passing references: to the patience, for example, with which Pachomius handled the bad-tempered, warning them six times before taking disciplinary action;[28] to the lenience shown toward those who were late, not only in the evening, after work, but even for morning prayer, unable to shake off their sleep.[29] Ignorance, as well as weakness, was always accepted as an excuse for failure: "anyone who sins through ignorance shall be easily forgiven."[30]

For it was the spiritual, interior welfare of his monks that preoc-

26. G[1] 54. Again, for "irreproachable" (ἀπρόσκοπος), I would prefer "will have no cause to stumble": see Chapter IV n. 3, on G[1] 25, where the same word is used. There is no exact equivalent in Bo. Festugière was unwise to regard the differences between the two versions as merely "banalités," *Première Vie grecque*, p. 32.

27. Ruppert, pp. 344f, sees this concern as another important example of the readiness to adapt.

28. *Plud* 2. Ruppert, pp. 258f, comments adversely on the Old Testament quality of this concern with numbers, but it is the postponement, rather than the punishment itself, that is thereby ritualized.

29. *P* 9 and 10.

30. *Plud* 16.

cupied Pachomius, not their exterior conformity. "He was full of mercy for the old men or the sick or for the younger ones, and he cared for their souls in every thing." [31] He was, as another passage puts it, "patient and loved the souls, especially the ones for whom he had been toiling for a long time"; the anecdote proceeds to demonstrate how much he was prepared to fast and pray, so that "each one of them received the understanding to be healed from his error." [32] It was not just a matter of temperament: the underlying theory is well defended in more general terms by a passage in the Bohairic *Life*. It ascribes important status to "the brothers who are the lowliest in the *Koinonia*, who do not give themselves up to great practices and to an excessive ascesis, but walk simply in the purity of their bodies and according to the established rules with obedience and obligingness." The statement comes at the climax of a long comparison between cenobites and hermits: self-effacing members of the community were "far superior to those who live as anchorites." [33]

Of course, it was possible for a monk to underestimate what he might achieve, failing to "carry the cross according to his capacity." [34] But variety of achievement was a fact of life: "there is not just one measure of piety, but many." [35] Between those two statements, Pachomius unfolds a crucial parable. The fruits of the Spirit fill, as it were, a series of cells within a monk. Each must be carefully guarded. To lose possession of any one, even deep within, is to risk the intrusion of the enemy and increasing weakness. But—and here we have an image peculiar to the *Vita Prima*—"if on the other hand he pulls himself together again [ἑαυτὸν συνσφίγξῃ], he will not only gain possession of the one fruit from which he was estranged, but will also make great progress." [36] The crucial aim, therefore, was self-knowledge and, even more important, self-possession: the willingness to admit one's faults, and the ability to identify and preserve one's strengths. On this basis one progressed from a healthy fear to the freedom of God's adopted sons. The purpose of the *synaxis*, as described in the *Rules*, could be taken as the purpose of the

31.   G¹ 28. Ἀσθενεῖς τῷ σώματι may just mean weak, unequal to physical rigor.

32.   G¹ 100; Bo 92 is similar: see n. 12.

33.   Bo 105, not in G¹. See the comments of Ruppert, p. 97 and, more generally, p. 167.

34.   G¹ 74, not in Bo. Note how Pachomius sensed here an individual shortcoming.

35.   G¹ 75.

36.   Ibid., and see Bo 67, where however "piety" (θεοσέβεια) becomes "service," and where God is not so much within as simply with. In G¹ it is almost as if the monastery itself has become the model of the soul.

whole of the common life: here was a rule that "God has given us in the light of the scriptures for the liberation of ignorant souls, so that they might glorify God in the light of the living."[37]

Two attitudes, then, in Pachomius's regime went hand in hand: a sympathetic attentiveness to the needs of the individual, and a firm belief in the possibility of growth and in the importance of an intelligent freedom that allows growth its scope. We must keep both in mind, not only when we examine what the *Rules* prescribed, but also when we assess the sanctions imposed for failure. In that case, too, we are dealing with an attempt, not to achieve rigid conformity, but to establish a school of self-knowledge and self-improvement.

Prior to punishment, even as formulated in the *Rules*, warnings were issued, the institutional equivalent of the personal pedagogy we have described, and in themselves a sign that formation and sympathy remained paramount preoccupations. We have already noted the six warnings in the case of persistent ill-temper, and other examples can be found. There was a place for preliminary counsel, even in the face of what was ominously described as the "pessima consuetudo," which we shall discuss again in a moment.[38]

When counsel proved fruitless or, in minor matters, unnecessary, the normal form of punishment (*increpatio solita*)[39] seems to have been a strong verbal rebuke. This the waverer received in a posture of sorrow and humiliation, standing with belt unfastened, his neck bent, his hands hanging loosely at his sides.[40] For certain offenses, serious enough to be specified in detail, more forceful punishments were imposed. Persistent false witness (which shows that monks might often have brought reports on one another to their superiors) could result in a week's separation from the community, presumably in one's cell, with only bread and water for refreshment.[41] To be late for a meal might result in having, for that one meal, no food at all.[42] Anger was obviously regarded as even more serious, since the ill-tempered monk who refused to change his ways could find himself demoted from his normal position in the strict monastic hierarchy; but repentance brought restoration.[43]

Only once is there reference in the *Rules* to corporal punishment: in connection with the "pessima consuetudo" mentioned above. This might have been homosexuality, or simply the fomentation of discord or rebellion: the text refers to a monk who has "the wicked habit of soliciting his

---

37. *PInst*, introduction, after Bacht, "Verkanntes Fragment," p. 9. Compare Horsiesios, *Liber* 19: "sed et vos omnes, fratres, qui subiecti estis per ordinem liberae servituti."

38. *PIud* 1, 2, 4. See n. 28.   39. *PLeg* 2.   40. *P* 8, 135.
41. *PIud* 1.   42. *P* 32.   43. *PIud* 2.

brothers by words and of perverting the souls of the simple." Even he, as we have said, received the benefit of three warnings, but then he was whipped outside the gate of the monastery and kept there on a diet of bread and water until cleansed of his impurity.[44]

Here we come very close to a sentence of expulsion. The evidence for such a drastic punishment, however, is confused. We have noted already, in the story of the "vulgar" brother wrongly accused, that expulsion could be considered. In that instance, however, Theodore was arbiter,[45] and we know from a Bohairic passage that he was not averse to the practice.[46] As for Pachomius, he expelled, as we noted also, some of his earliest disciples. Their "carnal mind" is no more informative a description of their offense than "pessima consuetudo," but the circumstances, at that early stage, were exceptional in other ways.[47] The case of Silvanos, discussed briefly in Chapter III, may help us more. He was at least threatened with expulsion, and the Arabic version makes it almost certain that Silvanos's shortcomings were of a sexual, and probably a homosexual, nature.[48] That aspect of the matter is consistently obscured in the *Vita Prima*. Titoue, for example, praying to be made perfect in the fear of God, is supposed by the Greek author to be tempted to greed;[49] but Sahidic and Arabic versions ascribe to him a weakness for pretty boys.[50] An old man accused of stealing (as also in the Bohairic) is, we might note, forgiven: "he confessed his fault and Pachomius corrected him according to his spiritual discernment, quoting the Scripture, 'We all err in many things; but let us pray to the merciful God, and he will heal us.'"[51] Yet Sahidic and Arabic versions are explicit in making the old man's failing sexual. They add that Pachomius would recommend both expulsion and severe beating in such a case.[52] The general conjunction here of Greek, Sahidic, and Arabic texts makes it very unlikely that we are dealing, in the sexual allusions, with some later development; it is much more credible that the *Vita Prima*, in such instances, modified the tone of its anecdotes. A point to note, however, is that the penitent in this last passage was not a member of Pachomius's community, but sent for his judgment by a bishop.

44.   *Plud* 4.   45.   G[1] 92, Bo 75.   46.   Bo 195.

47.   G[1] 38, and other texts described in n. 17.

48.   See Chapter III n. 64. The *Paral.* passage is 2 (2). Ruppert, pp. 178f, stresses the link between expulsion and sexual failings.

49.   G[1] 84, not in Bo. Note this conjunction with fear in such cases: the "carnal mind" of the early malcontents betokened an absence of spiritual fear, G[1] 38, and Silvanos lamented at length his loss of that fear, Am, p. 520 especially.

50.   S[10], trans. Lefort, *Vies*, p. 35; Am, pp. 435f. For this and the following passage, see Veilleux, *Liturgie*, p. 89.

51.   G[1] 76, echoed in Bo 68, which stresses the "light penance" imposed.

52.   S[10], trans. Lefort, *Vies*, pp. 33f; Am, pp. 427f.

Probably the most we can conclude is that expulsion was a rare sanction, and closely associated with concern for sexual discipline in the community. To suppose more widespread application would be to fly in the face of much else in the sources that emphasizes the pedagogic norm—namely, that *increpatio* of every sort was designed to guide and improve more than to humiliate. Of the angry monk demoted to the bottom of the ladder, the *Praecepta atque Iudicia* continue, "and he shall be given instruction, that he may be cleansed from this agitation of mind."[53] The principle is excellently illustrated in a widely reproduced anecdote.[54] A monk from a monastery not governed by Pachomius had demanded promotion; his superior had resisted, judging him unworthy. Pachomius was to arbitrate; he advised, in the face of intransigence and insults, that the man should get his way.

> When that brother had got what he wanted, he returned immediately to the great Pachomius, greatly sobered.[55] He embraced him and confessed, "O Man of God, you are much greater than we had heard. We have seen how you have conquered evil with good by sparing a foolish sinner like me. If you had not been truly patient and had said something against me, I would have rejected the monastic life and become estranged from God. Blessed are you, for thanks to you I live."

Pachomius's comment to the other superior explains that conduct: "If we do good to a bad man he comes thereby to have a perception of the good. This is God's love, to take pains for each other." Simply to reject the sinner, therefore, was to repudiate that responsibility: only within the *Koinonia* could the requisite healing, enlightenment, and growth take place.

Possibly the most brilliant illustration of that belief comes in an isolated fragment from some forgotten biography or ascetic florilegium.[56] Following a dispute, Pachomius expels one of the miscreants. An older member of the community promptly asserts, "I am a sinner, brothers, and I leave with him"; at which the whole community follows suit! Pachomius is forced to apologize; he then reflects upon passages from scripture that exhort to forgiveness, and upon the fact that many have come to the monastic life precisely to repent. Expulsion will rob them of that very opportunity; he acknowledges, therefore, that it can no longer

53. *Plud* 2, emphasized by Ruppert, pp. 378f.
54. Ruppert, pp. 171f, offers a very full commentary. The S² fragment probably represents the earliest version, trans. Lefort, *Vies*, p. 13, with references. I concentrate here on G¹ 42/Bo 42.
55. I find this a weak rendering of ἀνέκαμψεν εὐθέως μετὰ νήψεως σφόδρα, which includes also something immediate and perceptive, "a sudden awakening."
56. Inserted in a MS of the *Lausiac History*, it is now known as Draguet, Fragment 1: see Chapter II n. 41.

be taken as a logical course. Henceforward the integrity of a monastery will be measured by effort and growth and by renewed endeavor after weakness and failure, not by the achievement of some exclusive purity.

If there was a change in the period between that reflected in the *Lives* and that reflected in the *Rules*, it may be represented by the public nature of penance in the second case. Pachomius would on occasion issue rebukes in company, but he often gave his guidance in some place apart; later superiors would naturally do the same. But the *increpatio* in the *Rules* seems most commonly to have taken place in front of others, chiefly at the *synaxis* and during meals. Clothing left to spoil in the sun, other monks' property absconded with, laughter and conversation at prayer, and even lateness: all led to this *increpatio* before the whole community.[57] It could also take place in the house, presumably at the hands of the *praepositus*, during the "six prayers" of an evening: for lateness, again, for breakages, or for going to sleep during the *disputatio*.[58] The second venue has a particular significance, because although the gravity of the offenses may have been less, the atmosphere of the house would have been more familiar and intimate, exposing the wrongdoer to the correction of those who knew him best.[59]

What we sense here is that monks were encouraged to feel a responsibility for one another's behavior, a responsibility not surrendered entirely to superiors. Returning a third time to that angry monk, we note that, duly punished, he had to find three witnesses who would support him publicly in his promise of improved behavior. His repentance had to be social and convincing.[60] Such was the attitude and custom Horsiesios had in mind when he wrote in his *Liber*,

> We learn from all this that we must stand before the tribunal of Christ and be judged not only for each deed but also for each thought. And, after we have rendered an account of our own life, we shall likewise render an account for those who were entrusted to us. And not only is this to be understood of the housemasters [*praepositi*] but also of the superiors of the monasteries and of each of the brothers belonging to the rank and file, because all must carry each other's burdens and so fulfill the law of Christ.[61]

Such allusions may surface rarely in the legislative sources, and yet color still both the daily experience of the monastic life and later literary

57. *P* 8, 9, 10; *PInst* 6 (see *P* 70) and 8 (with the peculiar injunction that the thief should carry on his shoulders whatever he had stolen!).

58. *P* 21, 121 (which Veilleux takes as referring to the evening on the basis of the Coptic fragment: *Liturgie*, p. 122 n. 32, and *Koinonia*, 2:191) and 125.

59. For confusions as to who was responsible for punishment, see Ruppert, p. 293.

60. *PIud* 2.   61. Horsiesios, *Liber* 11.

interpretations of its nature and purpose. We have discovered enough already to suggest that the very function of the *Rules* could have been to encourage the development of a community in which mutual support would be made possible.[62] At the very least an avoidance of tension appears the aim in some passages. Pachomius wrote rules for the women's monastery at Tabennesi, "that they might govern themselves by keeping them";[63] when he founded Phbow, "he enjoined them in writing, as a form of memorial, that no one should hurt his neighbor, but each should keep to his rule of conduct."[64] The passage most crucial to our understanding of the *Rules*, however, occurs in the Bohairic *Life*.[65] Pachomius has reprehended a monk who may have thoughtlessly tempted his brethren to greed, and in a subsequent catechesis he remarks,

> He who makes progress in the *Koinonia* with purity, obedience, humility, and submissiveness, and puts no stumbling-block or scandal before anyone by his words or by his acts, that one will grow rich forever in imperishable and enduring riches. But should he be negligent, and should a soul be scandalized by him and perish from it, woe to that man; not only has he lost his soul and the troubles he took on himself, but he also will have to render an account to God for that soul he scandalized.

Turning then to the anchorite, Pachomius asserts by contrast,

> He does not bear the responsibility of other ascetics, but neither does he see those who practise exercises—a thing which would incite him to imitate their actions and the excellent practices they perform in order to do the same himself. Well, such a man will not rank high in the kingdom of heaven.

What gave the cenobitic life its excellence, therefore, were the opportunities it offered a monk to encourage those with whom he lived— although the privilege had its dangers, for he could just as easily find himself leading them astray!

We can admit, therefore, that there was in the Pachomian communities a degree of regimentation, and we recognize there the readiness to

62. See Ruppert, pp. 94f, 400.
63. G³ 42; Bo 27 is slightly different. The Greek vocabulary—ὅπως κατὰ κυβέρνησιν αὐτῶν στοιχήσωσι—is closely comparable to that of G¹ 112, μετὰ πολλοῦ μόχθου κυβερνῶσιν ἀλλήλους φόβῳ θεοῦ, discussed in Chapter III at n. 89, and to that of the passage discussed next, ἵνα μή τις βλάψῃ τὸν πλησίον, ἀλλ᾽ ἕκαστος τῷ ὅρῳ αὐτοῦ στοιχήσῃ, already mentioned above at n. 18.
64. G¹ 54, not reproduced in Bo.
65. Bo 105, supported, perhaps with greater simplicity, by Am, pp. 506f. See the extensive comment by Ruppert, pp. 93f. Compare the anxieties of Theodore, should his visiting mother gain her will, G¹ 37: "for instead of becoming enough of a man to reform others, I will set up a stumbling block in the way of so many," not reproduced in Bo 37.

punish and compel. What we value more, and what they valued more themselves, is the admission of human weakness and individual need, and the sense that growth was necessary and possible. Those were the convictions that governed community life above all else; they were based on much more than any genius in Pachomius for meticulous regulation. Hence, many of the *Rules* are of a general nature and point beyond themselves. They depend clearly on many activities and relationships about which, at the same time, they make no attempt to legislate in detail. For example: "those who spurn the precepts of the superiors and the rules of the monastery, which have been established by God's precept, and who make light of the counsels of the elders, shall be punished according to the established order until they amend."[66] Several factors are made to govern behavior here. Formal rules are only one of them, and are to be conjoined with "God's precept," with the advice of *maiores* and *seniores*, and with what is more generally described as the *ordo constitutus*. Yet the precept itself tells us little about the nature of such influences and how they were brought to bear upon members of the community. Within the houses, too, there were general principles at work, which reached beyond the specific prescriptions of the *Rules* themselves. Again, for example, "no one shall receive anything from another without the housemaster's permission," and "no one in the house shall do anything against the directive of the housemaster."[67] Such commands leave an enormous amount unsaid and offer great scope for individual initiative and temperament. And we must remember another general source of inspiration that lay beyond particularities: that of scripture. Its importance has been building up throughout this chapter, as in the one previous, and will continue to do so. The point was made at the beginning of Pachomius's career that both rules and traditions "he took from the holy scriptures."[68] It was a point repeated by Theodore after Pachomius's death: "You know how he used to gather us together daily and speak to us about the holy commandments so that we might observe each of the commandments in the holy Scriptures of Christ, and how he used first to put them into practice before giving them to us."[69] That point, too, is made in general terms by the *Rules*: monks are to avoid "whatever is contrary to the rule of the scriptures and the monastery's ordered routine"; in another passage, "those who minister well

66. *PIud* 8.
67. P 106; *PInst* 16. Veilleux defends the technical nature of the word here translated as "housemaster," *Koinonia*, 2:193; this is confirmed by Ruppert, p. 310, and see also 250f. The issue will recur in Chapter VI.
68. G¹ 25.
69. Bo 194; not in G¹.

are those who stand within the limits of the scriptures."[70] The morning *synaxis*, the practice of mental recitation, and the evening catechesis—all would carefully support that scriptural inspiration.

To live under rule, then, was to acknowledge that a variety of influences governed your life, or rather, provided for your weakness and fostered your spiritual growth: the scriptures, the elders of your community, your immediate superiors. It is vital to interpret aright the quality of submission implied by that acknowledgment. Even in the more forceful versions of incidents already discussed, we must allow full play to every aspect of the statements made. In the case of the monk who prayed and fasted to excess, the "Greek" Pachomius exclaims, "The Lord says, I have come down from heaven, not to do my own will, but to do the will of the one who sent me. Therefore listen also to him who says this through me." This could mean two things—closely related, of course: either the monk is to hear the voice of Christ, in which case he hears the advice of one who was himself obedient, or he obeys as Christ obeyed, hearing the Father, and so shares with Christ the closest relationship to the one who commands. Neither attitude implies a loss of dignity.[71] There is another passage in which Pachomius encourages obedience in similar terms. Concerning his rule of silence in the bakery, he remarks that some might think it merely "human . . . about a very small matter"; but the principle at stake was a great one. Scripture shows us, he says, in the fall of Jericho how the will of God might often be made clear through a human command. He presents himself as precisely an agent of that sort, with the similar task of communicating God's will; but let us note again the exact terms in which he makes the suggestion: "if that commandment were not profitable for their souls, we would not have given it."[72]

A similar story occurs in later *Lives* and in the *Paralipomena*. It may

70. The first quotation, *PInst* 10. M. M. van Molle doubted whether the reference to "rule" here and in *PInst* 17 was primitive. She is answered by Ruppert, p. 244, and, in more general terms, pp. 128f. The second quotation, from *PInst*, introduction, follows the text of Bacht, "Verkanntes Fragment," p. 9, which reads, "Qui bene ministrarunt, sunt illi qui steterunt in mensura Scripturarum." It avoids, in other words, Jerome's intruded word "regula." I have not translated with Veilleux; in particular, he does not explain why he omits the phrase "et monasterii disciplinam." It is surprising in the face of such general allusions that there is so little quotation from scripture in the *Rules*: see Ruppert, pp. 131f, 138f.

71. G[1] 69; but see n. 12.

72. G[1] 89, Bo 74. Comparable phrases in G[1] 42, already mentioned in n. 12, do not weaken the force of what follows, which *is* reproduced in Bo 42: "that by this means we may snatch his soul away from the enemy."

show how the heirs of Pachomius developed with some care those notions of obedience. The texts open with a note of tenderness. A young
monk complains to the visiting Pachomius about a shortage of food:
"Truly, Father, from the time you left to visit the brothers until now they
have not cooked either vegetables or porridge for us." "To this," we are
told, "the holy Old Man answered kindly, saying, 'Do not be afflicted,
my son, I will have these things cooked for you from now on.'"[73] Pachomius proceeds to the kitchen to investigate and finds that those on duty
had cut back on the cooking because "almost all the brothers practise
abstinence and do not eat cooked food." Such self-denial, in themselves
and in others, they thought it only right to encourage—not least on financial grounds! Moreover, in the time thus saved, they had worked
more productively, weaving mats. They presented Pachomius with a
double difficulty, therefore: one task commanded they had left undone,
and another they had taken upon themselves uninvited. In response to
the second, Pachomius gathers up the mats and burns them, "that you
may learn what it is to disregard the fathers' ordinances which were
given for the salvation of souls." It is striking that Pachomius does not
present the matter as an order of his own: again we have the notion of
profiting others—$\varepsilon\dot{\iota}\varsigma\ \sigma\omega\tau\eta\rho\dot{\iota}\alpha\nu\ \psi\nu\chi\hat{\omega}\nu$. He then turns to the first omis-
sion and points out that compulsion rules out merit. The eager cooks
have forced the brothers to abstain. Abstinence in the face of plenty
would have been much more desirable. "Do you not know that when a
man has the possibility of looking for something and he abstains from it
for God's sake, he will receive a great reward from God; but if he has not
such power over a thing and is forced by necessity to abstain from it because he does not have it, he will seek a reward for this in vain?" One
senses the exasperation in his voice at the *coup de grâce*: "For the sake of
eighty measures of oil you have cut off so great a harvest of virtues! May
the whole substance of the world be destroyed rather than one small virtue be cut off from the soul." It would have been hard to defend with
more subtlety, at one and the same time, a carefully contrived order and
the arena of individual freedom.

So it was the constant interaction between order and personal liberty
that characterized most the experience of Pachomian monasticism. Order, we know, could not mean simply the list of commands bequeathed
to us in Jerome's translation. The appeal was always to scripture as a
basis for the ascetic life. The additional point now borne in upon us concerns the circumstances of interaction between order and individual,

73. So *Paral.* 8 (15), which, with (16), is the text I follow for the most part
here. In G² 67 and Dion. 43 Pachomius says he will do the cooking himself! See
useful comments by Ruppert, pp. 153, 171f.

and the methods whereby it was sustained. Spiritual success, as it were, did not depend for Pachomius on the creation of some smooth-running, uniform community. That was not the meaning of the *Koinonia*. Success would occur within the individual, and there the force of scripture would meet with both needs and talents and lead to perfection. Hence derived Pachomius's own sense of freedom, which Horsiesios remembered. "He would often recall to them what Abba Pachomius had told him when he was head at Chenoboskion, 'Even if you have not received a great knowledge of God, tell them a parable, and God will make it work.'" Horsiesios remembered the point of the comment also: that the working of the scriptures within the heart counted for most. "Our father [Pachomius] strengthened us from the Scriptures through his perfect knowledge. But I think, in my poverty, that if a man does not guard his heart well, he forgets and neglects all that he has heard. And so the enemy finds a place in him and casts him down."[74]

So, in order to understand how life under rule was supported by that strength, that perfect knowledge, it is not enough to attend simply to the scriptural background in Pachomius's early instructions about dress, food, and sleep,[75] or to his subtle exegesis on the birth, death, and resurrection of Jesus.[76] It was the way he engaged with the scriptural text *within himself* that offered the most important model for his followers: "When he began to read or to write by heart the words of God, he did not do this in a loose way or as many do, but worked over each thing to assimilate it all with a humble mind in gentleness and in truth."[77] Palamon not only admired that skill, but saw it vividly in action. After hearing the voice at Tabennesi, Pachomius "in purity of heart discerned according to the Scriptures that the voice was holy" and "he returned to his father and told him about it."[78] In that conjunction of personal inspiration and respect for the authority of others, we are brought to the very foundations of those two great pillars, *meditatio* and *disputatio*, which, as we saw in Chapter IV, were so much a feature of the monastic day as Pachomius later defined it. Reflection upon scripture was to be the constant interior preoccupation of every member of the community and the most frequent topic of their conversation. It would be foolish to argue that the inception of the *Rules* depended upon some democratic consensus; but were it not for that persistent interior attitude, repro-

---

74. G¹ 118; but the *dictum* of Pachomius is not reproduced in Bo 209.
75. G¹ 25, Bo 23.
76. G¹ 56, not in Bo. See Veilleux, *Koinonia*, 1:414, for a characterization of Pachomius's habitual catechesis.
77. G¹ 9; Bo 15 is weaker.
78. G¹ 12; but not quite in Bo 17.

duced from individual to individual, no *Rules* more generally and formally proclaimed, however scriptural their style, could possibly have
gained adhesion. The *Rules* themselves insisted as much: "Everything
that is prescribed they must observe *coram Deo*—as if in the presence of
God." [79]

79.   *PLeg.* 8. Ruppert discusses inner obedience extensively, pp. 412f.

· VI ·

LEADERSHIP AND RESPONSIBILITY

We have yet one more level to penetrate if we are to understand justly the structure of monastic life under Pachomius. We observed in Chapter IV the visible level of that life, the carefully imposed activities that occupied a monk's day. In Chapter V we asked more precisely about the corresponding inner experience of the individual monk, the submission and docility which those external activities were most intended to prompt and support. We discovered not a series of regimented responses, but a program designed to expose weakness and to encourage growth in each member of the community, more under the influence of carefully meditated scripture than at the behest of autocratic superiors.[1] In the course of our inquiry, we have inevitably anticipated other topics: Pachomius's understanding of self-discipline and his broader conception of spiritual progress and human nature. Those will be studied further; but now, to complete our tripartite analysis of order, we need to know how the ascetic program was controlled. Who applied rules? Who identified needs? Who encouraged, who directed, who took blame or praise for order and achievement?

If Pachomius governed thousands, then he could not fulfill all those roles, certainly not in the life of every monk. Yet the writers of the *Lives* were interested only in the encounters that involved Pachomius himself. On very few occasions, most of them already noted, do we glimpse another leading figure advising or commanding. There were good reasons for that apparent limitation. We know already how mistaken it would be

1.   We cannot emphasize enough the judgment of Ruppert that "nowhere in the whole Pachomian corpus is obedience singled out as the highest or most characteristic Pachomian virtue," p. 373.

to depend on the *Rules* to describe the structure of authority in Pachomian communities. That awareness we share with the monks themselves. We should not underestimate, then, any more than they did, the
true value of the *Lives*, which were in a sense a legislative record also,
providing norms as well as narratives.[2] Nothing that Pachomius aimed
at, in terms of daily order or inner assent, could have rested on mere
legislation. Specific advice—on prayer, for example, or on the day-to-
day conduct of community life—was certainly necessary and was com-
mitted to writing at an early stage, but it was Pachomius himself who
was the "rule" in the fullest sense. The personal example of his service,
the fruit of his own experience, above all his insight into scripture, con-
veyed in frequent catechesis: those were the indispensable keys to his
enduring influence. It is leadership we are dealing with, more than legislation; and that was what the *Lives* portrayed. The formative quality of
his own character lay at the root of his own ascetic experiments and persisted in its effect throughout his lifetime, molding also the conduct of
successors and subordinates in every community of the federation.

Not that his monks, faced with that inspiring example, contented
themselves with mere admiration. They may have remembered him as
being, in Palladius's phrase, "a great lover of men and of his brothers."[3]
Early disciples had been attracted by a faith in the man that seemed
"healthy" (ὑγιαινούσης), capable of bringing complete restoration of
spirit to himself and to others.[4] That healing vocation obviously caught
on as a Pachomian characteristic. Those appointed to assist him in government were said to have as their chief function "to take care of the
brothers' souls";[5] an ability to cherish and console others was a hallmark
in Theodore, who "became a comforter to many who were grieved and a
corrector to his seniors."[6] But it was never considered enough to acknowl-

2.   I carry further the remarks of Ruppert, pp. 271f, linking biography and
rule.

3.   *HL* 32.1. That he "became" such might be the point (Palladius has ἐγέ-
νετο). Compare passages like G¹ 91, "Our Father Pachomius was perfect in everything, but fearful and always mournful," or Bo 77, "Straightway he laughed in
his face with great anger." But note the qualities described in Dion. 37, closely
parallel to G² 39: "He had received from the Lord the gift of being always the
same, never varying in any circumstance." The passage does not occur in either
G¹ or Bo. Compare the quality ascribed to Silvanos, ἀμετάβλητος.

4.   G¹ 26, also in Bo 24, but not quite in Am, p. 371. F. Nau presents an
analogous text (no. 217), ὡς καλὸς ἰατρὸς κατέπλασεν αὐτοῦ τὴν ψυχὴν ἐκ τῶν
θείων γραφῶν, *Revue d'Orient chrétien* 14 (1909): 357f. The anecdote recurs in the
Latin *Verba seniorum* 10.85, *PL* 73.928A–C.

5.   G¹ 28, as in Bo 26.

6.   G¹ 36. Bo 32 omits the second phrase, "corrector . . . ," but has "despite
his age." Note the comments of Ruppert, pp. 159f. A later passage states, "Abba

edge in Pachomius such a purely natural sympathy or desire to serve others. Disciples, readers of the *Lives*, were constantly encouraged to develop more formal interpretations of his skill. The monk returning from Tabennesi, destined to inspire Theodore, was supposedly sure that the justice of Pachomius would protect even himself in the sight of God. Theodore longed for the same assurance, praying that God would let him see the holy man, "that through him you may save my soul."[7] Pachomius more than once during moments of prayerful insight saw his monks blundering in darkness or amid many obstacles and dangers for want of clear teaching or firm leadership. We may with justice suspect that such anxieties were associated in his mind with what might happen after his death.[8] Jesus, too, he said himself, was a teacher and leader who cared for those in the darkness of error or obduracy. "Just as someone seeing a pit grabs the blind lest they fall into its deadly depth, so too the Lord revealed [the] evil conduct [of the Pharisees and the Scribes] to the believers, lest they become like them and die with them."[9] It was that kind of mercy that Theodore sought in his earliest years[10]—the mercy that, in Pachomius's eyes, was one of the qualities that distinguished his community from, say, the world of bishops, who were judges (under God) more than healers.[11]

We have, then, a series of texts that refer to Pachomius's natural sense of balance, his shrewdness, and his sympathy, but join that reference constantly to theological reflections on the saving role of Christ in the church. Something similar happens in the case of Pachomius's insight. He just knew, for example ("he realized in the spirit" [συνῆκεν τῷ πνεύματι]), that monks at Tabennesi were talking in the kitchen—not a

---

Theodore was very vigilant over souls, encouraging each one privately and tending them as a doctor [ὡς ἰατρὸς θεραπεύων]," G[1] 132; see also 106. On the key virtue of healing in a leader, compare the vocation recommended by Hermas, *The Shepherd, Similitudes* 1.8: "instead of lands, purchase afflicted souls [ψυχὰς θλιβομένας]." The significance of *The Shepherd* for an understanding of Pachomius's spirituality will be pursued further in Chapter VII.

7. G[1] 34. Bo 29 is not quite the same, but it does repeat the statement of Theodore's informant, "I am confident that the Lord will forgive some of my sins [Bo: "many"] because I have just now brought to mind a righteous man."

8. G[1] 71 and Bo 66, with repetitions in S[4] and S[10]. Compare G[1] 102, Bo 103. See also *CMR* 48 and 60, and the anxieties of Theodore, Bo 196. The issues will recur in Chapter IX.

9. G[1] 57, not in Bo. Note how the teaching was effected: "Let us also find strength, brothers, in the commandments that the Lord gave us through his conduct." The final twist corroborates so much said in Chapter V.

10. G[1] 33, Bo 31.

11. G[1] 27, not reproduced in Bo 25. Recall how Pachomius's sister sought mercy, G[3] 42.

long shot, to judge by some other references.[12] He just knew, on another occasion, that a monk was snoozing in his cell during community prayer: "His heart [καρδία] was suddenly so seized that he could no longer speak. Understanding in his spirit why this happened . . . [again, συνιεὶς τῷ πνεύματι]."[13] In an experienced superior, such facility need hardly have been miraculous, but the *Lives* theorize indefatigably. That skill—the ability to know above all who were the true monks, "which of them is walking aright and which has only the appearance of a monk"—flourished only when God wished it.[14] For that reason Pachomius could surprise even himself. He spoke accidentally one day in a way that aroused compunction in a monk who had stored up five figs for a secret feast—indeed, he went out of his way to say afterward, "I knew nothing and had not heard about it from anybody." Whatever the case, the blushing fruitlover blurted out his subterfuge. At which, "both [Pachomius] and the brothers marvelled. For it was not about him that he had spoken. Then he told them, 'You must realize that it is not when we want it that we see hidden things for the sake of salvation; it is when God's providence wishes.'"[15]

So all those instances of generosity, tenderness, and perception are recounted as part of a theology of leadership. Those responsible for preserving the biography of Pachomius knew well that a bald account of his skills and ambitions would not be enough to elicit loyalty and imitation in those who came after him. In this, we should note, they were not substituting institutional elements for a charismatic figure now dead. That may have happened—we shall return to the issue in Chapter IX—but in the instances mentioned here we observe more a shift of attention within each anecdote from a real to an ideal person, from the real to the ideal leader, from real to ideal disciples. Such a literary conceit, if we may call it that, was as necessary as the *Rules* to the maintenance of the Pachomian system after 346.

The question is, of course, whether Pachomius saw himself in the same light. We know that from an early stage he had to wrestle with a temptation to pride.[16] Some of the first demons in his ascetic experience

12. G[1] 89, not reproduced in Bo 74. See Chapter IV n. 33.

13. G[1] 74, not in Bo.

14. G[1] 112. The skill is referred to in Bo 107.

15. G[1] 97. Bo 72 makes Pachomius a little less human in that he does not admit it was an "accident"! G[1] 48 has much on clairvoyance.

16. It is hard to believe that the story in Bo 86 is strictly a historical narrative: Pachomius, during a catechesis, seats himself in the exact spot where, in a dream, he had seen Christ teaching! See also S[5], trans. Lefort, *Vies*, p. 86, and Am, pp. 469f. I was not sufficiently critical of this anecdote in my *Ascetics*, p. 30; the reference is faulty as printed, and the interpretation probably unjust.

taunted him with the phrase "Make way for the Man of God." [17] Yet he allowed himself to feel that sympathy and insight could give a man rights over others. Theodore, for example, once he had proved himself guided by God,[18] was said by Pachomius to possess the power that allowed him to give orders "as a father" (ὡς πατήρ). In so doing, he shared the authority of Pachomius himself: "Theodore and I fulfill the same service [τὴν αὐτὴν λειτουργίαν] for God." [19] Pachomius is also referred to as "father" throughout the *Lives*. It was a title that conjured up not simply rights and obedience, but a more emotional bond, a readier sense of mutual obligation: "should you, as sons, not bear with your father?" [20] Theodore, in the end, so Pachomius implied, took amiss the implications of that relationship, committing his great "fault" of thinking, "After him [Pachomius], I will be in charge." [21] "Just as a corpse," Pachomius said, "does not say to other corpses, 'I am your head,' so too I never considered that I am the father of the brothers. God himself alone is their father." [22] Entirely characteristic, therefore, was his first greeting to Theodore many years before: "Do not weep; I am a servant of your Father." "He meant," says the text with winning clarity, "God." [23]

Clearly there is a theology at work even in those statements. At the same time, we do seem to come closer to the "original" Pachomius in such passages that emphasize his patience and humility. The early pattern of his prayer and ministration was reinforced throughout his life. Subjects, meanwhile, came slowly to recognize their contrasting inadequacy.[24] No doubt the knowledge that Pachomius had been six days without food on someone's behalf, and forty nights without sleep, not to mention the sight of his body "extremely lean and feeble" as a result, would be enough to prompt in even the hardest heart a suspicion that

17.   They are said to have marched beside him, we might note, "as people do in escorting a commander"—so G[1] 18. The phrase in the text comes from Bo 21. There may be a trace of this incident in S[1] V (21); see also Am, p. 364. *Paral.* 8 (14) has a different phrase, but Dion. 17 and G[2] 17 follow what I take to be the earlier Greek tradition.

18.   G[1] 77, also Bo 69.

19.   G[1] 91. Bo 74 adds, "and he has power over everything, as father and as master." Bo 96–97 are also associated with this anecdote. Compare the observation of Poemen, after calling Agathon ἀββᾶ : ὅτι τὸ στόμα αὐτοῦ ἐποίησεν αὐτὸν καλεῖσθαι ἀββᾶν, *Apophthegmata patrum*, Poemen 61.

20.   G[1] 66; see Bo 62: it is a moving story, in which Theodore kindly "tricked" a dejected brother, and Pachomius apologized for his harshness. Compare the tenderness of Antony as described in *Life of Antony* 16.

21.   G[1] 106. The events will be discussed in Chapter IX.

22.   G[1] 108, not in Bo.

23.   G[1] 35; see Bo 30.

24.   G[1] 38. See Chapter V at n. 17.

there was room for improvement in someone's behavior. There are several examples of such a tactic.[25] Genuine humility, however, lay at the heart of the ruse. In a passage central for both Greek and Bohairic biographers, Pachomius gave apposite advice on the art of government to Theodore of Alexandria. Aspects already mentioned recur: Theodore should have particular regard for the sick, he should be the first to keep the rules, he should outstrip his subjects in the spiritual life, "since you hold the rank of father." Above all he should admonish the wrongdoer "privately with patience," letting him get away with a fault at first, "waiting for him to be touched by the Lord." He should learn, too, that an angry man is more influenced by patient silence than by harsh attempts to cure him.[26]

Recalling the story of the monk who sought responsibility beyond his deserts,[27] we are able now to appreciate another level of reflection in the anecdote. As he had advised Theodore, Pachomius let the man get away with it. He showed in so doing his own much-valued patience. He showed that superiors should demand in their subjects understanding and self-knowledge rather than submission. And now another point comes to the fore: the monk must acknowledge that he needs a master endowed with prudence and perception; he needs to unfold his inner thoughts to someone with γνῶσις, that special understanding given by God, "the therapy through discernment of spirits that the Lord has taught us."[28] So the patience and humility of the superior is still part of a theory of government. It not only achieves better results pedagogically, it also brings the subject into a healthier posture of his own, reinforcing a structure of command and response beneficial to both parties.

The "humble Pachomius," therefore, was not only part of a portrait in the *Lives* but also part of an argument. The biographies represent a clear attempt to make his interior experience a rule of life for thousands who never knew him. Nevertheless, those idealized interpretations could not eradicate wholly from the "humility image" a note of realism that may tell us something important about Pachomius as an individual. He could find prudence and perception sometimes elusive. There was in his "humility," in other words, the mark of a man to whom the art of

25.   E.g., G[1] 100. Here is another example of Pachomius leading subjects to understanding, as discussed in Chapter V: they "murmur" at first, in both G[1] and Bo 92, and "would not listen to the Man of God in faith." Bo is less explicit about Pachomius's appearance. In another version of the story, Bo 102, "impure thoughts" appear to be the issue; and G[1] may hint at this, with its apologetic phrase, "although they were chaste in body." For another instance of Pachomius's tears leading to repentance in others, see G[1] 55, Bo 59.

26.   G[1] 95, Bo 90.

27.   G[1] 42. See Chapter V n. 54.

28.   G[1] 96, not in Bo.

government sometimes proved difficult. He would issue commands that were contradictory or obscure. If, like Theodore, you obeyed him as you would God, you presumed that at such moments he had not lost touch with his original inspiration.[29] Most superiors had their unintelligible, even brutal, days; "but this we know, that men of God do nothing hurtful; and their severity as well as their goodness are measured by their knowledge of God."[30] In any case, there were always demons around intent on fostering such obscurities, setting monks at odds with those who governed them. Only patience and a "vigilant spirit" could defeat their ruse.[31] In such ways even self-doubt in a superior could encourage theology among those who later remembered his life. But the ambiguity is admitted in the man. Reading between the lines, we are able to acknowledge that while Pachomius was generous and shrewd—shrewd enough, especially, not to overreach himself in his dealings with the more recalcitrant—he could also at times estimate wrongly what was possible or expedient.

Those observations bring us to an important feature both of Pachomius's own approach to the problems of government and of the longer-term structure of his communities—namely, a carefully controlled system of delegation. It may have been, again, an aspect of his humility that he never pretended to be indispensable. Doubts could arise in his mind about the competence of probable successors, as we shall see, but they never entirely shook his early confidence that God would eventually raise up men with sufficient insight and generosity "to assist me," as he said, "in caring for the monastery."[32] It is true that he exercised at least a moral authority over other communities, even some outside his own federation. He certainly kept an eye on the foundations that sprang originally from Tabennesi. Phbow was given its own οἰκονόμος—meaning, in this case, its overall superior—and its house superiors, but Pachomius "used to [watch over] the two monasteries day and night as a servant of the Good Shepherd."[33] Šeneset and Thmoušons, already established centers of asceticism, received superiors in the same way,

29. G^1 50, not in Bo. In this instance, Theodore took comfort from an earlier and more accommodating prescription, which he was sure Pachomius would eventually recall.

30. G^1 103, as interpreted by Veilleux, Koinonia, vol. 1, and Festugière, Première Vie grecque; but variant readings—γνώσεως/γνώσει θεοῦ—make it uncertain whether the knowledge is theirs or God's. Bo 93 is slightly different: "solidly based on a perfect knowledge which is pleasing to our Lord Jesus." The long version in Paral. 3 (5–6) makes no such observation, nor do Dion. 39 and G^2 62f.

31. G^1 72, Bo 67.

32. G^1 25, echoed by Bo 23.

33. G^1 54. Veilleux's "visit" for ἐπεσκέπτετο seems not quite right, in conjunction with "day and night." See Bo 49.

"spiritually capable brothers"; but, once again, they were established there by Pachomius "to govern the brothers, as though he were present, until he should come."[34] In the early days there may have been sound reasons for retaining that direct supervision. That certainly seems to have been true in the case of the foundation at Panopolis, which was, unusually, fairly close to the city: even though the chosen superior, Samuel, was "cheerful in spirit and abstinent," Pachomius felt it necessary to stay with the new community, "until they were well established."[35]

But in spite of that sense of responsibility, Pachomius could hardly be described as a man who wanted a finger in every pie. Those whom he trusted with a share in his authority he trusted as collaborators. "Together," as he assured Theodore of Alexandria, "we shall try to find the exact answer to each one of the problems."[36] To the very moment of his death, he valued passionately his sense that he had no absolute power to command within the communities, indeed no office of any kind.[37] So he lived in a house like all his monks, subject to its *praepositus* and dutifully attending his catechesis.[38] A particularly striking example of combined self-effacement and self-confidence is provided in several versions by the *Lives*. Pachomius was sitting at Tabennesi, stripping flax for basket work, when a young monk, one of the duty house for the week, came by and said, " 'Not so, father. Do not turn the thread this way, for Abba Theodore has taught us another way of weaving.' He got up at once and said, 'Yes, teach me the way.'" A small thing, perhaps, and easy enough to moralize about, but almost certainly not apocryphal, and therefore central to any portrait of the man.[39]

Such humility implies chiefly what we have hinted at already in our analysis of the *Rules*: that Pachomius did not regard himself, and was not regarded by others, as the only source of authority in any community. To understand the matter fully we have to penetrate beyond any simple hierarchy of *patres* and *praepositi* governing in their turn either the monastery as a whole or the individual houses. The frequent use of terms like πατέρες or *maiores* involves often such vague definition that assuming always that they applied to the major superiors of the communities would be most unwise.[40] References can be very general, and al-

34. Ibid.

35. G¹ 81. It is here that Bo has "Many times he would come to visit them, for he was a keeper of flocks following Christ, the great Good Shepherd," 55.

36. G¹ 95, as in Bo 90.

37. S⁷, trans. Lefort, *Vies*, pp. 45f, and Am, pp. 597f.

38. G¹ 110; also S³, trans. Lefort, *Vies*, p. 57. Not in Bo, but see Am, p. 640.

39. G¹ 86. Bo 72 explains a little more why Theodore had suggested the change. See Am, p. 441, Dion. 47, and G² 79.

40. There has been much dispute over G¹ 122, and the phrase τὰς δια-

most always mention these functionaries in the plural—for example, "Let there be peace and concord among them, and let them willingly submit to the *maiores*,"[41] or the text already mentioned in Chapter V, that places the *praecepta maiorum* alongside the rules of the monastery and the advice of older monks as sources of authority under God.[42] *Praecepta* here could refer at most to *ad hoc* commands by the monastery superior, and certainly not to anything widely binding in the long term. At the other end of the scale come much less significant regulations, such as needing the permission of *maiores* to relieve oneself during the *collecta*.[43] In that case *maiores* were the men who, with the house *praepositi*, sang the psalms in the Sunday liturgy.[44] At times such leaders appear to rank above the *praepositus*. A house superior, absent for a night (presumably without permission), had to do penance before he could be readmitted, and even then was allowed back only "maioris imperio."[45] In another context, the *maiores* are clearly less important, taking the place of the *praepositus* when traveling with a group outside the monastery, teaching and admonishing as he would normally do himself.[46] In one early text, the impression is even given that the *maiores* might be dead, or at least absent: "these are the precepts of life handed down to us *a maioribus*."[47]

It is hard to judge how one might have qualified for inclusion in such a category. The *Lives* demonstrate how early and more favored disciples of Pachomius came to form an influential body within the federation,

τἀγὰς τῶν πατέρων. (There is no equivalent in Bo.) Veilleux, in *Koinonia*, vol. 1, is quite clear: "the rules of the Community which Abba Pachomius had established . . . as well as the decision of the fathers . . ." There is no doubt the Greek bears that meaning. Am, p. 661 is similar, though following G³. Festugière, *Première Vie grecque*, p. 50 n. 1, thought the phrase might mean decisions "*concernant* les pères;" and here he was influenced by Lefort's rendering of S³, "directives *aux* pères:" see *Vies*, pp. xlivf and 348–49. Veilleux, *Liturgie*, pp. 99f, is critical, and explains the confusion; but there he insists that πατέρες must mean "superiors." Only two of the relevant *Praecepta* have surviving Coptic equivalents: 112, with "absque iussione maioris," and 127, with "absque maioris imperio." The Coptic in each case makes no specific reference to persons at all, and the Greek *Excerpta* offer no assistance. It would be wise at this point to recall the discussion prompted in Chapter II, at nn. 26f, by the researches of M. M. van Molle.

41.   *PLeg* 3. Veilleux translates "superiors."
42.   *PIud* 8; Veilleux, "the precepts of the superiors." See Chapter V at n. 66. M. M. van Molle emphasizes the frequent plurals and the vagueness in *PIud*, "Vie commune," p. 197.
43.   *P* 11, no clarification in the *Excerpta*.
44.   *P* 16. Here Veilleux is quite happy with "elders of the monastery." The *Excerpta* again offer no help.
45.   *P* 137; Veilleux, "without the superior's order." The *Excerpta* are silent.
46.   *PLeg* 13; Veilleux again relapses to "elders."
47.   *P* 8; Veilleux, "by the elders." Nothing in the *Excerpta*.

even though they did not all become superiors of monasteries. We hear
first of Pšentaesi, Sourous, and Pšoi. Then come Pecoč, Cornelios, Paul,
another Pachomius, John, and Theodore.[48] Theodore's career and responsibility are well documented throughout the *Lives*. A Sourous was appointed general superior at Phnoum. There is no way of telling whether
he was the man already mentioned.[49] Cornelios is described in the Greek
tradition as an οἰκονόμος, and explicitly in the Bohairic as general superior of Thmoušons.[50] The *Vita Prima* mentions all these early figures
again, along with a Paphnouti, adding, "Pachomius . . . appointed most
of them as leaders and fathers [ἡγουμένους καὶ πατέρας] of the monasteries."[51] There is a certain institutional ambiguity even in that phrase,
and there must have been many others not so famous who exercised less
official authority. Such were the persons implied by the instruction of
Pachomius already mentioned, "join another who is living according to
the Gospel of Christ."[52] Such also was Psenamon, to whom Pachomius
entrusted the young Silvanos.[53] That relatively haphazard subjection of
monk to monk, of neophyte to elder, might often have softened the outlines of a rigid hierarchy of superiors and *praepositi*.

Even the *praepositi*, the superiors of the individual houses, key figures though they were in the Pachomian system, were not as mighty as
they may seem. If one were to believe a few texts, they wielded considerable power, although some in any one community were probably
more important than others:[54] "no one in the house shall do anything
against the directive of the housemaster."[55] Being a *hebdomadarius* (always a *praepositus*) gave a man some standing, even if only for a week.[56]
But behind those general statements, there lay a great many carefully
stipulated controls. Where the *Vita Prima* is able, for example, to emphasize in similar terms the absolute authority of the *praepositus* over many
aspects of life within his house, the passage ends with the tell-tale summary, "and all that government is written in detail in the book of the

48. G¹ 25f, Bo 23f. There is just a hint in the Bohairic *Life* that the last
named, excluding Theodore, may have been pursuing the ascetic life, in some
loose sense, jointly.

49. G¹ 114.

50. G¹ 61, 114; Bo 59 (ⲛ̅ⲅⲏⲅⲟⲩⲙⲉⲛⲟⲥ).

51. G¹ 79.

52. *CMR* 17. See Chapter V at n. 14.

53. G¹ 104–5. See Chapter III n. 64.

54. This seems to be the implication of *P* 59, "the housemaster of the first
house [*prioris domus*]," which G¹ 28 would support: "the first house [ἡ δὲ πρώτη
οἰκία] is the one of the lesser stewards who prepare the table. . . ." Also in Bo 26.

55. *PInst* 16. See Chapter V at n. 67.

56. See Veilleux, *Liturgie*, p. 127.

stewards."[57] That could cut both ways, of course. Where the matter was in writing, the authority of the housemaster was not open to question; but he, too, especially where teaching and punishment were at issue, was bound by what was written, while anything *not* covered in the book was to be judged by the superior of the monastery himself.[58] Even in the case of written regulations, *praepositi* were not made responsible for the general state of their subjects' souls. They simply reprimanded them offense by offense, as these occurred.[59]

So the *praepositus*, like his companions in the house, led a fairly regulated life. It was a general rule, as Pachomius had pointed out to Theodore of Alexandria, that superiors at any level should be bound by the same standards as their subjects.[60] Indeed, the development of a potential superior depended upon a lifetime of obedience. As an old monk said of Theodore, "Now, Pachomius, this man's father, by obeying God in all things became well-pleasing in his sight. And if this man too is steadfast after his likeness, then he will be his heir."[61] Interestingly, the *Rules* have more to say about the inner disposition of a superior than about the correct attitudes of his subjects. *Praepositi* were to be sober. That much one might expect. More surprising is the warning that they should resist bribes. They were to be moderate in their demands—"he shall not forget the distress of needy souls."[62] On the other hand, they should not be changeable in their commands. They should be attentive to the *senes*, follow the *praecepta maiorum*, and hold themselves above all subject to the law of God.[63]

57.   G¹ 59. "Stewards" here translates οἰκονόμοι, which Veilleux suggests must mean the *major* superiors of monasteries, the "book" in question being, according to him, the *Praecepta*, on which this chapter of the *Life* is based, *Koinonia*, 1:414. But even in the previous sentence, οἰκονόμος is used for the official to whom returning monks should hand in monies received, which would match rather more the subordinate delegate mentioned by, for example, *P* 65 and 81.

58.   *P* 133. Presumably "novel fault" is to be connected with "new matter" in 134, which appears (with the word "him") to refer back to the "superior of the monastery" in 133. Such disjointed references indicate not only wide variety of practice, but muddled construction in the *Rules* themselves: Ruppert, p. 263.

59.   *PLeg* 5. *Praepositi* had to report certain offenses to the father of the monastery within three days and the absence of deserters within three hours: *PInst* 11.

60.   See n. 26 above; Bo 79 shows him living up to this ideal. Note the prohibition against issuing materials to oneself, *P* 38, 41.

61.   G¹ 108.

62.   In the Latin, "those who need mercy."

63.   *PInst* 18. See Veilleux, *Liturgie*, pp. 89f. It is useful to speculate on possible links between the vocabulary of leadership here and in the province more at large. Ruppert offers a hint, p. 286. After all, the Prefect of Egypt was entitled ἡγεμών or ἡγούμενος, or occasionally ἄρχων. He exercised an overall judicial

At least by the end of the fourth century, everyone would have
known that that was what the *Rules* demanded; if the demand was not
met, remedies were by that time available. How quickly that degree of
formality and control developed is much harder to judge. According to
Jerome, all the brothers in a house, if they thought their *praepositus* was
overstepping his authority, could freely report him to the superior of the
monastery. That much liberty is perhaps a little surprising, and there
may be reason for supposing that only the housemasters of other houses
exercised the privilege.[64] But there must have been some basis for Jerome's version. Communities were well accustomed to argument, if we
can extrapolate from more formal references to anger and tale-bearing,
to lies, hatred, sourness, and backbiting, as well as to laziness and levity
in general.[65] Perhaps we can at least suggest that with time it became
necessary to define more precisely in what ways one might appeal over
the head of one's immediate superior. The *Praecepta ac Leges* describe a
disciplined process of mediation between *praepositus* and subjects, undertaken by "brothers of proven life and faith"—although this was allowed only in the absence of the major superior, so that unresolved tension might not give rise to even greater discord.[66] The *Praecepta atque
Iudicia* present us with an even tidier system: panels of monks who were
to settle disputes of this nature, even by the suspension of the superior
of the monastery himself.[67]

---

and administrative authority, made occasional ἐπιδημίαι, or visits of inspection,
and wrote letters to subordinates with the somewhat apophthegmatic introduction, "'Ο δεῖνος [name inserted] λέγει": Lallemand, *Administration*, pp. 60f, 68,
71, 75. More locally placed were the *praepositi pagi*, introduced by the Emperor
Maximin; mainly intent upon police activity, they made inquiries into acts of violence and generally helped to extend the influence of the cities over the surrounding *territoria* (described as πολιτεῖαι!), Lallemand, pp. 40, 98f, 131. It would
be silly to press the analogies too far, but to note what civil models were available
(and it is *civil* models we are talking about) may help to clarify the relatively remote
and surprisingly mobile style of administration of Pachomius and his successors
and the more restricted and slightly oppressive authority of housemasters.

64.   Jerome's *PInst* 17 is clear, with "omnes fratres qui in una domo sunt."
Veilleux, *Koinonia*, 2:193, argues for "housemasters." Ruppert, pp. 253f, is at
least cautious.

65.   *PInst* 9f.

66.   *PLeg* 14, as interpreted by Veilleux, *Liturgie*, p. 128: "une évolution al-
lant dans la direction d'une législation plus précise." On this and the following
text, see Ruppert, pp. 312f.

67.   *PIud* 11. Interpretation will depend partly on how one translates "de
maioribus et praepositis." The phrase "the aforementioned judges" takes us
back to *PIud* 9, which Ruppert (against M. M. van Molle) would ascribe to a very
late period, when superiors were more remote, pp. 295f. That passage reads as
follows: "If the one who is the judge of the sins of all [*qui iudex est omnium pec-*

However late these rules may have been, brotherhood counted in them for as much as hierarchy; to that extent, at least, they may not carry us far from the mind of Pachomius himself. In his anxiety about the future of his foundations, he dwelt in particular upon the discord he thought likely to develop and upon the way in which monks would fight among themselves to achieve positions of authority.[68] In a later version by Dionysius, Pachomius concluded one gloomy forecast, "and good men will no longer feel able to speak out for the benefit of the community, but will remain silent and still."[69] Such a cowed abandonment of informed freedom was never his ideal. Most persistent was his belief that each bore some responsibility for the welfare of others in the community, a belief dating from that early assertion of Hieracapollon, "If carelessness overtakes you, [the devil] will also dominate us."[70] It was a belief that came to affect superiors, perhaps, more than others. It was made clear to Theodore of Alexandria that his position of authority meant more was demanded of him.[71] *Praepositi* were held responsible for faults they did not report.[72] Even the more famous Theodore could be blamed for the waywardness of his subordinates. Pachomius shamed him publicly after a bout of talking in the bakery and warned him after three weeks of penance, "take care that you never again hereafter be negligent and that no transgression occur among the brothers, lest you be found guilty of sins before the Lord Jesus Christ."[73] But we have seen already how Horsiesios, for example, extended that line of thought in his *Liber*. Superiors would be answerable before Christ for their subjects, but "not only is this to be understood of the housemasters [*praepositi*] but also of the superiors of the monasteries and of each of the brothers belonging to the rank and file, because all must carry each other's burdens and so fulfill the law of Christ."[74]

We must conclude that the structure of authority both in Pachomius's lifetime and later was complex and fluid. Pachomius, presented

catorum, which Ruppert takes to mean the superior] abandon the truth, because of the perversity of his heart or out of negligence, he shall be judged by twenty holy and God-fearing men, or ten or even only five about whom all bear witness. They shall sit and judge him, and degrade him to the lowest place until he amends."

68.   G¹ 71, Bo 66; G¹ 88, Bo 73; G¹ 102, Bo 103. His attitude to the clergy is relevant here, G¹ 27. There will be further discussion in Chapter VIII. Note also the "lust for power" in G¹ 96. G¹ 126 shows the process well under way.

69.   Dion. 45. The equivalent G² 69 uses, for "speaking out," παρρησία. Corresponding is G¹ 102.

70.   G¹ 20. See Chapter III at n. 48.   71.   G¹ 95.   72.   *PInst* 13.

73.   Bo 77; not in G¹, but in Am, pp. 446f.

74.   Horsiesios, *Liber* 11. See Chapter V at n. 61.

by the texts in a variety of guises, many of them inspired by theoretical reflection, is nevertheless allowed to insist on his basic role of servant: servant of God, but also servant of his monks. So he seems to stand at times at the top of the ladder, at other times virtually at the bottom.[75] Authority otherwise was delegated downward along a chain of command—through superiors and *praepositi* especially, but with others in the communities enjoying important status.[76] The whole process was constantly subject in some degree to the judgment of the community at large, within which each monk felt responsible for the conduct of his colleagues and enjoyed some explicit if regulated power to criticize and judge.

One is brought back also to that basic experience which colored the monastic day and governed the understanding of what it was to live under rule: the whole community, superiors and subjects, thought of themselves constantly as living in the presence of God. It was from God that the line of command would always run; and it was that sense of confidence that gave authority its rights and submission its self-respect. Here again Pachomius was the prime example. Theodore was happy enough to follow him, the Father's servant, because Pachomius was himself, as the *Life* says, "an imitator of the saints."[77] And Theodore was not the first to seize upon that truth: "Then we, too, and all men," asserted his first disciples, "can follow him, for he follows the saints. . . . Let us die with this man and we shall also live with him, for he guides us straight to God."[78]

75.   As the writer of G[1] puts it, quoting Deuteronomy, he was like a land at once "mountainous and lowly," 110.

76.   Add to the instances already discussed *P* 63. Veilleux admits that the terminology is difficult, particularly "ductores fratrum," *Koinonia*, 2: p. 188. Neither the Coptic fragment nor the Greek *Excerpta* are any help. On the passing back and forth of responsibility, *PInst* 5 deserves quotation: "The minister [*minister*, ⲡⲉⲧⲇⲓⲁⲕⲟⲛⲉⲓ] shall not let anything be found spoiled in any of the shops where they work at each craft; neither shall he let any of the things outside the houses be spoiled. For all the things that will be found spoiled in the shops [Jerome adds, "and the damage is due to negligence"] he shall be punished by the steward [*a patre*, ϩⲓⲧⲏⲡⲟⲓⲕⲟⲛⲟⲙⲟⲥ] according to their rule [in the Coptic only]. He shall himself punish the one who is found to have spoiled the thing, according to the sentence of the steward [*iuxta voluntatem et sententiam principis*, or, more immediate and less judicial, ⲕⲁⲧⲁ ⲧⲉⲅⲛⲱⲙⲏ ⲙⲡⲟⲓⲕⲟⲛⲟⲙⲟⲥ], without whose order no one shall punish a man."

77.   G[1] 36, not explicit in Bo 30 or 32.

78.   G[1] 25, not included in Bo 23, nor in Am, pp. 369f.

· VII ·

THE ASCETIC GOAL

We are now in a position to judge the deeper purposes of Pachomius's enterprise. We have some understanding of how he went about his "cenobitic experiment." We know a little about the daily life of his monasteries, and we have examined how their order was maintained and how their leaders were defined and regarded. In the course of those inquiries, we have inevitably exposed and discussed some of the motives and attitudes of Pachomius and his associates. Key notions that we need now to recall from earlier chapters are the sense of mutual support and responsibility in the ascetic community; the importance of scripture, both as a source of ideas and, through recitation, as a means to tranquility and self-control; the value ascribed to individual freedom; the consequent desire, in counselor and superior, to lead the monk to a sense of his own needs and abilities; and the awareness of God's presence as both the context and the focus of work and prayer. All those ideas help us to define more clearly the inner landscape of Pachomian asceticism, as well as the visible boundaries of its practice.

So now we may ask more directly, what kind of human being was that monastic life designed to produce? What personal achievement was anticipated? And we cannot answer these questions with simple clarity—indeed, to do so might reduce to triviality the pain, doubt, and seriousness of Pachomius's lifelong effort.

There was, of course, a physical dimension to the enterprise. The monastic timetable, diet, and industry we have discussed were bound to foster a certain image of the self, and even, perhaps, a certain physical type. It is important, therefore, that, when referring to the visible, exterior circumstances of life, Pachomian sources are normally prosaic. About the regulations on clothing, for example, there is little that is surprising—unless it be the measured tone itself. The conformity involved may have had social effects, as we have already mentioned in Chapter IV, but in terms of warmth or comfort, the detailed allotment in the *Rules*—the linen tunics, the hoods, the scarf, the goatskin, and the shoes—can only be described as adequate and simple.[1] So also in the matter of food. We have noted the lenient regime recounted by Palladius, with herbs, olives, cheese, and vegetables.[2] Pachomian texts do not contradict that impression of moderate discipline, mentioning that there was often more than one meal a day,[3] that figs were tolerated, and cooked vegetables,[4] that permission was given to eat "a few" figs while picking them, although that was a dispensation that may have palled at times,[5] and that monks could eat their *tragematia* between meals.[6]

For the majority of monks, such a calm approach to refreshment would have made the statutory fasting twice a week a clearly separate and entirely tolerable exercise in self-discipline. Pachomius was in any case more interested in promoting self-denial by choice, although a choice always subject to the approval of superiors. The prick of conscience and the decision to go without were possible only when a measured indulgence, so to speak, was presumed to be the general norm.[7] And it was not mere going without that counted most. Ascetic struggle gave glory to God, yes; but if holy men wanted to boast, it was the inner result—their σωφροσύνη, or balanced self-control—that justified it.[8]

At the same time, life was not easy. We probably should not exaggerate the difference in standard of living between Pachomian monks and the peasants of neighboring districts, but there were particular attempts at self-denial. Monks had to work standing up unless they were actually ordered to sit.[9] In summer they slept in temporary shelters to keep cool, and in winter fires were allowed indoors.[10] Both were considerate relaxations; but the fires were not lit for every communal occasion, nor was one supposed to stand too close to them![11] Sleep itself was never regarded as a period of lost or wasted time: the ideal was to achieve a balanced alternation between rest and prayer. Hence those special seats

1.   *P* 81.   2.   *HL* 32.11.   3.   *P* 103.
4.   G¹ 53, Bo 48; G¹ 55, Bo 59.   5.   *P* 76.
6.   *P* 37f. All these features were discussed in Chapter IV.
7.   *Paral.* 8 (15–16); see Chapter V at n. 73.
8.   G¹ 84. The passage is recalled at n. 19 below. Variations in the texts (S¹⁰, trans. Lefort, *Vies*, p. 35; Am, pp. 435f) are noted by Veilleux, *Liturgie*, p. 89, but do not affect the point made in G¹. Chitty admitted that G¹ had its peculiarities here, but did not really solve them by appealing to G³, "Pachomian Sources Reconsidered," pp. 69f. Fasting, when it was imposed, extended through the night, and covered the drinking of water—a real hardship, *P* 88.
9.   *P* 62.   10.   *P* 87, 120.   11.   *P* 5, 22.

for monks in good health, to remind them that the hours of darkness were not to be written off completely.[12]

What Pachomius was able to achieve was a degree of hardship unspoiled by a competitive spirit, that pursuit of discomfort for its own sake which seems to have characterized some more solitary ascetics, and in particular the stylites of Syria a century later. He was not alone in that achievement. We need to remind ourselves that, in the earliest levels of the *Apophthegmata* also, there is very little that smacks of such extremism. Where we find pain apparently embraced on purpose, a motive beyond jealousy of others or hatred of self is normally apparent.[13] In other instances, we may suspect that the text has been modified to suit the taste or credulity of a later age.[14] In the *Lives*, the younger Pachomius endures the thorns that pierced his feet in the desert near Palamon's cell, but that was a circumstance accepted rather than sought after.[15] There is only one other incident reliably described in more than one text that suggests a misplaced zeal. Even there the accounts are confused. In the *Vita Prima*, a monk at prayer deliberately invites renewed attack by a scorpion he had disturbed and he refuses to attend to his wounds until sunrise. The anecdote is oddly intruded and lacks a moral. The Bohairic version appears more rational, and connects the endurance with admiration for the martyrs—"even if I was made to suffer the afflictions of the persecutions I would never deny you because of torments"—but that modification is perhaps weakened by the previous chapter, which tells how *Pachomius* was bitten in similar circumstances and displayed a comparable indifference! In the Arabic tradition, imitation of Pachomius is made the primary motive for the other monk's heroic gesture. Clearly the tale has been fitted to a variety of literary purposes.[16] More characteristic of Pachomius was his advice to Theodore about a nasty headache. It could have developed, he said, only because it was God's will. At the same time it was clearly abnormal, a fortuitous and temporary addition

12.   Balanced alternation, G[1] 60: the idea was to avoid undue weariness the following day. Seats, *P* 87f, and see Chapter IV at n. 4.

13.   E.g., *Apophthegmata patrum*, Zeno 6: the holy man, standing in the blazing sun, just wanted to see if he might be able to endure the pains of hell!

14.   E.g., *Apophthegmata patrum*, Eladius 1: in the Greek, he lived at the Kellia, in Lower Egypt, and guarded his eyes to such an extent as never to "look at the roof of the church"; but the sixth-century Latin version has misunderstood the word "Kellia," and put "cella," a cell, adding that he never "looked at *its* roof [*tectum eius*],"—a much more exaggerated virtue! There are many such shifts of emphasis.

15.   G[1] 11, Bo 15.

16.   G[1] 101, Bo 98f, Am, pp. 481f.

to the cross of his ascesis. There was certainly no call to prolong or deliberately induce such a condition. Nor did it compare with the heroism of
the sick. Its worth lay only in prompting Theodore, like Job, to give
thanks to God in adversity, and to acquire a greater degree of spiritual
vigor and long-suffering.[17]

So moderation and practicality seem to have been the hallmark of
ascetic practice. The Pachomian attitude to the body did prompt, at the
same time, wider theological reflection. A monk captured by desert
tribesmen agreed under duress to sacrifice to their gods. Pachomius regretted that the man had missed his chance. Martyrdom, therefore, he
may still have regarded as a possible ideal: the crown had been offered,
and refused. A more "modern," post-Diocletianic note is also sounded
in the passage. The missed chance should not be allowed to induce de-
spair: what God looked for was not death, but repentance. The air of
excitement created by an opportunity for the ultimate sacrifice and the
expression of regret when the opportunity was lost were both by this
time probably no more than a cultural habit. It contributed nevertheless
to a new and lasting conviction that the penance of any true convert
would show itself "not only in a contrite and humble spirit but also
through bodily toil [σώματος πόνῳ]."[18] In the previous chapter of the
Life, the prayer of Titoue made clear this transition from the sufferings of
the persecuted to the quieter achievements of ascetics: "'Lord, I am prepared not only to fast until I win your love, but truly even if they subject
me to martyrdom and burn me, I will not forsake temperance [τὴν
σωφροσύνην], in which all the saints are glorified. I pray you, make me
perfect in your fear.' And so he died, a pure and genuine monk."[19]

Then there are references to the resurrection. They are largely restricted to the *Vita Prima* and need to be unraveled carefully. Pachomius
found it hard to avoid morbid anxiety. The sound of mourners weeping
at a tomb was enough to disturb, at least, his strict confidence in a resurrection to come. Present circumstances were, by contrast, all the more
worthy of tears. "And if we often hear [the brothers] weeping, let us not
be surprised, because all the saints have been in the valley of weeping
. . . So these, who are the children of the saints, also weep." Then his

17. G[1] 90; Bo 36 is slightly harsher.
18. G[1] 85. Not in Bo, but see S[10] VII, Am, pp. 439f, and *Paral.* 5 (8–11).
Am is the most reasonable. In the *Paral.*, very long and late, Pachomius posi-
tively dissuades the man from a desire for martyrdom. G[1] says he was "from
another place," S[10] that he was an "anchorite." Festugière, *Première Vie grecque*,
p. 44, suggests we are dealing here only with "formules passe-partout" that recur in conjunction with many virtues. He harks back, as we do, to G[1] 84, and
also G[1] 101/Bo 99.
19. G[1] 84.

habitual sympathy for others and his relentless ability to think in social terms led him, even in that incident, to a sense of how the resurrection might come about. "They are weeping for the dead whom they cannot raise up. But let us weep first for ourselves and then for our neighbor. Perhaps through our weeping with those who weep, the Lord will raise them up." [20] The crucial passage on resurrection, however, occurs a little earlier. First, in the case of Jesus, a real continuity is asserted between his body before death and his body in the risen state: Thomas "touches the crucified [lit. "cross-bearing"] and risen flesh in which the Lord was as in a temple." As for the resurrection of other humans, it was to be seen as at once a future and a present event: "as the Lord rose so we also shall rise [ἀναστησόμεθα]—and we have already risen with him [καὶ ἤδη ἀνέστημεν]—since his crucified body is like ours," and "he himself raised us with his own body." [21] Here was an interpretation that stressed how the monk would share with Jesus a "cross-bearing body"; thus it linked the resurrection, like martyrdom, with the daily practice of the ascetic life. We should recognize, therefore, that it really did involve a statement about the body and not merely about some hidden grace. Pachomius appears perfectly willing to talk about "*spiritual* resurrection" (πνευματικὴ ἀνάστασις); but that was something entirely separate, referring to the life here and now that followed upon faith and repentance. [22] It did not mean, either, that the body, meanwhile, was to be repudiated, was doomed to disappear in the face of some such "spiritual" alternative. The body shared already in the triumph of Jesus and represented at the same time both the means and the token of that association.

It would be surprising if theological reflections of that nature had not occurred in the Pachomian corpus. In spite of toleration under Constantine, the earlier persecution of Christians was still a living memory; the conduct it had given rise to (sometimes heroic, sometimes otherwise) could still be a cause of conflict, as between the Melitians and the orthodox in Egypt. As for the resurrection, when the *Lives* in their present form were beginning to take shape at the end of the fourth century, controversy over the writings of Origen and his contemporary supporters would have made it a very live issue. What physical future might lie in store for a being so spiritual as an immortal soul was precisely one of the points of debate. How one rated suffering, or violent death, or the prospect of immortality for bodies as well as for spirits, clearly had important consequences in the field of physical asceticism. [23]

20. G¹ 62, not in Bo. There is no question of a miracle being meant.
21. G¹ 56, not in Bo.
22. G¹ 57.
23. About the Melitians, enough has been said in Chapter I. On martyr-

Those are not, however, the preoccupations that lie at the heart of the *Lives*. They probably tell us more about the circumstances and attitudes of the authors than they do about Pachomius himself. It would be foolish to suppose that Pachomius was completely ignorant of theological traditions or of ecclesiastical conflicts. His involvement, for example, in the liturgical life of local villages and his undoubted admiration for, and possible dependence upon, the patriarch Athanasius, both as churchman and as thinker, would have been enough to put him in touch with current ideas and controversies.[24] But that serves also to remind us that a rich theology and a keen sense of loyalty amid conflict could have been fostered in a Christian of the Thebaid through quite narrow channels: the occasional letters of distant bishops, or local traditions of exegesis.[25] It is a topic to which we shall return. In any case, Pachomius himself fought shy of theological controversy. Precisely because he was aware of the damage it could do, he would not allow his monks to be dragged into conflicts of no spiritual advantage. They were not to mimic in their own communities, by appeal either to rank or to doctrine, the schisms that would beset the church at large.[26] Even in his own "trial" at Latopolis, it was his status as a "clairvoyant" that was most at stake, rather than any corpus of ideas.[27] What interested him much more were the personal implications of ascetic practice: the way, for example, bodily behavior, such as the voluntary hardship or accidental suffering we

---

dom, E. E. Malone, *The Monk and the Martyr*, is frequently referred to, and perhaps more rarely read. The book offers a useful collection of references, but the few allusions to Pachomius are rendered worthless by the author's complete ignorance of the critical literature. It should be remembered that, by the time the most recent persecution came to an end, Christian asceticism was well established in Egypt. On Origen, Pachomius's opposition is recounted in G[1] 31, as augmented by MS Athos 1015—although with how much accuracy it would be risky to judge. The Origenist Controversy has not received the precisely focused attention it deserves. J. N. D. Kelly, *Jerome*, begins to present a context. For some of the theoretical issues at stake, see A. Guillaumont, *Les "Kephalaia gnostica" d'Évagre le Pontique*.

24.   Note his activities as liturgical reader, G[1] 29/Bo 25, and his praise of Athanasius, G[1] 136/Bo 134, perhaps reliably expanded in *Letter of Ammon* 12.

25.   A point made with particular force by Roberts, *Manuscript*, and discussed in Chapter I. The conversion of Antony may well have depended on an understanding of scripture inspired by local homilies: see *Life of Antony* 2f. For pointing out this particular connection, my thanks to Peter Brown.

26.   G[1] 27/Bo 25. Compare Athanasius's picture of Antony's involvement in the Arian conflict, *Life of Antony* 69, with Pachomius's "disappearance" into the crowd of his monks when faced with a visit by the patriarch, G[1] 30/Bo 28.

27.   G[1] 112.

have noted, bore inner fruit. What, he asked, was the connection between the two? If we are looking for theoretical reflection on his part, it is in his handling of that kind of question that we should expect him to make his most characteristic and useful contribution to Christian ascetic debate.

A subtle appreciation of the issue may have been displayed by Pachomius at a very early stage. Palamon was "amazed" to see his "open, intensive ascesis" (τὴν φανερὰν σύντονον ἄσκησιν), but admired even more his efforts "to cleanse his conscience perfectly" (τὸ συνειδὸς . . . τέλεον καθαρίσαι). The visible and the mental, if we may risk those terms for the moment, were closely connected: at the level of motivation by the way Pachomius placed his hope on heavenly things, at the level of self-mastery by his learning and reciting the text of scripture.[28]

Those are insights and skills we shall examine further. Entirely characteristic of Pachomius was the way they were quickly reflected, with even greater complexity, in his regulations concerning the sick. Ailing monks were separated from the life and work of the community[29] and there was always a team of healthy brethren on duty night and day to provide for their needs.[30] The regulations reflect a genuine compassion in Pachomius, which persisted throughout his life. (Jerome has a moving description of the sick monk "nursed by the old men with such care that he misses neither city luxuries nor a mother's affection.")[31] It was a compassion, furthermore, based on the sense that physical health was the natural condition within which the spirit would flourish.[32] From his earliest years Pachomius had learned that any capacity in himself or in others to endure hardship or to rise above the limits of physical nature had to point beyond itself to a spiritual purpose, or at least had to have a spiritual explanation. His mastery over animals, for example—and here one might recall the scorpions!—was achieved "through the uprightness of his heart" (ἐν εὐθύτητι καρδίας). And he would reach even further than that, acquiring in time a "perfect knowledge" (τελειότης γνώσεως). For his spectacular ability to escape injury from crocodiles was not to be the sum total of his achievement: "he was being preserved by the Lord who intended to teach him later how to act [καθὼς δεῖ

---

28. G¹ 9, not quite so explicit in Bo 15. S³ associates these statements with material in G¹ 18: see Festugière, *Première Vie grecque*, pp. 117f.

29. *P* 40f, esp. 42–43, 46–47.

30. *P* 129, after Jerome. The Coptic is briefer, but to the same point.

31. Jerome, *Ep.* 22.35.

32. G¹ 28 (Bo 26 is more cursory) and G¹ 51f. On the connection, if any, with Bo 47f, see Festugière, *Première Vie grecque*, p. 31.

ποιῆσαι].[33] Yet that final phrase shows that a firm link was still being maintained with the visible, outer life. Γνῶσις, the "perfect knowledge," was not presented as an *alternative* to action, any more than the "up-rightness of heart" mentioned above had displaced Pachomius's power over dangerous reptiles. It was simply that a rich store of spiritual and intellectual power was being constantly enhanced in order to keep pace with and further support a corresponding increase in physical energy and practical success. The same complementary descriptions are used for the sick. A monk who was apparently the victim of an entirely tangible disease might still be regarded most as suffering from a spiritual malady—perhaps, though not necessarily, one induced by demonic forces.[34] On the other hand, men who persistently betrayed an inner discontent were to be regarded as physically sick.[35] Infirmity was accepted as a legitimate excuse for failure to obey the *Rules*, but that failure, in its turn, was seen as a weakness that should be cured in the company of the sick before any further attempt was made at a more properly spiritual reform.[36]

So the recurrent theme throughout those passages is that the body and the inner man cannot be divided one from the other. There seems to have been no trace of reaction or controversy in the emphasis. It was born of Pachomius's earliest experience and found expression in incidents throughout his career. Once established in his mind as the fruit of what he saw happening in his own religious conversion and ascetic practice, it represented a view of human nature that would then distinguish the Pachomian disciple from any dualist, whether gnostic or Manichee. Not that it need have been in its original form a principle wielded deliberately against some consciously identified adversary. It survived in the Pachomian texts as a more reticent reproach amid the strident religious positions that characterized the controversial age in which those texts themselves were compiled. It might become interwoven with that "theology of the body" discussed earlier: the link with martyrdom through both inner self-mastery and corporal ascesis, the faith in the resurrection as both a fruit of repentance and a blessing bestowed upon the body even now. But in purer form it was a conviction proper to Pachomius, coloring the unbroken thread of practice that ran from his ear-

33.   G¹ 21. Dion. 19f comments more extensively; G² 20 makes the point a little clearer.

34.   G¹ 52; compare Bo 107, which has no equivalent in G¹ but corresponds to Am, pp. 510f (for sickness, see especially p. 516).

35.   *Plud* 5.

36.   *Plud* 12. Both this and the previous text could imply an attempt to shame a monk back to obedience, but that seems a less likely interpretation.

liest ascetic enthusiasm to the teaching of his final years and defining in part his constant sympathy and his urgent attention to the inner needs of those around him who labored, fasted, and prayed.

We have discussed so far what might be called the physical asceticism of Pachomius. We have examined some of the theoretical reflections upon that asceticism, both those typical of the age and those more peculiar to Pachomius himself. We have discovered emphasis upon a close alliance, so to speak, between the body and the inner life.

But we are not talking about a merely static relationship. An associated theme and principle, equally important, is that the monk did indeed have to pass from the outer to the inner world. It was within oneself that the most important courses were engaged upon, the most important goals achieved. To say as much was not to detract from the value of the body or of visible asceticism. The idea represented simply a desire to give the monastic life its proper momentum, its fullest sense of purpose. So it is perfectly just in the end that we should attend most to qualities of mind or spirit. At that level our question—what kind of human being did Pachomius wish to produce?—demands even greater caution, and to avoid prejudgment we shall be wise to content ourselves at first with a haphazard answer. We can weigh clues, for example, that emerge in various parts of the *Rules* already examined. Rules are inevitably concerned more with methods than with aims, and may not appear to contribute at once to a coherent system of spirituality; but the sense of purpose we are looking for will often be betrayed by the loose ends of thought, the suppositions, the implications, the allusions, which poke their way now and again above the surface of mere practicality.

Take for example the declaration that serves as opening to the *Praecepta et Instituta*: "that they may not be fuddled with passion of any kind,"[37] but maintain a balance that accords with the truth, as it has been handed down by the apostles and prophets."[38] To possess a firm footing is the central idea, and great importance is given to measuring oneself against tradition. Both Pachomius and his followers were well aware

37.   So Jerome. Lefort admitted to difficulty with the Coptic, which Veilleux translates, "not inebriated by what is pleasing to God."

38.   *PInst*, introduction. Jerome has "stent in mensura veritatis." Bacht uses almost the same words to translate the Coptic, which Lefort renders, "s'en tenant à une juste mesure." See Chapter V at nn. 37 and 70.

that such a balance, such a measured approach, might be difficult both to acquire and to maintain; from such a prescription, nervousness could follow just as easily as tranquility. The nervousness becomes explicit in some sources. The *Instruction Concerning a Spiteful Monk*, for example, warns, "Do not take one step forward, then a step backward, that God may not detest you; for the crown shall go to the one who perseveres." [39] The balance here has taken on a quite different quality. Only the most self-assured would escape a sense of being caught between two extremes, and the resulting tension would be connected more with fear of judgment to come than with any sense that a truth had been perceived, or a tradition inherited. Yet the more wholesome tranquility would also recur in other texts. Dionysius reported, echoing the *Vita Altera*, "He had received from the Lord the gift of being always the same, never varying in any circumstance; and he kept his soul carefully schooled, as the Lord had taught him." [40] The *Instruction* itself could strike a similar note: "Do not go from one place to another saying, 'I will find God here or there.' God has said, 'I fill the earth, I fill the heavens'; . . . My son, be aware that God is within you, so that you may dwell in his law and commandments." [41]

So, starting from the one passage, we can already glimpse an ideal in spite of attendant anxieties. The monk should aim at a degree of calm self-possession, which will open him to the presence of God but place him also more consciously within an ascetic tradition.

In our pursuit of clues let us follow up the last point first. We have noted already an anecdote widely reproduced, and included in the *Vita Prima*, which stresses the value of such a link with the past, while affirming also the possibility of fruitful personal effort. [42] Pachomius's first disciples, Pšentaesi and his companions, are filled with wonder at his asceticism. They conclude a speech of gratitude and admiration with the words, "Then we, too, and all men can follow him, for he follows the saints." The suggestion is clear that the church's tradition of holiness served to put a seal of authenticity on Pachomius's own holy life. Prior to that remark, however, comes the statement, "We used to think that all the saints were made holy and unswerving by God without regard to their free will, from their mothers' womb, and that sinners were not able to have life because they had been created that way. But now we see the goodness of God manifested in our father who, although born from pagan parents, has become so dear to God and has clothed himself with

39.   *CMR* 14.
40.   Dion. 37. There are variations, but the text is close to G² 39.
41.   *CMR* 25.
42.   Touched upon in Chapter III at n. 80 and in Chapter VI at nn. 48 and 78.

all God's commandments."[43] Thanks to their acquaintance with Pachomius, a real sense of personal freedom was being borne in upon those
early disciples, challenging them to reach out for untried goals. It was a
freedom, however, that did not isolate them or leave them to their own
devices. It rested precisely on their being placed in relationship to a *new*
past, to new traditions, in a new society. We should not take for granted
such liberty of spirit any more than they did themselves. So many of the
pagans around them, and some of the Christians too, were bound by an
astral fatalism or wedded to the notion of innate virtue that persisted
through life unchanged; that might gradually betray itself, but would
not be susceptible to modification or growth in the truest sense.[44]

Here was another conviction, therefore, that helps us again to make
sense of loose ends in the *Rules*—of that phrase in the *Praecepta et Instituta*, for example, which says that the *synaxis* was aimed at "the liberation of ignorant souls, so that they might glorify God in the light of the
living."[45] In that context, freedom is made to lean forward, as it were, to
become a movement from moral victory to final union with God. It is
freedom presented also as the fruit of prayer; Palladius, writing on that
very subject, may not have misunderstood the motives behind Pachomian discipline: "that they may fulfill the duties of their station in life
like house-servants and so enjoy a life of complete liberty."[46]

What we have described as self-possession, therefore, had its links
with ascetic tradition. It depended also upon keen awareness of the

43.   G^1 25. Festugière thought that the passage might be alluding to literary
antecedents: *Première Vie grecque*, p. 20 n. 1. Veilleux's phrase, "without regard to
their free will," weakens slightly the force of καὶ μὴ αὐτεξουσίους. God, they
thought, had *made* the saints *not* masters of themselves. Ἀυτεξουσία, therefore,
is the virtue or natural endowment here most defended. Ruppert builds much
upon the passage, pp. 356f. Theodore uses the term in G^1 141. Bo 107 reiterates
the belief that one may overcome the disadvantages of birth. The text is suspiciously prolix, but it does recur in Am, pp. 510f.

44.   The Greek tradition appears not wholly consistent. G^2 4 is explicit in
praising Pachomius's youthful virtue, before his conversion: "such a prelude,
even in his pagan state, fitted worthily with what he later became." But G^1 3,
with its phrase, "[Demons] saw that I hated evil even then" (as also in Bo 6),
places events in a different context. Appeal (in both those *Lives*, unlike G^2) is to
Eccles. 7.30, "God made man upright," implying simply that a rejection of demons was natural to anyone, Christian or otherwise. Conversion was still a reality, therefore: the transformation of spirit, the acquisition of fresh virtue. The
caution in this passage stems from a distinction between nature and morality,
between chosen behavior and the human endowment that makes it possible.
Other implications of G^1 25 will be pursued in Chapter IX.

45.   See Chapter V at n. 37.

46.   *HL* 32.7. Note the link with Dion. 32/G^2 34; and see Chapter V at
nn. 22f.

presence of God. On that connection we have the clear statement in the *Praecepta ac Leges* that all should obey "coram Deo."[47] Given the references above to spiritual balance and to freedom within a new society, we may risk for the moment interpreting that "presence of God" as the level of awareness or insight, the spiritual atmosphere, which, once gained or promoted, would open up for a monk the clearest views of himself and of his fellows.

That much we may gather from the following of clues, as we put it earlier. That much constitutes our haphazard answer, based only on the reasoning hinted at by practical demands, mainly in the *Rules*. What we have to do now is inquire of the *Lives* whether Pachomius himself grew in those convictions, formulating them with increasing clarity and putting them into practice more effectively. If we have been right to detect them as his overriding preoccupations, then they should help us to make greater sense of his career and to identify the general and persistent patterns of his thought.

A lasting impression, in spiritual matters as in his more strictly social experiments, was made upon Pachomius by his first experience of the Christian community.[48] Those compassionate visitors to the military billet at Thebes had been described to him as people who "do good to everyone, putting their hope in Him who made heaven and earth and us men."[49] Christians, in other words, were optimistic as well as generous; Pachomius very quickly made that optimism as much a part of his inner life as his determination to serve others. Palamon admired his clear-headed concern for the law of God even more than his visible asceticism and saw how it drew him to look "to the greater hope in heaven."[50] Pachomius himself made an interesting remark years later about the spiritual perceptiveness of children, which sprang partly, he said, from their greater readiness to obey, but also from their natural optimism. Like St. Paul, they "strain ahead to the things that are before."[51]

There would have been a natural connection between that optimism

47. *PLeg* 8. See Chapter V at n. 79 and the final paragraph of Chapter VI.
48. See the early chronology constructed in Chapter III.
49. G[1] 4, less explicit in Bo 7.
50. G[1] 9. The Sahidic tradition connects these events with G[1] 18: see Festugière, *Première Vie grecque*, pp. 117f.
51. G[1] 49, with allusion to Philippians 3.13. Pachomius had already felt the force of that Pauline passage in his own early experience, G[1] 15/Bo 19.

and what we have called the level of insight, the "presence of God." To look forward in such a way was inevitably to look upward also. For that very reason, it is not surprising to find an admixture of nervousness, of the fear discussed above and, more fully, in Chapter V. When Pachomius heard the description of the Theban Christians, "his heart was set on fire with the fear of God," as well as with "joy." [52] His progress under Palamon was accompanied by similar anxiety: "seeing this [the misfortunes of one possessed], Pachomius was stirred the more to fear for his own progress, and determined to take every precaution to keep watch over his heart." [53] Even his remarks about the virtues of children ended with an exhortation to vigilance. Those virtues had to be protected, as well as admired: "The man who cleanses his own conscience to perfection, in the fear of God and in truth, he it is who can keep the little ones with the Lord's help." [54]

Such fears seem often to have played upon Pachomius's mind. But we must understand them aright, hold fast to the distinctions he made himself, and do justice to the development of his ideas. For it is in this matter, perhaps more than in any other, that the man has been exposed to misinterpretation and presented as the dour and relentless architect of a discipline designed to assuage God's anger. That God, supposedly the God of the Old Testament, was "the God of justice and judgment, of law and legalism, whose anger was a burning fire, in the face of whose holiness no sinner could survive." [55]

Certainly we can find morbid statements in the sources. When Palamon, for example, admired Pachomius's watchful heart, the text admits also that his disciple "was always meditating on the fear of God, the thought of the judgment, and the torments of everlasting fire." [56] A later passage, alluding to Theodore's gracious temper, says that Pachomius, although "perfect in everything," was, by contrast, "fearful and always mournful, remembering the souls in torment." [57] In that case, perhaps, the reference to Theodore gives the game away: the passage may have

52.   G¹ 5, not explicit in Bo 7.
53.   G¹ 9. Even allowing for his textual adjustments, which are inspired by Festugière, I find Veilleux's translation awkward here.
54.   G¹ 49.
55.   So even the judicious Bacht, "Pakhôme et ses disciples," in *Théologie de la vie monastique*, p. 48.
56.   G¹ 18. Bo 21 proceeds directly to discuss a conflict with visible demons, on which more below.
57.   G¹ 91, not in Bo 74. S¹ makes amusing allowances: "From that day on he did not get angry again as fleshly men do, but if he happened once to be angry, he was angry as the saints are," III (9)! See further references in Chapter VI n. 3.

been designed to improve his reputation at Pachomius's expense, and spring from a biased "Theodoran" source.[58] The evidence concerning Theodore himself is not without confusion. He thought, according to another passage, that the presence (or possibly the final coming) of Christ would induce "fear and trembling,"[59] and he quite freely used fear of God's judgment to rouse the negligent.[60] But in other passages, particularly when he invoked the experience of Pachomius himself, Theodore made what must appear to be not only more wholesome, but almost certainly, historically speaking, more authentic emphases. A monk's greatest ambition should be union with the Holy Spirit, orthodox belief, and the observance of God's commandments—all of which would make him a temple of God, and gain him "all power and liberty" ($\pi\hat{\alpha}\sigma\alpha$ $\dot{\epsilon}\xi o v\sigma\acute{\iota}\alpha$ $\kappa\alpha\grave{\iota}$ $\pi\alpha\rho\rho\eta\sigma\acute{\iota}\alpha$).[61] That brings us much closer, in our reading of the *Lives*, to other accounts of the ascetic goal, closer also to the "clues" we had begun to follow earlier. And years before, Theodore's own declared ambitions had not been dissimilar: purity of heart, a measured and gracious tongue, unquestioning obedience until death.[62] Only the last, perhaps, left immediate room for fear: in that case, fear of judgment.

In the case of Pachomius, there are plenty of such hints at a more wholesome sense of caution. One section of the *Praecepta et Instituta* is packed with curses against the negligent *praepositus*. Almost every misfortune, it would seem, that the Old Testament in particular could suggest is heaped hopefully upon his head, but there also is the bland prescription, "he shall fear not death but God."[63] That fear Pachomius linked with other values—truth, for example, and joy.[64] It was a fear often inspired by the very sight of virtue in others; as part of a monk's social experience, it did not spring simply from confrontation with death and judgment. So, for example, it was the achievements of one's fellows that did most to prompt effort in one's own prayer. Prayer, for Pachomius, was clearly intimate, intense, and affective; that gives further and special point to his comment that the one thing he feared more than the fire of hell was to find himself estranged from "the humility and the

58. Festugière, *Première Vie grecque*, p. 47; Chitty, "Pachomian Sources Reconsidered," p. 64.

59. G¹ 131, not made explicit in Bo.

60. G¹ 132. Note also an anecdote dating from his accession as leader: "But as soon as he saw them [the leaders of the monasteries], he became very angry and they almost had to force him to embrace them. When they saw the expression on his face, they were seized by great fear," Bo 142, not in G¹ 131.

61. G¹ 135.   62. G¹ 36.   63. *PInst* 18.

64. See above at nn. 52–54.

sweetness of the Son of God, our Lord Jesus Christ."⁶⁵ There are times when he seems to have gone out of his way to avoid fear. That was why, for example, he was reluctant to talk about his visions. He certainly did not think that visions should be sought after: "For [the invisible things] are full of wonder and frighten those who seek and hear them."⁶⁶ He thought it much wiser that monks should marvel at the goodness in the world around them, rather than strive for an understanding beyond their normal perception. The fear of God, therefore, was not among the chief aims of a monk or the primary goal of religious experience. It was much more a means, helping him to maintain, for example, the necessary balance between service of others and watchfulness over his own perfection. Rejecting the attentions of Theodore during a brief illness, Pachomius exclaimed, "Because we have to administer the labor and the needs of the brothers, do we have the right to go to expenses for ourselves? Where is the fear of God [καὶ ποῦ ὁ φόβος τοῦ θεοῦ]?"⁶⁷ Its ultimate result was "purity of heart." Even the apparent morbidity of those early years—the concern with judgment and everlasting torment—had that preoccupation as context: "he paid great attention to the Beatitudes, striving especially to be found pure in heart."⁶⁸ And that purity would make a monk not only noble in the sight of God, but also—and here we have again the social emphasis—"ready for any good work."⁶⁹

What we are admitting, of course, is that Pachomius matured. From what may have been a naive generosity and a crude fear of hell, he progressed to a careful balance between many acknowledged social obligations and a self-effacing but ardent desire for union with God.

We should consider it even more important that he clearly expected others would be able to make the same transition. Palladius and Dionysius, at least, propagated without hesitation an image of the Pachomian community in which both novice and expert would find their place. The famous angel, bearing the *Rules* in bronze, proclaims, "I have laid down

65. G¹ 110. Note the *delectatio*, the "great delight," associated with evening prayer in *PLeg* 10. Veilleux writes warmly of the character of the Coptic evidence concerning Pachomius's prayer in, e.g., Bo 7: "une simplicité et une intimité qui annoncent le style d'un Bernard de Clairvaux," *Liturgie*, p. 132. Compare G¹ 5. On the example of others, G¹ 111.
66. G¹ 93. Bo 82f is more florid, echoed in Am, pp. 461f. One must have deep suspicions about so prolix an account, which could have come only from the lips of Pachomius. See the discussion of G¹ 88 below at n. 98.
67. G¹ 51, and exactly in Bo 47.
68. G¹ 18.
69. G¹ 96, omitted in Bo 72. The allusion is to 2 Tim. 2.21, with the same practical phrase, εἰς πᾶν ἔργον ἀγαθόν. Purity of heart we shall analyze further below.

these rules concerning prayer, so that weaker brethren may be able to perform them without undue effort. Those who are perfect, on the other hand, have no need of such a law, for they will stay in their own cells and pray without ceasing, nourished by their purity of mind and their contemplation of the divine."[70] The dubious historicity of the event may undermine the usefulness of the distinction, but there is no doubt, given the character of much earlier evidence, that Pachomius himself appreciated well enough the difference between the τέλειοι and those less successful in asceticism.[71] He appreciated also the possibility of increasing success in the spiritual life, of achieving perfection. His segregation of novices, his concern for the weak, his exhortation to seek first in the ascetic life the mercy of God, to renounce the world, one's relatives, and then oneself—all appear in one form or another in the more primitive record, and all suggest a clear conception of growth. Freedom was recognized and defended in those early passages precisely as the basis of such change in a monk's life. The point was made in the same context that tells us of the first rules, the organization of the common life, and the need for a simple appreciation of scripture—all instruments of progress. While Pachomius attended to the practical needs of the monastery, his disciples meditated, as it were, upon that promise of spiritual growth, slowly coming to see how they must achieve it.[72]

To understand better how Pachomius combined his readiness to foster growth and his preoccupation with the inner life, it is rewarding to examine his treatment of demons, of temptations, of spiritual conflict. It may seem an unlikely source of illumination, and is certainly a difficult topic to deal with. We should hardly be surprised, of course, to find de-

---

70. Dion. 22, echoing *HL* 32.7. We have already discussed this tradition in Chapter V at nn. 24f.

71. Apposite here was his famous ability to know who were the "true monks," G[1] 112. But monks would have had to be careful in using the word τέλειος, since it might smack of gnostic self-confidence. A Coptic analogue occurs in the *Apocryphon of John* = Nag Hammadi Codex II, p. 8; see the *Facsimile Edition*, Codex II, p. 18, line 29; English translation, p. 103. But Irenaeus was happy to use the word, *Adv. Haer.* 4.38.3, *PG* 7.1108; and he set the tone for an orthodox alternative: τοῦ δὲ ἀνθρώπου ἡμέρα προκόπτοντος; i.e., it was a quality you acquired in daily growth, almost by stealth.

72. All these points have been touched upon, especially in Chapters III and V. See G[1] 24–25, 28, 32 as constructed by Veilleux, *Koinonia*, vol. 1; and for novices, *P* 49.

mons in a fourth-century ascetic text, but before we jump to any conclusions about their significance or assume that conclusions are not possible we need to interpret the specific quality of "Pachomian demons"
very carefully. Even when we look at the early monastic world more generally, it is a mistake to assume some antithesis between the cultured
Hellene and the rural peasant and then to suggest further that demonology represented nothing more than the superstition of the unlettered
class.[73] One has only to think of the refined curiosity and speculation of
Porphyry, Iamblichus, or Calcidius, not to mention their extensive philosophical antecedents, to realize how ridiculous such a suggestion would
be. Pachomius, in his own catechesis, came closer than one might expect
to the rational measure of such men. He was not content, nor even
ready, to think of demons as deities dethroned, occupying the ruined
sites of pagan cult. He would not allow preoccupation with a demonic
adversary to distract him from the positive task of growing in the love of
God. He would not project into demonic terms, as a vivid phantasm or
escapist illusion, any sense he may have had of personal inadequacy.
When he spoke of demons, he was not merely expressing fear of the unintelligible or attempting to master a tension engendered by opponents
in the society around him. All those explanations have been suggested;
some of them can be illustrated, but none of them justly estimates the
moral seriousness of Pachomius's teaching.[74] The imaginative vigor of
any ascesis that involves, among other elements, a demonology is likely
to awaken the scientific suspicions of a modern student, but the last thing
we are thereby entitled to doubt is that consistency, purpose, and indeed
perception lay behind it. "Demon language" involves categories and descriptions that may be hard to translate into moral alternatives. But it is
not hard to discover at the psychological center of fourth-century Egyptian culture a genuine effort to achieve clarity of mind about the self and
about the world.

73. In what follows immediately, I take severe issue with A-J. Festugière,
Culture ou sainteté = *Les Moines d'Orient*, vol. 1, especially the chapter "Le Moine
et les démons," pp. 23–39. It is striking that most of his few allusions to Pachomius (and I include the whole book) refer to his association with Palamon. The
only exceptions are a misplaced comment on G¹ 94 (not wholly relevant in this
context), and his use of the less than reliable *Paral.* 12 (28–31). He makes scarcely
any use of the *Apophthegmata patrum*, and relies heavily on the more vivid passages of the *HM* and the *HL*.

74. Festugière's difficulty arises from the very distinction on which he
bases his study—"culture ou sainteté." At the conclusion of his chain of logic lie
inevitable absurdities: "Essayons de nous représenter les terreurs de l'homme
d'autrefois. Essayons de nous mettre dans la peau de ces gens-là, dont les modes
de penser et de sentir ne dépassent pas, au vrai, ceux du primitif le plus sauvage
perdu dans la forêt équatoriale," *Culture*, p. 33.

What are likely to have been the sources of Pachomius's view in such matters? Given his remote setting in Upper Egypt, and his no more than moderate erudition, it is all too easy to take refuge in generalities about "the temper of the age" or launch ourselves upon a broad discussion of late antique religion. It is, of course, perfectly reasonable to suppose that the intellectual proximity of Alexandria was of some importance to Pachomius's understanding of the cosmos and its forces, and that the speculations of Origen, or of Neoplatonism generally, would have penetrated to some degree even the towns and villages of the Thebaid. We have touched upon that possibility in mentioning the resurrection, and there are connections we shall explore further in a later section of this chapter.[75] But we may be brought surprisingly close to Pachomius himself by one ancient text in particular—because it was widely read in Egypt, because it has much to say about visions and the heart, because it appealed beyond the philosophic circle to all serious Christian lay people intent upon practical self-improvement, because its notion of spirit, law, and inner life had roots in Judaic as well as other traditions, and because it had influenced Origen, and taught the value of γνῶσις while maintaining an acceptable standard of orthodoxy: *The Shepherd* of Hermas.[76] More than the heady products of Alexandrian theology, it was such a work as this that could have influenced the homiletic exegesis of the local Egyptian churches and thus stirred the minds of Pachomius and of the peasants, artisans, and bureaucrats among whom he lived.

Several aspects of *The Shepherd* deserve our attention. First, a clear link is established between virtues and vices on the one hand, and an-

75. A useful beginning is François Vandenbroucke's article "Démon" in *Dictionnaire de spiritualité*, 18–19: 141–238, especially the sections on the early Fathers by J. Daniélou, 152–89, and on early monks by A. and C. Guillaumont, 189–212. More up-to-date, more extensive, but less informative on the monastic material, is C. D. G. Müller's corresponding article "Geister" in *Reallexikon für Antike und Christentum*, 9:546–797. Extremely useful also is E. C. E. Owen, "Δαίμων and Cognate Words," *Journal of Theological Studies* 32 (1931): 133–53, much of which contributed to the *Greek Patristic Lexicon*. Ruppert makes much of the Alexandrian connection, pp. 117f.

76. On its popularity in Egypt, see Roberts, *Manuscript*, esp. p. 63, but also 42, 45, and 59. Most readily accessible to English readers will be the translation I have used here, by Kirsopp Lake, *The Apostolic Fathers*, vol. 2. More information is supplied in his introduction by R. Joly, *Hermas, Le Pasteur*. The best edition of the text is by Molly Whittacker in the *GCS* series. See the Bibliography, Sources, under "Hermas," for full details. The *Shepherd* was considered sufficiently "canonical" to be included in part in the *Codex Sinaiticus*, the famous fourth-century and possibly Egyptian MS of the Bible. Clement of Alexandria had already accorded it influential praise, *Stromata*. 1.29. For guidance on this background, my particular thanks to Brian Daley and Massey H. Shepherd.

gels and demons on the other. The focus is for the most part on the moral quality, on activity and behavior. There is scarcely any attempt to name the various spirits so that they might be made to people some envisioned cosmology. That was one of the major distinctions between a work like *The Shepherd* and the more gnostic treatises among the Nag Hammadi codices. It was a book that set the reader to work, not to dream.[77] Second, Hermas makes it clear, amid his visions, that he is concerned most with inner events. The desire to purify his hearers' hearts (καθαρίσαι τὰς καρδίας ὑμῶν) and instill true wisdom (φρόνησις) distinguishes the Christian teacher from the "sorcerers," who "carry their charms in boxes."[78] Hermas makes constant allusion to "having the Lord in your heart." That there is only one heart modifies also the dualism for which he has been unjustly famous. When he writes, "there are two angels [ἄγγελοι] with man, one of righteousness and one of wickedness," he makes it clear that both make themselves known by entering the one heart (ἐπὶ τὴν καρδίαν) and by making an impact on the one conscious mind.[79] Hence the importance of a third aspect of his spirituality: an ascetic dynamism. There is movement in this heart, and in particular a mechanism for change. Knowledge of self leads to fear of God and induces repentance.[80] The Christian must therefore pack his heart, as it were, with good thoughts and virtues, and thus exclude those evil thoughts and vices that would otherwise force entry. With a call to that task, *The Shepherd* makes its dramatic opening. One evil desire (πονηρὰ ἐπιθυμία) is enough to subvert the soul: that is the ἁμαρτία μεγάλη, the great sin. "The righteous man has righteous designs [δίκαια βουλεύεται]. . . . But they who have evil designs in their hearts bring upon themselves death and captivity."[81] There is no room for "double-mindedness" (διψυχία), a constant emphasis:[82] whatever good we lay claim to within us must drive out the bad.[83]

77.   The practice of speaking evil of others is a δαιμόνιον, Shepherd, Mandates 2.3. Bad temper is a πονηρὸν πνεῦμα, ibid. 5.1.3. Hermas writes later of the "angel [ἄγγελος] of luxury and deceit," Similitudes 6.2.1. Maidens who appear to him in one vision are both good spirits, ἄγια πνεύματα, and virtues, as well as "powers [δυνάμεις] of the Son of God," ibid. 9.13 and 15. The variety of terms is both remarkable and characteristic.

78.   *Visions* 3.9.8.

79.   *Mand.* 6.2.1.

80.   *Simil.* 8.11.2. This is perhaps the most strikingly "Pachomian" passage in the whole work. Note also the earlier phrase, τὸ μετανοῆσαι . . . σύνεσίς ἐστιν μεγάλη, *Mand.* 4.2.2.

81.   *Vis.* 1.1.8.

82.   The most extensive explanation is in *Mand.* 9.

83.   Note the conflict between the πονηρὸν πνεῦμα and τὸ πνεῦμα τὸ ἄγιον, *Mand.* 5.1.2–3, and the development at 5.2.6–7.

Now it cannot be suggested with any security that Pachomius was directly influenced by those texts, although the possibility remains of close contact with Hermas's teaching. *The Shepherd*, with its known Egyptian audience, simply helps us to pinpoint certain attitudes, certain theological and ascetic categories, which, it will be obvious already, are reminiscent of much in the Pachomian corpus. It remains, therefore, to demonstrate how Pachomius might have made his own, not simply the general habits of mind characteristic of his age, but particular conceptions of the spiritual life available in his immediate surroundings.

One of the first things he taught his monks was how "to know blamelessly and without any ignorance the craftiness of the enemies [τῶν ἐχθρῶν], and to oppose them with the Lord's power [τῇ δυνάμει τοῦ Κυρίου]."[84] That δύναμις, the sheer strength of God himself, they would acquire by adopting a πολιτεία, a pattern of life, and specifically a program of ascesis, inspired by the life of Jesus and constantly enlivened by his grace and presence.[85] Each monk had to be, like Silvanos, "[a man] strong in the Spirit [δυνατὸν τῷ πνεύματι] and in whom was Christ."[86] In the corresponding passage of the *Paralipomena*, we find the same idea presented from a different angle: "Nothing so weakens the demon as humility coming with active power [μετὰ πρακτικῆς δυνάμεως] from the whole soul."[87]

That scarcely suggests that Pachomius and his followers were condemning themselves to a life of hallucination and anxiety. Yet the language alludes to demons: a "belief" in demons, if that is the correct word, was inextricably a part of that view of ascetic combat, together with a determination to resist their onslaughts. The belief and resolve had several important results of positive value. First, they encouraged introspection, a careful exploration of that self which the demons were supposedly intent upon destroying. Pachomius likened the self to a series of inner chambers. Within each one was nurtured some "fruit of the Spirit." Any weakness, no matter how deeply hidden in any one of those chambers, exposed the whole structure to the enemy. That very model encouraged also some clearer understanding of how to counter the threat. A monk would rule his heart, mount adequate guard, and

84. G¹ 56, not in Bo. Note the link between power and knowledge.
85. G¹ 73. There is obscurity in the phrase καὶ κατ᾽ αὐτῶν πολιτευόμενοι. Veilleux translates, with Halkin's text, "if you practise ascesis against them [referring back to the demons]." Festugière suggests αὐτόν for αὐτῶν and translates, "si vous vous conduisez conformément à lui [referring back to Christ]"; see *Première Vie grecque*, p. 38. Bo 67 is somewhat briefer, and offers no assistance.
86. G¹ 105.
87. *Paral.* 2 (4). There is a fainter echo in Am, p. 532.

achieve adequate control of the passageways within only when God was ruler there, "seated as upon a throne."[88]

At the same time the demons remained in important ways exterior to the self. Pachomius was not thinking here of literal possession, or of any radical subversion of the personality. Like other famous Egyptian ascetics, he believed that he and his colleagues were witnesses to a cosmic conflict between God and the spirits of evil, but it was a conflict for the most part quite independent of their own states of soul.[89] Dwelling in his mind on the evils that men wrought, for example, a monk might well lose touch with God, but awareness of demons and the evil done by them would leave his self-possession and potential openness to God unthreatened.[90] It was natural that demons should occasionally "appear" (with God's permission), as they did to Antony and Pachomius—mainly, let it be noted, during the early stages of their asceticism.[91] But that very "reality," as it was thought of, helped the ascetic to distinguish the demon from the λογισμοί, the thoughts that the demon might insinuate into his mind. That was the second positive result of Pachomius's careful reflection. Λογισμοί were not always, of course, the work of demons, nor always "bad." That, too, he knew well. The word refers to all processes of discursive reasoning. At times, however, they might provoke in a monk anxiety or false ambition and desire, they might intrude upon more intuitive experience, or they might simply disturb his tranquility or attention to the matter in hand. Not all ascetics at the time were able to distinguish so readily between the mental tension and inconsistency proper to the monk himself and the plots hatched against him by spiritual forces from "outside." Poemen warned that an ascetic might think he was engaging with evil spirits when he was victim of nothing more than his own ill-disciplined inclinations: "our desires [θελήματα] turn into demons."[92] In the Letter of Ammon, Theodore warns the monk Mou-

88. G[1] 75; virtually the same in Bo 67. God, displacing evil, is active in the monk's attempt to acquire virtue. The point will recur. But see Ruppert, pp. 110f.

89. See my "Desert Fathers"; and note Cassian, Conferences 8.12.

90. Apophthegmata patrum, Macarius 36.

91. Life of Antony 5f; G[1] 18f, Bo 21; God's permission necessary, G[1] 87. There may be some difference here between Antony and Pachomius. The latter appears to have experienced such vivid apparitions less and less. Antony suggested, by contrast, that they represented a lasting sense of frustration on the part of evil spirits, in the face of the self-possession achieved by an ascetic in his years of maturity. On the other hand, Antony implied that there might be an even later stage in ascetic experience, when demonic attack might take the form of pressure from one's fellow monks; that was a danger Pachomius would have appreciated. See Life of Antony 23 and 25.

92. Apophthegmata patrum, Poemen 67.

saios not to blame demons for his own "thoughts" (ἐνθυμήσεις, διαλο-
γισμοί): "the demons have not yet been permitted to attack you [another
important factor]; but by becoming so full of weeds, you prepare broad
pasture for demons, drawing them upon yourself by evil counsels."[93]

His clear view of inner thoughts and emotions was the point most at
issue during Pachomius's appearance at the Synod of Latopolis. His opponents were perfectly happy to take for granted his power over demons, even his ability to see them. What made them anxious was that
"great thing," his διορατικόν or clear-sightedness. That was the quality
in himself Pachomius was most concerned to defend: his ability to judge
character, to assess the quality of λογισμοί, and hence the spiritual
needs of his subjects. It was a gift that had brought him by that time
great peace of mind and kept him quite untouched by the turmoil of the
demonic world. Whatever perception did not spring from natural talent,
he said, or from long acquaintance with the ascetics concerned, was to
be attributed entirely to the generosity and inspiration of God.[94] One is
not surprised, therefore, to see what the mature Pachomius considered
as really dangerous λογισμοί, real threats to spiritual achievement:
temptations against chastity, predictably, but also the love of power, hesitation in the face of effort, hatred of the brethren, desire for money.
Faced with such inclinations, he could cry out against demons; we should
note in what terms: "How shall I join you apostates in a thought of blas-
phemy against the God who created me [πῶς . . . λογίζωμαι σὺν ὑμῖν]?
. . . These [thoughts] are not mine but yours." Those were also the
threats that sprang to his mind in symbolic form during his vivid nightmares about the future of his communities—love of power and desire
for money in particular. He may have called them visions, but neither he
nor anyone else was fooled into thinking that they were mere phan-
tasms conjured by evil spirits before his eyes.[95]

Both "events" in the ascetic's spiritual struggle, the inner λογισμοί
and the "appearance" of demons, were distinguished even further by
Pachomius from the ὀπτασία τῶν ἁγίων, the vision that a holy man
might be expected to enjoy. During such, one would lose consciousness
of the self: λογισμοί would be no longer present. It was easy to tell good
visions from bad ones, therefore. When a demon was involved, or a
phantasm projected, then λογισμοί would still disturb the mind. Pachomius was faced once suddenly with Christ himself, as it seemed, but he
reflected without hesitation, "Now here I am seeing this [apparition]

93. *Letter of Ammon* 24.
94. G¹ 112. See also *Letter of Ammon* 16.
95. G¹ 96, not in Bo's equivalent.

and conscious and reasoning [φρονῶ καὶ λογίζομαι]. It is clear that he deceives me."[96]

All of this could make precise self-knowledge still something of a fearful prospect, but the fear was now less naive. That was the third positive result of Pachomius's reflective power. The true vision of divine realities, not the demons, induced most fear. One fear, as it were, drove out the other.[97] The loss of self-consciousness just mentioned could be an unnerving experience—"I was so afraid that it was as if I were no more"—but it was a fear worth having. Pachomius prayed that both he and the brothers might experience it always, as had Moses and his companions when faced with the fire of God's presence on Mount Sinai. It was a fear linked also with experiences described in earlier sections of this chapter: the sense of God's presence and the arrival at a level of true insight shared carefully with one's disciples. Given "the hidden things [Pachomius] happened to see by the Lord's will," those disciples could only conclude, "it is as if, in their minds, the holy ones were in heaven always."[98]

Through familiarity, then, with a "demon culture," with its terminology and above all with its imagery, Pachomius and his followers arrived at other perceptions more intelligible in our time and in the long term more important to themselves. They recognized more keenly that the ascetic task was an inner one, that it called for patient effort over long periods, that it demanded, above all, the careful identification and control of λογισμοί, and that it would result in greater closeness to God, albeit a closeness touched by awe. Returning, therefore, to our earlier

96. G¹ 87, but notice how the incident ends with Pachomius reaching out his hand and breathing on the apparition. The deception was very real! Bo 113 is less precise; see also Am, p. 542. S² may provide a context, trans. Lefort, Vies, p. 8: so Festugière, Première Vie grecque, pp. 116f. Note the fear of God, a wall behind which a monk may lie hidden, Dion. 48/G² 81; this is an element added, perhaps, by following Paral. 10 (24–26).

97. Apophthegmata patrum, Serapion 3. Compare the two fears in Hermas, Shepherd, Mand. 6.2.

98. All in G¹ 88. Bo 73, which may be more reliable, is certainly more vivid: the vision is actually described, as in S¹⁰ and in Am pp. 442f. G¹ 88 only says that Pachomius did recount it, without providing details. See Festugière, Première Vie grecque, p. 46, and compare the problem alluded to in n. 66 above. Letter of Ammon 10f refers to the same event.

theme, we note that the Pachomian sources acknowledge a monk's capacity to grow in the spiritual life and that this growth is now seen to be predominantly a growth in self-knowledge. As Palamon had said at the very beginning, "We will be ready, in so far as our weakness allows, to labor with you until you get to know yourself."[99] The monk's understanding could involve a degree of fear, but it matured eventually in liberty, vision, and composure.

That inner achievement is described also in the texts as "purity of heart"; with that phrase we probably come closest to Pachomius's spiritual ambition. Early references are marked by simplicity, but anticipate clearly the ultimate achievement envisaged. The purity sought for, as we have noted, was that described in the Beatitudes: "blessed are the pure in heart, for they shall see God." The attempt to gain both the purity and the vision quickly inspired Pachomius to define the heart itself as an inner sanctum, upon which he felt obliged to mount constant watch, as if behind "a bronze door secured against robbers."[100] There was, again, fear involved—a fear inseparable from that all-important watchfulness, a fear also that helped to purge the heart: "Just as fire cleanses all rust and burnishes the objects, so the fear of God consumes every evil in man."[101] But Pachomius, somewhat like Hermas, was more intent upon substituting one state of mind for another: "In his struggle he did not allow a foul thought to settle in his heart . . . he set his mind intently upon gaining the fear of God."[102] The process was akin to that mentioned above, the careful occupation of each chamber in the heart by God "seated as upon a throne."[103] Here Pachomius came closest to the later and more schematic developments of Evagrius and Cassian, who emphasized in detail the steps whereby unacceptable inclinations— which they, too, often called λογισμοί—were to be gradually displaced by positive alternatives.[104] Pachomius may not have had direct access to

99.   Bo 10, not explicit in G^1 6.
100.   Both in G^1 18. Compare the handling of the inner and the outer man in *Life of Antony* 28, which I misinterpreted in my *Ascetics*, p. 47 n. 83.
101. G^1 104, not in Bo, but in some Sahidic texts. G^1 96, not in Bo 72. Note that in Dion. 46 there is a clearer understanding of how fear leads to self-knowledge. The text is independent of G^1, and even improves on G^2.
102. G^1 18.
103.   See n. 88 above.
104.   On philosophical antecedents, A. Guillaumont is exhaustive: *Évagre le Pontique, traité pratique ou le moine*, 1:63–84. Origen was central: see further H. Crouzel, "Origène, précurseur du monachisme," in *Théologie de la vie monastique*, pp. 15–38; his *Origène et la "connaissance mystique"*; and his *Théologie de l'image de Dieu chez Origène*; W. Seston, "Remarques sur le rôle de la pensée d'Origène dans les origines du monachisme," *Revue de l'histoire des religions* 108 (1933): 197–213;

the philosophical sources that inspired those later theorists, but the affinities remind us, again, that he almost certainly developed his ideas in the light of the same general traditions.[105]

Watchfulness, of course, was not identical with the spiritual goal, the purity. Rather, it was one of the means by which one achieved it. Method was never far from Pachomius's mind. Dionysius, expanding an early passage in the *Vita Prima*, points to the need for a dependence on scripture in this task of purging and of substitution; it was scripture Pachomius memorized with such care and sang aloud to keep the demons at bay.[106] In that light we can link our more interior-directed inquiry with all those prescriptions about *meditatio* in the *Rules* and the *Lives* and see how closely they contributed to Pachomius's strictly spiritual program.

W. Völker, *Das Vollkommenheitsideal des Origenes.* Λογισμός for Origen was chiefly demon-inspired, while for the Stoics, who valued psychic taxonomy, it was not; that may cast some light on Pachomius's greater openness to the "natural" aspects of growth in virtue. Attention to Stoic terminology is rewarding: not only λογισμός, but also, e.g., ἐνθυμήματα and its associates. See D. E. Hahm, *The Origins of Stoic Cosmology*; J. M. Rist, *Stoic Philosophy*; and M. Spanneut, *Le Stoicisme des pères de l'église*. It is also possible to associate some of Pachomius's language with that of the gnostics, but central to their conception of reality was the notion of dualism, a division within the individual as well as in the cosmos. Such division was forcefully opposed by Pachomius, as it was by the majority of Stoics. For both of them, reason could be both victim and master of passions and thoughts. Gnostics were not always secure in that conviction. Clement of Alexandria, in his criticism of Basilides and Valentinus, shows how cautious the orthodox had to be in identifying acceptable alternatives. Basilides may have been dismissed with relative ease, since he appears to have thought of passions as real spirits, clinging to reason in animal form (Clement, *Stromata* 2.20.112). Valentinus sounds much more like Pachomius: purity of heart means displacement of evil spirits by the presence of Jesus, neglect will lead to a repossession of the soul by its enemies, but the healing influence of God offers light and vision (*Stromata* 2.20.114). Clement makes it clear that, while the goals and categories—vision and purity—were acceptable enough, the real debate was about the methods whereby such changes were achieved. See, as an introduction, the article "Basilide" by G. Bardy in *Dictionnaire d'histoire et de géographie ecclésiastiques*, 6:1169–75.

105. In addition to the light thrown on these matters by our use of *The Shepherd*, we should recall also the importance of Athanasius, who seems to have inspired Pachomius directly. His treatise *On Charity and Temperance*, the source for much in the *CMR*, sounds exactly like the G¹ passage just alluded to: "We were given purity and watchfulness, through which God will dwell in us, for purity is God's temple and watchfulness his resting place," Athanasius, *Lettres festales et pastorales*, trans. Lefort, p. 95. The second phrase is omitted by Pachomius, *CMR* 43. Recall also Lefort, "S. Athanase écrivain copte." Further connections are discussed below.

106. Dion. 16.

He would have said, as Poemen did when questioned about purity of heart, that "the man who hears the word of God often, opens his heart to the fear of God."[107] That purging quality of God's word marked also the beginning of a theology of prayer: "The word of God had proved him [Theodore] through fire and strengthened him to mind the things which are above."[108] Moreover, the process of *meditatio* had to be constant. Silvanos was praised as a man who had passed beyond the need for watchfulness. In that, he could be contrasted with such avowedly great figures as Petronios, Cornelios, and even Theodore himself, who, once they relaxed their ascetic efforts, would fall victim to the devil and find themselves back where they started.[109] But that simply demonstrated how much of an exception Silvanos was. Another anecdote makes the point quite clear. Mauo, a *praepositus* of long standing, objected strongly to the suggestion by Pachomius that one might never achieve lasting success in the spiritual life, that one was condemned to work at one's problems again and again, without certain progress. Mauo thought himself "firmly set" ($\dot{\epsilon}\sigma\tau\eta\rho\iota\gamma\mu\acute{\epsilon}\nu o\nu$): "are we good only to fall every hour?" But, Pachomius said, insecurity, even when balanced by God's mercy, was the true, lasting, and inevitable state of the soul.[110]

So purity of heart was not a guarantee of spiritual achievement or a quality of the monk's final state of perfection, but rather a condition upon which that achievement was based. We have to take one final step in our inquiry, therefore, and ask what, given watchfulness, did purity of heart make possible?

A frequently quoted remark in the *Vita Prima* says of Pachomius, "because of the purity of his heart he was, as it were, seeing the invisible God as in a mirror [$\dot{\omega}\varsigma\ \dot{\epsilon}\nu\ \dot{\epsilon}\sigma\acute{o}\pi\tau\rho\omega$]."[111] Purity, therefore, appears to point beyond itself to vision. There is something, however, suspiciously literary about the final words in particular;[112] they prompt us to inquire

107. *Apophthegmata patrum*, Poemen 183.
108. G[1] 78, Bo 70.
109. G[1] 105. Among many variations, which tend to narrow the issue to one of sexuality, the point persists in *Paral.* 2 (4) and Am, pp. 531f. S[5] is missing at that point.
110. G[1] 76. Again, there are variations. S[10] is much fragmented, trans. Lefort, *Vies*, pp. 33f. Am, pp. 427f suggests that that textual tradition may have been rather different. The point does recur in Bo 68, although the phrase corresponding to $\dot{\epsilon}\sigma\tau\eta\rho\iota\gamma\mu\acute{\epsilon}\nu o\nu$ has been displaced, suggesting that one author was making a special point: see Festugière, *Première Vie grecque*, p. 40 n. 2.
111. G[1] 22.
112. Dion. and G[2] do not make, in their equivalent passage, quite that emphasis, and concentrate more on a transition from darkness to light, from ignorance to joy. See Dion. 19f, which also appeals to Heb. 11.27, "as seeing him who is invisible," but not to 1 Cor. 13.12, "now we see in a mirror dimly." Corresponding is G[2] 20.

what antecedents may have been available to the writer. The notion of "mirror" was inevitably linked, for a Greek, with that of "image." Besides its long history in the Origenist tradition, "image" was a concept about which the patriarch Athanasius had a lot to say, in ways that bring us close to the Pachomian point. He built specifically on the general connections he was able to make (in company with many others) between monastic retreat, tranquility, and vision.[113] In a *Festal Epistle*, he wrote of sinners, "They do not resemble the saints, reflecting the image neither of their way of life nor of that true wisdom by which a man becomes a reasonable being, conformed to the image of God."[114] In the treatise *On Charity and Temperance*, Athanasius used the phrase "humility in the face of a neighbor, the image of God."[115] Pachomius did not reproduce those words in the *Instruction Concerning a Spiteful Monk*, but he did echo the earlier passage: "It is the same with a man who hates his brother. He walks in darkness and does not know God because, with the hatred that comes from enmity blocking his eyes, he does not see the image of God."[116] In conjunction with those Athanasian references, we have to reflect also, as in other contexts, upon the gnostic associations of the same terminology. As they formulated their views on purity of heart, both Pachomius and his biographers had not only to seek orthodox inspiration but also to prevent confusion with less acceptable speculations. In some of the mythologies revealed in Nag Hammadi, for example, God might see his image in the mirror of creation, and in human beings above all.[117] Nor was Pachomius alone in so grappling with his own chosen tradition and with those who challenged it. At least one other Egyptian master, recommending silence and solitude to his companions, likened those blessings to a still pool that happened to be at hand: "and as they approached the water, they saw their faces there, as in a mirror [ὡς ἐν ἐσόπτρῳ]."[118]

Here we have another fascinating glimpse of the theoretical setting within which Pachomius may have worked and of the careful path he had to tread among the traditions available to him. In whatever way we interrelate our Athanasian and gnostic allusions with the teaching of Pachomius himself, it is clear that he sought after insight or vision of some sort. Those less advanced in the spiritual life were exhorted to seek

113. Athanasius, *Lettres festales* 24, trans. Lefort, pp. 9f. In this instance his models were taken from the Old Testament.

114. *Lettres festales* 2, trans. Lefort, p. 7.

115. Trans. Lefort, p. 98.

116. Trans. Lefort, p. 9. Compare *CMR* 36; see also the later phrase in 41, "You have not respected my image."

117. Doresse, *Livres secrets*, pp. 58, 231f.

118. Anonymous apophthegma 134, ed. F. Nau, *Revue d'Orient chrétien* 13 (1908): 47.

out "a man of experience" (τινὰ ἐπιστήμονα), and to open themselves
quickly "to someone who has knowledge" (τῷ ἔχοντι τὴν γνῶσιν). Such,
clearly, was the type of person Pachomius hoped they would themselves
eventually become.[119] Perception was a gift that flowed from the mercy
of Jesus himself,[120] a gift that would always be available to those rightly
disposed.[121] But the Athanasian passages quoted above point the way to
a spiritual insight specifically characteristic of Pachomius himself. The
gift of perception reached its full flowering not in the sight of God face to
face but in orthodox belief, in truth and justice, in good works and cautious self-discipline. Those were the true miracles, the visible proof of
God's presence and effect. They were also achieved with the help of others—followers were "instructed by men of God," or attained understanding "through the help of some servant of God."[122] So Pachomius
was able to carry his teaching to a conclusion not only logical but social,
too, in its emphasis: "When you see a man who is pure and humble, that
is a vision great enough. For what is greater than such a vision, to see
the invisible God in a visible man, his temple?"[123] Continuing, he made
it clear that that kind of vision depended precisely on the διορατικόν he
would later defend at Latopolis, the capacity for insight that enabled
holy men to see "the thoughts of souls" (τῶν ψυχῶν τὰ ἐνθυμήματα).
When we recall the earlier passage in the *Vita Prima* that spoke of the
"mirror" in which the pure-hearted might see the invisible God, the
similarity of thought is obvious. But the twist in the logic, away from
tranquil contemplation and toward involvement with others, is altogether startling.

So we are able to make a summary of this whole stage in our investigation. Fear, even of demons, could lead to self-awareness. Self-
awareness led to self-knowledge and self-discipline. Those when combined brought purity of heart. Purity of heart could make possible the
vision of God, yes; but also—and, for Pachomius, perhaps even more
so—it encouraged a keener understanding of one's fellows. Just as freedom came with commitment to a new society, so self-possession in the
presence of God was shared with others. It was to a great extent defined
by that very sharing.

Is that a tentative way of suggesting that the final goal for Pachomius, reached by way of vision, was love? Love is a notion that proves
elusive in the Pachomian corpus. Fear, purity, knowledge, freedom,

---

119.   G¹ 96.   120.   G¹ 57.   121.   G¹ 112.
122.   G¹ 47, equally Bo 46.
123.   G¹ 48. Veilleux, *Koinonia*, 1:330, has omitted the first sentence without
explanation. Note again the allusion to Hebrews 11.27. Compare the conviction
of Theodore, n. 61 above.

goodness, gentleness—all of them are present, but love is less frequently made explicit. "This is the love of God," said Pachomius, "to have compassion for each other." [124] In its context, the remark evoked tolerance, patience, allowing people time, recognizing their weaknesses: in other words, the qualities of the guide and leader that we noted particularly in Chapters V and VI. If there were "Pachomian lovers," their aim was to help others, to set them free, without necessarily obliging them by some more intimate relationship. "Blessed are you," said the monk unrebuked even in his misplaced ambition, "for thanks to you I live." [125] Your understanding, in other words, has borne fruit in my quite independent self-knowledge and self-control. We are certainly dealing with more than the common social emphasis of the cenobite. Antony could make similar assertions about mutual responsibility, after all: "If we gain our brother, we gain God: if we scandalize our brother, we sin against Christ." [126] In the case of Pachomius, it was rather more a question both of deciding how caution, self-knowledge, and self-control were to be linked with generosity, with selflessness, with surrender to the influence of God, and of determining how such a connection, once made, would affect one's daily conduct among one's fellows. "God," said Pachomius, "wants nothing from men but fear and love [φόβον καὶ ἀγάπην]." The simplicity of the statement may suggest authenticity. It is also aggravating that Pachomius should persist in combining with such enigmatic brevity one element apparently having more to do with method and another more concerned with ultimate spiritual goals. It is only his biographer who then proceeds, by way of explanation, to quote St. Paul, "Love does no wrong to a neighbor." [127] However, it may not be fair to make too forceful a distinction between the virtues aimed at and the means employed in attaining them. Fear, in some senses, was no less a goal, and love was a method as well as an aim. Pachomius was never able to leave love standing on its own. The *Praecepta atque Iudicia* made exactly the same point as the dictum in the *Vita Prima* just quoted, complete with allusion to the same text of St. Paul: "Love is the fulfilling of the law for those who know that the time has come for us to wake up and that our salvation is nearer now than it was when we came to the faith." Love, for Pachomius also, was bound up with the notion of law, of common observance, and

124. G¹ 42, also in Bo 42.
125. Ibid., to "live" here meaning to persevere in the monastic life: see Chapter V at n. 54.
126. *Life of Antony* 9.
127. G¹ 119, alluding to Romans 13.10. If there is, in the first phrase, another allusion, to Deuteronomy 10.12, it is so modified as to suggest memory in Pachomius rather than quotation by his biographer. Bo 199 may point to the source of this tradition, without repeating the phrase.

with a sense of constructive unease at the thought of the day of salvation now so challengingly at hand.[128]

What the sources provide us with, therefore, even when "tidied" in so analytic a way, is a spiritual pathway more than an account of the destination. The reticence, the economy involved was undoubtedly deliberate. It helped Pachomius to avoid, among other things, a false γνῶσις and a false mythology. He fully accepted responsibility as a teacher, anxious always for individuals, in all their variety, and never content merely to create or transmit an abstract and beautiful view of the cosmos. So the goal a monk aimed at—and love must have been very close to its center—was always implied, rarely revealed. The confidence of those early disciples sprang not from a sense of arrival, but from recognizing new possibilities in themselves and from seeing in Pachomius a man who would guide them "straight to God."[129] The fear, the hope, the freedom, even the purity and the insight, were no more than instruments, and often it is only by reading between the lines that we can see what they were intended to gain. The *delectatio* that came from prayer and companionship, the sense of "feasting in heaven," the desire for enduring contact with "the humility and the sweetness" of Jesus himself: those were not experiences that a rule could impose or even a biographer adequately describe. They had to be discovered and recognized by each monk personally, often in moments of unexpected loneliness and silence.

128.   *Plud*, introduction.
129.   G¹ 25.

· VIII ·

MONASTERY AND WORLD

So much for the inner, personal goals of the ascetic life as Pachomius envisaged it. But none of those goals was pursued in total isolation from society. It is doubtful whether even hermits were that remote in their endeavors, but certainly the members of Pachomius's monasteries were not. The formation of the communities, the conduct of daily life and the development of structure and authority, even the most intimate pursuit of spiritual ideals—all took place under the scrutiny of those who were not members of the *Koinonia*. Indeed, curiosity could be persistent and intrusive, drawing people of widely differing levels of talent or office, often from far afield, to visit the communities and see their way of life for themselves. The impact upon the founder and his followers was far from negligible.

So, having observed Pachomius's own development and that of his "cenobitic system," we must now return to the world of Chapter I, and in particular to the towns and villages of the Thebaid. We must show in more detail how our "portrait of a province" does supply a setting for the more specifically monastic information provided in our intervening chapters. What did people "outside" think of Pachomius's experiment? What did they contribute toward it? How were they regarded by the monks themselves?

Let us examine first the simple matter of hospitality. There seems to be some evidence for a certain nervousness in relations between the community and the world around it. One might speak almost of suspicion, of fear, of a constant desire to protect monks from outside influ-

ence. It was not a question of theoretical unease about the monastic vocation or about the degree of responsibility communities should accept
for the material needs or the spiritual improvement of local people. There
may have been ideological conflict among biographers on that point,
some supporting wide concern, others isolation. And there was always
a danger—readily acknowledged—that service to others would awaken
admiration or gratitude among the "worldly," which might lead a monk
in turn to conceit.[1] But even Pachomius himself, at least during his early
years, could offer practical assistance to those around him—entertaining
guests, visiting the sick, taking part in local worship.[2] It was much more
in detailed prescriptions for regular conduct that the anxieties appeared.
Monks were forbidden to go out alone,[3] and when they returned, they
were not allowed to speak about anything they had seen or heard,[4] even
if they had simply been visiting another monastery.[5]

Yet it is clear enough, even if we judge by nothing but the *Rules*, that
monks themselves could expect a constant stream of visitors. These were
received gladly, even if with caution. Priests and other clerics, for example, were to be shown due honor on such occasions. The monks were
willing to pray with them during the *synaxis*. They would not eat with
them,[6] but the visitors shared a separate eating place with many other
strangers, including laity as well as monks.[7] Indeed, even the community's own novices may have taken their meals in the same place.[8]

Such an arrangement raises interesting questions. How clear, for example, was the distinction, at least in the early days, between a visitor
and a recruit? Recruitment is scarcely mentioned in most of the sources.
It seems to have been taken for granted that prospective monks would
simply arrive at the gate in a guaranteed stream; for that very reason
visitors had to be welcomed as well as scrutinized. The careful arrangements made by Pachomius for the reception, instruction, and eventual
promotion of Theodore of Alexandria (already ἀναγνώστης καὶ ἀσκητής)
are clear illustration of that.[9]

1. Bo 35.
2. Some details were discussed, along with the underlying ideology, in
Chapter III at nn. 9f, 19, 31f.
3. *P* 56.
4. *P* 57, 86.
5. *P* 85: indeed, even if they had been visiting another house in their own
monastery! According to Palladius, Pachomius was afraid that Macarius of Alexandria might not be equal to the rigors of Tabennesi or to the virtues of its
monks: "you will be scandalized and you will leave, speaking ill of them," *HL*
18.13. That may have been partly why the absence of fugitives had to be reported
within three hours: there was a fear of what they might say elsewhere, *PInst* 12.
6. *P* 51.   7. *P* 50.   8. G¹ 28, Bo 26.
9. G¹ 94, Bo 89; see also G¹ 95, 111.

So, by maintaining in some instances a cautious segregation, what other distinctions was Pachomius intent upon enforcing? He was taken to task, on one occasion, by Dionysios, the priestly οἰκονόμος of the nearby church at Nitentori, because he would not allow visiting monks to eat with his own brethren. He replied that he was anxious to protect his *visitors*; visitors, that is, rather than, as one might have supposed, his own community. Many of his monks, he said, as beginners in the spiritual life, did not know how to behave without giving scandal.[10] So defensive an anecdote is not entirely convincing. Not just clergy and monks came to visit, or even potential monks. Certainly, relatives could be expected. A member of the community may have visited his family, although he would have been careful not to eat in their company. Such journeys were allowed if a relative was sick—indeed, it was easier to visit the sick than it was to attend the funerals of the dead. And so relatives would visit the monastery in return. Permission was required, of course, but it could be obtained, and one could expect relatives to bring even gifts of food.[11] Women, too, were received with great honor, although strictly segregated while present in the monastery precincts.[12]

Rarely would such comings and goings have been tolerated simply as a preliminary to enrollment in the community. At least by the end of the century, therefore, relaxation of the barriers separating monastery and world seems to have been afoot on other grounds, in spite of earlier emphasis that leaving the world meant, perhaps more than anything else, leaving one's family. Yet we may usefully recall the compromise, even the contradiction, when Theodore's mother came to call, demanding at least to see her son and flourishing the written support of bishops.[13] Perhaps, in that instance, it *was* the character of recruitment that was most at issue. Theodore's adhesion to the Pachomian cause may have provoked resentment. At least once, he thought himself of leaving. Now, perhaps, he was to be forcibly withdrawn. On the other hand, his own brother showed some inclination to join him, and perhaps even his mother had it in mind to stay in the women's community. The incident may explain in part why Pachomius was anxious that families should develop a sound understanding of why a relative might desire to join a monastic community, and that a family's attitude should be taken into account before a recruit could be admitted.[14] Openness to the world,

10.   G¹ 40, Bo 40. "Neophytes" here may not mean novices in a strict sense. Note the caution concerning *peregrini* (wanderers) in the rule presented by the angel, Dion. 22.

11.   P 53–55. For an example, G¹ 67, Bo 63. Visiting sick relatives within the community was also regulated, P 47.

12.   P 52.

13.   For both points, see Chapter III at nn. 68f, as also P 49.

14.   G¹ 24, also discussed in Chapter III.

therefore, and withdrawal of recruits from it, were policies that could be closely interwoven.

The story of Theodore's mother, so full of vigor and character, may usefully illustrate another influence upon the Pachomian experiment. The lady, as we have said, appeared at the monastery gate armed with a letter or letters, "ordering the boy to be given back to her."[15] The *Vita Prima* is strangely coy at this point, saying that "she came with letters from bishops." The Bohairic *Life* and the Arabic tradition are more explicit: she brought a personal letter, addressed to Pachomius, from the bishop of Sne (Latopolis).[16] Latopolis was quite possibly Theodore's home town; certainly it was in that area he first engaged in the ascetic life. If we may judge by the declaration of the Bohairic *Life* ("born into a prominent family"), by the Christianity of his parents, and by his distaste for their prosperity, it seems likely that his mother was an influential member of the church community there.[17] Latopolis lay well to the south of the two great centers of Pachomian endeavor, Phbow/Tabennesi and Šmin (Panopolis). Yet there, for no clear reason (beyond some reference to a vision), Pachomius made his last foundation, Phnoum. In doing so, he met with bitter opposition: "the bishop of that diocese got a large crowd together; they set out and rushed at [Pachomius] to drive him out of the place."[18] And there, of course, he faced his "trial," just before his death. We shall describe the events in detail shortly. They took place much later than the visit here discussed, but they may cast some light on the caution and reticence displayed by Pachomius toward Theodore's mother and underscore the dangerous naivety of Theodore's own intolerant adhesion to principle, namely his refusal to see her. Pachomius must have been at least slightly embarrassed by the interference of even so distant a bishop; it was perhaps partly for that reason that he was driven to compromise, trying for a time to persuade Theodore that he should change his mind. On the other hand, it may be that the differences between versions of the story point to the threats felt by later monks in different situations and to the uncertainties generated by Pachomius's problem. Well might Cassian have exclaimed, quite possibly on the basis of his Egyptian experience, "Avoid women and bishops."[19]

Three points should be clear so far. Monasteries, first, were on the

15.   So G¹ 37, but in Bo 37 Pachomius is asked simply, "that he might allow her son Theodore to come out and that she might see him."

16.   Bo 37, Am, p. 405.

17.   G¹ 33, Bo 31.

18.   Bo 58. G¹ omits that information, but Am, pp. 574f, is even more emphatic; see also S⁴ 58.

19.   Cassian, *Institutes* 11.18.

public map. Not only did people know and care where they were; they came to examine, to lodge, and to stay. Secondly, families were not entirely severed by the walls around the communities. Duty, as well as sentiment, retained its hold over those who had "left the world"—at least the duty of respect for elders, of material concern for living relatives, of remembrance of those dead. Finally, the office-holders of the church were beginning to express keen interest in monastic development. Not only did they visit, and even enroll themselves in the communities; they also attempted at least to monitor, even to control, the whole process whereby members were recruited.

That last feature will demand our further attention. We must examine now, however, the economic context. The visits, the enduring bonds of kinship, even the official interference, remind us how close the monasteries were to other settlements, whether village or town. That proximity, and the commerce it encouraged, made those other contacts both possible and less surprising.

A striking episode helps us to link the world of curiosity and recruitment with a more commercial *ambiance*. To the north of the early foundations, near Diospolis Parva, a certain Petronios had founded a monastery called Thbew. He came from a wealthy Christian family, like Theodore, and his monastery was built (the text is explicit) on his parents' lands. Ascetics gathered about him—"anyone who wanted to live in Christ." Two developments followed, although it is not entirely clear in what order. Thbew applied to join the *Koinonia*, receiving housemasters and seconds according to the familiar pattern, and Petronios's own family joined his community—his father, Pšenthbo, at least one brother, Pšenapahi, and some of his sisters and other relatives. Pachomius's federation inherited, therefore, at least part of a family estate, and also "slaves" (mentioned explicitly in the *Vita Prima*), together with "sheep, goats, cattle, camels, donkeys, carts, and all he possessed, including boats."[20] What matters here is not simply the influx of wealth, but the acquisition of what may have been a large and viable agricultural unit. Unless we are to believe that those assets were immediately sold off, it would have been hard to draw thereafter a clear line between the monastic community and the personnel and industry now drawn within its orbit.

20.   G¹ 89, Bo 56 (which is clearer and more detailed).

What we have in the instance of Thbew is something halfway between, on the one hand, the haphazard adhesion of runaways or men cast adrift by changes in patterns of employment, ownership, and loyalty in the villages of the Nile, and, on the other, the formal endowment of the federation, by gift or legacy, with land and other forms of wealth. The possibilities attaching to both were outlined in Chapter I, but we have to remind ourselves constantly that firm proof of either comes much later than Pachomius.[21] One arresting piece of independent evidence lies in a document dated 367/68, which includes a tax return paid for the ἐποίκιον μοναστηρίου Ταβεννῆσε, which probably meant a property held by the whole federation rather than by Tabennesi alone.[22] Responsibility for payment of the tax was registered in the name of one Anoub, presumably because of his original association with the ἐποίκιον concerned. That raises the possibility that he brought the property with him at the time of his enrollment in a Pachomian monastery, probably one of Theodore's foundations at Nouoi or Kahior, visited by Athanasius only a few years before.[23] A comparison with Petronios is not far-fetched.

Obviously a process of acquisition was under way, though hardly simple or consistent in form. (No doubt distinctions in the type of land-holding and exploitation implied by the different foundations would have been clearer to a perceptive or anxious eye, even before 346.) Yet more important than those incipient gestures of generosity toward the monastery by the world was a movement in the other direction, no less

21. So the warning of A.D. 370/373 against "ignaviae sectatores, desertis civitatum muneribus," in the *Theodosian Code* 12.1.63: see Chapter I n. 33. The examples of endowment provided by A. Steinwenter, "Aus dem kirchlichen Vermögensrechte der Papyri," *Zeitschrift der Savigny-Stiftung für Rechtsgeschichte 75*, Kanonistische Abteilung 44 (1958): 1–34, even in the early pages, are similarly post-Pachomian. The legal distinctions outlined by Steinwenter, 20f, would have taken time to develop, although the separation of deserted village, donated estate, and suburban site is clearly adumbrated in the quite different establishments of Tabennesi, Thbew, and Šmin. E. Wipszycka, in *Les Ressources et les activités économiques des églises en Égypte du IVe siècle*, avoids concentration on the monastic evidence, p. 8, admits, again, its later date, p. 154, and warns that the abundant references may have accidentally survived to make this still an exceptional feature of Egyptian church life, pp. 36f.

22. E. Wipszycka, "Les Terres de la congrégation pachômienne dans une liste de payements pour les apora," *Hommages à Claire Préaux*, pp. 625–36. Wipszycka thought ἐποίκιον might refer to some abandoned property, not unlike the *agri deserti* of earlier foundations. For wider possibilities attaching to the word, see Marianne Lewuillon-Blume, "Problèmes de la terre au IVe siècle après J-C.," in *Actes du XVe congrès international de papyrologie*, 4: 177–85. (See Bibliography under International Congress of Papyrologists.)

23. So Wipszycka; see Bo 201–2, and G¹ 134.

economic in character. We have already described it in part in Chapter IV: manufacture and marketing, mainly in basketwork and related crafts. At an early stage, Pachomius made formal arrangements to support such a system: "he appointed other faithful brothers noted for their devotion to sell the monks' handiwork [τὸ ἔργον, simply] and to buy what they needed." [24] The monasteries were productive, therefore, and had an eye to their income. What is more forcefully implied is that they were not self-sufficient. The two characteristics were, of course, interrelated.

The matter extended beyond "handiwork." When the monks set off in columns in the morning, as described in Chapter IV, with their tools on their shoulders, where did they go? We begin to see that the monasteries might not have grown all their own food; they might find themselves set, as at Thbew, on viable property well in excess of their immediate enclave, to be worked in alliance with other peasants, even slaves; they might oversee, at least, if not share in the development of, land some distance away, as perhaps at Nouoi or Kahior. All the more important, therefore, are the early hints of what may have been afoot. In the First Sahidic *Life*, it is made clear that Pachomius's followers hired themselves out as agricultural laborers, probably on a seasonal basis, perhaps for money, more likely for an eventual share in kind. [25] It is not unreasonable to compare the behavior of ascetics further north, disclosed in the *Apophthegmata*. As in the *Lives*, there are vague references to harvesting; we must now admit the possibility, even in the case of Pachomius and his followers, that this may have been on others' property. [26] More frequently the references are precise. Macarius and six companions work with seculars, at the service of the "owner of the field" (τὸν κύριον τοῦ χωρίου, which suggests a village community); three unnamed ascetics earn a "share" (μισθός) at harvest time; Isaac tells of another "harvesting in a field," talking to the "foreman of the field" (τῷ κυρίῳ τοῦ ἀγροῦ). The last instance is interesting in the very obscurity of the final point: the ascetic asks if he may eat an ear of wheat; the foreman replies, "Father, this field belongs to you [Σός ἐστιν ὁ ἀγρός]." The humility of the request would be less striking if the reply were not to be taken literally. [27]

---

24. G¹ 28, Bo 26 (which says simply "to transact sales"). For the boats thereby made necessary, see Chitty, *Desert*, p. 25.

25. S¹ III (14).

26. *Apophthegmata patrum*, Isaac of the Cells 7.

27. Macarius 7; Nau 350, *Revue d'Orient chrétien* 17 (1912): 298f, reproduced in the Latin, *Verba seniorum* 17.20, PL 73.976; Isaac of the Cells 4. The warning to Theodore, in G¹ 107, Bo 95, brings together different classes of ascetic; the moral force of the parable they are able to share in understanding could only have meant anything to them against such a background.

Such semi-eremitic experiences were probably not far removed from Pachomius's world.

When income dwindled, crops failed, or employment receded, the
precarious economy of Pachomius's community was laid bare. So also,
however, was the closeness of the non-ascetic world. The *Paralipomena*
describe a famine, during which Pachomius tries to "borrow" wheat
from the state granary at Hermonthis. He is known to the official in
charge. He promises to return it at the next harvest. His agent, however,
has other plans. He buys wheat at the low price allowed by the friendly
official, promptly sells it publicly at a considerable profit, and is thus
able to return with even more than Pachomius planned for! The sequel
describes a virtuous reversal of this embarrassing success and the humiliation of the zealous agent, but what we should note is the useful
contact at Hermonthis, the familiarity with the market and the fiscal system, and the confidence in the following harvest.[28] The story can be
linked back to the *Lives*, because the agent was replaced by Zacchaeus,
mentioned in their text.[29] There is a similar story in earlier chapters.
Again, the community faces a shortage. A benefactor arrives in the nick
of time, diverting to the monks grain he had intended to donate elsewhere. Again, he was a πολιτευόμενος, like the official in the *Paralipomena*, and had heard of Pachomius; and again, the latter insisted on
arranging a date for the return of the gift.[30]

So here we have extremely varied evidence of contact between the
Koinonia and the society around it. Two features of the situation claim
special attention. The contact was not clearly planned, nor even fully
understood, and, almost as a consequence, it often gave rise to anxiety
and embarrassment. We saw in our opening section how distraction by
the curious and itinerant prompted haphazard regulations about entertaining guests and admitting visitors. And the conflicting demands of
loyalty and detachment, only partially foreseen and considered, provoked a corresponding contradiction of caution and compromise in the
face of family affection, sickness, jealousy, and loneliness. Furthermore,
as we shall examine in more detail, a failure to define the precise distinction, if any, between asceticism and church life led inevitably to mixed
feelings about the advantages of clerical services and support, and about
the return contribution by ascetics to the official structure of the church.
Now we can see that any desire to develop a society visibly different
from that of town and village would have been constantly undermined

28.   *Paral.* 9 (21f).
29.   G¹ 109, Bo 96.
30.   G¹ 39, Bo 39. S⁵ 53 seems closely related; there is no parallel in G¹ (Bo is
missing), but there is in Am, p. 569.

by financial and material insecurity and compromised by the very closeness of the markets, the fields, and the supplies upon which it too
often depended. In sum, therefore, the bonds between ascetic and
world, far from being challenged by any clear-headed attempt at separation, were reinforced by short-term necessity or pragmatic adaptation to
circumstance.

Yet anxiety did persist, at least as far as the economic aspects were
concerned. The *Instruction Concerning a Spiteful Monk* inveighs against
the love of money, a love revealed not only by greed, but also by a willingness to engage in trade, and by too great a commitment to work, leaving no leisure for the service of God. When one hears it suggested that
material store should be laid up in order that alms and resources for the
needy be at hand, one should detect temptation, and "remember what is
written, 'Your granaries and all they contain shall be accursed.'" [31]

The absorption of those Athanasian sentiments into the Pachomian
corpus may well have represented comment upon the controversies that
broke out after the founder's death, and in particular those surrounding
the monastery at Thmoušons. We spoke briefly of its incorporation in
Chapter III. The community had "existed of old," less than a day's journey from Phbow, under its leader Jonas, and had applied, like Šeneset
nearby, for membership in the federation. [32] During the first period of
government by Horsiesios, and under a new superior of its own, Thmoušons initiated some form of rebellion.

> And it happened after this, as the brothers had greatly increased in
> numbers, that they began to expand in fields and many material things
> in order to feed the multitude. And each monastery began to be a little
> negligent as other preoccupations increased. A certain Apollonios, fa-
> ther of the monastery of Thmoušons, wanted—contrary to the rule of
> the *Koinonia*—to buy himself superfluous commodities. Questioned
> about this by Horsiesios and reprimanded by him, he was vexed. By
> the enemy's temptation, he wanted to separate his monastery from the
> Community and he persuaded many elders of the monastery to do so.
> Many other monasteries were harmed by him because he had seceded,
> saying, "We no longer belong to the *Koinonia* of the brothers." [33]

These events, as we shall see in the final chapter, set in motion the resignation of Horsiesios. The Bohairic *Life* is not so explicit in linking the
crisis with a temptation to ownership and trade, and it fails to mention
that one of Theodore's first tasks on his appointment as successor to

31.   *CMR* 53.
32.   G^1 54. Bo 51 mentions Jonas, but then lacks some pages, to be supplied
by S^5 51f, trans. Lefort, *Vies*, pp. 246f.
33.   G^1 127. It was at Thmoušons that Pachomius killed off a fig tree to punish too zealous a cultivation, *Paral.* 12 (28–30).

Horsiesios was to regain, "after much struggle and spiritual understanding," the allegiance of Apollonios.[34] But the Bohairic writer does admit, with much greater detail, that the issue remained a long-term problem, even for Theodore, one that he came to admit he could not resolve any better than his predecessor. "When he observed that, owing to the excuse of needing food and other bodily needs, the monasteries had acquired numerous fields, animals, and boats—in a word, numerous possessions—he was deeply distressed. He felt certain that the feet of many had slipped from the right path because of material concerns and the empty cares of this world."[35] The two successors of Pachomius could do little but weep together. Horsiesios declared with resignation, "It is the Lord who has blessed the *Koinonia* and has expanded it. He also has the power to constrict it again." Theodore prayed and mourned by night at the tomb of Pachomius: "We have turned from the paths of life and from your laws and your commandments which you gave to our righteous father, over whose holy body I am now standing." He began to prepare at once for his own death.[36]

At the root of all such difficulties connected with location, family relationships, authority, and commerce, there lay an inability, perhaps even a reluctance, to make clear distinctions—not exactly a failure, but a caution, we might say, at the level of theory. For a long time it was far from clear what divided—what *should* divide—the *Koinonia*, in economic terms, from the villages around it. And what was to be the relationship between the ascetic community, which could be regarded as a relatively enclosed school of self-improvement, and the Christian body more generally, which was "apostolic" by virtue of an equally close relationship with God and Jesus, and by virtue of its wish to convert and assist the world around it?

34.   Bo 139, to correspond with G[1] 127; see G[1] 131 for Theodore's success. There may be a hint in Theodore's long catechesis that property had become a source of division: "now then, my brothers, you who are leaders of the holy places of God which he gave to our righteous father, I hear perverted words issuing from your mouths. Some in fact are saying, 'This monastery is mine,' others, 'This object is mine.' Now things of this sort ought not to take place here," Bo 142.
35.   Bo 197, G[1] 146. Note his reaction to widespread dismay when a boatload of monastic flax sank in the Nile, Bo 183.
36.   Bo 197–98.

The two obscurities were connected. Pachomius was still attempting to clarify, late in his life, the difference between his own endeavors and those of other ascetics. The *Koinonia* did not enjoy a monopoly of the evangelical life. That in itself blurred the edges between desert hermits, cenobites who lived close to the fertile valley, and religious devotees within the secular community. These last, in particular, made it hard for Pachomius to distance himself from the urban world. Our rich information about Oxyrhynchus tells us that there were twelve churches in the town, a large Christian population, and at least some ascetics, if not as many as the *Historia Monachorum* would like to suggest.[37] Oxyrhynchus was exceptional, but not unique. Christianity meant, for its citizens, not just asceticism, but the wider-ranging charity and hospitality that had attracted Pachomius at Thebes and that came to characterize his own communities. Other references confirm that we are dealing here with a level of religious order and dedication typical of the Egyptian church in its normal urban setting. The earliest so-named μοναχός we know of seems to have lived in a village and associated closely with local clergy.[38] Jerome, in his letter to Eustochium, mentions urban ascetics, if not entirely with approval.[39] The supposed *Canons of Athanasius* mention domestic virgins, and include ascetics generally in regulations concerning public order and fasting. These *Canons* may well represent fourth-century attitudes and practice.[40] More certainly genuine is Athanasius's tenth *Festal Epistle*, which insists that the word of God is addressed to all, and bears fruit in all, not just among ascetics: "all of us are within the wall, and all of us enter within the same fence."[41]

When we pursue this issue in the sources, what we discover, as in the passage just quoted, is ecclesiology—a debate not about monasticism but about the very nature of the church. That is not accidental. It is striking, for example, that in the *Instruction Concerning a Spiteful Monk*, where scriptural allusion and theological imagery had had time to crystallize around the growing social prescriptions of Egyptian Christianity, Pachomius is made to say, "If you are in the desert, do battle with prayers, fasting, and mortification. If you are among men, be wise as serpents and simple as doves."[42] This could have been taken as a distinction be-

---

37. *HM* (Greek) 5.1, tempered by Roberts, *Manuscript*, pp. 70f. See, for exhaustive material, *The Oxyrhynchus Papyri*.

38. E. A. Judge, "The Earliest Use of Monachos for 'Monk' (P. Coll. Youtie 77) and the Origins of Monasticism," *Jahrbuch für Antike und Christentum* 20 (1977): 72–89.

39. *Ep.* 22.35.   40. *Canons* 92, 98.

41. *Festal Epistles* 10, English translation, p. 71. Pachomius used the same image, with a gloss, G¹ 113: ἐκτὸς γενομένοις τοῦ τείχους ἤτοι τοῦ νόμου.

42. *CMR* 22.

tween the solitary and the cenobitic life. Yet the quotation from *Matthew* occurs originally in an apostolic, missionary context. In several early confrontations between Pachomius and other ascetics or churchmen, those two themes emerge. It is not our task to unravel them, as if we might thereby expose conscious contradictions in Pachomius's own mind. We use them only to show that a dialogue with the world was inevitable. It was part of the attempt to define rightly both the social status and what we may call the theological destiny of the Pachomian monk. Pachomius was intent upon serving God, but humanity also.[43] Specifically, he wished to save it as God wished it to be saved.[44] While he was with Palamon and his brother John, working out his own transition from the solitary to the cenobitic life, Pachomius cared for the poor and gave his surplus to those in need.[45] He worried whether it was right to involve himself in the problems of nearby villagers.[46] He was reminded that his own spiritual trials and successes were public events capable of encouraging others around him.[47] By the time a communal way of life had become established, Pachomius could take a simple Christian inclination—his own natural readiness to concern himself with the sufferings and needs of those outside his community—and show that it was not a distraction or a temptation, but an incentive to be equally generous toward the ascetic brethren with whom he lived *inside* the community each day. "We offer help to others, as God does himself—strangers, and the needy. Shall we not serve you with the same eagerness—one of our own, and so advanced in years?"[48]

It was not just a question of practical solicitude or of the resulting willingness to lay the ascetic community open to wider economic responsibilities. There was a truly pastoral motive at work. During his trial at Latopolis, Pachomius referred obliquely to himself as "someone trembling with all his heart for the loss of his neighbor."[49] And neighbor here was not defined by the monastery walls. Pachomius was one of those "saints" through whom the Lord would provide for "the salvation of souls" and perform "many . . . healings," "both among the worldlings [ἐν τοῖς κοσμικοῖς] and among the brothers."[50] In summing up his early teaching on the incarnation, the *Vita Prima* alludes to texts with a pastoral note, stressing that God reaches out to his people: from Isaiah, "I am coming to gather all the nations"; and from the Gospel, "The Word was made flesh and he lived among us."[51]

43. G^1 5, Bo 7; see the discussion in Chapter III at nn. 6 and 31f.
44. G^1 29, not explicit in Bo 25.   45. G^1 6, Bo 10.   46. Bo 9.
47. G^1 20.   48. G^2 87, also in *Paral.* 16 (35).   49. G^1 112.
50. G^1 45; Bo 45 is briefer.
51. G^1 56, not in Bo.

The inner disposition to pastoral concern must claim our attention just as much as particular instances of contact with this village or that. It was inevitable that a person like Pachomius would find himself "preaching the gospel." That was another reason why he and his associates would fall immediately under the observation, if not the control, of the Egyptian clergy. So, in what we can describe as his first pastoral enterprise, Pachomius was careful not to encroach upon the clergy's field of action. It was the occasion when he built near Tabennesi "a church in the deserted village for the shepherds of the surrounding region, who were common folk, so that they might assemble on Sunday and Saturday to hear the word of God."[52] It is made perfectly clear that Pachomius was intent upon converting the people to Christianity, although the need of a small core of Christians for church services may first have prompted his concern. He wished "to save all men if he could." Moreover, his role in the new church was quite a formidable one. He fulfilled the duties of lector and accepted the deacon-like responsibility of providing at least for the liturgical materials in the building, if not for food and clothing in the neighborhood. At the same time it is carefully emphasized that the church was built in a "deserted village." The impression is given also that Pachomius would perform his duties in the area only "until a priest was appointed there." He was careful how he trod. And the *Vita Prima* introduces the crucial addition, "This he did not on his own accord, but on the advice [γνώμη] of Sarapion, the bishop of the Church of Nitentori."[53]

In the *Vita Prima*, at least, it is that event that prepares the stage for the attempt by Sarapion to ordain Pachomius priest.[54] It was on the occasion of a visit south by Athanasius in 329 or 330; we may see combined in the event the new patriarch's attempts to counter his Melitian enemies and a local bishop's desire to extend his authority beyond the limits of

52. G[1] 29; see Bo 25.

53. Γνώμη is pretty vague. Bo 25, like all other texts, omits this detail, and proceeds directly to express anxiety about clerical office within the communities, like G[1] 27—passages to be discussed shortly. Veilleux was unhappy about what seemed to him a tendentious addition in G[1], *Liturgie*, p. 193; see also Festugière, *Première Vie grecque*, p. 22. The correct name of the bishop may be Saprion, Chitty, *Desert*, p. 40 n. 43. He should not be confused with the bishop mentioned in S[1] IV (19), probably of Diospolis Parva, who supported Pachomius when he expelled his first rebels; see Veilleux, *Koinonia*, 1:443. But he may appear in Draguet's Fragment 2, 9, on a visit to Oxyrhynchus, and is there suitably concerned with monastic behavior. Note also the later allusion in Bo 49, "Later he built the little celebration room [at Phbow], with the permission of the bishop of Diospolis."

54. G[1] 30, Bo 28.

his town.[55] Sarapion had already approached Athanasius, recommending Pachomius, pointing out that he now had a number of monks in his diocese, and asking the patriarch "to set him over all the monks in my diocese as father and priest [πατέρα καὶ πρεσβύτερον]." Not only did the bishop wish to exert better control over monastic developments; he probably hoped to formalize the local pastoral initiative we have already described, and even to impart a new and more general quality to Pachomius's leadership among his own and nearby ascetics. The Bohairic version implies that discussion on those points had been going on for some time: "he refuses to obey me in this matter." However, when the patriarch actually arrived, Pachomius "hid from the pope among the brothers until he had passed by." Athanasius recognized and respected that reticence: "You chose for yourself that which is better and which will always abide in Christ! Our Lord, therefore, will accede to your wish."[56]

Yet Pachomius retained a close connection with the church at Nitentori. The οἰκονόμος there, Dionysios, is described in the *Vita Prima* as "one of the closest friends of Pachomius," who would visit the town to talk to him.[57] Both the friendship and the consequent ecclesiastical association brought pressure to bear. As we have noted, Dionysios saw fit to criticize the way in which Pachomius ran his monastery. Coming from a priest, it may not have been a purely personal observation! And the wife of a local person of note, a πολιτευόμενος, used Dionysios as a mediator between herself and Pachomius, seeking—with success—a cure from sickness.[58]

The situation at Nitentori in particular illustrates the degree of success with which Pachomius related to local bishops. Events surrounding his later foundations at Panopolis appear to touch upon the same issue, but they introduce us also to the fascinating topic of Pachomius's atti-

55. Both aspirations were touched upon in Chapter I. See Frend, "Athanasius," pp. 30f, Lallemand, *Administration*, p. 96, Hardy, *Christian Egypt*, p. 41.

56. The final text here is restored with the help of other versions; see Veilleux, *Koinonia*, 1:272. We have mentioned already the possibility that the foundation of Phbow was an attempt to escape the jurisdiction of Sarapion: Chitty, "Chronology," p. 381. For interesting examples of forced ordination, see *Apophthegmata patrum*, Macarius 1, Moses 4, Matoes 9.

57. G¹ 40f. Bo 40 is less insistent on the friendship. Bo 41 says the conversations took place at Tabennesi, as does Dion., but Festugière preferred the Greek, *Première Vie grecque*, pp. 27f.

58. G¹ 40f.

tude toward paganism. Our understanding of those events is affected by some uncertainty as to how many monasteries were built in the area.[59] A defensible chronology would run as follows: the community at Tse, "in Tkahšmin" (i.e., the present Ahkmîm, Panopolis), under Pesso;[60] then that of Panopolis, otherwise unnamed, "near" the city, under Samuel;[61] and finally that at Tsmine, in "the vicinity of the city of Šmin," under Petronios, who was transferred from Thbew and given some responsibility also for "the other two monasteries near him."[62] The number and order are important because the second foundation is said by both Greek and Coptic writers to have been made at the invitation of the coadjutor bishop, Arios, who even designated a site. Apparently a community already existed nearby to awaken and inform Arios's enthusiasm. And that enthusiasm may have been augmented by his being himself an ἀσκητής, as the sources call him, although it is impossible to gauge how formal a monastic background the word might imply. His declared motive suggests that the new community was to be somewhat closer to the city than Tse: "I beseech you to rise and come to me and organize a monastery at our place so that the blessing of the Lord may come to our land because of you." Pachomius took great care in the appointment of Samuel, the superior of this second community, "for they were near a city." The subsequent foundation of Tsmine suggests that the experiment had been deemed a success, and with the appointment of Petronios as the third and most important superior in the district, a considerable Pachomian empire had been established some hundred kilometers north of Phbow.

Whatever may have been the role of Bishop Arios, not everyone in the city viewed these developments with the same enthusiasm: "Some people who did not know God's designs and were moved by envy, kept throwing down by night what was being built." The exact identity of the saboteurs is not made clear. Nor do the Lives explain with any conviction how the tension was eventually resolved. The question does arise, however, whether we should equate that opposition with the arrival of a "philosopher" at one of the new monasteries, perhaps with companions; he wished "to see what kind of men they were."[63] In that confrontation we have a good opportunity to examine the religious and cultural profile of the Pachomian community as it would have appeared to

59.   There has been little room for change since the generally convincing disagreement by Chitty, "Chronology," with the conclusions of Lefort, "Premiers Monastères" and Vies, esp. p. 247. Problems arise partly from the failure of the Coptic texts, obscured in Koinonia, vol. 1.

60. G¹ 83, S⁵ 52.   61. G¹ 81, 83, S⁵ 54.   62. G¹ 83, Bo 57.
63. G¹ 82.

others equally serious about the practice of their religion. We may also
discover a little more about Panopolis itself, which we know from other
sources to have been a strong center of pagan and gnostic activity.[64]

Two conversations are recorded with the visitors from the city. The
first, conducted with Cornelios, reflected little more than anxious curiosity on the part of the locals—curiosity about the monks' way of life, or,
in the Coptic/Arabic tradition, about their "sayings." By the same token,
a certain equality was admitted. The "philosopher" saw Cornelios and
his associates as "monks who are intelligent and speak wisdom [συνετοὶ
καὶ σοφὰ λαλοῦντες]." It was what they had in common that prompted
his famous question, "Who would ever bring olives from elsewhere to
sell them in Panopolis?" The implication could only have been that the
local market in wisdom had been saturated already. But Cornelios took
up the light-hearted image, to insist on a difference between them: "We
are the salt; we have come to salt you." The Coptic/Arabic texts make
much more of this attempted contrast. Pachomius, detecting a "snare"
in the philosopher's approach, exhorted Cornelios, "Answer to those
senseless men who think only of the body whatever the Lord will put

64.   Rich background information on the earlier fourth century is provided
by T. C. Skeat, ed., *Papyri from Panopolis*, not least in his own excellent introduction. For the gnostic connection, as well as allusion to "pagan practices and
pagan cultural life," see Roberts, *Manuscript*, pp. 70f, based mainly on a prepon-
derance of the sub-Akhmimic dialect in gnostic material of the period. Doresse,
Livres secrets, pp. 155f, specifically mentions our dialogue, and suggests that
Cornelios's and Theodore's questioners could have been "plus ou moins gnostiques," or "pas absolument des païens, mais plus probablement des hérétiques."
General observations on pagan priesthood in Barns, "Egyptians and Greeks,"
may now be illustrated more particularly by G. M. Browne, "A Panegyrist from
Panopolis," *Proceedings of the XIV International Congress of Papyrologists*, pp. 29–
33, and W. H. Willis, "The Letter of Ammon of Panopolis to his Mother," *Actes du
XVᵉ congrès international de papyrologie*, 2:98–115. Both reveal a flourishing pagan
society, anxious in particular to retain its hold, within certain families, over
priestly temple offices. Ammon says of himself in addition that he is among οἱ ἐν
φιλοσοφίᾳ καὶ λόγοις ἀνηγμένοι, Browne, p. 31. Our questioners may have been
counted among such men of erudition. Threats are not unknown, however.
Ammon warns, μαθετωσ[α]ν οὖν τὴν ἑαυτῶν [τ]ύχην ἐκεῖνοι οἱ θεοῖς ἐχθροί,
Willis, col. iv, lines 21–22. Some, no doubt, would have seen our monks as "enemies of the gods." Both commentators have extended their interpretation of the
texts: Browne, "Harpocration Panegyrista," *Illinois Classical Studies* 2 (1977):
184–96; Willis, "Two Literary Papyri in an Archive from Panopolis," ibid. 3
(1978): 140–53. Also useful is van Haelst, "Sources papyrologiques," with references to "un hellénisme violent chez des groupuscules d'intellectuels," p. 501,
and to an early domestic church in Panopolis, p. 498. Note also, ibid., how a
pagan lawyer in Hermoupolis can refer to Christianity in the early 320s in the
phrase τῶν ἄλλως φρονούντων, "those who think differently."

into your heart"; this encouraged Cornelios to assert, "[Pachomius's] spirit indeed is upon us. Now speak your empty word," and to add to his *dictum* on salt, "For you pride yourselves on being teachers and now what you say is vain. All discourse of this sort is very bad." The incident ended on a similar note: "By their vain learning they could not overcome those who possess the true knowledge of the Lord dwelling in them."

A moral distinction between the monks and the philosophers, therefore, and a pedagogical one, emerge already. The visitors lacked spiritual perception, and they laid claim to a teaching authority which their words could not substantiate. The second reported conversation, with Theodore, reinforced that point. "Now utter your carnal words" was the Christian challenge, "and he who is spiritual will answer you." [65] This time events took a new and specific turn. The leader of the second delegation, "the greatest of them all," announced, "I will go and test their understanding of the scriptures [τῶν γραφῶν]." Discussion centered on a riddle: "Who was not born and died? And who was born and did not die? And who died and did not stink?" In spite of initial misgivings—"I was afraid, not knowing how to answer a philosopher"—Theodore replied with confidence: Adam, Enoch, and Lot's wife. The philosophers were full of admiration; they wished the Pachomian enterprise every success, and they delivered the interesting accolade, "You have been granted a bright mind equal to the universal demiurge."

It might be rash to attempt too precise a definition of those questioners—as "pagans," for instance, or "gnostics." It is certain that they were not orthodox Christians as Pachomius would have understood that category, but a number of possibilities—or possible combinations—remain. The reputation of the city and the tone of the exchange with Cornelios may suggest they were the devotees of local cults, though it would be just as reasonable to think of them as earnest Pythagoreans or Neoplatonists. Reference to "the scriptures" would not exclude a learned non-Christian either, especially when such an interest was combined with allusion to the "universal demiurge." But it does introduce the possibility of gnostic, heretical, or Jewish influence—perhaps combined, perhaps distinct. The monks' responses also create an oddly gnostic impression, with their references to the one who is "spiritual" and to "those who possess the true knowledge of the Lord." The possibly rabbinic character of the visitors' riddle, on the other hand, is matched well by Pachomius's reaction to Theodore's success: "Blessed may you be,

65.   G² 66, close to Dion. 42, closes its account with an exhortation to leave verbal tricks and arguments, τὰς προτάσεις σου ταύτας καὶ τοὺς συλλογισμούς, and to turn to Christ.

Lord my God, for having confounded Goliath and all who hate Zion!"[66] Indeed there are so many facets to the account it is hard to know whether we are dealing with a literary composite or with religious syncretism. We may deduce that adhesion to religious principle was still not a cut-and-dried affair in Panopolis, or indeed in any "intellectual center" of the Eastern Empire. We may also suggest that biographers were simply intent upon creating an all-purpose adversary in order to highlight qualities peculiar to the Pachomian community—in this case a true insight that produced authentic teaching.

If the second was the case, then we have to admit that the biographers failed. To assert a distinction of this sort between monks and philosophers was not enough. What stands out most clearly is that the distinction, although bravely attempted by the writers, did not strike contemporaries with anything like the same force. It was easy enough to scrawl on a temple wall, "The cross has conquered! Victory forever!" Others with more time on their hands listed more carefully in similar places the supposed advantages of their success. To a pagan eye, they would have seemed immediately less novel. "Faith, hope, love, justice, peace, truth, generosity, restraint"—those were values that many would subscribe to beyond the Christian fold.[67] Incidents in the *Apophthegmata* offer useful comment. Macarius deplored in his disciple a readiness to call a pagan "demon." After a gentler exchange, the pagan became a monk himself, saying, "I realize that you are on God's side [τοῦ μέρους τοῦ θεοῦ]."[68] Olympius had an even more striking experience, worth quoting in full.

> One of the pagan priests came down from Scetis one day and came to my cell and slept there. Having reflected on the monks' way of life [διαγωγήν], he said to me, "Since you live like this, do you not receive any visions from your God [οὐδὲν θεωρεῖτε]?" I said to him, "No." Then the priest said to me, "Yet when we make a sacrifice to our God, he hides nothing from us, but discloses his mysteries [μυστήρια]; and you, giving yourselves so much hardship, vigils, prayer and asceticism, say that you see nothing? Truly, if you see nothing, then it is because you have impure thoughts in your hearts, which separate you from your God [λογισμοὺς πονηροὺς ἔχετε εἰς τὰς καρδίας ὑμῶν, τοὺς χωρίζοντας

66. For sharpening my awareness on this point, I owe particular thanks to Marie Taylor Davis. She pointed out to me the remarkably similar riddles presented to Solomon by the Queen of Sheba, as preserved in Louis Ginzberg, *The Legends of the Jews*, 4:146–48. Also useful are the notes on the Midrash na-Hefez, 6:290f.

67. G. Lefebvre, *Recueil des inscriptions grecques-chrétiennes d'Égypte*, no. 590 at Philae, p. 110; and no. 613 at Tâféh, p. 115.

68. *Apophthegmata patrum*, Macarius 39.

ὑμᾶς ἀπὸ τοῦ θεοῦ ὑμῶν], and for this reason his mysteries are not revealed to you." So I went to report the priest's words to the old men
[i.e., to other Christian ascetics]. They were filled with admiration and
said this was true. For impure thoughts separated God from man.[69]

What must strike the reader most is how much those ascetics had in
common with their pagan visitor. To assert anything else at any level of
Roman religious life in that period would have been immensely difficult,
whatever Pachomius's biographers might have wished. Athanasius, not
surprisingly, in his *Life of Antony*, made a more subtle attempt; it is worth
drawing the comparison at some length because it helps us to measure
both the determination of the later Pachomian biographers and the precise distinction they were trying to make.[70]

Antony, too, is presented as a man with "practical wisdom" (φρό-
νιμος), of "ready wit and understanding" (ἀγχίνους . . . καὶ συνετός).
The φιλόσοφοι approach him "thinking they could put Antony to the
test." But he immediately seizes the advantage. It is he who asks the
riddles here! He pretends at first to foolishness. No, they insist, he is
wise. So then, says Antony, if I am foolish, why bother to approach me?
But if I am truly wise, then why not imitate me (μιμεῖσθαι)—"make
yourselves what I am"? Others come to question him. Again, they receive instead a question from Antony: "Which is first, the mind or letters
[νοῦς ἢ γράμματα]?" The mind, they say. "Therefore, one who has a
sound mind [ᾧ τοίνυν ὁ νοῦς ὑγιαίνει] has no need of letters." A further
party arrives. Explain, they say, your faith, especially in this Cross,
which deserves only ridicule. "Which is better"—a question from Antony, as before—"to confess the Cross, or to attribute adulteries and
pederasties to your so-called gods?"

The method is clear and ingenious. Play upon the common ground,
the unavoidable agreement between yourself and your adversary; then,
on that basis, enforce your own distinction. "To maintain what we maintain is a sign of manly spirit [ἀνδρίας] and betokens disregard for death,
whereas your claims bespeak but wanton passions [ἀσελγείας . . .
πάθη]."

At that point in the *Life*, Antony is made to launch upon a more specifically philosophical discussion, the central theme of which is cosmology, in particular the best way to relate the divine and the visible worlds
in terms both of their structure and of consequent moral demands.
Athanasius called into play anxieties and arguments beyond the local

69. Olympius 1. We need not take "visions" too dramatically; it is not, perhaps, the best translation of θεωρεῖτε, as the rest of the anecdote will suggest.
70. *Life of Antony* 72–80.

confusions of the Thebaid: the deeper implications of the Arian theology, and the challenge of pagan antagonists more familiar to an Alexandrine churchman. Antony becomes immediately concrete: the Word was completely enfolded in a body, yet unchanged. How much more intelligible, how much tidier, than those confused gradations of divinity, linked, to the detriment of both clarity and sentiment, with beasts, reptiles, and the images of cult. Above all, how much more compelling than the myths in which they couch their doctrine. Away, he said, with any plea that "such things are spoken figuratively [μυθικῶς]." They should think less of the building and more of the architect! Pachomian ascetics, even at their most literary, either felt no need of such vigorous and protective self-definition, or were afraid to display it.

But then Antony changes tack. Once again he seeks the common ground. "You pin your faith on demonstrative proofs [τοῖς ἀποδεικτικοῖς λόγοις] . . . and you want us also not to worship God without demonstrative arguments." We will adopt that pose—and ask another question! "How does precise knowledge [γνῶσις] of things come about, especially knowledge about God? Is it by verbal proof or by an act of faith [δι' ἀποδείξεως λόγων, ἢ δι' ἐνεργείας πίστεως]?" They all agree with Antony that faith comes first. That was the trap! Antony's distinction was not so much between πίστις and λόγος as between ἀπόδειξις and ἐνέργεια, between argument and action. It was a question of the level within a man at which true γνῶσις came into play. His opponents prided themselves on a mere "skill" whereas he was talking about a "disposition of the soul." So comes the crucial retort: "What we apprehend by faith [ἐκ πίστεως νοοῦμεν], that you attempt to construct by arguments [διὰ λόγων κατασκευάζειν]; and often you cannot even express [οὐδὲ φράσαι . . . δύνασθε] what we perceive [νοοῦμεν]."

The rest of the dialogue points to the context within which the argument was conducted. Antony proceeds to list the practical results of the inner faith he had been talking about—faith in mind and soul. The pagan cults were in retreat, and above all in the face of a teaching and a moral code. "It is by faith that we persuade men [τῇ δὲ πίστει πείθομεν]," a "faith through love that works for Christ." And he cured some there who were possessed, to prove it!

That final gesture might seem unworthy of the elevated discourse that had gone before. But the careful combination of elements in Antony's appeal was as old as Christianity itself: "Go and tell John what you have seen and heard: the blind receive their sight, the lame walk, lepers are cleansed, and the deaf hear, the dead are raised up, the poor have good news preached to them." It was the last, the preaching, that one had constantly to justify, a duty that had also become a privilege difficult to lay claim to. That was true for Pachomius no less than for Antony. Whether by word or example, their aim was to proclaim a principle and to invite adhesion. Someone at Panopolis had considered that a threatening trespass. The actual opposition (the persistent philosophers) and the way the opponents are presented in the text have to be held constantly in juxtaposition. We should not attend more to the difference asserted between monk and philosopher than we do to the similarity this assertion is designed to obscure or counter. Behind the aim of proclamation, which Pachomius shared with his challengers, there lay a confidence in γνῶσις. Pachomius did not regard his own "knowledge" as greater or more privileged than that of his rivals, but it was, he felt, more deeply rooted, closer to the heart, and thus a source of action as well as of insight. Biographers may not have been equal to the occasion, and the confrontations that took place may have been confused or ambiguous in ways they obscured. But we can observe, in those conversations outside Panopolis, the very self-understanding we discussed in Chapter VII now being marshaled to affect a monk's relations with the secular and non-Christian world, just as it did with members of his own community.

———————

Another aspect of the Panopolis narrative calls to mind an issue already touched upon. The bishop Arios is described as ἀσκητής, which may mean that he was, or had been, a member of some religious community. One need not imagine anything as formal as a Pachomian monastery, although we shall meet in a moment bishops who did have that background. Cases like Arios are known from other sources. An Apphy, bishop of Oxyrhynchus, is mentioned in the *Apophthegmata* as a former ascetic; so also is a Netras of Pharan, certainly fifth-century. Ammonas, disciple of Antony, became a bishop, apparently quite happily.[71] Other examples can be found as the century progressed, notably two of the "Tall Brothers," protagonists in the Origenist dispute of the 390s, whom successive patriarchs of Alexandria attempted to consecrate—in one case, at least, with success.[72]

Evidence of such "monk-bishops," particularly when close to the Pachomian world, forces us to reflect rather more carefully upon those

71.   *Apophthegmata patrum*, Ammonas 8 and 10: delightful stories, projecting a startling view of episcopacy!

72.   For narrative and the many scattered references, see Chitty, *Desert*, pp. 53f. On the wider view of ascetic ordination, see my *Ascetics*, pp. 56f.

passages in which Pachomius debated, and gravely doubted, the pro-
priety of ordaining monks as priests.[73] In spite of his aversion, there
were undoubtedly priests in his monasteries. Should we regard their
presence as part of some attempt by bishops to exercise control over
those communities, or at least a growing opportunity for them to do so?
Or should we see them more as signs of an expanding pool of recruits
from which a new type of bishop could be drawn, a bishop, like Arios,
more sympathetic to the progress and principles of the monastic movement generally?

When Pachomius learned of Sarapion's plan to ordain him, he hid
himself from the visiting patriarch among his fellow monks.[74] In saying
that none of his followers should aim at priesthood any more than he
did, his main argument was that the prospect of ordination could encourage ambition and conflict. His anxieties were remarkably similar to
those expressed somewhat later by Athanasius himself.[75] The issue in
the case of the patriarch was ordination by a bishop outside his own diocese, but the terminology is almost identical: "such lawlessness results
constantly in argument, jealousy, frustration, and gives rise to schisms
that affect not only the churches but also the monasteries, for such li-
cence has reached them also." What specifically worried Pachomius was
the *seeking* of clerical rank: "the clerical dignity is the beginning of a
temptation to love of power." He accepted the fact that his communities
would need the ministry of priests, although he preferred to trust in
providence to fill that need—"to consider as minister of this sacred rite
the one we find at any time." On the other hand, he did not pass judgment on monks ordained in other communities. Most important of all
was how he was perfectly willing to accept into his own monasteries
those already members of the clergy, provided they obeyed the rules like
any other monk.[76]

The point to note most is that Pachomius, while respectful of priests
and bishops, wished always to call the tune in his association with them.
That characterized even his response to Theodore's mother, at least in
the *Vita Prima*. She had arrived, we may remember, with written authority from one or more bishops. Theodore, however, refused to ac-
quiesce in her request—to see her, or to leave with her, whatever may
have been the case. Pachomius may not have been certain that that was a

73.   Chief assertions are made in G¹ 27, Bo 25.
74.   G¹ 30, Bo 28.
75.   Athanasius, *Lettres pastorales* 11 (A.D. 368), trans. Lefort, pp. 40f.
76.   The monk that sought a rank beyond his deserts is said by G¹ 42 to
have wanted the post of "steward." Bo 42 and Am, p. 555 are vague, but G² 37
and Dion. 35 say he aspired to clerical, if not priestly office.

wise response, but deference to episcopal browbeating played no part in his judgment. "Certainly our fathers the bishops," he said—almost, one feels, with a wink—"will not be vexed when they hear about this, but will rather rejoice at your progress."[77] So, although having priests in the community was inevitably going to involve him in difficult, even ambiguous, relations with the church at large, the *Lives* are content to prescribe for those relations in surprisingly general terms: "It is better to be subject modestly [ἐπιεικῶς] to the Church of God."[78] All this suggests that, far from seeing priests in his communities as resident representatives of extraneous authority, Pachomius persistently kept church officials at arm's length, and would probably have regarded his own priestly subjects, especially if promoted to the episcopate, as emissaries to a world beyond.

———————

That reflection prepares us naturally for his last confrontation with that world: his foundation at Latopolis, and his subsequent trial. Pachomius had faced opposition at Panopolis, but in this case of Phnoum (the new community at Latopolis), it was the local bishop himself who led the opposing party, not without violence.[79] None of the *Lives* tells us how the disagreement was resolved, but there is good reason to suppose that events at the Synod of 345 held in the city should be seen as part of that resolution.[80]

We know almost nothing about the Synod save what is told us in the *Vita Prima*. The Arabic account simply confirms an underlying Coptic tradition. The dispute involved every level of civil and ecclesiastical society. Pachomius himself attended with the support of "some ancient brothers" and other monks, whose physical protection he would need soon enough, together with "those living in the villages surrounding [his monasteries]," "a great multitude." That was his somewhat intimidating response to being "summoned" by bishops who were anxious, according to one version, to expel him and his followers from their dio-

77. G¹ 37.
78. Bo has "respectfully." It is interesting that, with ἐπιεικῶς, it is the *Vita Prima* that should retain the nuance of rational independence.
79. Bo 58; G¹ 83 is silent.
80. The best known account is in G¹ 112f. Lefort thought that S¹ᵃ might refer to that event, *Vies*, pp. lxxiii and 371f, according to which Pachomius was both fearful and unrepentant. Am, pp. 591f gives a full account also, which Chitty was too ready to dismiss as "less reliable," *Desert*, p. 41 n. 57.

ceses. The issue, then, was not just one of antagonism at Sne/Latopolis. Ultimately, it was the charge that Pachomius laid claim to the ability to see into men's hearts, distinguishing good from evil. It would seem we are dealing with a straightforward case of trial by the church of an upstart monk. But, quite apart from what may be implied by the presence of villagers in his own train, Pachomius faced not only bishops, but also soldiers and monks on the other side. It may have been a monk, "filled wholly with pride," that testified most clearly against him. Two of the bishops present, Philo of Thebes and a certain Mouei (perhaps of Latopolis itself), had been monks at Tabennesi; there may have been two others with the same background. It may even have been a monk who, following his testimony and the uproar that it caused, ran at Pachomius with a sword to kill him. That much alone suggests an interesting diversity of personnel, but Pachomius had gained also the protection of one Sabinus, who acted as agent or manager for leading figures in the city and helped to save Pachomius from the mob, not least by warning that officials in Alexandria might well interpret the events as a seditious riot.

It would seem that, in spite of the disorder which characterized the meeting, positions were at least clarified, and disagreements may even have been overcome. "When they heard these things [Pachomius's testimony in his own defense], they marvelled at the confidence and the humility of the man [τήν τε παρρησίαν καὶ τὴν ταπεινοφροσύνην]." Pachomius calmly reflected later, "We ought to endure every trial, for it does not hurt. Those who inquire into our affairs are orthodox fathers and brothers [so events had little to do with the shifting fortunes of Athanasius, faced with Arian usurpers]; and though the enemy has wrought evil in some who belonged to us but who were outside the wall—that is the law—for a little while, God has saved us and them." Surely no one could have been present in Latopolis that day and still have thought, even in 345, that monks had "left the world"! All the elements touched upon in this chapter are brilliantly illustrated by the event: the liaison, indeed the alliance of Pachomius and his brethren with the local rural population, their possession of powerful patrons in the city, the cautious collaboration of monks with officials of the church, and their growing incorporation among the clergy itself.

It is fortunate that we can end with so arresting and complete a picture. But it is still only one image, and it does not tell us as much about other foundations as it does about Phnoum. Nor does it explain or describe Pachomius's growing self-confidence, his mature sense of independence, since his brush with Sarapion some fifteen years before. We need not discount the evidence of the Synod simply because of its unusual place in Pachomius's career and its appearance virtually in a single source or within a single tradition. But that exceptional quality does remind us that "relations with the world" were not a preoccupation of the biographers. They focused their attention mainly on life within the monastery, not to say within the monk. So, on these other matters, we are given only a few hints, a few isolated incidents. We have to avoid the temptation of building from those hints a tidy generality. In particular, we have to proceed very carefully when relating the communities, taken as a whole and throughout Pachomius's career, to the life of village and church as described in Chapter I. The chief certainty we can lay claim to—and the one that matters most—is that the monasteries were not cut off from the society around them. There was traffic from the one to the other. Indeed, one might say that the monastery, or rather the description of the monastery provided in the sources, acts for us like a fish-eye lens through which we can observe a multitude of activities and attitudes characteristic of the Thebaid more generally. The lens may be idiosyncratic in structure, and therefore even distorting, but it gives us access not simply to some private world, but, through the eyes of a few, to society at large. And yet, when we add them together, the fragments collected in this chapter give us only a discontinuous view of the channels along which that traffic passed. Kinship, the acquisition of property, the deployment of labor, the exchange of goods, and the activities and aspirations of priests and those with authority in the church: those are perhaps the five most prominent strands in our fragile web. They conspired to prompt anxious vigilance and admiration among the civil and religious leaders of the towns of the Upper Nile. They guaranteed, in a complementary way, a certain wealth among the monks themselves, but also a certain dependence, emotional as well as economic, upon the wider community. Neither sort of intimacy had been originally planned, and neither was consistently welcomed. But the siting of the communities, and the concept of service that lay at their heart, made both unavoidable.

· IX ·

CONTINUITY

With the death of Pachomius in 346, we come in a sense full circle because we are forced to assess again the value and purpose of his biographies. While there may be controversy, as described in Chapter II, about the sources of those texts and about the different levels within them, no one can doubt their close association, from the point of view of style, with the *Apophthegmata Patrum*. Despite a certain literary polish, and a degree of propagandist axe-grinding, one can still recognize at their core a series of surprisingly disjointed anecdotes and pithy sayings. To that extent the basic motive underlying them, and indeed the chief reason for their importance, remains clear. They were designed to preserve in memorable form the most significant actions and insights of a beloved master. They recounted in particular those events and sayings that revealed his inner life, and they did so, as he had tried to do himself, in a manner that could form the inner life of others.[1]

There is a chapter in the *Vita Prima* where the writer is usefully explicit about his motives and about the background to his work.[2] He reminds us that Pachomius himself had set out rules and spiritual instructions. Some of the superiors of his monasteries had created texts also, expanding the advice of their founder. That material had survived in part to the writer's own day, but, he says, it was not enough, for at least three reasons. First, while "God always glorifies his own servants," it did no harm to lend a helping hand. It would have been a pity to see the reputation of a good man fade away by default, simply because his admirers omitted to enhance it for subsequent generations. That was particularly important if you felt that such a holy man was your true an-

1. For example G¹ 46, not in Bo ("even his personal thoughts"); G¹ 71, Bo 66; G¹ 102, Bo 103. These last will be discussed further below.
2. G¹ 99 for what follows.

cestor, the central figure in an authentic tradition: "We have been writing as children eagerly desiring to recall the memory of the fathers who brought us up." Second, it was necessary to compete with, or at least take advantage of, the now thriving literary tradition represented by the lives and letters of other holy men, martyrs, monks, and bishops—not least those of Antony. Third, it was important to prove that monks were worthy subjects for literature. Although relatively new upon the scene, their lives were no less significant, and had no less to offer the more leisured and literate Christian, than did those of the great theologians and statesmen who governed the church in the leading cities of the empire.

In other words, the *Lives*, in whatever language, were themselves instruments of continuity—much more so than were the *Rules*. Pachomius and his successors strove to achieve permanence and clarity in institutional matters, but this other urge, to write *history*, was equally deliberate, impassioned, and formative—as indeed it had become in the wider development of Christianity. For we are not just dealing with a portrait, the presentation of a model to be imitated. The *Lives* were designed to provide the reader with a narrative account of his *own* past, a past—and this is the point of most significance—offered as a secure basis for moral growth and disciplined freedom. Perhaps more than all else, that was the attitude that distinguished Pachomian writers from any gnostic competitor. Gnostics were content to allow morality to flow from myth, or at least from an ordered cosmology. In that, of course, they were not entirely alone. But in our *Lives*, it was a documented past, made up of persons and events, that defined and guaranteed salvation. To that degree, they did not stand apart from the rest of Christian literature. Orthodoxy, interpreted as attachment to the past, to antecedents and progenitors, was the hallmark of Eusebius and his long train of imitators and continuators. It was to become increasingly the touchstone also for every reliable exegete and homilist.

Pachomius was presented, therefore, as the heir of prophets, apostles, and martyrs: as a part of the same past that any Christian could now look to for guidance.

> What we have heard and known and our fathers have told us should not be hidden from the next generation. For, as we have been taught, we know that these words of the psalm are about the signs and portents accomplished by God for Moses and those after him. And after the model of the benefit given by them, we have also recognized in the fathers of our time their children and imitators, so that to us and to the rising generation, until the end of the world, it might be made known that Jesus Christ is the same yesterday, today and for ever.[3]

3.   G¹ 17, not in Bo. See also G¹ 1f.

But Pachomius did not simply fulfill prophecy. His initiative, his monastic genius, tipped that tradition forward, into the reader's lap, so to speak, so that the *Koinonia* became a current legacy, demanding affection, loyalty, labor. It was worth preserving. That was why *Lives* were written. Their authors were careful also to define exactly what it was that should be preserved. Exactly what was the authentic tradition, and who were its custodians? They wished to make it clear, furthermore, that monasticism was not a fringe phenomenon. Both socially and ideologically, it was just as characteristic of Christian life in the Roman Empire as the structure, ritual, and morality of the urban and diocesan community. Perhaps even more surprising, it was just as much endowed with intellectual interest and refinement.

That is not to say, however, that Pachomius shared such confidence. Indeed, it may not always have been clear to him that he had initiated a firm tradition or that he had anything specific in the way of institution or teaching to bequeath to the next generation. We can say this in spite of his reputation as a "writer" because, as we discussed in Chapter II, so much of his *corpus* was piecemeal and *ad hoc*. His successors imposed order upon his stipulations precisely because they felt a greater need than he had for secure conformity and transmission.[4] It is true, as we noted in Chapter VI, that from a very early stage he displayed a certain humility, a readiness to delegate authority, and an associated optimism that worthy delegates would appear.[5] But from an equally early stage he was beset by considerable anxieties, which came to infect permanently his vision of the future.[6] Reference to that insecurity was not merely a conceit of his biographers. Take, for example, the *Instruction Concerning a Spiteful Monk.*

> Struggle, my beloved, for the time is near and the days have been shortened. There is no father who instructs his children, there is no child who obeys its father; good virgins are no longer; the holy fathers have died on all sides; the mothers and the widows are no longer, and we have become like orphans; the humble are crushed underfoot; and blows are showered upon the head of the poor. Therefore there is little to hold back the wrath of God from grieving us, with no one to console us. All this has befallen us because we have not practised mortification.

Or again, in a broader context:

4. It is striking that the G¹ 99 references to writing concern interpretations and visions. Although "ordinances" are mentioned, they are conflated with "talks" and "letters," with emphasis on "edification" and "spiritual writings"; all of which sounds much more like the *Instructions* than the *Rules*.

5. G¹ 25, Bo 23. See Chapter VI at nn. 32f.

6. Compare G¹ 18, Bo 21 with G¹ 71: Pachomius experiences a kind of vertigo when demons dig a pit just where he is about to kneel.

The churches are filled with quarrellers and wrathful people; monastic communities have become ambitious; pride reigns; there is no one left who is dedicated to his neighbor; on the contrary, every man has crushed his neighbor. We are plunged into suffering. There is no prophet nor gnostic. No one wins over another, for hardness of heart abounds. Those who understand keep silence, for the times are evil. Each one is his own lord.[7]

Even the next generation, therefore, could not disguise the fact that Pachomius harbored such sentiments. The biographies recount an analogous pessimism. On one occasion, Pachomius was observed transfixed in obvious distress. Asked later what he had witnessed in his ecstasy, he spoke of having seen the brothers trapped by fire, or terrified into immobility on a steep rock face. "He told them about his vision and they all wept with great fear. And as they asked him what this meant, he said, 'I perceive that after my death this will happen to my brothers, who will not find anyone capable of comforting them rightly in the Lord from their afflictions.'"[8] Another time he had a dream or vision very obviously concerned with leadership and guidance. He saw brothers lost in a dark, pillared building. They could not reach the light, but were taunted by voices crying, "Behold! Here is the Light!" At last a lamp appeared, borne by four monks, whom the others followed, each one's hands upon the shoulders of the man in front. In the Bohairic version, only those first four monks could clearly see, and the long procession of those they thus helped to save represented the *Koinonia* itself.[9]

Of course, when the written accounts were formed, such nightmares or visions were subjected to further interpretation and colored by wisdom after the event. The story just referred to is a case in point. "He told these things to some brothers in private. And we heard it from them much later, along with the following interpretation: 'This world is the dark place, which is dark because of error, each heretic thinking to have the true path. The lamp is the faith in Christ, which saves those who believe aright and leads to the kingdom of God.'"[10] But it seems entirely reasonable to believe that the anxiety itself was original, prompted

7. *CMR* 49 and 60.

8. G[1] 71. The last phrase is not in Bo 66, but occurs in S[4] and in the Arabic tradition.

9. G[1] 102, Bo 103. *Letter of Ammon* 12 would suggest that this vision was an early event. *Paral.* 9 (17f) has conflated all these passages, and even echoes the *CMR*.

10. G[1] 102. In Bo 103, Pachomius receives this interpretation himself, as part of the vision. There, too, some lose their hold on the shoulder in front, or even refuse to follow. They "stand for bishops who are in the right faith of Christ, but are in communion with the heretics." Clearly, conflicting interpretations of the vision were already at work.

in Pachomius by the thought of what might happen to his followers after his death. The dreams and visions themselves, with their vivid and detailed imagery, spring almost certainly from an oral tradition that is relatively untouched by subsequent interpretation, and they are easily distinguished from the uses to which biographers later put them. The fire, the thorny thickets, the cliffs above the river, the crocodiles below, even the dark, enormous building with all the appearance of a derelict temple from pagan days: all lay close to the daily experience of the Thebaid.[11]

So here we have two attitudes of mind—humility and fear in the founder, and a studied theology and a gift for special pleading among his literary champions. They marked the beginning and the end of a process whereby Pachomius's personal sense of vocation was transformed within fifty years into the self-assured and historically secure phenomenon of Egyptian cenobitism. There is, however, a shorter process, which fortunately we are able to document also—that whereby Pachomius's fears about succession were indeed realized and then overcome. That story, naturally, is not concerned only with Pachomius, but it does tell us more about his own attitude to authority, as well as about the motives of some of his disciples.

Central to the later history of Pachomian monasticism was the figure of Theodore.[12] Putting his career in a nutshell, we can have little doubt that he was Pachomius's favorite disciple and his designated successor. For reasons we shall see, he fell from favor and saw himself passed over by alternative leaders, but eventually he succeeded to what many regarded as his properly destined status as leader of the Pachomian communities.

That status is asserted very early in the *Vita Prima*. He was Pachomius's "true child," formed "after his likeness."[13] The likeness was a result of imitation, and a quality of sonship, of legal descent and inheritance, lay at the heart of Theodore's claim to respectability and leadership. Here again we find a concern characteristic of the sources themselves. A favorable and carefully constructed biography of Theodore was part and parcel of the literary tradition that was allowed to survive. References to his imitation of the founder, and to a carefully defined

---

11.   Gnostics could express their fears in comparable terms, Doresse, *Livres secrets*, pp. 170f, 240f, but they lack the Pachomian touch—a firm link with institutions. Note also the fears expressed by Pachomius much closer to the time of his death, in Veilleux's Bo 118 = S[7], trans. Lefort, *Vies*, pp. 45f.

12.   Still an excellent account of the years after 346 is Bacht's *Vermächtnis*.

13.   G[1] 26. The Bohairic equivalent is not in 24 or 30, as one might expect, but in 32: "He was also growing up in the instructions he would hear from the lips of our father Pachomius, after whose image he was walking in all things." G[1] 36 does not quite echo this. The emphasis recurs in Bo 190.

genealogy, recur in a number of passages; they clearly constituted the most important elements in any legitimate succession.[14] Even the great Antony was brought onto the stage to echo the theme. After Pachomius had died, he addressed a group of monks on their way to Alexandria. They included Theodore, but not Pachomius's immediate successors. "Do not weep," the great hermit said, "all of you have become as Abba Pachomius."[15]

Theodore himself was equally careful to stress the importance of legitimate genealogies, not entirely to his own disadvantage. "He believed he would obtain mercy through the compassion of the Lord and the tears and righteousness of our father Pachomius, since he had come to know God through him." So he was able to assure his monks, "we also believe that the blessing of our father will remain with us and with those who come after us before God for ever."[16] Such was the belief that inspired Theodore to encourage the creation of biography, as we have described in Chapter II. The theme of descent recurs in the *Instructions* attributed to him, particularly the familiar line from the apostles through Pachomius to the present generation.[17] And such habits of mind were not peculiar to Theodore. Horsiesios is presented in the same way by all the *Lives*, not least by the Sahidic biography which seems especially a chronicle of his career.[18] A Bohairic passage is also striking, in which Horsiesios is made to declare:

14. See G^1 99, as referred to in n. 2 above, where imitation is part of the process of succession. More examples will occur below, but see especially Bo 208.

15. Accounts of this journey are very confused. G^1 120, and further reference back to the event in G^1 136, appear reliable. Bo is missing at this point. Veilleux, *Koinonia*, vol. 1, has supplied the gap with complex substitutions, in this case from S^5 118–32. I shall refer to the chapters in his translation as VBo 124f, to make clear this process of compilation. In G^1 120, Theodore and Zacchaeus visit Antony *en route* to Alexandria. According to this version, both Pachomius and his immediate successor Petronios were already dead. Antony, after the conversation referred to here, recommends his visitors to Athanasius by letter. In VBo 124 = S^5 118, however, it is *Petronios* who sends Theodore on his journey to Alexandria, also with a letter to Athanasius. While in Alexandria, Theodore hears of Petronios's death. He has already visited Antony (VBo 132 = S^5 126). Antony does write a letter, but in this case addressed to the monks themselves, still in Alexandria, and he writes about Petronios (VBo 133 = S^5 127). Certainly the statement that Theodore had been sent by Petronios is an error, Veilleux, *Koinonia*, 1:287. So also, probably, are many other details in this Coptic account.

16. Bo 190, 194; neither is in G^1. See also the careful statements in G^1 135f.

17. Although by this time the inheritance is symbolized most by the *Rules*: Theodore, *Instruction Three*, 2, 5, and 26. The *Instruction* is translated by Veilleux, *Koinonia*, 3:92–122.

18. Namely S^{3b}. See G^1 118f. Bo 209, the corresponding version, omits allusion to Horsiesios's dependence on Pachomius; but see Bo 199.

May our turn come for [the apostles] to say of us, "Welcome are the sons who obeyed their father and kept the commandments which he gave them. Come, inherit eternal life with your fathers because you walked in their footsteps and in the commandments which they gave you." The bones of our righteous father actually remain in our midst today—that is, the laws he gave us, that through them we might be victorious over the evil one. Then the hearts of our fathers may be at peace about us, when they see their offspring producing spiritual fruit for God their creator.[19]

Not surprisingly, therefore, the *Lives* are just as swift to point explicitly to Theodore's expectations of being Pachomius's successor: "Seeing his remarkable progress, our father Pachomius realized in his heart that God would entrust him with souls after himself."[20] The moment of transition is vividly described, at a time when Theodore had been in the community for about ten years.

Some days later [Pachomius] called Theodore and said to him, "When the brothers come out from table in the evening, give your ministry to someone else and come to where we gather for the instruction on Sunday." And when Theodore came to the instruction, he told him, "Stand here in the midst of the brothers and speak the word of God to us"—as he used to do himself. He obeyed him and stood up, though unwillingly; and he began to speak what the Lord gave him. All stood, including Abba Pachomius who listened as one of them. But some, out of pride, were vexed and they returned to their tents so as not to listen to him. The one who stood [to speak] was younger in human age.

After the instruction and the prayer Pachomius sat down as was his custom and began saying, "You have heard what was said. Whose was it? The speaker's or the Lord's? And those who were vexed, for what reason were they vexed? Because he is younger? But we find that the Lord said about a child, *Anyone who receives a child like this in my name receives me.* Was I not standing and listening as one of you? And I tell you that I did not only pretend but I was listening with all my heart, as one thirsty for water. For worthy indeed of all acceptance is the word of the Lord, as it is written. Wretched are those who went away; they have estranged themselves from God's mercies. And if they do not repent of their pride, it will be difficult for them to have Life."[21]

Obviously the whole event was carefully staged. Immediately after, Pachomius made Theodore the οἰκονόμος at Tabennesi, "considering him capable in spirit [ἱκανὸν . . . τῷ πνεύματι]."[22]

Theodore maintained very close links with Phbow, coming there every day to hear Pachomius teach so that he might then return to Ta-

19.   Bo 208.
20.   G¹ 36, Bo 32.
21.   G¹ 77; Bo 69 is substantially the same.
22.   G¹ 78, Bo 70.

bennesi and repeat that teaching to his own community.[23] At some later stage he was given the additional task of traveling around to the other monasteries to check on their observance. That had been for a long time Pachomius's most characteristic preoccupation, and marked out Theodore in an even more obvious way as his successor. The custom was retained by Horsiesios. As Pachomius said himself, "Theodore and I fulfil the same service for God; and he also has the authority [in the Bohairic text, "power over everything"] to give orders as father."[24]

Those demonstrations of trust should have given Theodore every justification for supposing that when Pachomius died he would take his place as leader of all the communities. Then came what was perhaps an error of judgment.[25] Pachomius had fallen ill, and the *Vita Prima* says, in a careful phrase, that "some ancient fathers and heads of the monasteries" (ἀρχαῖοι πατέρες καὶ κεφαλαὶ τῶν μονῶν) came to Theodore and said that they thought Pachomius might die, leaving them dangerously leaderless. (The Bohairic text refers to "all the fathers of the communities and all the brothers who were at Phbow.")[26] They asked Theodore to promise that he would take up the leadership after him. Theodore refused many times to accede to such a request, but he eventually saw that he could not dissuade them, and gave his word. When Pachomius heard of this, he refused to countenance the bargain. He called to his bedside—and here again the phraseology may be important—"all the leaders of the monasteries," many of whom are listed by name: Sourous of Phnoum, Pšentaesi, Paphnouti (Theodore's brother, and steward at Phbow), and Cornelios of Thmoušons. Theodore was also present.[27] Pachomius then demanded a general confession of errors, starting with himself. Theodore, when it came to his turn, felt forced to admit, "For seven years now I have been sent by you to visit the monasteries and to settle everything as you do. And never did it enter my heart that 'after him, I will be in charge.' But now I am plagued by this thought and I have not been able to conquer it yet." Pachomius then stripped him of all authority and told him to pray for forgiveness. He endured that penance, according to the Greek text, for two full years.[28]

23.   G¹ 88, Bo 73.
24.   G¹ 91, Bo 74. For Pachomius's regular visits, see G¹ 54, Bo 49f. He was at times accompanied by Theodore, G¹ 106, Bo 94. For the same practice by Horsiesios, G¹ 118, Bo 208.
25.   For all that follows, G¹ 106, Bo 94.
26.   Following the correction of Lefort, *Vies*, p. 157 n. 1.
27.   One notes the absence of Petronios. Bo is not so specific, and mentions no names.
28.   G¹ 107.

There are several interesting points to the story. To begin with, it is not entirely clear who actually suggested to Theodore that he should lay claim formally to the succession. Are the ἀρχαῖοι πατέρες and others who met, as it were secretly, the same as the ἡγούμενοι whom Pachomius called to his sickbed? When Theodore was enduring his period of disgrace, he continued to receive frequent assurances of support from monks in whose eyes "what had occurred was not a sin." Those allies are again described in rather vague terms, as the "great brothers" (μεγάλοι ἀδελφοί). The Bohairic *Life* refers to "many ancient brothers," who were moreover, much to Theodore's distress, quite explicit in their criticism of Pachomius.[29] A dangerous division was beginning to appear.

Even more interesting is the way in which the whole event, having been described, had then to be recast by the writers, almost certainly in order to explain why Theodore eventually succeeded. Pachomius is said to have issued his reprimand "because he wanted to make [Theodore] perfect and completely free of ambition for power [τέλειον καὶ ἀφίλαρχον παντελῶς]."[30] That point is repeated when Theodore makes his first trip to Alexandria with Zacchaeus (not to be confused with the second trip, which we have mentioned already).[31] Pachomius entrusted to them a letter to Athanasius, and in a reply the patriarch had much praise for Theodore. Was he already intervening in those developing disputes? The Bohairic *Life* makes Pachomius then praise Theodore also, as a result of that exchange of letters, and repeats the phrase we noted earlier about the two of them performing the "same service." The *Vita Prima* also records the praise, although it makes no reference to letters or the patriarch.[32] It is possible to discern in these accounts both the additions of the biographers and the beginnings of a genuine rehabilitation at the time.

But Theodore had already displayed some new independence. He said to Pachomius before the first trip to Alexandria, "I have some business to wind up in Thmoušons; send me and I will come back quickly."[33] On the journey, he met two old men in a boat, who told him a parable about humility and obedience. It concerned a harsh farmer who, after a series of apparently irrational trials, declared in the end to his loyal la-

29.   G¹ 107, Bo 94. The latter betrays a rumor, denied, that Theodore considered leaving the *Koinonia* altogether. Titoue of Phbow (see G¹ 84) prophesies his eventual restoration to authority.

30.   G¹ 107.

31.   G¹ 109, 113, 135; Bo 96f. It was on the second journey that Theodore spoke with Antony: see above, at n. 15.

32.   The praise, G¹ 109; the travelers' return, without comment, G¹ 113. Bo 97 borrows from Bo 74, equivalent to G¹ 91.

33.   He did, to Phbow, G¹ 107f. Bo 95 says that this journey was Pachomius's idea, prompted by a vision—a less convincing apology.

borer, "You shall no longer be my hired servant, but my son and heir." The old men then explained, not surprisingly, that the farmer stood for God, that Pachomius himself had been formed precisely in such a school of obedience, that he was to be seen as Theodore's father, and that if Theodore himself behaved in a similar fashion, he would become the heir. The two men, it transpired, were angels, who had appeared to Theodore to set his opinions right and offer him comfort. Pachomius himself later said as much![34] Again, some special pleading must lie at the heart of this tale. Yet Theodore's status at the time does seem to have improved. And when he arrived at Thmoušons, "they all embraced him with great cheerfulness while congratulating him." On what? And in that center of later rebellion!

All those hints and obscurities have to be kept in mind when we come to examine what happened at the time of Pachomius's death.[35] He was a victim, along with "many other great brothers," of a widespread epidemic of plague. Among those who died before him were at least three of the superiors whom he had called to his earlier sickbed—Sourous, Cornelios, and Paphnouti. The *Koinonia* was facing, therefore, a serious crisis of leadership. The Sahidic texts suggest that from the earliest stages of his illness, Pachomius was worried, "grieving and sighing within himself, so that the unity of the *Koinonia* might not be dissolved." "He gathered all the brothers about him," including "many of the leaders of the monasteries" and Theodore, and spoke at length about the quality of his own leadership, particularly its unobtrusive emphasis on service and strict adherence to the common rule.[36] Once death became imminent, Theodore was particularly assiduous in his attendance upon the founder. Two days before his death, Pachomius summoned what the *Vita Prima* describes as "the other fathers of the monasteries and the other leaders" (in the Sahidic version, "all the great ones among the brothers").[37] He sent them off to choose a successor, but they could not decide. He called Horsiesios, surely a significant choice, to his bedside to inquire how the deliberations were proceeding. Horsiesios had to report continuing failure. In the Sahidic account, the leaders say that the choice must rest with Pachomius himself.[38] "Believe me in this," he then

34. G¹ 108. See Veilleux, *Liturgie*, pp. 64–67. The son-and-heir motif occurs in G¹ 26, 130. Bo 95 is not so tendentious in its interpretation of the story.

35. G¹ 114–16; VBo 117–23, mainly from S⁷, trans. Lefort, *Vies*, pp. 45f.

36. VBo 118f = S⁷, trans. Lefort, *Vies*, pp. 45f. The humility of G¹ 115 is transferred to VBo 117 = S⁷, Lefort, ibid.

37. Why "other" in G¹? Other than whom? And is this supposed to be the same gathering as in VBo 118f?

38. That humility may have become "une sorte de rite obligatoire"; it certainly seems so in the Coptic text: see Festugière, *Première Vie grecque*, p. 89.

says, "I think that Petronios, if he lives, is able to take care of you"; and "some of the ancients" are sent to inform Petronios accordingly.[39]

Yet, after all those negotiations, it was still Theodore who stood closest to the dying founder. It was to Theodore that Pachomius imparted his final instructions and breathed his dying words. The *Vita Prima* betrays some embarrassment. Pachomius, anxious to avoid a cult focused upon his tomb, took Theodore by the beard and told him to bury him secretly. He then added, "I say not only this to you but also this." The Greek biographer feels forced to add, "What he also told him was not to neglect the negligent brothers, but to rouse them by God's law." The Sahidic tradition, however, is more explicit. It is Pachomius himself who makes that explanatory declaration. Theodore, not surprisingly, then wonders whether "after a time" he will therefore be superior. Whereat Pachomius adds, "Do not be hesitant. Do not waver. I am referring not only to what I am saying to you [about the burial] but what you are thinking in your heart."[40] That dialogue was to be recalled, as we shall see. For the moment, Theodore contented himself with the privilege of laying Pachomius to rest beside his own brother Paphnouti.[41]

So Theodore remained a person of significance, and even of power, despite his earlier demotion. Pachomius, to the very moment of his death, was clearly unable to make up his mind where the legitimate succession should lie. He had given a variety of signals: suggesting election by a group of leaders, giving, perhaps, a hint in his attention to Horsiesios, attempting a somewhat oblique cession to Petronios, and showing, throughout it all, his inability to dismiss entirely the natural claims of his true intimate, Theodore. However, it was with the ailing Petronios that power now lay, albeit for a few days only. (Theodore, meanwhile, was again *en route* for Alexandria, the accolades of Antony, and further consolation by the patriarch!) When his own death was clearly at hand, Petronios asked an unspecified group of monks who they thought should succeed him. Again, no one was willing to take the responsibility. The choice, they said, must be Petronios's. He named Horsiesios.[42]

The biographers are very subtle in their treatment of Horsiesios's initial career.[43] Their work, prior to Theodore's ultimate triumph about four

39.   VBo 121 = S[7], trans. Lefort, *Vies*, p. 49, includes a confusing addition, involving some conflict of chronology between S[7] and S[3]. Another assembly, totally indecisive, had taken place, and here it is Theodore who is sent to assess their progress!
40.   VBo 122 = S[7], trans. Lefort, *Vies*, p. 50; compare G[1] 116.
41.   Only VBo 123 = S[7], trans. Lefort, *Vies*, p. 51, mentions Paphnouti.
42.   G[1] 117. VBo 130 = S[5] 124 is essentially the same.
43.   In addition to Bacht, *Vermächtnis*, see Ruppert, pp. 201f. The danger of depending on Horsiesios and Theodore for an understanding of Pachomian spirituality is clear from pp. 104f.

years later, becomes a history of Theodore under Horsiesios.[44] The existence of a "Theodoran party" is constantly hinted at—the men whom one author would later describe as "those who knew him from the beginning as a true child of Abba Pachomius, and knew that his word had the grace and power of healing for a soul in affliction."[45] Immediately after his own appointment, Horsiesios placed Theodore in the fairly unimportant position of οἰκιακός to the carpenters at Phbow. If there had been some rehabilitation under Pachomius, this would have had to be taken as a calculated demotion. Yet it was at Phbow that "the brothers were having recourse to [Theodore] more and more."[46] Then Macarios, the new abbot of Phnoum, persuaded Horsiesios to let him take Theodore into his own community. Phnoum, of course, lay in Theodore's home territory, just outside Latopolis.[47] Here he was greeted with great joy. This may have been a monastery where he enjoyed much more overt support, "for they knew him from before, when he was a comforter of souls together with our father."[48] It was Theodore also whom the brothers asked to explain the teachings and visions of Pachomius. Although he was always careful to refer them to Horsiesios, nothing could disguise the implications of this admiration, for this was the man "whom the Lord had spiritually tested through fire by Abba Pachomius, so that he would become a vessel of election."[49]

It quickly became apparent that Horsiesios was not equal to his task. He "nurtured the brothers," as the *Vita Prima* put it, but the author had to add, "according to the grace of God that was given him."[50] There was obvious relief that "many of the ancients," Pachomius's early disciples, were still alive—Pšentaesi, Samuel, Paul, John, Hieracapollon, Titoue, Jonas, Theodore of Alexandria, and Theodore himself. "Therefore, since there were so many lamps among the brothers, there was no darkness in sight."[51] Psahref, successor to Paphnouti as steward at Phbow, was also described as "one of the ancients."[52]

It is likely that Horsiesios knew his own shortcomings. His first reac-

---

44.   In VBo 132 = S⁵ 126, Theodore is very vocal in his praise of Horsiesios! But in G¹ 120, the very same words are placed on the lips of Antony. The quality of the Coptic tradition where Bo is missing may not inspire confidence. Should we suspect the Greek of exaggerating tension between Horsiesios and Theodore? Or has the Sahidic avoided an embarrassing truth? A characteristic obscurity, probably beyond solution, but one of the authors, certainly, has rewritten events!

45.   G¹ 130, not in the Coptic.   46.   VBo 137 = S⁵ 131.

47.   In VBo 137 = S⁵ 131, the move is Theodore's own idea.

48.   G¹ 121; not explicit in S⁵.

49.   So the G¹ writer, 123, 125, not in the Coptic.

50.   G¹ 122, not in the Coptic.   51.   G¹ 123, not in the Coptic.

52.   G¹ 124.

tion to his appointment had been to cry, "This is beyond my power." [53]
His subsequent statements about authority not only stress humility, as
Pachomius had done, but prepare the way for his own abdication. "It
does not belong to all to govern souls," he said, "but only to perfect
men." Even more important in this regard is his remark, "It is good for a
man who knows his own limits to lay down the burden of authority after
he is established, that he may not run into greater danger. . . . Knowing
our own limits, let us also strive; for even so we will scarcely escape
God's judgement." [54]

As we have seen in the previous chapter, Horsiesios finally came to
grief over a specific issue—the move for commercial expansion by the
superior of Thmoušons, Apollonios. There may also have been more
personal antagonisms at work; a Coptic version has the rebels declare,
"We will have nothing to do with Horsiesios nor will we have anything
to do with the rules which he lays down." [55] Faced with that situation,
Horsiesios's first reaction seems to have been to split the federation in
two, or at least to seek a "collaborator" (ἄλλον σύνεργον ἔχειν). [56] Then
he had a dream in which it was suggested that he should involve Theodore in the leadership of the communities. Without actually consulting
Theodore, he gathered together "all the leaders"; [57] he told them he intended to resign and that Theodore seemed to him the man best able to
assume his office. Indeed, he suggested that Theodore had already enjoyed some such authority, saying of him (in the Coptic version), "he
was formerly a father to us," or (in the Greek account) referring to him as
"the same one who was in the past and is again our father Theodore." [58]
On that cryptic note, he withdrew to Šeneset, while "all the brothers,
hearing it, took Theodore as their father with joy and exultation."

Theodore now took command, but, as an act of humility, he asked
Horsiesios to come back and help him. [59] Horsiesios then made the interesting declaration that neither he nor anyone else had appointed Theodore, except only Pachomius, on his deathbed, when he had taken him
by the beard and told him to bury his bones in a secret place. [60] Theodore
was willing to accept this new interpretation of Pachomian history and

53. G[1] 117, VBo 130 = S[5] 124.
54. G[1] 126, not in the Coptic.
55. VBo 139 = S[6], trans. Lefort, Vies, p. 324.
56. G[1] 128.
57. S[6]. Lefort, Vies, p. 325, suggests by his translation that this means "all
the ancients" in the monastery where he was.
58. G[1] 129, VBo 139 = S[6], trans. Lefort, Vies, p. 325. Festugière preferred
the Greek, Première Vie grecque, 89.
59. For this period, see Ruppert, pp. 209f.
60. G[1] 130, not in the Coptic.

of the genealogical succession of authority that would persist until his own death. Horsiesios returned to Šeneset. There does seem to have been a short period of ambiguity, however. Although Horsiesios obviously considered himself to have resigned completely, Theodore would act as if he were no more than a deputy, asking the former leader constantly for instructions—so much so that Horsiesios could say, "I rule now more than when I was alone." [61] Even Theodore's later foundations were made "with our father Horsiesios's approval." [62]

The new superior was faced with a situation very different from that of his predecessor. When Horsiesios had first acceded to supreme authority, many of Pachomius's early disciples had still been alive, making Horsiesios himself much more a *primus inter pares*. Indeed, this may have contributed to his apparent weakness as a leader. Theodore felt much more isolated, and therefore more exposed. That, in its turn, may tell us something about his apparent humility. He opened his first address to his new subjects with the words, "Where are the ancient ones?" [63] There are signs in what followed that he wished to return to an older system of government more reminiscent of Pachomius's earliest foundations. The "primitive" vocabulary reasserted itself, with emphasis on mutual help and sympathy. Those, he said, were the chief fruits of Pachomius's work, which the devil now threatened to scatter. "Now it is not yet five years since he passed away and we have forgotten that very great joy and peace which we then had with each other . . . But how are we now? Let us, however, all return; we do believe that God will renew us in his mercy." [64] So Theodore intended his exercise of authority to be much more personal and direct. His preoccupation was to heal, to cure. He did this, necessarily, person to person, counseling each monk in turn, while monks approached him also individually. [65] Another early task that he successfully achieved was the reconciliation of Apollonius, who was persuaded to make his peace with other members of the federation. [66]

The Coptic account of Theodore's initial address is much more detailed, and certain aspects of it deserve credence. [67] Even greater emphasis is laid there on the renewal of a covenant among the monks—an idea

61. G¹ 130.
62. G¹ 134.
63. G¹ 131, not in the Coptic. Here I would disagree with Chitty, "Chronology," p. 385. He felt that these "ancient ones" were Theodore's long-standing supporters, now witnesses to his triumph.
64. G¹ 131.
65. G¹ 132. See Bo 191.
66. G¹ 131.
67. VBo 141f are based on a complex interweaving of S⁵, S⁶, and some later passages of Bo, as explained by Veilleux, *Koinonia*, 1:4.

that had been central to Pachomius's first endeavor.[68] It is clear also that Theodore felt able to appeal to some canon of behavior initiated by Pachomius and probably by his own time written down. He was able to measure, as a consequence, what he interpreted as current decline. His views on that matter, however, had not inspired him to revolt against Horsiesios directly. If it is true that Horsiesios had been, as the text puts it, "removed from his position," the terms of Theodore's speech make it clear that it was none of his doing. Nor indeed do the "leaders of the monasteries" appear to have been responsible, for they arrived upon the scene somewhat later in response to a summons from Theodore. Initially they were unperturbed, but they became subsequently fearful when they found themselves victims of Theodore's anger.[69] He commanded them to remain at Phbow, humbly weaving mats, while he went to visit all the monasteries inquiring into their current standards of observance. As a result, so it seems, he moved all the superiors to new positions. The text even adds, "He used to do this twice a year for their own good and their salvation."[70] That last piece of information is hard to believe. Yet at some stage it was thought fitting or convenient to create that drastic impression of Theodore's new regime.

In formulating his own notions of authority, Theodore could echo the vocabulary of Horsiesios. "As for us, brothers, understanding these things, let us keep each to his own measure, both the one who is considered a shepherd of souls as well as the one who is considered a sheep." But he added a touch more reminiscent of Pachomius: "Let us all pray to be sheep, for no one is the shepherd save he who said, I am the Good Shepherd." Theodore is made to appear at once more realistic than Horsiesios and more organized in his reflections. God had initiated a tradition of authority. By the incarnation, man gained knowledge of God's truth. Then Peter was given the command, "Feed my lambs," and in each generation there would emerge others responsible for this feeding of the Lord's flock. First came the apostles, then what Theodore called "the bishops who are the fathers." Finally Theodore would add, as Pachomius had done, "All those who listen to Christ who is in them are also his children, although they do not belong to the clergy and have no ecclesiastical rank."[71]

Theodore, albeit slowly, was eventually reconciled with Horsiesios.

68. See Chapter III, at nn. 47f.
69. VBo 142 = S⁶, trans. Lefort, *Vies*, p. 327.
70. So S⁶ trans. Lefort, *Vies*, pp. 330f.
71. G¹ 135. These statements are reminiscent of much said by Pachomius at Latopolis, G¹ 112; indeed, the Synod is recalled at the beginning of the very chapter here quoted.

Harmony seems to have been aided by the intervention of the patriarch Athanasius. We know it was not the first time he had taken an interest in the fortunes of Pachomius's foundations. Now, following his triumphant return in 363 to the see from which he had been temporarily exiled by the Arian emperor Constantius, he was making an important tour of Upper Egypt. It was more than ten years, therefore, since Horsiesios had resigned. Theodore and companions went to meet the patriarch. Having expressed his admiration for the way the monasteries were run, and having publicly acknowledged Theodore's outstanding merits as a leader, Athanasius wrote a letter to Horsiesios, entrusting it to Theodore as mere messenger. In the letter, he referred to Theodore as "your assistant [σύνεργόν σου] and the father of the brothers," although he admitted also that he saw in him "the Lord of your father Pachomius."[72] Quite apart from reviving the notion of shared government, toyed with at the end of Horsiesios's first period of rule and during the early months after Theodore's accession, the letter seems to have inaugurated a new relationship between the two men. Whether Athanasius intended as much is impossible to judge. Theodore met with Horsiesios at Šeneset amid demonstrations of humility and reconciliation.[73] There was a sense too, in Theodore, that his own death might not be far distant. He persuaded the former superior to return with him permanently to Phbow. There Horsiesios resumed a regular teaching role. Theodore insisted again on his own status as "assistant," but the two are asserted to have been "as one man." They certainly exercised some joint authority, or at least took turn and turn about, delivering catecheses, and even, according to the *Vita Prima*, sharing the task of visiting the other monasteries.[74]

We shall probably never unravel completely the intricacies of their relationship. Quite possibly Theodore and Horsiesios themselves did not fully understand its implications. It is also striking that precisely at that moment there recurred those institutional anxieties that had beset Horsiesios during his original term of office. The communities started once again to buy up large areas of land and to deploy upon the river an increasing amount of commercial traffic. Theodore was saddened and worried, but, as we noted in the previous chapter, he could offer no solution beyond solitary prayer in the night hours.[75]

Soon after, in 368, he died. In marked contrast to the events follow-

---

72. G¹ 144. Bo 202 is not quite so explicit, but Bo 204 is, and 201 makes a similar point more vaguely.

73. The G¹ 145 reference to Thmoušons must be an error: see 129. Bo 204 captures well the atmosphere of the occasion.

74. G¹ 145, Bo 204f.

75. G¹ 146, Bo 187f. See Chapter VIII at n. 36.

ing the deaths of Pachomius and Petronios or after the resignation of
Horsiesios, there was no question of an election or of the designation of
any successor. Horsiesios was there; Horsiesios continued to rule. Only
in the Bohairic *Life* is there a deathbed scene, with a formal cession of
power by Theodore expressed in terms of the newly revived ambiguity:
"For the inheritance is his; I am only his assistant."[76] Once again it was
Athanasius who made more formal suggestions, in his letter of condo-
lence. Horsiesios, he said, represented Theodore so closely, it was as if
the great disciple were still living in his community. Their identity was
now the key to a smooth succession. On that final note of patriarchal
solicitude and interpretation, the biographies come to an end.

It is hard to know entirely what to make of those transitions. As we
saw in earlier chapters, Pachomius was never happy with any rigidly defined system of government. On the other hand, he had long been beset
by anxiety as to what would happen to his communities after his death.
When death was imminent, he was confused as to how to achieve a
smooth succession. It was not just that he could not decide whom to
choose: he could not decide *how* to choose, either.

It is also clear that the texts upon which we depend have taken up a
position on several issues. They are careful to suggest that a legitimate
tradition of monastic authority did exist. It is doubtful whether even that
much could have been clear in 346. Further, they champion the causes of
various pretenders to legitimacy, especially Theodore. Perhaps even
more important, they suggest that the patriarch of Alexandria was taking an increasingly close interest in what was going on among the Pachomian monasteries and was showing an unashamed readiness to be-
stow his accolade on this or that potential leader. Such hints are not
confined to the *Vita Prima*. More than one of the *Lives*, therefore, may
indeed have been an instrument in that attempted exercise of episcopal
authority. As we saw at the beginning of our story, there was a tendency,
at least in some of the biographies, to merge the legitimate tradition of
the ascetic communities with another legitimate tradition, which flowed
from the apostolic church to the fourth-century episcopate.

As a contribution to the history of asceticism and to our understanding of Pachomius's own ambitions and achievements, the leadership crisis reveals a conflict of ideas about authority, about poverty, and about
the very possibility of holding together so large a number of communities. The struggle for petty office, which Pachomius had supposedly
foreseen and which obviously distressed Horsiesios, making the exer-

76. Bo 206.

cise of his own office increasingly difficult, was in marked contrast to the
founder's ideal of mutual responsibility and support. Theodore seems to
have been intent upon restoring that ideal, even to the extent of admitting Horsiesios once more to a position of responsibility at Phbow, and
perhaps over other communities. Apollonius's rebellion at Thmoušons
was based, by contrast, on the conviction that survival depended on expansion—on the exploitation of land, and on the increased and more
efficient sale of monastic produce. Both Horsiesios and Theodore had
grave misgivings about such a policy. Yet there is no evidence that they
ever gained their point. The communities eventually described by Palladius bear a much closer resemblance to the grandiose ambitions of Apollonius than to any community Pachomius would have recognized. It is
entirely possible that considerable conflict continued between the communities on those issues throughout the rest of the century. Hints are
offered by events in the leadership crisis itself—by Theodore's retire-
ment to his "home" community of Phnoum, for example, or by his later
radical policy of regularly transferring superiors from one monastery to
another. They make it very likely that individual foundations—Phbow,
Tabennesi, Thmoušons, or Šeneset—remained for a long time surprisingly different centers of ascetic experiment, with ideals that conflicted
not least in matters of authority and economics. At least up to the time
of Theodore's death, real power seems to have resided most in the hands
of those at Phbow. It was only by persuading Horsiesios to come and live
there that Theodore could effectively resolve his disagreements with his
eventual successor. From there, perhaps, Horsiesios had then to establish anew the wider authority over the other monasteries that had once
been characteristic of Pachomius. His *Liber* and his own *Rules* may tell us
how easy he found the task and how successfully he achieved it, but
that has to be another story.

BIBLIOGRAPHY

For an understanding of the Roman Empire in general, consult Fergus Millar, *The Roman Empire and Its Neighbours*; Ramsay MacMullen, *Roman Government's Response to Crisis*; A. H. M. Jones, *The Later Roman Empire*. Wider surveys are given by Peter Brown, *The World of Late Antiquity*, and Roger Rémondon, *La Crise de l'Empire romain*. Still very useful is Ernst Stein, *Geschichte des spätrömischen Reiches*. The section of the work most relevant to this study has been translated from the German by Jean-Rémy Palanque, *Histoire du Bas-Empire*, vol. 1.

On late Roman religion, the following are excellent: Franz Cumont, *Astrology and Religion among the Greeks and Romans*, and *The Oriental Religions in Roman Paganism*; E. R. Dodds, *Pagan and Christian in an Age of Anxiety*; A. J. Festugière, *La Révélation d'Hermes-Trismégiste*; Johannes Geffcken, *The Last Days of Greco-Roman Paganism*; and A. D. Nock, *Essays on Religion and the Ancient World*.

On Egypt more particularly, I have been closely guided by Jacqueline Lallemand, *L'Administration civile de l'Égypte*. Inescapable is H. I. Bell, *Egypt from Alexander the Great to the Arab Conquest*. Also useful are A. C. Johnson, *Egypt and the Roman Empire*, and, with L. C. West, *Byzantine Egypt*; the chapter "Egypt" in the revised edition of A. H. M. Jones, *The Cities of the East Roman Provinces*; P. Jouguet, *La Vie municipale dans l'Empire romain*; and Germaine Rouillard, *L'Administration civile de l'Égypte byzantine*.

A discussion of Christianity in Egypt will be dominated by H. I. Bell, *Cults and Creeds in Graeco-Roman Egypt*; E. R. Hardy, *Christian Egypt*; and C. H. Roberts, *Manuscript, Society, and Belief in Early Christian Egypt*.

Some of the problems associated with the source material can also be deduced from a reading of André Bataille, *Les Papyrus*; Paul Eric

Kahle, *Bala'izah*. *Coptic Texts from Deir el-Bala'izah*; and Gustave Lefebvre, *Recueil des inscriptions grecques-chrétiennes d'Égypte*. Also instructive is J. G. Winter, *Life and Letters in the Papyri*.

Full references to all these works will be found in the sections of the Bibliography that follow.

SOURCES

Adam, Alfred. *Texte zum Manichäismus*. 2d ed. Kleine Texte für Vorlesungen und Übungen, no. 175. Berlin: Walter de Gruyter, 1969.

Alexander of Lycopolis. *An Alexandrian Platonist against Dualism: Alexander of Lycopolis' Treatise, "Critique of the Doctrines of Manichaeus"* [Disputatio]. Translated and with an introduction and notes by P. W. van der Horst and J. Mansfeld. Leiden: Brill, 1974.

————. *Contra Manichaei opiniones disputatio*. Edited by Augustus Brinkmann. Leipzig: Teubner, 1895.

Allberry, Charles Robert Cecil. *A Manichaean Psalm-Book*, part 2. With a contribution by Hugo Ibscher. Vol. 2 of *Manichaean Manuscripts in the Chester Beatty Collection*. Stuttgart: Kohlhammer, 1938.

Amélineau, Émile. *Vie de Pakhôme*. Arabic text and French translation in *Monuments pour servir à l'histoire de l'Égypte chrétienne au IVᵉ siècle: histoire de saint Pakhôme et de ses communautés*: 335–711. Annales du Musée Guimet, no. 17. Paris: E. Leroux, 1889.

Ammon, Letter of. See *Letter of Ammon*.

Andreas, Friedrich Carl, and Walter Henning. *Mitteliranische Manichäica aus Chinesisch-Turkestan*, vol. 2. Sonderausgabe aus den Sitzungsberichten der preussischen Akademie der Wissenschaften, phil.-hist. Klasse, 1933, no. 7. Berlin: Walter de Gruyter, 1933.

Apophthegmata patrum [The Sayings of the Fathers]. Alphabetical collection. In J. P. Migne, *PG* 65.72–440.

————. Anonymous collection [The Sayings of the Fathers]. "Histoire des solitaires égyptiens (MS Coislin 126, fol. 158f.)," nos. 133–369. Edited by F. Nau. *Revue d'Orient chrétien* 13 (1908): 47–57, 266–83; 14 (1909): 357–79; 17 (1912): 204–11, 294–301; 18 (1913): 137–40.

————. *The Desert Christian: Sayings of the Desert Fathers: The Alphabetical Collection*. Translated and with a foreword by Benedicta Ward. Cistercian Studies, no. 59. New York: Cistercian Publications, 1975.

————. Latin collection [The Sayings of the Fathers]. *Verba seniorum* [*Vitae patrum*, books V–VII]. In J. P. Migne, *PL* 73.851–1062.

Athanasius. *The Canons of Athanasius, Patriarch of Alexandria*. Edited and translated by Wilhelm Riedel and W. E. Crum. London: Williams and Norgate, 1904. Reprint. Amsterdam: Philo Press, 1973.

————. *The Festal Epistles of S. Athanasius, Bishop of Alexandria*. Edited by H. G. Williams. Translated from the Syriac by Henry Burgess. Oxford: J. H. Parker, 1854.

————. *The Festal Letters of Athanasius*. Syriac text edited and with extensive preface by William Cureton. London: Society for the Publication of Oriental Texts, 1848.

————. *S. Athanase: lettres festales et pastorales en copte.* Coptic text edited and with a French translation by Louis-Théophile Lefort. *CSCO* 150, 151, script. copt. 19, 20. Louvain: L. Durbecq, 1955.

————. *Athanase d'Alexandrie: lettres à Sérapion sur la divinité du Saint-Esprit* [Letters to Serapion]. Edited and with a French translation by Joseph Lebon. Sources chrétiennes, no. 15. Paris: Éditions du Cerf, 1947.

————. *The Letters of Saint Athanasius Concerning the Holy Spirit* [Letters to Serapion]. Translated by C. R. B. Shapland. London: Epworth Press, 1951.

————. *The Life of Saint Antony.* Translated by R. C. Gregg. Classics of Western Spirituality. New York: Paulist Press, 1980.

————. *The Life of Saint Antony.* Translated and with notes by Robert T. Meyer. Ancient Christian Writers, no. 10. London: Longman, Green and Co.; Westminster, Md.: Newman Press, 1950.

————. *Vita Antonii* [Life of Antony]. In J. P. Migne, *PG* 26.837–976.

————. "Lettre de saint Athanase au sujet de l'amour et de la tempérance" [On Charity and Temperance]. Coptic text edited and with a French translation by Arn van Lantschoot. *Le Muséon* 40 (1927): 265–92. *See also* Lefort, "Saint Athanase écrivain copte."

Bacht, Heinrich. "Ein verkanntes Fragment der koptischen Pachomius-Regel." *Le Muséon* 75 (1962): 5–18.

————. *Das Vermächtnis des Ursprungs.* Studien zum frühen Mönchtum, no. 1. Würzburg: Echter, 1972.

Barns, John W. B., Gerald M. Browne, and John C. Shelton. *Nag Hammadi Codices: Greek and Coptic Papyri from the Cartonnage of the Covers.* Nag Hammadi Studies, no. 16. Leiden: Brill, 1981.

Boak, Arthur E. R., and Herbert Chayyim Youtie. *The Archive of Aurelius Isidorus in the Egyptian Museum, Cairo, and the University of Michigan (P. Cair. Isidor.).* Ann Arbor: University of Michigan Press, 1960.

Bohairic Life of Pachomius. Coptic text in *Sancti Pachomii vita bohairice scripta. See* Lefort.

————. English translation in *Pachomian Koinonia*, 1:23–295. *See* Veilleux.

Boon, Amand. *Pachomiana Latina.* Bibliothèque de la Revue d'histoire ecclésiastique, no. 7. Louvain: Bureaux de la Revue, 1932.

Cassian, John. *Conferences.* Translated and with prolegomena, preface, and notes by Edgar C. S. Gibson. In *The Works of Sulpitius Severus*, etc. (A Select Library of Nicene and Post-Nicene Fathers, n.s., no. 11), pp. 161–641. Oxford: Parker and Co., 1894.

————. *Conlationes* [Conferences]. Vol. 2 of *J. Cassiani Opera*, edited by M. Petschenig. *CSEL* 13. Vienna: apud C. Geroldi filium, 1886.

————. *Jean Cassien: Conférences.* Latin text with French translation by E. Pichery. Sources chrétiennes, nos. 42, 54, 64. Paris: Éditions du Cerf, 1955, 1958, 1959.

————. *Institutes.* In *The Works of Sulpitius Severus. See* Cassian, *Conferences.*

————. *Institutiones* [Institutes]. In *J. Cassiani de institutis coenobiorum et de octo principalium vitiorum remediis libri XII*, edited by M. Petschenig, *CSEL* 17:1–231. Vienna and Prague: F. Tempsky; Leipzig: G. Freytag, 1888.

————. *Jean Cassien: Institutions cénobitiques.* Latin text with French translation by Jean-Claude Guy. Sources chrétiennes, no. 109. Paris: Éditions du Cerf, 1965.

Clement of Alexandria. *Opera*. Edited by O. Stahlin. *GCS* vols. 12, 15, 17, 39.
    Leipzig: J. C. Hinrichs, 1905–36.
————. *Clément d'Alexandrie: Les Stromates*. Greek text with French translation by
    Marcel Castor and with an introduction by Claude Mondésert. Sources
    chrétiennes, nos. 30, 38. Paris: Éditions du Cerf, 1951–. Further volumes
    to appear.
Codex Theodosianus. Edited by Theodor Mommsen and Paul M. Meyer. Berlin:
    Weidmann, 1905.
————. *The Theodosian Code and Novels and the Sirmondian Constitutions*. Trans-
    lated and with commentary, glossary, and bibliography by Clyde Pharr,
    Theresa Sherrer Davidson, and Mary Brown Pharr and with an introduc-
    tion by C. Dickermann William. The Corpus of Roman Law, no. 1. Prince-
    ton, N.J.: Princeton University Press, 1952. Reprint. New York: Green-
    wood Press, 1969.
Dionysius Exiguus. Latin *Life* of Pachomius. *See* van Cranenburgh.
Draguet, René. Fragment 1. "Un Morceau grec inédit des vies de Pachôme ap-
    parié à un texte d'Évagre en partie inconnu." *Le Muséon* 70 (1957): 267–
    306. [An English translation of the fragment is given in *Pachomian Koino-
    nia*, 2:111–14. *See* Veilleux.]
————. Fragment 2. "Un Paralipomenon pachômien inconnu dans le Karakallou
    251." In *Mélanges Eugène Tisserant* (q.v. under "Secondary Works"), vol. 2,
    part 1:55–61. [An English translation of the fragment is given in *Pacho-
    mian Koinonia*, 2:115–19. *See* Veilleux.]
Epiphanius of Constantia and Salamis. *Panarion*. In Epiphanius, *Opera*, edited by
    K. Holl, 3:1–496. *GCS* 37. Leipzig: J. C. Hinrichs, 1933.
Eusebius of Caesarea. *Historia ecclesiastica*. 2 vols. Translated by Roy Joseph
    Deferrari. Fathers of the Church, vols. 19, 29. New York: Fathers of the
    Church, Inc., 1953–55.
————. *Historia ecclesiastica*. 2 vols. Greek text with English translation by Kir-
    sopp Lake and J. E. L. Oulton. Loeb Classical Library. London: Heine-
    mann; Cambridge, Mass.: Harvard University Press, 1926–32.
————. *Opera*. 8 vols. in 18. Edited by J. A. Heikel, E. Schwartz, E. Klostermann,
    et al. *GCS*, vols. 7, 7:1, 9, 11, 14 [*bis*], 20, 23–24, 34, 43, 47, 53b. Leipzig:
    J. C. Hinrichs, 1902–26; Berlin: Akademie Verlag, 1956–75.
————. *Eusèbe de Césarée: la préparation évangélique*. Greek text with French trans-
    lation by Edouard des Places. Sources chrétiennes, nos. 206, 228. Paris:
    Éditions du Cerf, 1974–. Further volumes to appear.
Eutychius. *Annales*. In J. P. Migne, *PG* 111:889–1155.
Evagrius of Pontus. *Praktikos*. In *Évagre le Pontique: traité pratique ou le moine*. *See*
    Secondary Works: Guillaumont.
————. *Les Six Centuries des "Kephalaia gnostica."* Two Syriac versions edited and
    with a French translation by Antoine Guillaumont. Patrologia orientalis,
    vol. 28, part 1. Paris: Firmin-Didot, 1958.
Excerpta. See Pachomius.
The Facsimile Edition of the Nag Hammadi Codices. 12 vols. Leiden: Brill, 1972–79.
Festugière, André Marie Jean. *La Première Vie grecque de saint Pachôme, introduc-
    tion critique et traduction*. Vol. 4, part 2 of *Les Moines d'Orient*. Paris: Édi-
    tions du Cerf, 1965.
Ginzberg, Louis. *The Legends of the Jews*. Vol. 4, *Biblical Times and Characters from*

Joshua to Esther. Vol. 6, *Notes.* Philadelphia: Jewish Publication Society of America, 1913, 1928.

Grobel, Kendrick, trans. and comm. *The Gospel of Truth: A Valentinian Meditation on the Gospel.* London: Adam and Charles Black, 1960.

Halkin, François. *Sancti Pachomii vitae graecae.* Subsidia hagiographica, no. 19. Brussels: Société des Bollandistes, 1932.

Henrichs, Albert, and Ludwig Koenen. "Ein griechischer Mani-Codex (P. Colon. inv. gr. 4780)." *Zeitschrift für Papyrologie und Epigraphik* 5 (1970): 97–216.

Hermas. *Hermas: Le Pasteur.* Greek and Latin texts with French translation by Robert Joly. Sources chrétiennes, no. 53. 2d ed. Paris: Éditions du Cerf, 1968.

———. *Der Hirt des Hermas.* Edited by Molly Whittacker. 2d ed. *GCS* 48. Berlin: Akademie Verlag, 1967.

———. *The Shepherd of Hermas.* Greek and Latin texts with an English translation by Kirsopp Lake. In *The Apostolic Fathers*, 2 : 6–305. Loeb Classical Library. London: Heinemann; New York: Macmillan, 1913.

Horsiesios. *Liber.* Latin text with German translation and introduction in *Das Vermächtnis des Ursprungs*: 58–188. *See* Bacht.

———. *Liber.* English translation in *Pachomian Koinonia*, 3 : 171–224. *See* Veilleux.

Jerome. *De viris illustribus.* In J. P. Migne, *PL* 23.631–759.

———. *Letters.* Edited by Isidor Hilberg. 3 vols. *CSEL* 54–56. Vienna: F. Tempsky; Leipzig: G. Freytag, 1910–18.

Kahle, Paul Eric. *Bala'izah: Coptic Texts from Deir el-Bala'izah in Upper Egypt.* 2 vols. London: Oxford University Press, 1954.

Kramer, B., and R. Hubner, eds. *Kölner Papyri*, vol. 3. Papyrologica Coloniensia, no. 7, part 3. Opladen: Westdeutscher Verlag, 1980.

Lefebvre, Gustave. *Recueil des inscriptions grecques-chrétiennes d'Égypte.* Cairo: Institut français d'archéologie orientale, 1907.

Lefort, Louis-Théophile. "Saint Athanase écrivain copte." *Le Muséon* 46 (1933): 1–33.

———, ed. and trans. *Oeuvres de s. Pachôme et de ses disciples.* Coptic texts with French translations. *CSCO* 159, 160, script. copt. 23, 24. Louvain: L. Durbecq, 1956.

———, ed. and trans. *Sancti Pachomii vita bohairice scripta.* Coptic text with Latin translation. *CSCO* 89, 107, script. copt. 7. Paris: e Typographeo Reipublicae, 1925–36. Reprint. Louvain: L. Durbecq, 1953.

———, ed. *Sancti Pachomii vitae sahidice scriptae.* Coptic texts only. *CSCO* 99, 100, script. copt. 8. Paris: e Typographeo Reipublicae, 1933. Reprint. Louvain: L. Durbecq, 1952.

———, trans. *Les Vies coptes de s. Pachôme et de ses premiers successeurs.* French translations only, with extensive introduction. Bibliothèque du *Muséon*, no. 16. Louvain: Bureaux du *Muséon*, 1943.

Letter of Ammon. Greek text in *Sancti Pachomii vitae graecae*: 97–121. *See* Halkin.

———. English translation in *Pachomian Koinonia*, 2 : 71–109. *See* Veilleux.

Lewis, Naphtali, ed. and trans. *Leitourgia Papyri: Documents on Compulsory Public Service in Egypt under Roman Rule.* Transactions of the American Philosophical Society, n.s., 53, 9. Philadelphia: American Philosophical Society, 1963.

Liber Orsiesii [The Testament of Horsiesios]. *See* Horsiesios.

Lives of Antony, Pachomius. See *Vita Antonii, Vitae Pachomii.*

Nag Hammadi Codices. See *The Facsimile Edition of the Nag Hammadi Codices.*

Nag Hammadi Codices: Cartonnage. See Barns.

Nag Hammadi Library in English. See Robinson.

Nau, F. See *Apophthegmata Patrum,* Anonymous Collection.

Origen. *Opera.* Edited by P. Koetschau, E. Klostermann, et al. *GCS* vols. 2, 3, 6, 10, 22, 29, 30, 33, 35, 38, 40, 41. Leipzig: J. C. Hinrichs, 1899–1919.

―――. *The Writings of Origen.* Translated by F. Crombie. Ante-Nicene Christian Library, vols. 10, 23. Edinburgh: T. & T. Clark, 1869–78.

The Oxyrhynchus Papyri. Edited by Bernard P. Grenfell, Arthur S. Hunt, et al. 49 vols. London: Oxford University Press, 1898–. Further volumes to appear.

Pachomius. *Catecheses.* See Pachomius, *Instruction.*

―――. *Excerpta. See* Pachomius, *Rules.*

―――. *Instruction Concerning a Spiteful Monk* [CMR]. Coptic text and French translation in *Oeuvres de s. Pachôme et de ses disciples,* CSCO 159:1–24 (text); 160:1–26 (translation). *See* Lefort, *Oeuvres.*

―――. *Instruction Concerning a Spiteful Monk* [CMR]. English translation in *Pachomian Koinonia,* 3:13–46. See Veilleux.

―――. *Instruction on the Six Days of the Passover* [CJP]. Coptic text and French translation in *Oeuvres de s. Pachôme et de ses disciples,* CSCO 159:24–26 (text); 160:26–27 (translation). *See* Lefort, *Oeuvres.*

―――. *Instruction on the Six Days of the Passover* [CJP]. English translation in *Pachomian Koinonia,* 3:47–49. See Veilleux.

―――. *Letters.* Texts in *Die Briefe Pachoms. See* Quecke. [It is in the light of Quecke's work that one should read the texts presented in Amand Boon, *Pachomiana Latina. See* Boon.]

―――. *Letters.* English translation in *Pachomian Koinonia,* 3:51–83. *See* Veilleux.

―――. *Praecepta* [P], *Praecepta et Instituta* [PInst], *Praecepta atque Iudicia* [PIud], and *Praecepta ac Leges* [PLeg]. *See* Pachomius, *Rules.*

―――. *Rules.* Coptic fragments and French translation in *Oeuvres de s. Pachôme et de ses disciples,* CSCO 159:30–36 (text); 160:30–37 (translation). *See* Lefort, *Oeuvres.*

―――. *Rules.* Latin text in *Pachomiana Latina:* 11–74. *See* Boon.

―――. *Rules.* Greek *Excerpta* in *Pachomiana Latina:* 169–82. *See* Boon.

―――. *Rules.* English translation in *Pachomian Koinonia,* 2:145–85. *See* Veilleux.

Palladius. *The Lausiac History* [*Historia Lausiaca*]. Translated into English and annotated by Robert T. Meyer. Ancient Christian Writers, no. 34. Westminster, Md., and London: Newman Press, 1965.

―――. *The Lausiac History of Palladius. A Critical Discussion, Together with Notes on Early Monachism.* Edited and with an introduction by Cuthbert Butler. Texts and Studies, vol. 6, parts 1 and 2. Cambridge: Cambridge University Press, 1898–1904. Reprint. Hildesheim: Olms, 1967.

Paralipomena. Greek text in *Sancti Pachomii vitae graecae:* 122–65. *See* Halkin.

―――. English translation in *Pachomian Koinonia,* 2:19–70. *See* Veilleux.

Philo. *De vita contemplativa.* Greek text edited and wi'h English translation by F. H. Colson in *Philo: Works,* 9:113–69. Loeb Classical Library. Cambridge, Mass.: Harvard University Press; London: Heinemann, 1941.

―――. *Quod omnis probus liber sit.* Greek text edited and with English translation by F. H. Colson in *Philo: Works,* 9:11–101. Loeb Classical Library. Cambridge, Mass.: Harvard University Press; London: Heinemann, 1941.

Philostorgius. *Historia ecclesiastica*. Edited by Joseph Bidez. 2d ed. *GCS* 21. Berlin: Akademie Verlag, 1972.

Plotinus. *The Enneads*. 6 vols. Greek text edited and with English translation by Arthur Hilary Armstrong. Loeb Classical Library. Cambridge, Mass.: Harvard University Press; London: Heinemann, 1966–.

———. *The Enneads*. Translated into English by Stephen MacKenna. 2d ed. rev. London: Faber and Faber, 1956.

———. [The Enneads] *Plotini Opera*. Vol. 1, *Enneads* I–III. Vol. 2, *Enneads* IV–V. Vol. 3, *Enneads* VI. Edited by Paul Henry and Hans-Rudolf Schwyzer. Oxford Classical Texts. Oxford: Clarendon Press, 1964, 1977, 1982. Further volumes to appear.

Polotsky, Hans Jakob. *Manichäische Homilien*. With a contribution by Hugo Ibscher. Vol. 1 of *Manichäische Handschriften der Sammlung A. Chester Beatty*. Stuttgart: Kohlhammer, 1934.

Polotsky, Hans Jakob, and Alexander Bohlig. *Kephalaia*. With a contribution by Hugo Ibscher. Vol. 1 of *Manichäische Handschriften der staatlichen Museen Berlin*, edited by Carl Schmidt. Stuttgart: Kohlhammer, 1940.

Porphyry. *Life of Plotinus* [*Vita Plotini*]. In *Plotini Opera*, 1:1–38. *See* Plotinus.

———. *Life of Plotinus*. In *Plotinus: The Enneads*, vol. 1, translated by Arthur Hilary Armstrong. *See* Plotinus.

Quecke, Hans. *Die Briefe Pachoms. Griechischer Text der Handschrift W. 145 der Chester Beatty Library*. Textus Patristici et Liturgici, no. 11. Regensburg: Friedrich Pustet, 1975.

Robinson, James M., gen. ed. *The Nag Hammadi Library in English*. Translated by members of the Coptic Gnostic Library project of the Institute for Antiquity and Christianity. Leiden: Brill, 1977.

Rufinus. *Historia monachorum*. In J. P. Migne, *PL* 21.387–462.

Rules of Pachomius. *See* Pachomius, *Rules*.

Sayings of the Fathers. *See Apophthegmata patrum*.

Schmidt, Carl, and Hans Jakob Polotsky. *Ein Mani-Fund in Ägypten. Originalschriften des Mani und seiner Schüler*. Sonderausgabe aus den Sitzungsberichten der preussischen Akademie der Wissenschaften, phil.-hist. Klasse, 1933, no. 1. Berlin: Walter de Gruyter, 1933.

Serapion of Thmuis. *Against the Manichees*. Edited by Robert Pierce Casey. Harvard Theological Studies, no. 15. Cambridge, Mass.: Harvard University Press, 1931.

———. *Epistola ad monachos*. In J. P. Migne, *PG* 40.925–42.

Skeat, Theodore C., ed. *Papyri from Panopolis in the Chester Beatty Library*. Chester Beatty Monographs, no. 10. Dublin: Hodges Figgis, 1964.

Socrates. *Historia ecclesiastica*. In J. P. Migne, *PG* 67.29–842.

———. *Historia ecclesiastica*. Anonymous English translation. Bohn's ecclesiastical Library. London: G. Bell and Sons, 1853.

The Testament of Horsiesios [*Liber Orsiesii*]. *See* Horsiesios.

Theodore. *Instructions* [*Catecheses*] and *Letters*. Coptic texts and French translations in *Oeuvres de s. Pachôme et de ses disciples*, *CSCO* 159:37–59 (texts); 160:38–61 (translations). *See* Lefort, *Oeuvres*.

———. *Instructions* [*Catecheses*] and *Letters*. English translation in *Pachomian Koinonia*, 3:91–134. *See* Veilleux.

The Theodosian Code. *See Codex Theodosianus*.

van Cranenburgh, H. *La Vie latine de saint Pachôme, traduite du grec par Denys le*

Petit. Subsidia hagiographica, no. 46. Brussels: Société des Bollandistes, 1969.

van Lantschoot, Arn. "Lettre de saint Athanase au sujet de l'amour et de la tempérance" [On Charity and Temperance]. *See* Athanasius.

Veilleux, Armand, trans. *Pachomian Koinonia. The Lives, Rules, and Other Writings of Saint Pachomius and His Disciples.* With a foreword by Adalbert de Vogüé. Vol. 1, *The Life of Saint Pachomius and His Disciples.* Cistercian Studies, no. 45. Kalamazoo: Cistercian Publications, 1980. [Contains Bo, G¹, S¹, S², and S¹⁰.] Vol. 2, *Pachomian Chronicles and Rules.* Cistercian Studies, no. 46. Kalamazoo: Cistercian Publications, 1981. [Contains the *Paralipomena,* the *Letter of Ammon,* Draguet's "Fragments," extracts from the *Historia monachorum,* the *Lausiac History,* and the *Apophthegmata patrum,* the *Rules* of Pachomius, and the *Rules* of Horsiesios.] Vol. 3, *Instructions, Letters, and Other Writings of Saint Pachomius and His Disciples.* Cistercian Studies, no. 47. Kalamazoo: Cistercian Publications, 1982. [Contains Pachomius's *Instructions* and *Letters,* together with those of Theodore and Horsiesios, and the latter's *Liber,* or *The Testament of Horsiesios.*]

Verba seniorum [The Sayings of the Fathers]. See *Apophthegmata patrum.*

Vita Altera [G²]. Greek text in *Sancti Pachomii vitae graecae:* 166–271. *See* Halkin.

Vita Antonii [Life of Antony]. *See* Athanasius.

Vita Prima [G¹]. Greek text in *Sancti Pachomii vitae graecae:* 1–96. *See* Halkin.

————. English translation in *Pachomian Koinonia,* 1:297–423. *See* Veilleux.

Vitae Pachomii [*Lives of Pachomius*]. *See* Amélineau, Festugière, Halkin, Lefort, van Cranenburgh, Veilleux.

Vitae patrum. For the *Verba seniorum* [The Sayings of the Fathers], see *Apophthegmata patrum.*

Winter, John Garrett. *Papyri in the University of Michigan Collection: Miscellaneous Papyri.* Michigan Papyri, no. 3. Ann Arbor: University of Michigan Press, 1936.

SECONDARY WORKS

Actes du XVᵉ congrès international de papyrologie. See International Congress of Papyrologists.

Akten des VIII. internationalen Kongresses für Papyrologie. See International Congress of Papyrologists.

Aland, Barbara, ed. *Gnosis. Festschrift für Hans Jonas.* Gottingen: Vandenhoeck and Ruprecht, 1978.

Anderson, J. G. C. "The Genesis of Diocletian's Provincial Re-organization." *Journal of Roman Studies* 22 (1932): 24–32.

Armstrong, Arthur Hilary. "Man in the Cosmos: A Study of Some Differences between Pagan Neoplatonism and Christianity." In Arthur Hilary Armstrong, *Plotinian and Christian Studies,* paper XXII. London: Variorum Reprints, 1979. [First published in *Romanitas et Christianitas,* edited by W. den Boer, 5–14. Amsterdam and London: North-Holland, 1973.]

Arslan, Edoardo, ed. *Studi in onore di Aristide Calderini e Roberto Paribeni.* 3 vols. Milan: Casa editrice Ceschina, 1956–57.

Asmussen, Jes Peter. *XᵁĀSTVĀNĪFT. Studies in Manichaeism.* Translated by Niels Haisland. Acta Theologica Danica, no. 7. Copenhagen: Munksgaard, 1965.

Atti dell'XI congresso internazionale di papyrologia. See International Congress of Papyrologists.

Bacht, Heinrich. "Antonius und Pachomius: von der Anachorese zum Cönobitentum." In *Antonius Magnus Eremita*, edited by B. Steidle, 66–107. Studia Anselmiana, no. 38. Rome: Orbis Catholicus, 1956.

――――. "Pakhôme et ses disciples." In *Théologie de la vie monastique*, edited by Gabriel Le Maitre, 39–71. Théologie, no. 49. Paris: Aubier, 1961.

――――. *Das Vermächtnis des Ursprungs. See* Sources: Bacht.

Bang, W. "Manichaeische Hymnen." *Le Muséon* 38 (1925): 1–55.

Bardy, Gustave. "Basilide." In *Dictionnaire d'histoire et de géographie ecclésiastiques*, 6:1169–75. Paris: Letouzey and Ané, 1932.

Barnes, Timothy D. *The Sources of the Historia Augusta*. Collection Latomus, no. 155. Brussels: Éditions Latomus, 1978.

Barns, John Wintour Baldwin. "Egyptians and Greeks." Inaugural lecture, University of Oxford, 1966. Papyrologica Bruxellensia, no. 14. Brussels: Fondation égyptologique Reine Élisabeth, 1978.

――――. "Greek and Coptic Papyri from the Covers of the Nag Hammadi Codices." In *Essays on the Nag Hammadi Texts in Honour of Pahor Labib*: 9–17. *See* Krause.

Bataille, André. *Les Papyrus*. Traité d'études byzantines, edited by Paul Lemerle, no. 2. Paris: Presses universitaires de France, 1955.

Bauer, Walter Felix. *Rechtgläubigkeit und Ketzerei im ältesten Christentum*. Beiträge zur historischen Theologie, no. 10. Tubingen: Mohr, 1934. Translated under the editorship of Robert A. Kraft and Gerhard Krodel, under the title *Orthodoxy and Heresy in Earliest Christianity*. London: S. C. M., 1972.

Bell, Harold Idris. *Cults and Creeds in Graeco-Roman Egypt*. Forwood Lectures, 1952. Liverpool: Liverpool University Press, 1953.

――――. "The Economic Crisis in Egypt under Nero." *Journal of Roman Studies* 28 (1938): 1–8.

――――. *Egypt from Alexander the Great to the Arab Conquest. A Study in the Diffusion and Decay of Hellenism*. Gregynog Lectures, 1946. Oxford: Clarendon Press, 1948.

――――. "Evidences of Christianity in Egypt during the Roman Period." *Harvard Theological Review* 37 (1944): 185–208.

――――. *Jews and Christians in Egypt. The Jewish Troubles in Alexandria, and the Athanasian Controversy*. London: Oxford University Press, 1924. Reprint. Milan: Cisalpino-La Goliardica, 1977.

――――. Review of *Byzantine Egypt*, by Allan Chester Johnson and Louis C. West. *Journal of Roman Studies* 40 (1950): 123–28.

Bernand, Etienne. "Épigraphie grecque et histoire des cultes au Fayoum." In *Hommages à la mémoire de Serge Sauneron*, 2:57–76. *See* Vercoutter.

Bingen, Jean, Guy Cambier, and Georges Nachtergael, eds. *Le monde grec. Hommages à Claire Préaux*. Université libre de Bruxelles, Faculté de philosophie et lettres, Travaux, no. 62. Brussels: Éditions de l'Université de Bruxelles, 1975.

Blackman, Winifred S. *The Fellāhīn of Upper Egypt. Their Religious, Social, and Industrial Life To-day, with Special Reference to Survivals from Ancient Times*. London: Harrap, 1927.

Boak, Arthur E. R. "An Egyptian Farmer of the Age of Diocletian and Constantine." *Byzantina Metabyzantina* 1 (1946): 39–53.

————. "'Tesserarii' and 'Quadrarii' as Village Officials in Egypt of the Fourth Century." In *Studies in Roman Economic and Social History in Honor of Allan Chester Johnson*: 322–35. *See* Coleman-Norton.

————. "Village Liturgies in Fourth Century Karanis." In *Akten des VIII. internationalen Kongresses für Papyrologie*: 37–40. *See* International Congress of Papyrologists.

Boak, Arthur E. R., and Herbert Chayyim Youtie. "Flight and Oppression in Fourth-Century Egypt." In *Studi in onore di Aristide Calderini e Roberto Paribeni*, 2:325–37. *See* Arslan.

Bousset, Wilhelm. *Apophthegmata. Studien zur Geschichte des ältesten Mönchtums.* Tubingen: Mohr, 1923.

Bowman, Alan K. "The Economy of Egypt in the Earlier Fourth Century." In *Imperial Revenue, Expenditure, and Monetary Policy in the Fourth Century A.D.*, edited by C. E. King, 21–40. British Archaeological Reports, International series, no. 76. London, 1980.

————. *The Town Councils of Egypt.* American Studies in Papyrology, no. 11. Toronto: Hakkert, 1971.

Brown, Peter. "The Diffusion of Manichaeism in the Roman Empire." In *Religion and Society in the Age of Saint Augustine*, by Peter Brown, 94–118. London: Faber and Faber, 1972. [First published in *Journal of Roman Studies* 59 (1969): 92–103.]

————. *The World of Late Antiquity.* London: Thames and Hudson, 1971.

Browne, Gerald M. "Harpocration Panegyrista." *Illinois Classical Studies* 2 (1977): 184–96.

————. "A Panegyrist from Panopolis." In *Proceedings of the XIV International Congress of Papyrologists*, 29–33. *See* International Congress of Papyrologists.

Büchler, Bernward. *Die Armut der Armen. Über den ursprünglichen Sinn der mönchischen Armut.* Munich: Kösel, 1980.

Cameron, Alan. "Wandering Poets: A Literary Movement in Byzantine Egypt." *Historia* 14 (1965): 470–509.

Casey, Robert Pierce. "The Text of the Anti-Manichaean Writings of Titus of Bosra and Serapion of Thmuis." *Harvard Theological Review* 21 (1928): 97–111.

Castel, Georges. "Étude d'une momie copte." In *Hommages à la mémoire de Serge Sauneron*, 121–43. *See* Vercoutter.

Chadwick, Henry. "The Relativity of Moral Codes: Rome and Persia in Late Antiquity." In *Early Christian Literature and the Classical Intellectual Tradition*, edited by William R. Schoedel and Robert L. Wilken, 135–53. Théologie historique, no. 54. Paris: Éditions Beauchesne, 1979.

Chitty, Derwas James. *The Desert a City. An Introduction to the Study of Egyptian and Palestinian Monasticism under the Christian Empire.* Oxford: Blackwell, 1966. Reprint. Oxford: Mowbray, 1977.

————. "A Note on the Chronology of the Pachomian Foundations." In *Studia patristica* (q.v.), no. 2: 379–85.

————. "Pachomian Sources Once More." In *Studia patristica* (q.v.), no. 10:54–64.

————. "Pachomian Sources Reconsidered." *Journal of Ecclesiastical History* 5 (1954): 38–77.

Coleman-Norton, Paul Robinson, ed. *Studies in Roman Economic and Social History in Honor of Allan Chester Johnson.* Princeton, N.J.: Princeton University Press, 1951.

203

Crouzel, Henri. *Origène et la "connaissance mystique."* Museum Lessianum, section théologique, no. 56. Paris: Desclée de Brouwer, 1961.

———. "Origène, précurseur du monachisme." In *Théologie de la vie monastique,* edited by Gabriel Le Maitre, 15–38. Théologie, no. 49. Lyon-Fourvière, 1961. Paris: Aubier, 1961.

———. *Théologie de l'image de Dieu chez Origène.* Théologie, no. 34. Paris: Aubier, 1956.

Cumont, Franz Valéry Marie. *Astrology and Religion among the Greeks and Romans.* American Lectures on the History of Religion, ser. 8. New York and London: G. P. Putnam's Sons, 1912. Reprint. New York: Dover Books, 1960.

———. *Les Religions orientales dans le paganisme romain.* Annales du Musée Guimet, Bibliothèque de vulgarisation, no. 24. Paris: E. Leroux, 1906. Authorized English translation published under the title *The Oriental Religions in Roman Paganism.* Chicago: Open Court, 1911. Reprint. New York: Dover Books, 1956.

de Cenival, Françoise. "Les Associations dans les temples égyptiens d'après les données fournies par les papyrus démotiques." In *Religions en Égypte hellénistique et romaine* (q.v.), 5–19.

de Lange, Nicholas. *Origen and the Jews. Studies in Jewish-Christian Relations in Third-Century Palestine.* University of Cambridge Oriental Publications, no. 25. Cambridge: Cambridge University Press, 1976.

de Mendieta, E. Amand. "Le Système cénobitique basilien comparé au système cénobitique pachômien." *Revue de l'histoire des religions* 152 (1957): 31–80.

Demicheli, A. M. *Rapporti di pace e di guerra dell'Egitto romano con le popolazioni dei deserti africani.* Università di Genova, Fondazione nobile Agostino Poggi, Pubblicazioni, no. 12. Milan: A. Giuffrè, 1976.

Deseille, Placide. *L'Esprit du monachisme pachômien.* Spiritualité orientale et vie monastique, no. 2. Abbaye de Bellefontaine, 1973.

de Vogüé, Adalbert. "L'Anecdote pachômienne du 'Vaticanus graecus' 2091: son origine et ses sources." *Revue d'histoire de la spiritualité* 49 (1973): 401–19.

———. Foreword to *Pachomian Koinonia,* by Armand Veilleux, 1:vii–xxiii. Translated by Denyse Lavigne. *See* Sources: Veilleux.

———. "Les Pièces latines du dossier pachômien: remarques sur quelques publications récentes." *Revue d'histoire ecclésiastique* 67 (1972): 26–67.

———. "La Vie arabe de saint Pachôme et ses deux sources présumées." *Analecta Bollandiana* 91 (1973): 379–90.

Dodds, Eric Robertson. *Pagan and Christian in an Age of Anxiety.* Wiles Lectures, 1962–63. Cambridge: Cambridge University Press, 1965.

Doresse, Jean. *Des hiéroglyphes à la croix: ce que le passé pharaonique a légué au christianisme.* Uitgaven van het Nederlands Historisch-Archaeologisch Instituut te Istanbul, no. 7. Istanbul: Nederlands Historisch-Archaeologisch Instituut in het Nabije Oosten, 1960.

———. "Deux monastères coptes oubliés: Saint-Antoine et Saint-Paul dans le désert de la Mer Rouge." *La Revue des arts* 2 (1952): 3–14.

———. *Les Livres secrets des gnostiques d'Égypte.* Vol. 1: *Introduction aux écrits gnostiques coptes découvertes à Khénoboskion.* Paris: Librairie Plon, 1958. Translated by Philip Mairet, under the title *The Secret Books of the Egyptian Gnostics.* New York: Viking Press, 1970.

Draguet, René. "Le Chapitre de l'*Histoire Lausiaque* sur les Tabennésiotes dérive-t-il d'une source copte?" *Le Muséon* 57 (1944): 53–145; 58 (1945): 15–95.

————. "L' 'Histoire Lausiaque,' une oeuvre écrite dans l'esprit d'Évagre." *Revue d'histoire ecclésiastique* 41 (1946): 321–64; 42 (1947): 5–49.

Essays in Honour of Pahor Labib. See Krause.

Ex orbe religionum: Studia Geo Widengren. 2 vols. Studies in the History of Religions (Supplements to *Numen*), nos. 21–22. Leiden: Brill, 1972.

Festschrift Jonas. See Aland.

Festugière, André Marie Jean. *Antioche païenne et chrétienne: Libanius, Chrysostome et les moines de Syrie.* Bibliothèque des Écoles françaises d'Athènes et de Rome, no. 194. Paris: E. de Boccard, 1959.

————. *Les Moines d'Orient.* Vol. 1, *Culture ou sainteté. Introduction au monachisme oriental.* Paris: Éditions du Cerf, 1961.

————. *La Révélation d'Hermes-Trismégiste.* 4 vols. Paris: J. Gabalda, 1944–54.

Fikhman, I. F. "Quelques données sur la genèse de la grande propriété foncière à Oxyrhynchus." In *Le Monde grec. Hommages à Claire Préaux*, 784–90. See Bingen.

Frank, Suso. *ΑΓΓΕΛΙΚΟΣ ΒΙΟΣ. Begriffsanalytische und begriffsgeschichtliche Untersuchung zum "engelgleichen Leben" im frühen Mönchtum.* Beiträge zur Geschichte des alten Mönchtums und des Benediktinerordens, no. 26. Munster Westfalen: Aschendorff, 1964.

Frend, William Hugh Clifford. "Athanasius as an Egyptian Christian Leader in the Fourth Century." In his *Religion Popular and Unpopular in the Early Christian Centuries* (q.v.), paper XVI. [First published in *New College Bulletin* 8 (Edinburgh, 1974): 20–37.]

————. *The Donatist Church. A Movement of Protest in Roman North Africa.* 2d ed. Oxford: Clarendon Press, 1971.

————. "The Gnostic-Manichaean Tradition in Roman North Africa." In his *Religion Popular and Unpopular in the Early Christian Centuries* (q.v.), paper XII. [First published in *Journal of Ecclesiastical History* 4 (1953): 13–26.]

————. "The Gnostic Sects and the Roman Empire." In his *Religion Popular and Unpopular in the Early Christian Centuries* (q.v.), paper II. [First published in *Journal of Ecclesiastical History* 5 (1954): 25–37.]

————. *Martyrdom and Persecution in the Early Christian Church. A Study of a Conflict from the Macabees to Donatus.* Oxford: Blackwell, 1965.

————. "Religion and Social Change in the Late Roman Empire." In his *Religion Popular and Unpopular in the Early Christian Centuries* (q.v.), paper XI. [First published in *Cambridge Journal* 2 (1949): 487–96.]

————. *Religion Popular and Unpopular in the Early Christian Centuries.* London: Variorum Reprints, 1976.

————. Review of *Manuscript, Society, and Belief in Early Christian Egypt*, by Colin H. Roberts. *Journal of Ecclesiastical History* 31 (1980): 207–8.

Frye, Richard Nelson. "The Cologne Greek Codex about Mani." In *Ex orbe religionum: Studia Geo Widengren* (q.v.), 1:424–29.

Geffcken, Johannes. *Der Ausgang des griechisch-römischen Heidentums.* Religionswissenschaftliche Bibliothek, no. 6. Heidelberg: Carl Winter, 1920. Translated and with revisions and commentary by Sabine MacCormack, under the title *The Last Days of Greco-Roman Paganism.* Amsterdam: North-Holland, 1978.

Gnosis. Festschrift für Hans Jonas. See Aland.

Grant, Robert McQueen. "Early Alexandrian Christianity." *Church History* 40 (1971): 133–44.

————. *Early Christianity and Society. Seven Studies.* New York: Harper and Row, 1977.

————. *Eusebius as Church Historian.* Oxford: Clarendon Press, 1980.

————. "Manichees and Christians in the Third and Early Fourth Centuries." In *Ex orbe religionum: Studia Geo Widengren* (q.v.), 1:430–39.

Grützmacher, Georg. *Pachomius und das älteste Klosterleben. Ein Beitrag zur Mönchsgeschichte.* Freiburg im Breisgau: Mohr, 1896.

Guillaumont, Antoine. *Aux origines du monachisme chrétien. Pour une phénoménologie du monachisme.* Spiritualité orientale et vie monastique, no. 30. Abbaye de Bellefontaine, 1979.

————. "Esquisse d'une phénoménologie du monachisme." *Numen* 25 (1978): 40–51.

————. *Les "Kephalaia gnostica" d'Évagre le Pontique et l'histoire de l'origénisme chez les grecs et chez les syriens.* Patristica Sorbonensia, no. 5. Paris: Éditions du Seuil, 1962.

————. "Philon et les origines du monachisme." In his *Aux origines du monachisme* (q.v.), 25–37.

Guillaumont, Antoine, and Claire Guillaumont. *Évagre le Pontique: traité pratique ou le moine.* 2 vols. Greek text and French translation with an introduction and commentary. Sources chrétiennes, nos. 170, 171. Paris: Éditions du Cerf, 1971.

Haardt, Robert. *Die Gnosis. Wesen und Zeugnisse.* Salzburg: O. Müller, 1967. Translated by J. F. Hendry, under the title *Gnosis.* Leiden: Brill, 1971.

Hahm, David E. *The Origins of Stoic Cosmology.* Columbus, Ohio: Ohio State University Press, 1977.

Harder, Richard. "Eine neue Schrift Plotins." *Hermes* 71 (1936): 1–10.

Hardy, Edward Rochie. *Christian Egypt, Church and People.* New York: Oxford University Press, 1952.

Hausherr, Irénée. "Spiritualité monacale et unité chrétienne." *Orientalia Christiana Periodica* 153 (1958): 13–32.

Henne, Henri. "Documents et travaux sur l'anachôrésis." In *Akten des VIII. internationalen Kongresses für Papyrologie*, 59–66. *See* International Congress of Papyrologists.

Heussi, Karl. *Der Ursprung des Mönchtums.* Tubingen: Mohr, 1936.

Hommages à Claire Préaux. See Bingen.

Hommages à la mémoire de Serge Sauneron. See Vercoutter.

Husson, Geneviève. "L'Habitat monastique en Égypte à la lumière des papyrus grecs, des textes chrétiens et de l'archéologie." In *Hommages à la mémoire de Serge Sauneron*, 2:191–207. *See* Vercoutter.

International Congress of Papyrologists. *Akten des VIII. internationalen Kongresses für Papyrologie.* Mitteilungen aus der Papyrussammlung der österreichischen Nationalbibliothek (Papyrus Erzherzog Rainer), n.s., 5. Vienna: R. M. Rohrer, 1956.

————. *Atti dell'XI congresso internazionale di papyrologia.* Milan: Istituto lombardo di scienze e lettere, 1966.

————. *Proceedings of the Twelfth International Congress of Papyrologists.* Edited by Deborah Samuel. American Studies in Papyrology, no. 7. Toronto: Hakkert, 1970.

————. *Proceedings of the XIV International Congress of Papyrologists.* British Academy, Graeco-Roman Memorials, no. 61. London: Egypt Exploration Society, 1975.

————. *Actes du XVe congrès international de papyrologie.* 3 vols. Edited by Jean Bingen and Georges Nachtergael. Papyrologica Bruxellensia, nos. 16–19. Brussels: Fondation égyptologique Reine Élisabeth, 1978–79.

————. *Proceedings of the Sixteenth International Congress of Papyrologists.* Edited by Robert S. Bagnall, et al. Chico, California: Scholars Press, 1981.

Johnson, Allan Chester. *Egypt and the Roman Empire.* Jerome Lectures, 2d series, 1949. Ann Arbor: University of Michigan Press, 1951.

Johnson, Allan Chester, and Louis C. West. *Byzantine Egypt: Economic Studies.* Princeton University Studies in Papyrology, no. 6. Princeton, N.J.: Princeton University Press, 1949. [Reviewed by Harold Idris Bell. *See* Bell.]

Jones, Arnold Hugh Martin. "Egypt." With revisions by J. David Thomas. In *The Cities of the East Roman Provinces,* by A. H. M. Jones, 2d ed. rev., 295–348. Oxford: Clarendon Press, 1971.

————. *The Later Roman Empire.* 4 vols., with maps. Oxford: Blackwell, 1964.

————. "Were Ancient Heresies National or Social Movements in Disguise?" *Journal of Theological Studies,* n.s., 10 (1959): 280–98.

Jouguet, Pierre. *La Vie municipale dans l'Égypte romaine.* Bibliothèques des Écoles françaises d'Athènes et de Rome, no. 104. Paris: Fontemoing, 1911.

Judge, Edwin Arthur. "The Earliest Use of Monachos for 'Monk' (P. Coll. Youtie 77) and the Origins of Monasticism." *Jahrbuch für Antike und Christentum* 20 (1977): 72–89.

————. "Fourth-Century Monasticism in the Papyri." In *Proceedings of the Sixteenth International Congress of Papyrologists,* 613–20. *See* International Congress of Papyrologists.

Karayannopulos, Johannes. "Collective Fiscal Responsibility in Egypt, Particularly in the Byzantine Period." *Bulletin of the American Society of Papyrologists* 3 (1965): 16.

————. "Entstehung und Bedeutung des Nomos Georgikos." *Byzantinische Zeitschrift* 51 (1958): 357–73.

Kasser, Rodolphe. "Les Dialectes coptes et les versions coptes bibliques." *Biblica* 46 (1965): 287–310. English summary by Bruce M. Metzger in *The Early Versions of the New Testament,* 127–32. *See* Metzger.

————. *Kellia 1965.* 2 vols. Recherches suisses d'archéologie copte, nos. 1–2. Geneva: Georg, 1967.

————. "Y a-t-il une généalogie des dialectes coptes?" In *Mélanges d'histoire des religions offerts à Henri-Charles Puech* (q.v.), 431–36.

Kelly, John Norman Davidson. *Jerome: His Life, Writings, and Controversies.* London: Duckworth, 1975.

Kopecek, Thomas A. *A History of Neo-Arianism.* 2 vols. Patristic Monographs, no. 8. Cambridge, Mass.: Philadelphia Patristic Foundation, 1979.

Koschorke, Klaus. *Die Polemik der Gnostiker gegen das kirchliche Christentum.* Nag Hammadi Studies, no. 12. Leiden: Brill, 1978.

Kraft, Robert A., and Janet A. Timbie. Review of *The Nag Hammadi Library in English,* edited by James M. Robinson. *Religious Studies Review* 8 (1982): 32–51.

Krause, Martin, ed. *Essays on the Nag Hammadi Texts in Honour of Pahor Labib.* Nag Hammadi Studies, no. 6. Leiden: Brill, 1975.

Ladeuze, Paulin. *Étude sur le cénobitisme pakhômien pendant le IVe siècle et la première moitié du Ve.* Paris and Louvain: van Liuthout, 1898.

Lallemand, Jacqueline. *L'Administration civile de l'Égypte de l'avénement de Dioclé-*

tien à la création du diocèse (284–382). Contribution à l'étude des rapports entre l'Égypte et l'Empire à la fin du IIIe et au IVe siècle. Academie royale de Belgique, Classe des lettres et des sciences morales et politiques, Mémoires, 2d ser., no. 57, part 2. Brussels: Palais des Académies, 1964.

——. "Lucius Domitius Domitianus." *Aegyptus* 33 (1953): 97–104.

Lefort, Louis-Théophile. "Les Premiers Monastères pachômiens: exploration topographique." *Le Muséon* 52 (1939): 379–407.

——. "Saint Athanase écrivain copte." *Le Muséon* 46 (1933): 1–33.

——. "Les Sources coptes pachômiennes." *Le Muséon* 67 (1954): 217–29.

Le Maitre, Gabriel, ed. *Théologie de la vie monastique: études sur la tradition patristique.* Théologie, no. 49. Paris: Aubier, 1961.

Lewis, Naphtali. "Exemption from Liturgy in Roman Egypt." In *Atti dell'XI congresso internazionale di papyrologia,* 508–41. See International Congress of Papyrologists.

Lewuillon-Blume, Marianne. "Problèmes de la terre au IVe siècle après Jésus-Christ." In *Actes du XVe congrès international de papyrologie,* 4:177–85. See International Congress of Papyrologists.

Lieu, Samuel N. C. "Precept and Practice in Manichaean Monasticism." *Journal of Theological Studies,* n.s., 32 (1981): 153–73.

Loos, M. "Quelques remarques sur les communautés rurales et la grande propriété terrienne à Byzance (VIIe–XIe siècles)." *Byzantinoslavica* 39 (1978): 3–18.

Lorenz, Rudolf. *Arius Judaizans?* Gottingen: Vandenhoeck and Ruprecht, 1979.

McCue, James F. "Walter Bauer and the Valentinians." *Vigiliae Christianae* 33 (1979): 118–30.

MacMullen, Ramsay. *Roman Government's Response to Crisis, 235–337.* New Haven, Conn.: Yale University Press, 1976.

Malone, Edward E. *The Monk and the Martyr. The Monk as the Successor of the Martyr.* Studies in Christian Antiquity, no. 12. Washington, D.C.: Catholic University of America Press, 1950.

Meijering, Eginhard Peter. *Orthodoxy and Platonism in Athanasius: Synthesis or Antithesis?* Leiden: Brill, 1968.

Mélanges d'histoire des religions offerts à Henri-Charles Puech. Paris: Presses universitaires de France, 1974.

Mélanges Eugène Tisserant. 7 vols. Studi e testi, nos. 231–37. Vatican City: Biblioteca Apostolica Vaticana, 1964–67.

Meredith, Anthony. "Asceticism—Christian and Greek." *Journal of Theological Studies,* n.s., 27 (1976): 312–32.

Mertens, Paul. *Les Services de l'état civil et le contrôle de la population à Oxyrhynchus au IIIe siècle de notre ère.* Academie royale de Belgique, Classe des lettres et des sciences morales et politiques, Mémoires, 2d ser., no. 53, part 2. Brussels: Palais des Académies, 1958.

Metzger, Bruce M. *The Early Versions of the New Testament: Their Origin, Transmission, and Limitations.* Oxford: Clarendon Press, 1977.

Millar, Fergus. *The Roman Empire and Its Neighbours.* London: Weidenfeld and Nicolson, 1967.

Miscellanea Coptica. See Torp.

Le Monde grec. Hommages à Claire Préaux. See Bingen.

Müller, C. D. G. "Geister." *Reallexikon für Antike und Christentum,* 9:546–797. Stuttgart: Anton Hiersemann, 1976.

Musurillo, Herbert. "Early Christian Economy. A Reconsideration of P. Amherst 3(a)." *Chronique d'Égypte* 31 (1956): 124–34.

Nelson, Carroll A. *Status Declarations in Roman Egypt.* American Studies in Papyrology, no. 19. Amsterdam: Hakkert, 1979.

Nock, Arthur Darby. "A Coptic Library of Gnostic Writings." *Journal of Theological Studies*, n.s., 9 (1958): 314–24.

――――. *Essays on Religion and the Ancient World.* 2 vols. Edited by Zeph Stewart. Oxford: Clarendon Press, 1972.

Oates, John F. "The Romanization of the Greek East: The Evidence of Egypt." *Bulletin of the American Society of Papyrologists* 11 (1965): 57–64.

Ort, L. J. R. *Mani: A Religio-Historical Description of His Personality.* Supplementa ad *Numen*, 2d ser., no. 1. Leiden: Brill, 1967.

Owen, E. C. E. "Δαίμων and Cognate Words." *Journal of Theological Studies* 32 (1931): 133–53.

Pagels, Elaine. *The Gnostic Gospels.* New York: Random House, 1979.

――――. *The Gnostic Paul.* Philadelphia: Fortress Press, 1975.

Parássoglou, George M. *The Archive of Aurelius Sakaon. Papers of an Egyptian Farmer in the Last Century of Theodelphia.* Papyrologische Texte und Abhandlungen, no. 23. Bonn: Habelt, 1978.

Peeters, Paul. "Le Dossier copte de saint Pachôme." *Analecta Bollandiana* 64 (1946): 263–67.

――――. Review of *Ein Mani-Fund in Ägypten*, by Carl Schmidt and Hans Jakob Polotsky. *Analecta Bollandiana* 51 (1933): 396–99. *See* Sources: Schmidt.

Puech, Henri-Charles. "La Conception manichéenne du salut." In his *Sur le manichéisme* (q.v.), 5–101.

――――. *En quête de la gnose.* 2 vols. Paris: Gallimard, 1978.

――――. "La Gnose et le temps." In his *En quête de la gnose* (q.v.), 215–70. [First published in *Eranos Jahrbuch* 20 (1951): 57–113.]

――――. *Le Manichéisme: son fondateur, sa doctrine.* Musée Guimet, Bibliothèque de diffusion, no. 56. Paris: Civilisations du Sud (S.A.E.P.), 1949.

――――. "Plotin et les gnostiques." In his *En quête de la gnose* (q.v.), 81–116. [First published in *Les Sources de Plotin* (q.v.), 161–90.]

――――. *Sur le manichéisme, et autres essais.* Paris: Flammarion, 1979.

Quispel, Gilles. *Gnostic Studies.* 2 vols. Uitgaven van het Nederlands Historisch-Archaeologisch Instituut te Istanbul, no. 34, part 1. Istanbul: Nederlands Historisch-Archaeologisch Instituut in het Nabije Oosten, 1974–75.

Redfield, Robert. *Peasant Society and Culture. An Anthropological Approach to Civilization.* Chicago: University of Chicago Press, 1956.

――――. *The Primitive World and Its Transformations.* Ithaca, N.Y.: Cornell University Press, 1953.

Religions en Égypte hellénistique et romaine. Colloque de Strasbourg, 16–18 Mai 1967. Centre d'études supérieures specialisé de l'histoire des religions de Strasbourg. Paris: Presses universitaires de France, 1969.

Rémondon, Roger. *La Crise de l'Empire romaine de Marc-Aurèle à Anastase.* Nouvelle Clio, no. 11. Paris: Presses universitaires de France, 1964.

Rist, John Michael. *Stoic Philosophy.* Cambridge: Cambridge University Press, 1969.

Roberts, Colin H. "The Codex." *Proceedings of the British Academy* 40 (1954): 169–204.

――――. *Manuscript, Society, and Belief in Early Christian Egypt.* Schweich Lectures, 1977. London: Oxford University Press, 1979.

————. Review of *Cartonnage*, vol. 11 of *The Facsimile Edition of the Nag Hammadi Codices*. *Journal of Theological Studies*, n.s., 32 (1981): 265–66.

Roldanus, Johannes. *Le Christ et l'homme dans la théologie d'Athanase d'Alexandrie*. 2d ed. Studies in the History of Christian Thought, no. 4. Leiden: Brill, 1977.

Rouillard, Germaine. *L'Administration civile de l'Égypte byzantine*. 2d ed. rev. Paris: Geuthner, 1928.

Rousseau, Philip. *Ascetics, Authority, and the Church in the Age of Jerome and Cassian*. Oxford Historical Monographs. Oxford: Oxford University Press, 1978.

————. "The Desert Fathers." In *The Study of Spirituality*, edited by C. P. M. Jones, G. Wainwright, and Edward J. Yarnold. London: S. P. C. K., forthcoming.

Rudolph, Kurt. "Die Bedeutung des kölner Mani-Codex für die Manichäismus-forschung: vorläufige Anmerkungen." In *Mélanges d'histoire des religions offerts à Henri-Charles Puech* (q.v.), 471–86.

————. *Die Gnosis. Wesen und Geschichte einer spätantiken Religion*. Gottingen: Vandenhoeck and Ruprecht, 1977.

————. *Die Mandäer*. 2 vols. Forschungen zur Religion und Literatur des alten und neuen Testamentes, nos. 56–57. Gottingen: Vandenhoeck and Ruprecht, 1960–61.

————. *Theogonie, Kosmogonie und Anthropogonie in den mandäischen Schriften*. Forschungen zur Religion und Literatur des alten und neuen Testamentes, no. 88. Gottingen: Vandenhoeck and Ruprecht, 1965.

Ruppert, Fidelis. *Das pachomianische Mönchtum und die Anfänge klösterlichen Gehorsams*. Münsterschwarzacher Studien, no. 20. Munsterschwarzach: Vier Türme, 1971.

Säve-Söderbergh, Torgny. "Holy Scriptures or Apocalyptic Documentations? The 'Sitz im Leben' of the Nag Hammadi Library." In *Les Textes de Nag Hammadi*, edited by Jacques Ménard, 3–14. Nag Hammadi Studies, no. 7. Leiden: Brill, 1975.

Schaeder, Hans Heinrich. *Iranica*. Abhandlungen der Gesellschaft der Wissenschaften zu Göttingen, philologisch-historische Klasse, ser. 3, no. 10. Berlin: Weidmann, 1934.

Schwartz, Jacques. *L. Domitius Domitianus. Étude numismatique et papyrologique*. Papyrologica Bruxellensia, no. 12. Brussels: Fondation égyptologique Reine Élisabeth, 1975.

————. "La Place de l'Égypte dans l'*Histoire Auguste*." In *Bonner Historia-Augusta Colloquium (1975/1976)*, edited by Johannes Straub, 175–86. *Antiquitas*, Reihe 4: Beiträge zur Historia-Augusta-Forschung, edited by A. Alföldi, no. 13. Bonn: Habelt, 1978.

Segal, Alan F. *Two Powers in Heaven. Early Rabbinic Reports about Christianity and Gnosticism*. Studies in Judaism in Late Antiquity, edited by Jacob Neusner, no. 25. Leiden: Brill, 1977.

Seston, William. "Achilleus et la révolte de l'Égypte sous Dioclétian d'après les papyrus et l'*Histoire Auguste*." *Mélanges d'archéologie et d'histoire de l'École française de Rome* 55 (1938): 184–200.

————. "L'Égypte manichéenne." *Chronique d'Égypte* 14 (1939): 362–72.

————. "Remarques sur le rôle de la pensée d'Origène dans les origines du monachisme." *Revue de l'histoire des religions* 108 (1933): 197–213.

Shelton, John C. Introduction to *Nag Hammadi Codices*, by J. W. B. Barns, et al. *See* Sources: Barns.

Simonetti, Manlio. *La Crisi ariana nel IV secolo.* Rome: Institutum patristicum Augustinianum, 1975.

Skeat, Theodore C. Review of *Manuscript, Society, and Belief in Early Christian Egypt,* by Colin H. Roberts. *Journal of Theological Studies,* n.s., 31 (1980): 183–86. *See* Roberts.

Les Sources de Plotin. Entretiens sur l'antiquité classique, no. 5. Vandoeuvres-Geneva, Fondation Hardt, 1957.

Spanneut, Michel. *Le Stoicisme des pères de l'église de Clément de Rome à Clément d'Alexandrie.* 2d ed. Patristica Sorbonensia, no. 1. Paris: Éditions du Seuil, 1969.

Stein, Ernst. *Geschichte des spätrömischen Reiches.* Vienna: Seidel, 1928. French translation by Jean-Rémy Palanque, under the title *Histoire du Bas-Empire.* Paris: Desclée de Brouwer, 1959.

Steinwenter, Arthur. "Aus dem kirchlicher Vermögensrechte der Papyri." *Zeitschrift der Savigny-Stiftung für Rechtsgeschichte* 75, Kanonistische Abteilung 44 (1958): 1–34.

Studia patristica, vol. 2. Papers presented to the Second International Conference on Patristic Studies held at Christ Church, Oxford, 1955. Edited by Kurt Aland and Frank Leslie Cross. Texte und Untersuchungen, no. 64. Berlin: Akademie Verlag, 1957.

———, vol. 10. Papers presented to the Fifth International Conference on Patristic Studies, Oxford, 1967. Edited by Frank Leslie Cross. Texte und Untersuchungen, no. 107. Berlin: Akademie Verlag, 1970.

Studi in onore di Aristide Calderini. *See* Arslan.

Studia Widengren. *See* Ex orbe religionum.

Studies in Honor of Allan Chester Johnson. *See* Coleman-Norton.

Taft, Robert. "Praise in the Desert: The Coptic Monastic Office Yesterday and Today." *Worship* 56 (1982): 513–36.

Telfer, W. "Episcopal Succession in Egypt." *Journal of Ecclesiastical History* 3 (1951): 1–13.

Théologie de la vie monastique. *See* Le Maitre.

Torp, Hjalmar, J. Rasmus Brandt, and Leif Hohn Moussen, eds. *Miscellanea Coptica.* Institutum Romanum Norvegiae, Acta ad archaeologiam et artium historiam pertinentia, no. 9. Rome: Bretschneider, 1981.

Vandenbroucke, François. "Démon." *Dictionnaire de spiritualité,* fasc. 18–19: 141–238. Paris: Éditions Beauchesne, 1954.

van Haelst, J. "Les Sources papyrologiques concernant l'église en Égypte à l'époque de Constantin." In *Proceedings of the Twelfth International Congress of Papyrologists,* 497–503. *See* International Congress of Papyrologists.

van Molle, M. M. "Confrontation entre les règles et la littérature pachômienne postérieure." *Supplément de La Vie spirituelle* 86 (September, 1968): 394–424.

———. "Essai de classement chronologique des premières règles de vie commune connue en chrétienté." *Supplément de La Vie spirituelle* 84 (February, 1968): 108–27.

———. "Vie commune et obéissance d'après les institutions premières de Pachôme et Basile." *Supplément de La Vie spirituelle* 93 (May, 1970): 196–225.

Veilleux, Armand. *La Liturgie dans le cénobitisme pachômien au quatrième siècle.* Studia Anselmiana, no. 57. Rome: Herder, 1968.

Vercoutter, Jean, ed. *Hommages à la mémoire de Serge Sauneron, 1927–1976.* Vol. 2:

Égypte post-pharaonique. Institut français d'archéologie orientale, Bibliothèque d'étude, no. 81. Cairo, 1979.

Vergote, Joseph A. L. "Der Manichäismus in Ägypten." Translated by Ernst Leonardy in *Der Manichäismus*, edited by Geo Widengren, 385–99. Wege der Forschung, no. 168. Darmstadt: Wissenschaftliche Buchgesellschaft, 1977.

Vermes, Geza. "Essenes and Therapeutai." *Revue de Qumran* 3 (1962): 495–504.

———. "Essenes—Therapeutai—Qumran." *Durham University Journal* 52, n.s. 21 (1960): 97–115.

Vogt, Joseph. *The Decline of Rome. The Metamorphosis of Ancient Civilisation*. Translated by Janet Sondheimer. London: Weidenfeld and Nicolson, 1967.

Völker, Walther. *Das Vollkommenheitsideal des Origenes*. Tubingen: Mohr, 1931.

———. *Der wahre Gnostiker nach Clemens Alexandrinus*. Texte und Untersuchungen, no. 57. Berlin: Akademie Verlag, 1952.

von Campenhausen, Hans. *Die Entstehung der christlichen Bibel*. Beiträge zur historischen Theologie, no. 39. Tubingen: Mohr (Siebeck), 1968. Translated by J. A. Baker, under the title *The Formation of the Christian Bible*. Philadelphia: Fortress Press, 1972.

Wallace-Hadrill, David Sutherland. *Eusebius of Caesarea*. London: Mowbray, 1960.

Walters, Colin Christopher. *Monastic Archaeology in Egypt*. Warminster: Aris and Phillips, 1974.

Welles, C. Bradford. "The Garden of Ptolemagrius at Panopolis." *Transactions of the American Philological Association* 77 (1946): 192–206.

Whittacker, C. R. "Agri deserti." In *Studies in Roman Property*, edited by Moses I. Finley, 137–65. Cambridge: Cambridge University Press, 1976.

Widengren, Geo. *Mani und der Manichäismus*. Stuttgart: Kohlhammer, 1961. Translated by Charles Kessler, under the title *Mani and Manichaeism*. London: Weidenfeld and Nicolson, 1965.

Willis, William H. "The Letter of Ammon of Panopolis to His Mother." In *Actes du XVe congrès international de papyrologie*, 2:98–115. See International Congress of Papyrologists.

———. "Two Literary Papyri in an Archive from Panopolis." *Illinois Classical Studies* 3 (1978): 140–53.

Wilson, Robert McLachlan. "From Gnosis to Gnosticism." In *Mélanges d'histoire des religions offerts à Henri-Charles Puech* (q.v.), 423–29.

———. *The Gnostic Problem. A Study of the Relations between Hellenistic Judaism and the Gnostic Heresy*. London: Mowbray, 1958.

Winter, John Garrett. *Life and Letters in the Papyri*. Ann Arbor: University of Michigan Press, 1933.

Wipszycka, Ewa. "Les Confréries dans la vie religieuse de l'Égypte chrétienne." In *Proceedings of the Twelfth International Congress of Papyrologists*, 511–25. See International Congress of Papyrologists.

———. *Les Ressources et les activités économiques des églises en Égypte du IVe au VIIIe siècle*. Papyrologica Bruxellensia, no. 10. Brussels: Fondation égyptologique Reine Élisabeth, 1972.

———. "Les Terres de la congrégation pachômienne dans une liste de payements pour les apora." In *Le Monde grec. Hommages à Claire Préaux*, 625–36. See Bingen.

Wisse, Frederick. "Gnosticism and Early Monasticism in Egypt." In *Gnosis. Festschrift für Hans Jonas*, 431–40. *See* Aland.

Youtie, Herbert Chayyim. "Ἀπάτορες: Law vs. Custom in Roman Egypt." In *Le Monde grec. Hommages à Claire Préaux*, 723–40. *See* Bingen.

Index

Compositor: G & S Typesetters, Inc.
Text: Linotron 202 Palatino
Display: Phototypositor Palatino
Printer: Maple-Vail Book Mfg. Group
Binder: Maple-Vail Book Mfg. Group